CRACK THE CASE SYSTEM

Complete Case Interview Prep

David Ohrvall

Founder of **MBACASE.com**

Crack the Case System is dedicated to my amazing wife Shiloah,
whose patience, perseverance and passion made it all possible.

Many thanks to . . .

Carole Driscoll, for making every detail right; Sarah Kinnard, for her sharp editing and (no longer) hidden acting skills;
John Miller for working his video magic with much creativity; Chip Root, for being the one to figure it out;
Michael Rohani, for his expertly crafted design; and all my coaching clients for their insight, advice and encouragement.

Crack the Case System: Complete Case Interview Prep

Library of Congress Control Number: 2011916655
ISBN: 978-0-9744428-4-6 (Paperback, black & white: Complete one-volume edition)
ISBN: 978-0-9744428-5-3 (Hardcover, color edition: Volume 1)
ISBN: 978-0-9744428-6-0 (Hardcover, color edition: Volume 2)

Printed in the United States of America
Book design by DesignForBooks.com

Credits. *Cover photography*: iStockphoto © uschools, iStockphoto © phildate, iStockphoto © Ashwin82, iStockphoto © Yuri_Arcurs, © Brandon Ritter (author photo of David Ohrvall); *Pages (photography)*: iStockphoto © 4x6 (300, 320, 352, 372, 390, 416, 456, 484, 504, 520), iStockphoto © Adrianhillman (385); iStockphoto © Aleaimage (463); iStockphoto © Andrewjohnson (313); pixmac © Yuri Arcurs (16, 18, 19, 20, 21, 22, 24, 25, 26, 27, 286, 304, 324, 356, 376, 394, 420, 432, 462, 492, 508); iStockphoto © Ariwasabi (395); iStockphoto © Asiseeit (82); iStockphoto © Billnoll (353); iStockphoto © Blondiegirl (476); iStockphoto © Brown54486 (353); iStockphoto © CAP53 (536, 456, 478); iStockphoto © Danishkhan (377); iStockphoto © Davidcallan (321); iStockphoto © Diane39 (v, xi, 281, 296, 288, 306, 314, 326, 342, 358, 370, 378, 386, 418, 434, 396, 442, 458, 486, 498, 506, 518, 526); iStockphoto © Diego_cervo (381); iStockphoto © Dny59 (331); iStockphoto © Dobrinov (421); iStockphoto © Dolnikow (388); iStockphoto © Elenathewise (457); iStockphoto © Erlucho (525); iStockphoto © Fotosipsak (82); iStockphoto © Frankydemeyer (357); iStockphoto © Georgijevic (82); iStockphoto © Grafissimo (291); iStockphoto © H-Gall (341); iStockphoto © Hafizov (391); iStockphoto © Halbergman (467); iStockphoto © StephanHoerold (320, 352, 412, 432, 492, 440, 445, 492); iStockphoto © Izusek (82, 309); iStockphoto © Jgroup (280); iStockphoto © jaroon (16, 18, 19, 20, 21, 22, 24, 25, 26, 27); iStockphoto ©laflor (284, 292, 302, 310, 322, 332, 354, 375, 382, 362, 392, 404, 414, 422, 446, 464, 470, 480, 494, 502, 510, 522); iStockphoto © Lawrencekarn (417); iStockphoto © Leezsnow (433); iStockphoto © Ldf (287); iStockphoto © Maica (295); iStockphoto © Michaelsvoboda (280); iStockphoto © Mammuth (353); iStockphoto © Moodboard_images (403); iStockphoto © Msrphoto (244); iStockphoto © Muratkoc (369); iStockphoto © Naes (305); iStockphoto © Neustockimages (v, xi, 281, 294, 312, 340, 368, 384, 412, 444, 478, 500, 536); iStockphoto © Petdcat (82); iStockphoto © Petreplesea (82); iStockphoto © Plastic_buddha (280); iStockphoto © Renphoto (225); iStockphoto © Rhyman007 (469); iStockphoto © Rickszczechowsk (534); © Brandon Ritter (v, xi, 104, 281, 286, 290, 294, 298, 304, 308, 312, 317, 324, 328, 334, 345, 356, 360, 364, 372, 376, 380, 384, 387, 394, 398, 407, 416, 420, 425, 437, 449, 460, 468, 473, 481, 489, 444, 496, 500, 504, 508, 514, 520, 529, 524); iStockphoto © Sambarfotos (410); iStockphoto © Seraficus (373); iStockphoto © Sgv (361); iStockphoto © ShutterWorx (290, 308, 330, 360, 380, 402, 440, 468, 496, 516, 524); iStockphoto © Snapphoto (82); iStockphoto © Spxchrome (206); iStockphoto © Stephenmeese (280); iStockphoto © Thelinke (441); iStockphoto © Track5 (301); iStockphoto © Urbancow (150); iStockphoto © Uschools (445); iStockphoto © Veni (479); iStockphoto © Ytwong (413); iStockphoto © Yuri_arcurs (82); iStockphoto © Zig4photo (283); iStockphoto © Zilli (338); *Pages (illustration)*: iStockphoto © johnwoodcock (58, 92, (tree, modified)); (heads) coolillustration.com © Michael Rohani (69); iStockphoto © ildogesto (274–275 (world map, modified)); iStockphoto © VecDog (278: industry icons, modified)); coolillustration.com © Michael Rohani (278 (industry icons, modified))

This publication is designed to provide accurate and authoritative information with regard to the subject matter covered. It is sold with the understanding that the author and/or publisher are not engaged in rendering legal, accounting, or other professional advice. If legal advice or other expert assistance is required, the services of a competent professional person should be sought.

—From a Declaration of Principles jointly adopted by a Committee of the American Bar Association and a Committee of Publishers and Associations

This book is available at quantity discounts for bulk purchases.
For information, please contact: service@mbacase.com

Crack the Case System
At a Glance

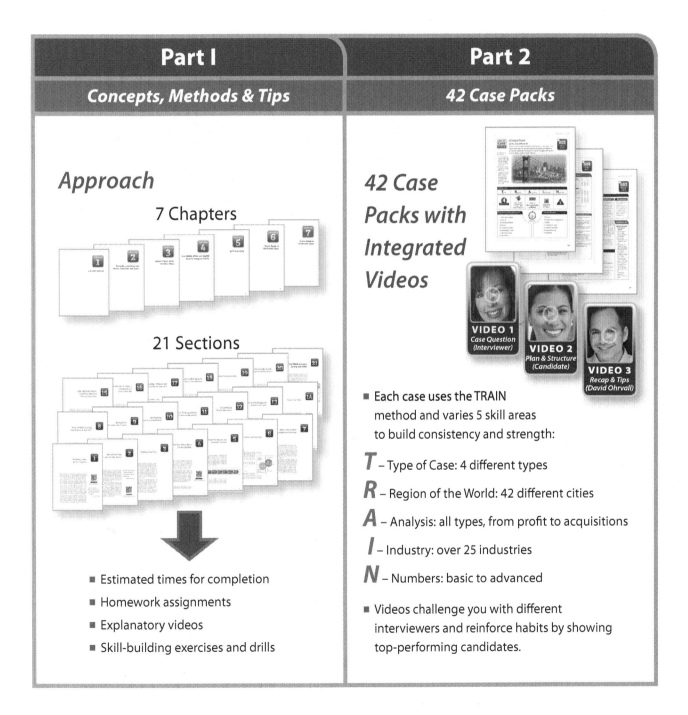

Part I	Part 2
Concepts, Methods & Tips	*42 Case Packs*

Part I — Concepts, Methods & Tips

Approach

7 Chapters

21 Sections

- Estimated times for completion
- Homework assignments
- Explanatory videos
- Skill-building exercises and drills

Part 2 — 42 Case Packs

42 Case Packs with Integrated Videos

VIDEO 1 Case Question (Interviewer)

VIDEO 2 Plan & Structure (Candidate)

VIDEO 3 Recap & Tips (David Ohrvall)

- Each case uses the TRAIN method and varies 5 skill areas to build consistency and strength:

T – Type of Case: 4 different types

R – Region of the World: 42 different cities

A – Analysis: all types, from profit to acquisitions

I – Industry: over 25 industries

N – Numbers: basic to advanced

- Videos challenge you with different interviewers and reinforce habits by showing top-performing candidates.

Crack the Case System **Content Guide**

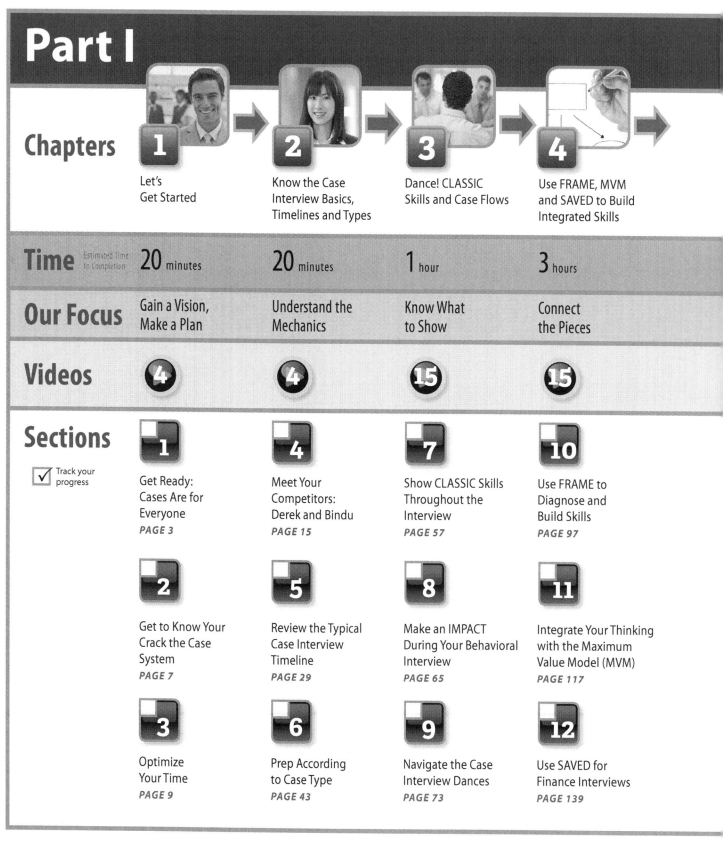

Part I

Chapters

1 Let's Get Started

2 Know the Case Interview Basics, Timelines and Types

3 Dance! CLASSIC Skills and Case Flows

4 Use FRAME, MVM and SAVED to Build Integrated Skills

Time — Estimated Time to Completion

20 minutes | 20 minutes | 1 hour | 3 hours

Our Focus

Gain a Vision, Make a Plan | Understand the Mechanics | Know What to Show | Connect the Pieces

Videos

4 | 4 | 15 | 15

Sections

☑ Track your progress

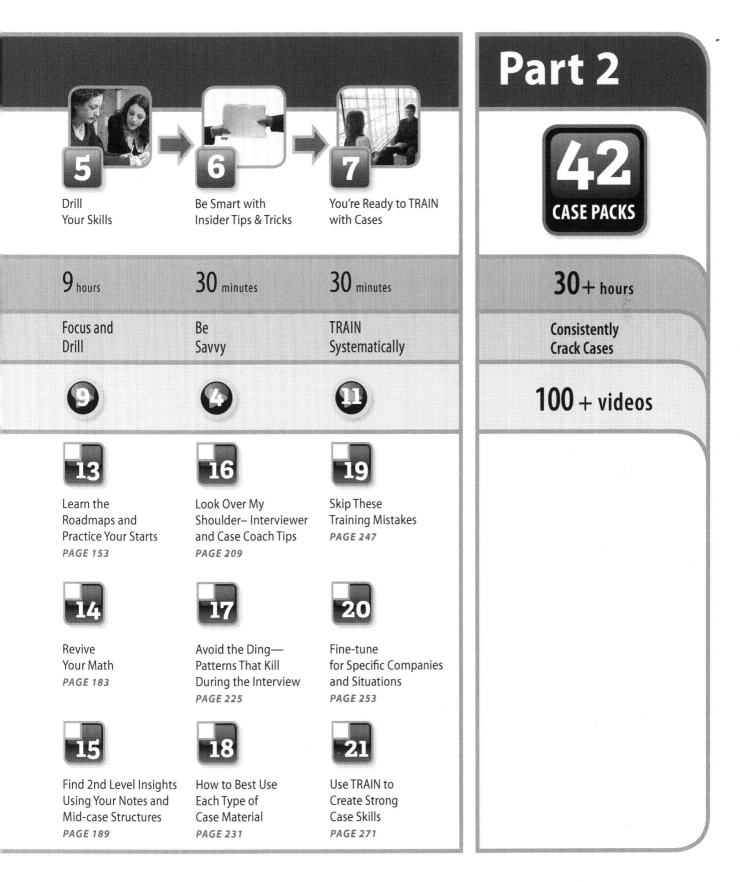

5 Drill
Your Skills

6 Be Smart with
Insider Tips & Tricks

7 You're Ready to TRAIN
with Cases

Part 2

42 CASE PACKS

9 hours

30 minutes

30 minutes

30+ hours

Focus and
Drill

Be
Savvy

TRAIN
Systematically

Consistently
Crack Cases

9

4

11

100+ videos

Crack the Case **Skill Progression Map**

Skills You'll Build	Content/ Method	Section
1 Case Interview Basics	■ Case Types ■ Interview Timeline ■ Competitor Profiles	**1–6**
2 Interview Skill Self Awareness	■ CLASSIC Skills you'll show every interview	**7**
3 Answer First Communication	■ IMPACT stories about yourself	**8**
4 Understanding Case Steps for Market Sizing and Business Cases	S P E **+** MBACASE Path A K	**9**
5 Business Case Step by Step Mastery	FRAME	**10, 13**
6 Integrated Thinking	MVM SAVED	**11–12**
7 Math Fitness	Drills	**14**
8 Ability to Find 2nd Level Insights	Mid-case Structures	**15**
9 Savvy Perspective	■ Coaching insights ■ Interviewer tips ■ Case material guidelines ■ Company specific prep	**16–20**
10 Case Mastery	■ 42 cases covering all business problem with varied regions and industries	**21** Back half of the book

Introduction

"Did you crack the case?"

About five minutes had passed in my first interview with a Bain & Company partner. It was the first of two interviews I would have that morning—the "fit" interview, to be followed by a case interview. The partner's job was easy: he would determine whether I suited the Bain culture and might make a good summer intern. I thought the interview was going very well. We had a nice exchange about the firm, why I was interested in management consulting, and why he thought Bain was the best place to work. And then I felt things start to slip.

I couldn't put my finger on it. Maybe it was intuition from several years of client meetings. Maybe it was a slight change in his body language. Whatever the source, I knew he was mentally tossing me in the "ding" bucket. And there was no way I would let that happen without a fight. My blood pressure rising by the second, I risked a point-blank question: "What problem do you have with my working for Bain this summer?"

He blinked in surprise, then paused awkwardly. "Well, let me see," he said, pulling out my resumé again. "You seem like a person who would fit well at EDS [systems consulting] or Andersen [Ouch! I had just come from there]. My question is: did you crack the case?"

I could only smile and say, "We'll find out soon. My next interview is the case." We shook hands and I left. I cracked that first case, and went on to cack three more and got the job offer.

My own entrance into management consulting is a lesson in how quickly an interviewer can make decisions about a candidate. It is also a lesson in how each candidate has the power to change the course of an interview. Like everyone else, I had prepared for my case interviews using whatever materials and mock interview partners I could find. But to be honest, I still felt unprepared and incredibly nervous.

"Did you crack the case?" This question sums up the purpose of the case interview. Cracking a case is not a matter of finding the one right answer or simply saying all the expected things during the interview. To crack a case is to systematically solve a business problem using logic and data in an organized manner. It is one of the few objective criteria firms can use to evaluate and compare you to other candidates.

Some schools do not disclose MBA grades. Undergraduate performance is somewhat dated and is considered before interviews, not afterward. GMAT scores help, but most candidates are above the "high" threshold. Looks, personality, style and manners play minor roles, as I'll discuss later. But in the end, the case matters most.

Over time, as I interviewed MBAs and undergraduates and talked with other interviewers, I found the "crack the case" mentality to be a constant theme. Why? Because a case interview is a unique tool that allows the firms to "test drive" their candidates, to assess their mental horsepower, and to preview their ability to communicate with clients. In the firms' view, your case interview is the best predictor of your ability to solve tough business problems.

Crack the Case System is the product of many years in the trenches of the interview process. As a manager and consultant at Bain & Company, I regularly interviewed and evaluated candidates. Also, in my role at Bain I had to continually evaluate the consultants on my team and assess their skill sets. Since writing my first *Crack the Case* book in 2003 and launching MBACASE, I've trained thousands of MBAs and undergrads around the world in the areas of logic, analysis and communication through my Crack the Case workshops and private coaching practice. During that time I have learned what it takes to build strong case solving skills. I am pleased to introduce *Crack the Case System*, the first truly comprehensive training system for case interviews. CTCS delivers a common-sense approach to business issues, combining practical instruction, skill building drills, and companion videos that show you how to master every aspect of the case interview. Take your practice seriously, work hard, and good luck!

But in the end, it always comes down to the case.

x

USING THE CRACK THE CASE SYSTEM VIDEOS

As you practice, you'll want to recreate the real interview experience as much as possible. You should also find good mentors to learn from and imitate. The MBACASE videos will help you start to meet both of those goals. We have videos placed throughout Crack the Case System to help you at just the right point, providing insights, tips and good role models. You'll face over 40 case questions from an interviewer and then see how a top candidate would approach the problem. At the end of each case I will help you understand the second level insights.

Types of Videos

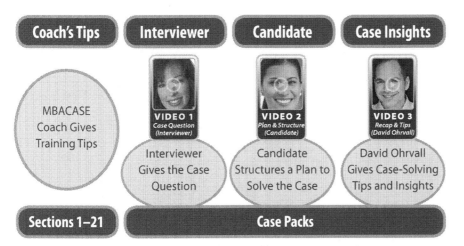

How to Access the Videos

Use your smart phone to scan the QR Code and watch the video. Download a QR Code reader app if it is not pre-installed on your device.

You can also visit www.mbacase.com
and scroll through our easy-to-use video library.

CHAPTER 1

Let's Get Started

Get Ready: Cases Are for Everyone

VIDEO 1-01

What is a Case Interview?

If you're hoping to avoid case interviews, I'm going to have to break it to you: you're out of luck. Case problems are showing up in all kinds of interview situations, and solving them is now considered a basic skill for entering many businesses. Companies like giving cases because they are a great way to test your skills and get a feel for what it's like to work with you. The exact nature of these interviews varies by company. Some companies give general cases that just test your logic and thinking, while others get specific by focusing the case on situations they face or on products and industries that matter to them.

Case interviews are exploding in popularity, and they are not just designed to torture you. For one thing, putting you in a real business situation is simply the best test of your thinking and logic skills. Ideally, a company would like to hire you for 2 to 3 weeks, work with you and then have the option to fire you if you can't perform. Of course it's doubtful that anyone would want to work for a company like that. So the case is the best way to replicate a company's typical daily work, and to find out if you can solve their kinds of problems.

Giving cases is also useful for measuring how well you deal with ambiguity. One of the most challenging parts of an analytical job is coping with incomplete facts and numbers. Interviewers know that someday you will face a tough problem, have limited sources and information, but still have to find a solution. The best way to predict your performance in that kind of situation is to give you a case with limited data. That's why many interviewers use market sizing cases, or business cases

"Success is more a function of consistent common sense than it is of genius."
— An Wang

with virtually no information and nothing you can rely on from your previous experience, because they want to see how you work through the challenge.

Another reason for giving cases is to pressure-test you. Some companies are intentionally raising the stress level in their interviews. Variations on the case interview include: multiple candidates in a room, multiple interviewers, and even creating a presentation within a tight time-frame. All of these interview styles are designed to test how you'll perform under pressure and to recreate some of the tension you'll feel on the real job. Hiring firms want to know that you'll be able to produce results despite the stress around you.

It's natural to want to focus on a specific interview that's coming up. You may ask, "How does this firm want me to perform?" and then attempt to mold yourself into their culture. But I strongly encourage you to first work through this book systematically, building good logic, analytical and communication skills that are applicable to many firms and companies, and then work on focused preparation for certain firms. (You can learn how to tune up for specific companies and situations in section 21.) By preparing systematically, you'll be ready to face your near-term challenges and reach your long-term goals.

The skills you build in this process of training for cases will be invaluable throughout your career. This 20-minute interview is a miniature version of how you would attack a real-life problem. You'll be able to apply the concepts learned here in many situations—whether on a consulting project or sitting around a table with friends discussing whether they should start a business. By preparing for case interviews you are investing in your communication, analytical and advisory skills. So think not only about your short-term interview goals, but also consider your long-term career goals, and you'll have a stronger vision for your time commitment.

Fill out the table opposite by listing some of your short-term and long-term goals. What types of cases are you prepping for specifically? Which of your skills need the most improvement? Do you need to work on your chart-reading skills, or do you need to revive your math? What communication and analytical skills do you want to develop for the long term?

VIDEO 1-02

Cases Are for Everyone

Putting you in a real business situation is simply the best test of your thinking and logic skills.

1

HOMEWORK ➡

CRACK THE CASE GOAL SHEET

Time Period	Goal	Skills	Concerns
0–3 Months			
4–9 Months			
9+ Months			

Get to Know Your
Crack the Case System

Crack the Case System (CTCS) is packed with unique features that will take your preparation to the next level. The book and accompanying videos are designed to help you improve your case skills rapidly. But to get the most out of this system, you'll need to make it your own. I strongly encourage you to flip through the book, check out the At a Glance page and Content Guide, review the TRAIN method for cases, skim a case or two, and watch a few videos. I want the material to engage your curiosity and motivate you to build your skills. And I want this case prep to be fun and energizing, not a chore to complete. Let's walk through some of the key features.

I developed *Crack the Case System* to help interview candidates train systematically, focusing on foundational skills for solving moderate to advanced cases. First you must understand how a typical business case flows and how you perform in it, and then you need to *drill* to strengthen your weak areas. Most people practice plenty of full cases with peer partners, but never drill on specific elements of the case. That's like playing lots of tennis matches but never working on specific strokes. Really good players know that to get better they have to work on basic skills: a more consistent serve, more accurate volleys, or hitting a backhand down the line. Preparing for your cases is no different. You need to drill and practice each skill before you can put them all together for an outstanding case performance.

"Everything should be made as simple as possible, but not one bit simpler."
—Albert Einstein

VIDEO 2-01

Crack the Case System **Overview**

The problem with case interview practice is that you often find yourself working with other people who have little experience giving and solving cases. Since it's not exactly feasible to have an expert with you at all times, the CTCS videos will serve as your virtual coach.

Review the At a Glance page and understand how the front and back halves of the book work together. Then go to the Content Guide and review it. Circle any number or section that is a high priority for you and plan how you'll implement your systematic practice.

This is a system, so we've thought about every aspect of the process: fit interview questions, initial case structure, doing analysis, and closing the case with a recommendation. To fast-track your improvement we've included videos of interviewers and sample candidates, along with drills and homework assignments that reinforce your skills.

It's modular, allowing you to work on the pieces you find most important. I strongly encourage you to follow the system in order, but if necessary, you can drill in quickly on areas where you need work.

It is focused on building skills, with each module progressing level by level. For example, to improve your structuring skills you'll start training with Case Starts—the first 5-7 minutes of the case in which you present your plan to solve the problem. In a similar way, the MBACASE Math Pyramid starts out with multiplication, division and fractions to review your basic math facts. As the cases progress, you'll encounter more complicated equations and advanced concepts.

CTCS includes crucial reinforcement activities. Any time I've learned something very well—whether I was studying Japanese kanji or working on a new math concept—I found that I mastered the material more quickly when I used several different learning strategies, such as writing, listening, and speaking. With CTCS, you do the homework assignments, take notes on your progress, and practice out loud by yourself. You also train with others using our TRAIN methodology, an approach that reinforces the most important skills with every case. Each piece of the system makes the material go deeper and helps the knowledge last beyond your short-term goals.

Finally, CTCS includes videos that will give you an extra edge in your preparation. Most people who are preparing for cases are very bright and good at pattern recognition. Once they see something done they can replicate it rather quickly. The problem with case interview practice is that you often find yourself working with other people who have little experience giving and solving cases. It's a disaster, because you have no good patterns to model. You need a balance between real-time practice with peers and instruction from professionals. Since it's not exactly feasible to have an expert with you at all times, the CTCS videos will serve as your virtual coach. We created them to give you insight into how great candidates solve cases, from presenting their structure to closing with recommendations. We believe these video models are the missing link in the case interview preparation process.

Optimize Your Time

If you're reading this book, chances are you're short on time. Typically, my clients have less than two months to prepare for their interviews. It's vital to use your time wisely. Most candidates prepare by doing a large volume of cases. They burn through one case book after another in a constant quest for new material. By contrast, I am a big believer in repetition. I advise my coaching clients to repeat their cases two to three times. After you have finished a case, go back and do it again. When you repeat a case, you begin to understand it at a new level. You see how it flows; you grasp how the interviewer may lead at points and then step back. And you learn how to transition smoothly from one section to another, using your notes and analysis to guide the discussion. These deeper insights don't come alive the first time you practice a case. Repeat and use those old cases.

Another way to optimize your time is to watch the CTCS videos and use that material to take each case's content deeper. After you do a case, go back through and watch the introductory video. Respond to the interviewer. Pull together your own plan for the case and present it out loud. Also, review the video that helps show you how to structure the case. Don't be afraid to copy someone else's style at first, as it will help you communicate more clearly over time. You will develop your own personal approach as you practice each element of the case.

Be sure to do your homework after every section. Don't tell yourself you are fine without the exercises and skip over them. Put dates next to your chapters and cases, and write down your thoughts as you go

VIDEO 3-01

Optimize Your Time

3A

HOMEWORK →

When you repeat a case, you begin to understand it at a new level.

along. It will help you to learn from the hours you've invested and to see your progress over time.

Finally, don't burn out. Set up time to practice and make a schedule for yourself. To help you get started, we've created the blank timeline that follows. Write down your interview dates and goals, and plot out your practice sessions. Prepare consistently over a long period of time rather than cramming at the end. If you do have a very short time period to prepare, then you will have to schedule some longer blocks of practice time. In either case, it will be important to track your progress.

What are your risk spots? What skills do you need to work on the most? Fill out the case interview preparation timeline and think through your strategy to be fully prepared. Here are some tips as you get started.

Weeks—Most people start seriously preparing with less than 8 weeks to go. If you are prepping sooner than that, take it easy at first and then ramp up more aggressively as your interview date nears. I don't believe you can over-prepare as long you are careful to not sound robotic and memorized. (We will cover this in later sections.) Professional pianists, skiers, painters and architects don't over-prepare; they just get better and better. As you invest more time in case interview prep you, too, will only get better.

Hours—If you don't carefully plan your case interview prep, you won't do it. Put the training hours in your calendar and stick to your schedule. When you are 6-8 weeks away, start by finding 3-5 hours of prep time. Plan to build up to about 1 hour a day in the last 1-2 weeks.

Skills—Make sure these skills are on your short list:

- Basic math (multiplication, division, growth rates)
- Estimating in thousands, millions and billions
- Reading basic bar charts (go to *www.mekkographics.com* to find just about every chart you'll ever see)
- Speaking answer-first (see Section 7)
- Telling your story (see Section 8)
- Using your notes effectively (See Chapter 5)
- Closing the case persuasively, with data

Materials—Check out Section 18 for tips on how to best use the variety of case materials that are on the market and available from schools.

These tips are based on my experience of working with hundreds of successful clients, but skills and time frames vary, so adjust accordingly.

CRACK THE CASE PREP TIMELINE				
Weeks Until Interview	**Hours I Have Set Aside For Practice**	**My Practice Partners**	**Skill Focus**	**Cases & Materials I'll Use**
8				
7				
6				
5				
4				
3				
2				
1				

Know the Case Interview Basics, Timelines and Types

Meet Your Competitors: Derek and Bindu

I want you to be excited about what's ahead of you. You are going to improve your logic, analytical and communication skills rapidly as you use *Crack the Case System*. Ultimately, we want to bring all of these skills together under pressure to crack the case and get the job! But consistently doing well in an oral, logic-based, problem-solving interview will require quite a bit of practice and time. As your skills progress, we'll need to keep in mind another critical factor: the competition. Let's face it—a lot of people want the job that you want.

To learn a little more about those you'll be up against and how you might compare, I'd like to give you a glimpse into the mind of a typical interviewer talking with two different candidates. Both look great on paper, with comparable backgrounds and experience. They are from the same school and have similar GPAs and GMAT scores. And they both worked hard preparing for their cases. What will differentiate them as they try to solve this basic profitability case? With which of them do you identify most as you observe their skills? Each person was interviewed separately, but let's do our best to put them side by side and see some differences through the interviewer's eyes.

VIDEO 4-01

What Do Interviewers Want?

Interview Day

As I'm walking down the hall to the interview holding room, my mind is racing a mile a minute. We're half-way through the day and we still

haven't found "the one". We've been tasked by HR to keep our picks to two people and under, since we have several good schools to visit. You'd think with the top-tier brand of this school, we'd have found at least one good person by now! But if we strike out here it's not the end of world. We don't have to take anyone from this place.

I turn the corner and it's the same scene as always. Dark suits, nervous smiles and hopeful eyes—unfortunately, they all look the same at this point. Here we go . . .

"Hi, Derek; I'm David Ohrvall."

"Hi, Bindu; I'm David Ohrvall."

INTRODUCTION TO CASE

Minutes 1–2

Derek Ding

Derek looks like a nice guy: haircut not too trendy, no facial hair (my pet peeve), nice suit, sloppy tie knot, but overall, very client-ready. He steps forward quickly after I call his name in the waiting room where twenty-five candidates are sitting, making small talk with the greeters. Firm handshake, a little wet. Good eye contact. Nice smile and a few pleasant comments about the weather. He seems excited and a little high-strung. But I like this guy; we're off to a good start as we walk to the interview room.

   Today we're in a fancy hotel suite as our firm chose not to interview on campus. I motion for him to take the seat across the desk from me.

Bindu Bright

My initial encounter with Bindu is similar to that with Derek. She has a calm demeanor but a 1,000 watt smile. I notice some extra bracelets that she should have left at home and her hair is a little messy, but overall she looks client-ready. She gives direct answers to my questions and seems to be keeping up with my peppy pace. Some of the candidates today have felt a little sluggish—or worse, giddy. But not Bindu; she's clearly bringing her "A" game.

   So far, they are on an equal footing. Unlike some of the others, I sense she feels very comfortable talking to me despite our roles. She doesn't seem nervous; she takes her seat and looks eager to begin.

"As you know, we're here today to have you do a case. I'd like to take a brief minute to introduce myself and then we'll get started. After the case, we'll have some time to discuss any questions you have about the firm. Your next interview is with Amy; it will be a case as well."

After a brief review of my background, I begin. I try to make sure that I start the case in exactly the same way for each candidate: "Today's case is about durable medical equipment distribution. My client is going through a number of changes, and I would like you to help with the situation. Here is a description of the problem. Let me know when you want to start." I show a slide (below) that contains a mix of bullets, some relevant and some meaningless. At the bottom of the slide is the bold-type question, "How can DuraMed Depot maximize profitability?"

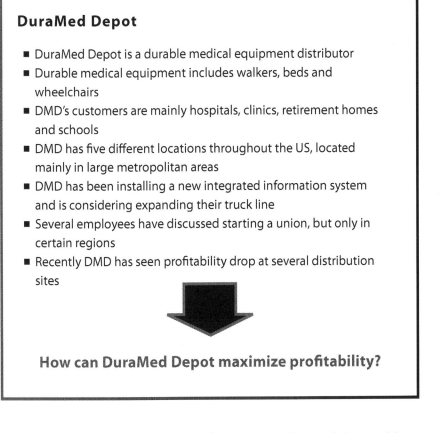

DuraMed Depot

- DuraMed Depot is a durable medical equipment distributor
- Durable medical equipment includes walkers, beds and wheelchairs
- DMD's customers are mainly hospitals, clinics, retirement homes and schools
- DMD has five different locations throughout the US, located mainly in large metropolitan areas
- DMD has been installing a new integrated information system and is considering expanding their truck line
- Several employees have discussed starting a union, but only in certain regions
- Recently DMD has seen profitability drop at several distribution sites

How can DuraMed Depot maximize profitability?

I'm interested to see how many of the points the candidates address in their analysis.

CREATING THE PLAN

Minute 3

Derek Ding

Bindu Bright

It's clear Bindu is ready to get down to work, but she is still very relaxed.

Derek pulls the slide closer and says he'd like to take a minute to review the information. He holds it tightly and I notice his left hand leaves a sweat mark on the desk. That's not a good sign. Then the red flags start flying.

Tense Posture: The head drops, the shoulders round and the eyes dart across the page with an intensity that could bore holes into the paper. It's apparent that the slide is unnerving him.

Erratic Notes: While looking at the slide, he scrambles for his notepad and nervously begins to jot down a few points. His chicken scratch is sloppy and erratic. I doubt the notes will help him later. I'm trying hard not to pre-judge, but I have seen this all many, many times before.

Stressed Face: Derek is not enjoying himself much; his face is full of tension. I'm sure he knows better than to get this worked up during an interview, but his anxiety is getting the better of him. Would he be this bad in front of clients?

I try to help him out: "All of the information I give you will always be available, so you don't need to copy down the bullets if you don't want to."

He mumbles a quick *"Thanks,"* and continues reading. He then asks for a minute to *"structure out a framework."*

It does not take Bindu long to distinguish herself from the other candidates. After glancing at the slide, she asks, *"Will I be able to look at this information later in the interview?"* She scans the data and takes a few notes.

Relaxed Posture: Bindu seems like she does this every day. It's clear she is ready to get down to work but she is still very relaxed. I'm starting to get a good feeling about her abilities.

Organized Notes: As she scans the data, Bindu quickly takes down a few notes. I notice that she already jotted down a few questions for herself. Her writing is neat enough to read from across the table and she keeps me in the loop.

Relaxed Face: Bindu is easily looking back and forth between me and her notes. She is calm and I could see her doing well in one of our more stressful client meetings. I'm hoping that she can back this up with some good smarts.

Bindu takes charge quickly: *"This information is helpful. I'd like to take a minute or so and lay out an approach that we can discuss together. We're focused on profit, so I'll be looking at revenue and cost drivers that will lead us to some solutions."*

CREATING THE PLAN (*continued*)

Minute 4

Derek Ding

After about two minutes (a little long, but acceptable), he lifts his head and begins to speak.

Weak Plan to Solve the Case

"It seems that DuraMed Depot wants to maximize profit. And profit is revenues minus costs. Can you tell me a little more about how DuraMed makes money in this business?"

That's it? I'm a little shocked at how limited Derek's plan is. I sense that I'm going to have to do a lot of digging to better understand how Derek thinks. He didn't do himself any favors by not making clear how he's thinking through the situation.

As with a lot of candidates, I didn't hear any case-specific language, like the words "medical equipment" or "hospital". There's also no case-specific logic about why a durable medical equipment company, which seems stable with clients like hospitals and healthcare facilities, would see a drop in profit.

I'm glad Derek wants to have a discussion, but his initial question is so elementary and broad, I'm not sure he won't hit me with more questions soon. I'm ready for the interview equivalent of the game show *20 Questions*.

Bindu Bright

Bindu is ready to go in about one minute. She is pointing to her paper and ready to explain her thinking.

Comprehensive Plan to Solve the Case

"Thanks for the minute. Since DuraMed Depot wants to focus on profit I have laid out a profit tree.

"My hunch is that over time DuraMed Depot has lost control of their costs, since it would be a little unusual for revenue from hospitals and clinics to drop across the board. Of course revenue is driven by price and volume, so I would like to find out if there have been price point drops, perhaps to competition. Volume decline could happen because a few large customers could be ordering from different vendors. As for costs, it will be interesting to see if my theory holds. On the fixed side they may have seen an increase in utilities, rent or warehouse expenses. As for variable costs, I'm curious about labor and the suppliers they use for items like wheelchairs and crutches.

"If it's OK with you, I'd like to test my hunch by looking at costs first. Do you have costs broken down by fixed and variable over the last 12 months?"

> *As with a lot of candidates, I didn't hear any case-specific language.*

Minutes 5–6

Derek Ding

Bindu Bright

Derek presented his approach fairly well; but overall, he's a little jittery. He seems to be reading formulas in his head as he's talking. I get the sense that he prepared for this interview, but the conversation doesn't feel natural and I'm not sure I'm going to see solid thinking. The friendliness and comfortable rapport that Derek established a few minutes ago have all but evaporated. I decide to give him a little push to find out what's going on in his head.

Interviewer Drills on a Part of the Plan

"Derek, I think you've covered the most important categories with your approach. Let's step back. What are two key profit drivers for a durable equipment distributor?" I ask. Now he's back in the game.

"Okay, I think one is having good relationships with equipment manufacturers to ensure low cost and good variety. Another driver would be maintaining strong relationships with the customers, like hospitals and urgent care facilities. They could charge a premium for the service they provide, as well as for distribution and storage."

Okay, I think we're getting somewhere. I feel like I'm seeing the thinking Derek rather than the stressed one. Maybe he's finally calming down and is about to show me how he can think through some analysis and deeper questions.

Overall Bindu seems to be thinking deeply about the topic, much like any of the top performers at my firm. I'm already imagining her in front of one of my toughest clients. She seems quick on her feet! But I need to push on her thinking a little.

I'm not quite sure if I buy Bindu's "costs are out of control" theory, but her hypothesis and solid structure give us a good framework for discussing the problem. She also mentioned data that she needs.

Interviewer Drills on Something Said

"Before we dig into any specific data, could you tell me more about the costs that may have crept up?" I ask.

She seems glad I asked. *"Sure, I'm thinking right away about costs that are hard to detect, like delivery charges, fuel, across-the-board supplier increases on component parts (like wheelchair accessories), and, finally, administration that could have caused across-the-board increases that would lower profit on all product lines."*

Wow! We're on our way. I'm impressed with her clock speed, as she's processing information very quickly and thinking specifically about this type of business.

She put a stake in the ground about where she thinks the value is, and she appears ready to test it. Let's see if she's equally good with numbers.

> *She put a stake in the ground about where she thinks the value is, and she appears ready to test it.*

DIVING FOR DATA—2ND SLIDE AND CALCULATIONS

Minutes 7–12

 Derek Ding

 Bindu Bright

Diving for General Data

Before we get into the data I have, I want to see where Derek's head is. "Can you give me some reasons why a distributor might have problems being profitable?" I ask.

"Uh, I suppose their cost structure might be too high. Or their revenues have decreased due to an industry-wide drop in demand for medical equipment. Do you have any more information about their revenues?" he asks.

Revenue is a fine place to start, but I have cost data, so I want to start there.

It will be easier to compare him to other candidates if we follow a similar flow.

"You can assume revenues have stayed constant over the past five years," I say.

Derek switches gears immediately: *"Okay. Do you have any information about costs? It would be best if we could see it over time."*

But what about location, Derek? I think he forgot about the first handout in front of him.

Missing Several Insights

I give Derek my handout. The variability in costs by distribution site practically jumps off the page; I'm hoping Derek will identify those differences between locations and

Diving for Specific Data

I'm eager for her to analyze the data I have, but want to see if she'll continue to drive the case. "What would you like to look at first?" I ask.

"Can we start with variable and fixed costs by location over the last 12 months or so? Going back to the original handout you gave me, it says that profit is down at several locations. It would make sense to see if there are any issues by location as we look at the data. They have the new IT system in motion, so it would be natural to see increased costs related to the technology."

I like how Bindu is working with the information in front of her, using her own approach and the initial handout I gave her.

She basically asked for the data I'm about to give her, so I hand over the new slide. I'll be able to compare her with the other candidates after she reviews this data and does a few calculations.

Highlighting Key Insights

"Here is some data I would like you to review. What jumps out to you?"

She doesn't stay silent for long before sharing her insights: *"This data slide is a good way to analyze each distribution center . . . what jumps out to me the most is such high cost variability by location. I see three areas that seem to be driving the*

It will be easier to compare him to other candidates if we follow a similar flow.

DIVING FOR DATA—2ND SLIDE AND CALCULATIONS *(continued)*

 Derek Ding

 Bindu Bright

She doesn't jump around in her thinking, but instead moves very intentionally from one section to the next.

then drill down into the causes.

"It seems like costs vary a lot by service center."

Good; he got the main insight.

"What do you think is causing such disparities?" I ask.

"Well, some of the service centers might be in more expensive areas, where the leasing costs are higher. Or they might need to pay their employees more because it's harder to find good people."

These are decent speculations, but Derek needs to focus on the slide and the three areas with the most variability: direct labor, administration, and truck maintenance. Instead of driving the interview forward by analyzing the data in front of him, he is taking shots in the dark and hoping he'll hit the target.

variability: direct labor, administration, and truck maintenance. I would like to look at each one and ask you a few questions."

Bindu then goes on to systematically examine each category by asking about changes in the last 12 months in order to prove or disprove her original hypothesis.

She doesn't jump around in her thinking, but instead moves very intentionally from one section to the next. I could see her doing well with a complicated work stream for one of our clients and not going off on tangents. That is an important skill with our work, as we need her to be consistently productive and to meet tight deadlines.

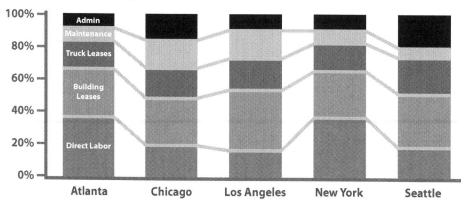

Total Monthly Expenses by Location

DIVING FOR DATA—2ND SLIDE AND CALCULATIONS (*continued*)

 Derek Ding

 Bindu Bright

Slow Math and Limited Insights

Now it's time to really find out who can hold it together under pressure. I'm expecting Derek to shine here with his engineering experience. I know his math training would have been rigorous and I see he spent three years in a German school system, so I'm even more hopeful. I need to move fast as he has burned up some extra time with longer pauses than most candidates.

I start in quickly: "Your insights on the data were helpful. Management wants to analyze the Direct Labor area. Could you do a few calculations for me?"

Derek grabs another sheet of paper and seems ready.

I make sure I give him the numbers without pause. "Total revenue for the company is about $780M, with total expenses representing 65%. Within total expenses, Direct Labor is about 35%. If they have an opportunity to reduce Direct Labor expenses by about $25M per year, is that significant?"

Derek shifts into complete HDDM mode—Head Down Doing Math. After a few seconds he asks, *"Could you repeat the Direct Labor number?"* I wonder if he's stalling, because I was pretty clear with the numbers. He seems a little flustered. I think he's starting to get psyched out. For about a minute I get a nice view of

Quick Estimates, Accurate Analysis and Insights

So far, Bindu has proven that she is a step ahead of the other candidates by thinking specifically about the data she needs. But I'm still not certain that she has the analytical prowess to handle our work. Her marketing research background should have built some solid quant skills, but you never know until a candidate does the math.

I attempt to say the same thing I've said with every candidate today: "Management wants to explore opportunities in Direct Labor. I need you to do a few calculations."

Bindu is already poised with a clean sheet and ready to go.

I spit out the numbers like I have done all day. Afterward she interjects, *"Do you mind if I do some quick estimates and then I'll be glad to be more accurate if that's helpful?"* I tell her that it's fine. I'm a little tired of watching people struggle with basic math and am wondering if anyone will get to second level insights today.

Rather than go completely silent during her math, Bindu pulls me into her thinking. *"So if we round 780 to 800, we're looking at 60% which is 480 plus 5% which is 40, so about 520. 30% would be 156 and add in about 8 for the 5% and the total is $164. So in the range of $165 to $170."*

DIVING FOR DATA—2ND SLIDE AND CALCULATIONS *(continued)*

Derek Ding

Bindu Bright

the top of his head until he finally blurts out, *"Well, I think Direct Labor would be about $200M. So their savings would be greater than 10%."*

Derek is close enough, but awkward silence follows as it's clear that he has no idea where to take the conversation. I prompt him to think about what would constitute "significance" for a company when choosing to pursue cost savings projects. He mentions the size of the savings and the difficulty of achieving them, but misses timing and the balance of the savings across locations. He's not thinking about making each service center stronger, which will be an important part of rolling out some changes.

Unfortunately we're out of time and we can't solve the break-even calculation. I debate whether or not to give it to him, but I don't think it will sway my opinion of his analytics, and I don't think it's worth the added stress. I push Derek for a conclusion despite his incomplete data set. I'm hoping he'll recognize a few gaps and at least put those in his next steps.

I know he's giving it his best, but the pressure seems to have affected his ability to think deeply about the situation. I feel that he has performed fairly well on the different tasks I posed, like "Do this math," or "Tell me your thoughts," but he lacks the ability to solve the whole prob-

I feel that he has performed fairly well on the different tasks I posed, like "Do this math," or "Tell me your thoughts," but he lacks the ability to solve the whole problem on his own.

OK, so Bindu can do math in her head. She would be great to have along when splitting the dinner bill among five friends, but what will she do with this data?

"You asked if saving $25M would be significant. With these numbers I would say that they would be reducing total Direct Labor by 15%, which seems to be strong given labor cuts I've seen in other industries. But if they have to choose where to put their energy they'll need to consider several factors, like implementation difficulty, savings across locations, and the potential to support additional savings projects."

I sense she's onto something. "How would you compare multiple projects?" I ask.

"Doing break-even calculations after including project-specific fixed costs could be one way … but since these are cost reduction projects there may not be much of an initial investment."

With that comment I give Bindu my final data question. She's only the second person to get this far in the case today and her efficient work earlier in the case is giving her another chance to shine. With ease, she calculates two break-evens and does a solid compare-and-contrast. She finds that the cost reduction project in the Admin area is going to be easier to implement and provide a better foundation for additional savings projects. Pursuing

FINAL RECOMMENDATION

Derek Ding

Bindu Bright

lem on his own. He hasn't owned the case issue and acted like this was his company and his problem. He is at best an average analyst, and I want someone who will quickly grow into manager material. I think he needs a little more experience and seasoning before he'd be ready for my firm.

Direct Labor still makes sense and requires no investment up front, but the potential employee unrest, union issues and risk of declining service make it the second choice.

Weak, Vague Conclusion

"Well, Derek, we've talked about several things. What's your final recommendation?"

Derek slides his papers around and tries to compose a summary. *"Given that DuraMed Depot is looking to increase profitability, I would recommend that they focus on the Direct Labor issue. They can save about $25M, or over 10% of current costs. They should also consider looking at Admin costs as they show some variability across regions; however, we didn't have time to explore that in detail. It would be good to look at that soon. Finally, even though revenues have been constant over the last five years, they should also consider looking for new opportunities for growth. With the aging population, there should be several new areas they can enter."*

I'm pleased that Derek pulled together a brief and fairly data-oriented conclusion; but honestly, much of it sounded like something

Practical, Data-Driven Conclusion

"OK, Bindu; let's wrap it up."

"Sure," she starts in without much hesitation. *"To increase profitability DuraMed Depot has several options. Their first priority should be pursuing the Admin project. Even though the payback period is slightly longer than the Direct Labor option, it offers almost the same savings, $23M or about 4.5% of total costs.*

"We also learned that by eliminating some of the inefficient and overlapping processes, the Admin project sets the stage to remove two redundant IT systems next year, which could save another $15M.

"A second priority would be to implement phased Direct Labor reductions in Atlanta and New York, our most out-of-line centers. These locations have had uneven hiring practices and wage rates that should be standardized going forward.

"Finally, we touched briefly at the end

Minutes 13–15

INTERVIEWER'S DECISION

 Derek Ding

 Bindu Bright

he could have said before the case began. Yes, the population is aging, but it's not a topic we mentioned, so bringing it in at the end wasn't wise. As for not having time to explore the Admin area, that was Derek's fault. A successful candidate has to use the data from the case and Derek just didn't go deep enough to find the right insights.

Derek was definitely doing his best throughout the case, but by minute ten I knew he was a ding. Overall, I would rate him as very inconsistent. He's obviously an intelligent person, but he just didn't consistently show the structured thinking, tenacity, analytical rigor and ability to see the big picture that I need in my employees.

When I knew that Derek was no longer in the running to get passed to the next round, my job was to make sure he had a good time. I want to give him a favorable impression of my firm. After all, he's getting his MBA from one of the top programs, and in the future he may be a buyer of our services.

In fact, I think that Derek may have walked away thinking he did well. After all, he got through the data, did some fairly accurate math and gave a firm recommendation at the end. But it just wasn't at the level

of our discussion on the potential to lock in a new customer, a chain of urgent care facilities. If they are successful, that may boost revenue by 12% over the next two years."

Home run! Bindu successfully wove together all the data we had discussed and did it in a very practical way. She was solid throughout and definitely cracked my case.

I am impressed with Bindu. She is truly bright, a quick thinker who is willing to challenge her own assumptions. When she recognizes a weak spot in her thinking, she points it out and makes adjustments.

Throughout the case she was consistently logical and stayed focused on the data. I liked how she worked her way through each section of the second handout and explained the potential drivers of the issue.

She also relied on her business sense where appropriate. I could tell that some of the additional comments she pulled in at the end were not fluff and that she is truly interested in business.

Also, it seems that she is enjoying the challenge of solving the problem. She stayed upbeat throughout, and even when she hit a bump in the break-even calculation, she stayed calm and worked it out. I

It seems that she is enjoying the challenge of solving the problem.

INTERVIEWER'S DECISION (*continued*)

Derek Ding

Bindu Bright

necessary to move ahead.

Since we can pass only two of our fourteen candidates to the final round, I'm confident in my decision to ding Derek. When I compare notes with my interview partner at the end of the day, it turns out that Derek did a little better on his second case. I had him ranked 7th out of 12 candidates, and my interview partner had him in 5th place. Usually we only have deeper discussions about the top three to four, so he is clearly out of the race. He needed to crack both cases to make it to the next round. Since he did worse on my case, I have to do the ding call tonight. I'll do my best to give him some feedback, but there's only so much coaching I can give in a five-minute call. I have a lot of other people to ding as well.

think she'd be game to solve any case I could throw her way and would have interest in a lot of different business problems.

My interview partner ranks Bindu second out of fourteen candidates and I rank her first. Basically, that's an even match and we both agree that she is a final round candidate. We pass her along with confidence. He was a little concerned about her leadership experience and we both flagged a few math hiccups. We'll note these issues for the next set of interviewers. To get a full-time offer she'll need to exhibit brilliance at cracking cases in three more interviews with partners from the firm. I hope she makes it, but you never can tell. Her chances are about 50/50 in the final round. Good luck, Bindu!

VIDEO 4-02

Types of Competitors

Take a highlighter and mark sections of the Derek and Bindu interviews that match traits you have shown in the past when doing analysis or solving a problem. Do you sometimes fumble with math? Are you quick on your feet or good at connecting different pieces of information? How do you perform under pressure? It's important to start recognizing patterns in your previous performance as you prepare to improve your skills.

4

← HOMEWORK

Review the Typical Case Interview Timeline

In the last section you got a close-up view of two candidates taking on an average case. You also probably know by now that you must crack your case in each and every interview to get an offer. But you may have noticed with Derek and Bindu that the interviewer rarely waits until the end of the case to determine how you are doing. In fact, every step of the case interview holds tests that highlight the differences between candidates and ultimately determine who wins out. Here is an account of every event along the interview timeline, along with some tips on how to come out on top.

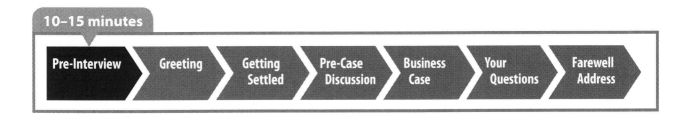

10–15 minutes

Pre-Interview ▸ Greeting ▸ Getting Settled ▸ Pre-Case Discussion ▸ Business Case ▸ Your Questions ▸ Farewell Address

CHECKING IN

Interviews can take place in the school interview rooms or off-site hotels. Sometimes firms need to go off campus because of timing, space restrictions or flexibility. It also gives them more control than using the career center and provides a more elegant atmosphere. They

typically will rent out a floor of deluxe rooms and set up a waiting room in a large suite. They'll stock it with assorted breakfast or snack foods (that no one has the stomach to eat) and station a pack of first-year associates to make small talk with the candidates. The firms are highly concerned with brand association, so booking rooms at the Ritz-Carlton or the Four Seasons adds to their image. If your interview does not take place in a hotel, you'll encounter a similar check-in process at your school's career planning and placement center.

After you arrive and sign in, you should ditch everything but your notebook and pen. You may find an array of tempting foodstuffs, but it is best to have eaten carefully beforehand. Avoid eating anything right before the interview; you don't want to be caught with a mouth full of muffin when they call your name. And food and drink can do funny things to your voice when you're nervous. Plan what you'll eat on interview day and manage it outside of the interview process (e.g., take your favorite protein bar in your bag). You may have to interview with 3–4 people in one day so managing your energy is important.

These people will not ultimately decide whether you move on, but they can create a favorable buzz about you.

Be sure to turn your attention quickly to the greeters. They are probably bored out of their minds and wouldn't mind a little small talk (see guidelines on page 34). Your job with them is simply to make a good impression. If you spot someone you've met at a reception or dinner, then by all means focus on building that relationship. These people will not ultimately decide whether you move on, but they can create a favorable buzz about you. This could help you later—if you make it to the final round—as the recruiting staff and partners often talk about the candidates they liked best.

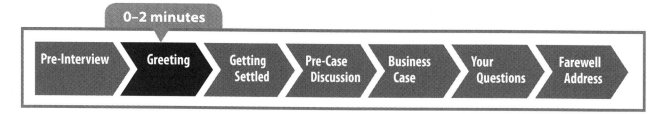

THE HANDSHAKE AND GREETING

Finally, someone calls your name and you stand to greet him or her with a handshake. This is your first point of contact with your interviewer and, therefore, an important event.

A handshake is very personal. You are taking the palm of a stranger's hand and pressing it against your own—a weird custom, when you think about it. Although some germaphobes would like to see the handshake disappear, it is not going anywhere soon. The best handshake is dry, firm and very brief. Wet or moist ones are the worst. Lengthy handshakes are too personal. No exceptions.

Any deviation from "dry, firm and brief" will leave a negative impression. Here are a few folks that no interviewer wants to encounter.

Limp Linda or Lifeless Luke

Her grip couldn't pull a parachute cord to save her life. You know who I'm talking about: the woman apparently afraid to shake hands. She puts it out there like a gentle flower, and as soon as you grab hold you realize it's already wilted. You're afraid that you may have hurt her. Or there is the guy who feels like he has a doughnut for a hand—you can't help but think he's weak. If you have a soft handshake and you don't have time to hit the weights, at least give it your all when you shake hands. Lean into it if necessary.

Sweaty Sam or Sticky Sally

"Hi, nice to meet you, Sam. I'm David." Hands meet and we stick together for what seems like an eternity. Your hand feels like a wet sponge. Yuck! Finally we separate, and I'm looking for a sink or a wet wipe. I used to know a consultant who cleaned his hands with a gel sanitizer after every handshake—in front of the candidates! He told them it was to ward off the common cold, but I'll bet he was really just trying to remove the feel of Sweaty Sams and Sticky Sallys. There is no more disgusting way to start an interview.

We've all had the sweaty-hands problem. Getting nervous and sweating is inevitable. Honestly, if you're a big-time sweater and there's nothing you can do about it, then here's a simple solution: in the waiting room press your palm to the couch or your pant leg to keep it dry. For the rest of us, a quick (and subtle) wipe of your hand on your pants or jacket should do the trick.

Any deviation from "dry, firm and brief" will leave a negative impression. Here are a few folks that no interviewer wants to encounter.

> *There is a huge difference between firmly squeezing a hand and pulverizing a hand.*

Bone-Crusher Bob or Bruiser Barb

"Hello, Bob, I'm David." I reach for the hand and then: crunch. Wow—are my bones still intact? Bone-Crusher Bobs out there, take it easy. There is a huge difference between firmly squeezing a hand and pulverizing a hand. Be especially careful if you're shaking a female partner's hand: a little goes a long way. If you find that the handshake coming back at you is a little weaker than expected, back off quickly. Disabling the interviewer is not a good start to your discussion.

How do you perfect your handshake? As with everything else, practice. Find an understanding friend and keep testing your handshake until you get it right. Along with your warm smile, it is perhaps the strongest part of your first impression, and it matters more than you might think.

YOUR CLOTHING

Some of my strangest moments as a candidate involved interviewers scanning my appearance from top to bottom, without an ounce of subtlety. We'd meet and say hello, and then their eyes would travel from my hair down to my shoes and back up again. It felt bizarre to be so overtly checked out. But it happened for good reason: the interviewer just wanted to know whether I fit the part.

Appearance and first impressions are important in the business world, as clients—whether internal or external—expect you to be professional and produce results. Let's hope your interviewers won't be so brazen when checking your appearance, but expect it to happen occasionally.

You didn't buy this book for fashion advice, so I won't attempt to adjust your closet. But if you want to get hired, you must remember one simple rule: don't wear or carry anything that distracts attention from you and what you have to say. Here is my Avoid-At-All-Costs list. Believe it or not, I have seen each of these mistakes—more than once.

Men	Women
Avoid the following...	***Avoid the following...***
■ Cologne (just skip it; your interviewer might be allergic)	■ Perfume (just skip it; your interviewer might be allergic)
■ Loud ties (no cute symbols or characters)	■ Too much jewelry (less is more)
■ Jewelry or rings of any type, except a wedding band	■ Over-styled, crazy hair
■ Facial hair (some firms are more accepting than others, but why not find out after you're hired?)	■ Weird pens or notebooks (keep it simple; no one is impressed by a Mont Blanc)
■ Weird pens or notebooks (keep it simple; no one is impressed by a Mont Blanc)	■ Loud scarves or suits (what would you wear to a manufacturing client in a conservative town?)
■ Any suit color other than black, blue or gray	■ Overly decorated shoes
■ Any shirt color other than white or French blue (why risk it?)	■ Purses or bags (store them in the waiting room)
■ Really bold pinstripes in your suit	■ Red or long fake fingernails
■ Unkempt or unprofessional hair (one partner I knew nicknamed a candidate the "Beatles haircut kid")	■ Bright lipstick or too much make-up

THE WALK TO THE ROOM

You have avoided the food but are holding a small juice to calm your nerves. A minute or two before your official interview time, you set it down, dry your hand and wait. After hearing your name called you step forward, offer a huge smile, make solid eye contact, say hello, shake hands and then proceed to the interview room. In some cases, my room was a good fifteen to twenty hotel doors away from the waiting room. Some interviewers will do their best to immediately begin engaging you with small talk on the way; others will walk quickly, saying little, solely focused on getting you into the room and starting the case. This is your first glimpse of the interviewer's communication style. Is he pleasant and friendly? Is she quiet and a little brusque? It's a good bet that what you see here will be similar to what you experience when you start the case.

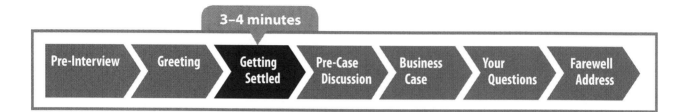

SMALL TALK

A little chatter here and there is natural with any interview. Try to stay relaxed, but keep in mind that you are being evaluated at all times. It is amazing what pops out of the mouths of nervous candidates! If you tend to say silly things in such situations, try to say as little as possible.

To give yourself a head start and to calm your nerves, below are some suggested topics. Your tone should always be positive. Do not complain about anything, or you may appear to be high-maintenance, a definite turn-off among co-workers.

Bounds	Out of Bounds
■ The weather ("The town is beautiful when covered with two feet of snow . . .")	■ Your or your interviewer's appearance
■ Your commute to the interview ("No problem, traffic was light today . . .")	■ Your or your interviewer's family
	■ Your health
■ The interviewer's city ("I got a chance to spend the weekend there . . . it was great!")	■ The details of other firms' activities (top-notch firms do not talk about their competitors)
■ Your school, including your classes ("It has been better than I expected . . .")	■ Your lack of experience with cases
	■ Your desire to work only in one city (wait until asked, then be careful)
■ Interview week ("I've had a chance to meet a lot of interesting people . . .")	■ Where you are headed after the interview (be vague; it's none of his or her business)
	■ Your grades or GMAT scores (they probably have them, so wait until asked directly)

Getting Settled in the Room

If you are interviewing in a hotel room, you might be a little unsettled to see a bed about seven feet from the interview desk. Try not to feel uncomfortable. Many interviewers keep the door ajar with the metal safety latch. The room should be perfectly neat since the hotels offer early maid service. As an interviewer, I always had to be up and out of the room by 7:00 A.M. to ensure ample clean-up time. You may see an open suitcase or a pile of dirty clothes in the corner. Try to ignore them.

Typically, the room will contain a desk or table. The interviewer will point to where you should sit. If you are solving a case, position yourself to write on the table. This means you'll need to assume what I call the "attentive pose", sitting on the front half of the chair, leaning slightly forward, ready to respond to whatever comes your way. Try to get comfortable, since you will probably be in that position for most of the interview. If you move around too much you'll seem fidgety and nervous. Your interviewer may move around quite a bit. You, however, are expected to stay in good form, so do not relax, even if the interviewer does.

PRE-CASE DISCUSSION
(WHAT THEY REALLY WANT TO KNOW)

Do I Like You?

If there is a pre-case discussion about your background, it happens right now. This part of the interview can go in several different directions. The interviewer's main purpose is to get a feel for your personality. Some people like to call it the Airport Test or the Pizza Test, as in "If I got stuck at the airport with you, or had to work late and share a pizza with you, would I want you on my team?" If you think this is incredibly subjective and judgmental, you're right. The interviewer

is determining whether you would fit into the firm's social circle. Do your best to be engaging with the following mental checklist:

- Am I making eye contact?
- Am I listening well?
- Do I appear pleased to be here and interested in what is being said?
- Am I smiling consistently (not like a crazed clown, but pleasantly)?
- Am I matching conversational pace (in sync with the interviewer)?

Why do you want to work for us?

Some people like to jump right into the case, since they know it will take about 20 minutes and they don't want to run out of time. Others start the discussion with a few questions about you and your career aspirations. Here are the basics:

Are you interested only in my industry?

This is a very tricky question. If you say yes, it shows you are focused. But it also shows that you are probably lying. Most people have a backup plan in another industry. If you say no it might indicate that you are not focused.

Answer with confidence along these lines: "My primary focus is consulting / marketing / high tech, but I'm interested in a few other areas as well." No one can fault you for having a variety of interests.

Why consulting? Why banking?
Why this industry (e.g., consumer goods)?

The best answers are direct and tight, as in "I love to solve problems, learn about lots of different businesses and face tough challenges on a regular basis. Consulting seems like a good fit." If you are interested in marketing, launching new products might be where you want to put your energy. Or if banking or finance attracts you, emphasize the

quant and deal nature of the work. Think carefully about why you really like something: your responses will ring true and you'll be able to answer with confidence.

Be prepared with a couple of crisp bullets for each of the categories you are pursuing.

What other firms are you pursuing?

You will hear this question infrequently during your first round of interviewing, but in the later rounds it is usually asked. Don't lie, but keep it vague at first. You want to assure them that they are not your only opportunity and that you are pursuing their competitors. Don't tell a McKinsey interviewer that you are also interested in a small boutique IT shop, for example; he might question your fit.

Who Are You?

Some interviewers may use this warm-up time to learn whether you're sharp and on the ball. They might ask you to talk about your resumé. Short, focused answers are better than long ones. Keep your answers to the point, and let the interviewer ask you a follow-up question if he wants to know more. This discussion may take one of the following paths:

Coolness/Uniqueness Factor

Partners love to find the next cool superstar. You know that person: he's bright, attractive, fun and an Olympic gymnast! Or she's smart, outgoing, friendly, and was a backup singer for Beyoncé! One partner I know prided himself on nabbing the "top student" of each program. Some interviewers love athletes. Others notice musicians. All of these campus celebrities still have to crack the case like everyone else. If they do, the interviewers and recruiting staff have more to talk (and gossip) about back at the office. But these candidates also have a slight disadvantage, as their extra uniqueness can sometimes lead to conversations that burn up precious time that should be spent on the case. If you don't consider yourself to be exceptional, take a fresh look at your resumé. Think about your graduate school essays. Remind yourself how amazing you really are.

Quantitative Quickie

This could be anything from a simple math question to something quantitative on your resumé. Look through your resumé and think about the analytical tasks you may have done at different points in your school and work experience. Test yourself to see if you can describe what the goal was, how you structured the analysis, what you did and what the final result was.

Strengths, Weaknesses and Other Basic Questions

Much has been written on how to best respond to these questions. My main advice is to prepare answers in advance and practice saying them out loud. Hearing yourself answer will reveal any awkwardness or difficulties. You never know when they will come up and you don't want to be caught off guard. For more detailed prep on these types of questions check out Section 7.

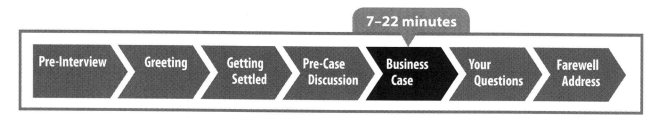

THE BUSINESS CASE QUESTION

The case will usually last about twenty minutes. Most interviewers want to have time at the end to talk about your conclusion and answer your questions about the firm.

Although your case can last a full fifteen to twenty minutes, it is usually decided within the first five to ten. By that time, the interviewer knows whether you are in the bottom, middle or top third of the roster. Even if yours is the first interview of the day, the interviewer has likely given this case many times before, so it's easy to bucket you. If you fall into the middle or bottom third, there is no hope. If you are in the top third, you have a fighting chance.

23–25 minutes

| Pre-Interview | Greeting | Getting Settled | Pre-Case Discussion | Business Case | Your Questions | Farewell Address |

YOUR QUESTIONS ABOUT THE FIRM

You need to do your homework in advance. Your best resources are the firm's website, company literature, company representatives and, especially, past employees of the firm. Make sure you take the time to develop questions that will give you additional insight about the firm. Many students do not prepare in advance and miss this opportunity. They are often flustered or mentally wiped out after the case, but a simple question written in their notebooks ahead of time would keep them on track. One rule of thumb is to focus on the interviewer's experience. Even if you get dinged, you can at least learn something from someone who is living the life you want to lead. Here are some questions to consider and some to avoid.

Good Questions	Not-so-good Questions
	(you should already have the answers)
■ What was your biggest lesson from your first year of work?	
■ What skills were most important to your success during your first year here (at the firm or company)?	■ How much training does a first year associate/analyst receive?
■ Do you still find your work to be challenging?	■ Do new hires in your office travel much?
■ What part of the lifestyle has been the biggest surprise?	■ How long does a typical project last?
	■ What would some of my main responsibilities be as a first-year?
■ What types of projects is your office focusing on right now? (strategy vs. operational)	■ Will there be a chance to interact with the client or customer over the summer?
■ What kind of problem are you trying to solve for your client/customer presently?	■ How has your office grown over the last couple of years?
■ How has your role changed, in terms of dealing with your clients/customers, over the last two years?	■ How many years does it take to make partner or director?
	■ How did I do on the case?

26–27 minutes

| Pre-Interview | Greeting | Getting Settled | Pre-Case Discussion | Business Case | Your Questions | Farewell Address |

THE FAREWELL ADDRESS

Well, it's over—not just the case, but also the decision about whether you will go on to the next round (or get an offer). At best, the interviewer has placed you in one of the top three positions in the pile. Each interviewer completes a score sheet rating each candidate's performance. Some try to do it during the interview and fill in the gaps after the candidate leaves, while others start the process at the end of the interview. In either case, they usually end the conversation a little early to finish it. You can expect to be out of the room a few minutes before the official end of your time slot.

Normally the interviewer will bid you adieu at the door of the hotel room. By now you have asked all of your questions, and the whole experience is truly over. A warm smile, a brief handshake and a "thanks for your time" are all that is required. You will head back to the reception area and encounter the greeters again. If you get a dopey question like "How did it go?" respond with a huge smile and say, "Great!" If nothing else, you will further unnerve the candidates-in-waiting.

VIDEO 5-01

Case Interview Timeline Tips

Let's get started on a piece of output that you'll definitely need later: your key questions for the firms. Think about your top choices of where you want to work and the type of information you want to understand better. For starters, you may want to know about training, hours, types of projects, timelines, length of projects, industries of focus and overall growth trajectory for the team, group or firm. Jot down these topics and then think carefully about where you'll get this information. If you can research it on your own, you'll now be smarter about the company. What remains will give you the topics for your questions. Now begin crafting the questions you'll want to ask. These will come in handy during quick chats with company personnel or throughout the interview process.

MY QUESTIONS FOR THE COMPANY

Company Name	Key Topics	Questions	Sources (Web Site, Peers, Company Rep)

Prep According to Case Type

BASIC CASE TYPES

As the 2x2 matrix below illustrates, you may face a variety of cases throughout the interview process. It's important to not only be aware of all the case types, but also allocate your preparation time carefully. Thus, as you read through this chapter, try to understand your present classification as a candidate, the position you want, what cases you would typically be expected to do, and your present skills.

Referring to the matrix on this page, there are four basic ways that you may be tested during the interview:

- Resumé, Leadership & Persuasion
- Business Case
- Fit & Personality
- Market Sizing & Brainteaser Cases

These four interview types will vary by interviewer, firm, interview location and, of course, your experience and education level. Some of them may overlap. A calm resumé discussion could heat up quickly as your interviewer turns your experience at Ford Motor Company into a mini business case. Or a market

sizing case can easily be embedded into a business case (e.g., estimate how big the toothbrush market is while discussing the launch of a new type of toothpaste).

Depending upon the position you are seeking and your current status, you will receive a different set of cases during your interviews. On the 2x2 matrix, one bubble represents the typical set of cases that a more senior candidate would receive. For MBAs, Lateral Hires, PhDs and graduate students, the interview will likely include a heavy emphasis on the business case, a review of your resumé and a discussion of your leadership experience. They will also seriously assess how your personality will fit with the company culture. Everyone in this group can expect to encounter tough, business-oriented analytical cases that are.

The second bubble represents undergraduates, or candidates who have not completed graduate-level work. They would be entry-level analysts in the consulting firm, marketing organization or industry department. Cases for these candidates may involve some business cases, but they will tend to emphasize math and analytics in a Market Sizing or Brainteaser format. Additionally, leadership and fit will play a big part in the decision process.

As much as you would like the interview process to be very straightforward and consistent (like an SAT or GMAT exam), it's not and never will be. So my best recommendation is that you become aware of the full set of cases you could encounter and then prioritize your preparation according to your skills and available study time. Your main objective should be to remove all variability in your interview performance. As you become more consistent with each problem format, you will find that your confidence grows and your excitement about the interview process will increase. Interviewers are most impressed with someone who is at ease during the interview and appears to be enjoying the case analysis and discussion. And of course, when you relax, your best thinking and personality traits come out. Let's move through each case type and review what will be expected of you.

RESUME, LEADERSHIP & PERSUASION

What is it?

Just as the title implies, companies want to understand you better by reviewing your resume and drilling in on your experience as a persua-

sive leader. A simple resumé review could include discussing where you worked and for how long. You will be expected to explain the type of work you did and the impact you and your team (or division) had on the company. You may also have to recount a detailed example of how you applied your leadership skills to a tough situation.

How should I prepare?

Here is a practical approach that will take the story of your experience and leadership to a whole new level:

- Save your resumé as a new electronic document. Name it something like "My Resumé Long Version".

- For each major section in your resumé, write out answers to the following questions. Don't worry about being too precise at first.

  - What did I do during this time of work? What was my main job and output?

  - How was I a leader? Give an example of how you persuaded a person or group to do something. Examples that describe a tough situation are best.

  - What did my team (or group) do? What was our main objective and how did our work influence the company?

  - What was going on at the company level while I worked there? Were there any shifts in the industry or major changes in the company?

- Now that you have taken the time to write out your main ideas, refine each answer into a tight one- to two-sentence response. Be sure to bring your main idea to the front part of your statement in order to be as answer-first as possible.

- Once you have written up your best answers, print out the document and put it in your briefcase or backpack. When you have free moments throughout the day, read through the document. Soon these well-written, concise answers will flow freely anytime you're asked about your experience. In a sense, you've methodically re-wired your mind to give the best responses when asked.

Where do candidates typically go wrong?

- Most candidates under-prepare for this type of interview. They

You will be expected to explain the type of work you did and the impact you and your team (or division) had on the company.

incorrectly assume that because they know their own experience, they'll give good responses.

■ Interviewers want to understand how you think. Be ready to give details when asked. An interviewer might ask, "So, what did you say next?" If the conversation happened three years ago, of course you won't remember exactly. But you need to convey what you think was said and how you were thinking. The interviewer is trying to predict how you might act in future situations, so help him with details.

MARKET SIZING & BRAINTEASER CASES

What are they?

These cases are basically math problems that you have to solve. The challenge is that typically you are given very little information and few facts upon which to base your calculations. You will be expected to make logical assumptions, build some basic facts and then do some calculations. For market sizing problems, you'll need to determine the size of a market (e.g., the number of people who will buy a new shampoo). For brainteaser questions, you'll have to solve a tough "riddle" that may even seem silly (e.g., how many ping pong balls would fit in an SUV?). You will be expected to give an answer at the end of the calculation.

How should I prepare?

Solving quite a few is the key here. You need to solve a significant number of market sizing and brainteaser cases to ensure your comfort with making assumptions about each situation. For market sizing problems, be prepared to give assumptions about population size (e.g., US population), number of consumers (e.g., dogs that eat dry dog food) and typical caveats (e.g., some children may be allergic to the new product). Brainteasers can also be conquered over time once you master the ability to make good assumptions. Most people who study for these types of cases become consistently good at solving them.

We've dedicated half of Section 9 to training you on how to handle the communication and analytical challenges that market sizing cases present. Years ago, they were isolated to undergraduate interviews, as that type of interview tests math skills well. Now they crop up in the middle of longer cases and as stand-alone cases for MBAs and graduate students. I believe they are excellent at training you in how

to speak and how to communicate your assumptions and logic. In the back of the book we have eight market sizing cases. I would recommend training with those and then looking for an additional ten in other resources. Undergraduates should spend more time preparing for these types of problems.

Where do candidates typically go wrong?

I find that candidates are hesitant to throw stones at their own assumptions. Since it is a problem that requires estimating, be prepared to explain how your analysis may under- or over-estimate the answer. Also be prepared to explain how you would refine the answer if you had more time. Check out Section 9 to better understand SPEAK, my method for solving market sizing cases.

FIT & PERSONALITY

What is it?

There is no precise test for this category. Instead, members of the company are trying to understand your background and your personality and whether or not you fit well with their firm. They will do this through questioning and observation.

How should I prepare?

As cliché as it sounds, be yourself. In the end, if you are not a personality fit for your target company, it will be an unhappy situation for both you and the company. Do your best to understand the typical personality and culture of each company to which you apply. Keep in mind that a company is made up of many people, so if you run across someone you don't like or fit with, give them a few more chances.

Where do candidates typically go wrong?

Candidates often do not take the time to learn about each company. Remember, interviewers are most interested in their own company, not your aspirations to "join an industry". If you prepare ahead of time, you are more likely to ask good questions and get along well

with the company culture. Learning each company's particular lingo (e.g., case vs. study vs. project, or deck vs. slide vs. storyboard) can also help you fit a little better.

BUSINESS CASE BASICS

Background

The top companies want to put your brainpower to the test. As a result, business case questions are becoming more complex and multi-layered. You should expect to be asked a question that involves an industry you may know very little about (e.g., hedge funds) or one that you have never thought much about (e.g., diamond mining). You should also expect to have to cover several business concepts in one case: for instance, introducing a new product and discussing the supply chain changes necessary to support it.

If study time permits, you can pursue expertise at fitting ping-pong balls into football stadiums or counting the number of pigeons in New York city seven different ways, but be sure to fully prepare for the type of case you will most likely encounter during your interviews: the business case question.

What is it exactly?

In a case interview you typically receive a business problem to solve. You are asked to work your way to a solution in about twenty minutes. These cases are often drawn from real-life problems that the interviewers have helped solve in the course of a client engagement.

Obviously, no one can expect you to solve in twenty minutes a problem that took a team of people four months to conquer. Because of this time constraint, the interviewer is often prepared to dole out data to assist you with your analysis. Sometimes this data is given verbally, and sometimes it takes the form of charts and graphs (called "slides" in the consulting biz). There's one catch: you typically must figure out what kind of information you need and ask for it. The interviewer will not necessarily hand it over without you asking first.

When I was preparing for my case interviews, I often heard that there is "no wrong answer" to a case. This is completely false. Several right answers may exist, but—trust me—there is an infinite variety of

wrong answers. While your approach to the case and your agility with facts and figures can leave a great impression with the interviewer, you must reach a well-reasoned and supported answer to achieve success.

Is it effective?

Companies seek candidates who can consistently think on their feet, be logical in their problem-solving approach, and handle unexpected curve balls with aplomb. A case question does a pretty good job of giving the interviewers a glimpse of how to rate the candidate on these skills. Most companies offer positions only to those candidates who have cracked all of their cases (typically four or five); this practice assures the firms that they have found the best available candidates during a very short and intensive interview process.

Many firms expect their interviewers to have cases prepared in advance and pre-tested by other members of their team. This method ensures that the cases are neither too long nor too simple. Nevertheless, it's not uncommon for a partner to show up unprepared and invent a case on the fly. These spontaneous cases can result in very easy or very difficult interviews.

Several right answers may exist, but—trust me—there is an infinite variety of wrong answers.

TYPES OF BUSINESS CASES

Despite the hundreds of case variations, they tend to fall into a few broad categories. To keep all the case types straight, I will use five categories, or zones; most of your interview cases will fall into the first two zones. We'll discuss these groupings in greater detail later in the book. In the meantime, remember that your ultimate goal is to maximize the value of the company being discussed in your case question. Keeping this goal in mind will broaden your perspective on your cases and help you think more like a business advisor. Rather than getting caught up in the details of only one aspect of the business, you must take on the perspective of the CEO.

Zone 1—Strategic Cases

Many people in the business world disagree on the true definition of strategy. As you prepare for your cases, you will find the word "strategy" slapped on the back of almost any case title (e.g., pricing strategy, systems strategy and operational strategy). A good working defini-

ZONE 1	STRATEGIC CASES

Expand Scope

- Merge
- Acquire
- Form a joint venture

Change Direction

- Enter/Exit a market (add/eliminate a product line)
- Develop and sell new products/services
- Reposition the company (brand/image)

Reduce Scope

- Divest a business or division

Maintain Status Quo

- Keep the business the same

tion of strategy is "maximizing value with a limited set of resources." With strategic cases, you are making a change that will have a large impact on the business as a whole, not a small adjustment like changing a product's price or launching a new advertising campaign.

Zone 2—Operations Cases

Operations cases focus on the internal operations of the company. Since we want to maximize the value of the company at all times, operations cases have two major drivers: revenue and cost. What emerges are various ways to impact those drivers. It would be easy to call any of these cases a strategy case (e.g., pricing strategy), but I find that naming them as such prevents you from focusing on the key value levers themselves. Revenue and cost are the most basic levers in business, so you should expect to see a lot of cases touch on them.

ZONE 2	OPERATIONS CASES

Increase Revenue (Price x Volume):

Increase pricing:

- Change pricing by segment
- Increase volume
- Keep present customers (loyalty)
- Acquire new customers
- Increase share of wallet with present customers
- Sell more in new places and ways

Reduce Costs:

- Assess fixed vs. variable
- Assess internal vs. external costs
- Benchmark costs to other companies
- Assess operational minimum costs

Zone 3—Organization, Systems and Process Cases

We are now entering the "fuzzy" zone. The categories in Zone 3 represent real potential business issues, but they don't necessarily offer clear-cut ways to increase overall company value. For instance, a new computer system may provide more insight into how the business is performing, but unless it eventually results in more revenue or fewer costs, it does not maximize company value. Solving these cases involves donning your CEO hat. Make sure that you do not get stuck in the minutiae and forget about the larger goal of making money.

Zone 4—Finance Cases

Cases in the finance zone cover a company's financing and balance sheet items. Strategy cases often touch on this area, so you should be prepared to incorporate some basic finance principles into your analysis. In Section 12 we'll go through the SAVED model for those cases that dive deep into finance.

Zone 5—External Forces

Another term for this zone might be the Reaction Zone, as the issues here demand that the company react in some manner. For example, a competitive threat case can result in an acquisition strategy, a pricing reduction or an exit from the industry. Zone 5 cases always result in the company taking some type of action.

THE MOST LIKELY SCENARIO

Now that you're panicking over the laundry list of case types listed on the previous pages, let's apply a little 80/20 logic to focus your efforts. Later in the book you will see how the Maximum Value Model pulls these zones together in a way that is easy to remember and apply in your interviews.

ZONE 3 | ORGANIZATION, SYSTEMS AND PROCESS CASES

Impact the People:

- Change the organizational structure
- Change people's roles
- Change people's incentives
- Change the management team (or Board of Directors)

Change the Process/Systems:

- Change information technology (broad or narrow)
- Change procurement
- Change sales
- Change inventory
- Change distribution (including Internet)

Measure the Organization's Capabilities:

- Assess skill sets
- Assess and streamline processes
- Centralize or decentralize
- Assess production capacities

ZONE 4 | FINANCE CASES

Impact the Balance Sheet:

- Assess inventory/ receivables
- Assess debt/equity mix of the company
- Assess cash management
- Buy back shares of the company
- Execute off-balance sheet financing

Increase Equity Returns:

- Improve capital efficiency
- Increase shareholder value

ZONE 5 | EXTERNAL FORCES

- Respond to supplier issues
- Respond to public attitude/ perception changes
- Respond to economic changes
- Respond to a competitive threat
- Respond to an industry shift
- Respond to auditor issues & concerns
- Address legislative and regulatory changes
- Respond to technological changes

Within the business case question category lie a variety of potential case questions. Keep in mind that the purpose of the interview is to ascertain whether you can think like a business advisor. In order to measure your skills and also to make sure they offer a case that most people can solve in a reasonable time frame, most interviewers will stick to Strategy Cases (Zone 1) and Operations Cases (Zone 2). These areas provide a rich set of issues that will put your abilities to the test. The beauty of being familiar with the other zones is that if the interview jumps into those other areas, you won't get lost.

Keep in mind that each case a firm gives provides a glimpse into the type of work they do. No firm wants to be seen as non-strategic or focused on mere support issues. Therefore, most questions you receive will be deemed strategic, even if they more properly fall into another zone.

Zone 1 and Zone 2 Favorites

Within the strategy and operations zones, a few issues appear frequently. They are, in no particular order, the following:

- Maximize profit ("Help! My company is losing money.")
- Enter a new market
- Develop / Launch a new product
- Sell more of the same stuff to more people (products or services)
- Reduce costs
- Respond to competitors
- Merge two companies

VIDEO 6-01

Case Interview Types

All of these cases work well in a case interview format because their problems are clear and their answers center on core business concepts. These cases are effective in revealing which candidates can frame a solution and which can't. Also, many of the interviewing companies' actual client problems (the source for most case interview questions) relate to these issues.

6

HOMEWORK →

Fill out the short quiz opposite on case types. Knowing the different ways you'll need to prepare will be helpful as you manage your practice time.

CASE TYPE QUIZ

Question	My Answer	What Did I Forget?
What types of cases will I likely face in Zones 1 and 2?		
Where do candidates usually go wrong with resumé, leadership & persuasion questions?		
What are some basic steps to solving a market sizing question?		

CHAPTER

3

Dance! Classic Skills and Case Flows

Show CLASSIC Skills
throughout the Interview

It may sound like an odd comparison, but when you meet some¬one during an interview, you are a lot like a tree. Much of you is above the surface—your appearance, your interactions and your overall personality. As they observe you on this level, interviewers are thinking about how you'll fit into their culture. But they also know that beneath that surface is a deep root structure that drives the output of the tree. Interviewers want to find out what your root structure is made of, what it has produced in the past, and what it will produce going forward—because in order to do well on the job day after day, you must have strong roots. The interview is their chance to "test the roots" with questions and problems.

When I talk about testing the roots, I'm describing how a company assesses the strength of the basic root structure that supports how you think, act and solve problems. So when you get behavioral questions that deal with leadership, teamwork or failure, the interviewer is also testing your root skills in communication and logic. Companies use behavioral questions and case questions during the interview to test for the kind of skills they need to see every day. They want to see you produce output that is similar to what they do at work. For instance, if the firm is focused on financial analysis, you can expect to see heavy testing on the analytics root skill. Other firms may need you to show a balance between communication, logic and analysis. Their cases will still focus on analysis, but will also require you to think through how

you might roll out your solution in the most successful way, and the kind of message to communicate to the employees. Ultimately, every firm tests for the root structure that shows you can consistently produce the results they need for their business. And since there are multiple rounds of interviews, different people will have the chance to test different skills.

I believe there are six key roots that you should show off during the interview. Together they spell out the word CLASSIC—because these are the clas¬sic skills that you need to demonstrate in every interview. Let's look first at the skills and how to strengthen them; later I'll explain how to weave them into the flow of the case interview.

Communication

Every company needs strong communicators. When I work with my private coaching clients on their communication, I stress being answer-first. I didn't invent this phrase, and it can encompass a variety of definitions. But we'll use it here to mean "Get to the point!" Most of us are very good at telling stories that are interesting (we hope) and, unfortunately, full of detail. We typically tell our stories in an answer-last approach, with a big "Aha!" or interesting punch line at the end. Details make stories come alive, and we use answer-last communication because we know those details help us bond with others as we share our experiences. Also, our natural storytelling instincts lead us to build the suspense and then hit our listener with the funny ending: ". . . So when we finally got to the party, it was completely deserted. We had the wrong night!" Interview communication, however, requires a completely different approach. Interviewers don't have time to wait for your answer-last stories. They want you to get right to the point because there is so much to cover between getting to know you, skimming your resumé, and giving you a case. Also, interviewers tend to come from work worlds in which their day-to-day customers and clients are very impatient. This has forced them to get to the point quickly; whether they're executives or senior leaders, they have learned to be answer-first. During the interview, you need to respond to that pattern and be answer-first with your behavioral and case questions.

VIDEO 7-01

Building CLASSIC skills

You may be using the STAR method for telling your behavioral stories: Situation, Task, Action and Results. Although this is good for making sure you cover every point in your story, your interviewer may become frustrated waiting for the results at the end, and may lose her focus. Instead of using a strict STAR approach, I recommend you summarize with a quick, answer-first executive sentence or tag line that lets the interviewer know where you're going with your story; then move into the details. You'll practice using tag lines with your IMPACT stories later, as you establish the habit of answer-first communication.

Logic

Logic is all about breadth and depth. In the case interview, you need to show the ability to think both broadly and deeply about a topic. You'll be expected to quickly break a problem down into a broad set of categories and to put those pieces in some kind of prioritized order. I call that breadth of thinking. Many firms will then ask you for additional ideas: "What else? What else?" They'll keep asking, pushing you to show breadth. Sometimes after your sixth or seventh idea, they'll still ask, "What else?", even though they know you can't have any other ideas. You'll also be expected to drill deep into any of those categories and explain your thoughts fully. This is showing depth of thought. Interviewers want to see depth and breadth of thinking on all kinds of questions, whether business scenarios or simple brain teasers. You know you're facing a depth question when the interviewer pushes in one area: "Tell me more about communications. Tell me more about the competitors." She's looking for specific areas where you can go deep. One of her highest priorities is to test your logic skills by understanding how broadly and deeply you can explore a topic. That's because day in and day out on the job, you'll be asked to face some kind of business problem, think broadly to organize a complicated set of topics, prioritize them, and then drill in and solve them one by one. Interviewers replicate this basic pattern during the interview.

VIDEO 7-02

Logic = Breadth and Depth

Analytics

Your analytics skills show that you can find the right kind of data, interpret it, and come up with ways to use that data to make changes. During the interview you'll need to demonstrate your ability to pull data out of the discussion, slide, or handout, and then interpret it in a way that helps you solve the problem. Early in your discussion, show that you're very concerned about numbers and that you want to think about how the data would show you more information. When you close, you also need to show how the data had an impact on the situation. So when you think about analytics, remember that it's your ability to show how you used numbers to solve problems. We'll work on how to pull together an analytical story for your behavioral interviews, and most of the case packs in the book will test your analytics.

Social Skills

You also need to stand out in your social skills. Interviewers look for candidates who excel in speaking and listening, and in socializing with all kinds of people. And as you talk, they're assessing whether they could see themselves having an effective working relationship with you. If you go on to be an analyst or consultant, you'll be meeting all sorts of people who hold keys to the data that you need. Even if you don't want to be a consultant, your future career will likely include leading teams to solve problems in which you'll encounter many of the same social challenges. You will also have to work with all levels of people. And some scenarios will require the ability to pull good information out of those people. For instance, in one project you may have to interview everyone—from the lowest-level accounting clerk or machine operator all the way up to the most senior VP of operations. You'll need the social skills to handle yourself in all kinds of situations and be effective with all types of people.

Integration

Interviewers are looking for integration skills—or, in their day-to-day work, the ability to take several pieces of disparate data and pull them together quickly. This means that at the beginning of the case interview, you'll be given random information about a problem; then in the middle of the case you'll probably be asked to analyze some data in the form of slides or charts. After doing analysis and learning more, you'll then be expected to pull together the major insights and end the case in an integrated manner. This integration skill will be valuable as you gather data in all kinds of jobs. One of your primary tasks in the near future will be to bring meaningful insights out of seemingly unrelated facts and numbers. It's different than just doing straight analytics because often there's no guide to the analysis and no pre-determined output. You may not be able to refer to any framework or road map from previous work. You'll have to pull together a solution using your business instincts, problem-solving skills and solid analytics. The *Crack the Case System* materials will build your integration skills as you solve problems, learn to sum up insights quickly, and understand how to read and interpret several charts and graphs.

Creativity

Creativity is a root skill and it will be tested overtly from time to time, but it is secondary to communication and logic for most companies. From the candidate's perspective, it can feel like the only way to stand out from the pack is to be creative. But some people overdo it by thinking that they have to add a fascinating comment to every piece of the case. Realistically, in order to build a company or firm that consistently produces, interviewers have to fill it with employees who show reliable results in the areas of logic, analytics and communication. Creativity is important, but you should save it for the end of your problem-solving time—after you've already proven that you have the other, more fundamental, skills. Once you're solid in terms of your thinking, bring in your creativity to set yourself apart. When it comes to creativity, save it for the end of the case or discussion.

7A
HOMEWORK →

Next to each of the CLASSIC letters below, jot down one strength and one weakness in your own skill set. Consider people's comments on your past performance. For instance, next to Communication you might write: "Upbeat, interesting tone and pace," and "A little too verbose".

	Strength	Weakness
C		
L		
A		
S S		
I		
C		

BLOCK AND BREAK DRILLS—
HOW TO BUILD BREADTH AND DEPTH SKILLS

Begin to build your breadth and depth skills with these drills:

Drill 1

Breadth: Your friend wants to open a pizza parlor (or sushi restaurant or hamburger joint) in your local town. You've been asked to be the business advisor. You are excited about the idea, but want to be thorough. In the boxes below, write key categories or areas you would want to explore in order to determine whether this restaurant is a good idea. Write down any idea. Don't hold back, and if you need more space, take it. For instance, one box might be "competitors". I call this blocking out your topics.

Depth: Below each box, write two sub-categories that you want to explore. Think about the data you'll need or the questions you want to ask. For instance, under "competitors" you might write "same type, other pizza places" and "new competitors, ice cream". I call this breaking your blocks. Your goal should be to have a simple A and B, or two breaks per block. Breaks can be questions, pieces of data you need, or sub-topics. Being able to do this quickly for any topic will highlight your depth of thinking.

On your own paper, do this same drill with the questions below. By pushing yourself to block out clean topics (breadth) and then break them into at least two parts (depth), you are warming up for case structures.

DRILL 1	BLOCKING OUT YOUR TOPICS

Open Pizza Parlor

Drill 2

The mayor of San Francisco wants his city to host the Olympics in the near future. Assuming the city gets approved, what does he need to think about to prepare the city to succeed? After you have listed out your broad set of categories, be sure to list at least 2 questions you'd like answered, or 2 pieces of data you want found, to resolve this sub-category.

Drill 3

You and your team of 5 have been asked to make changes to improve your current campus or company. Don't suggest the changes; instead, list out the elements or factors to consider. To go deep, below each category write 2 pieces of data or 2 questions you would like answered.

Make an IMPACT during Your Behavioral Interview

You need to make a highly positive impact during your behavioral or fit interview. One of the fastest ways for an interviewer to get to know you is to have you talk about yourself. Sometimes you'll get a general question like "Walk me through your resume," or "Tell me about your career so far," or "Walk me through the choices you've made." Other times you get more specific questions about leadership, teamwork or failure. It's easy to think that these questions are just fluffy warm-up questions and that the case is all that matters. But in reality, these questions are key to setting the interviewer's mind in a positive or negative attitude toward you. As an interviewer listening to you start on one of your memorized stories, I am either thinking, "Great, this will be a good case," or "Wow, this is going to be the longest 30 minutes of my life." If you are using answer-first communication skills, telling your stories with the right amount of details and results, and embedding natural logic with comments like "first," "second," and "third," I'm feeling that you will probably do well on the upcoming case. But if you bore me with answer-last stories, too much detail, and a disorganized approach, I conclude you will probably not do well in the case. Remember, you have a very short time in which to make an impact with your behavioral stories, and they are important because people judge you long before the case even begins.

So let's start with that term: IMPACT. Each of the letters in this acronym represents a story that you need to build. (In fact, you will build

2 stories for each letter—this will give you a nice base from which to choose.) After you master your individual stories, you'll be able to blend them with other stories in order to answer vague questions like "Tell me about a time you made a difference" (ugh!). With these IMPACT stories as your foundation, you can handle any kind of question, whether vague or specific. Keep in mind that your communication is also under scrutiny, so be answer-first with all of your IMPACT stories. We'll work through some exercises to hone your skill of getting to the point quickly.

IMPACT

Individual Contribution

The letter "I" stands for individual contribution. Make sure you prepare stories highlighting your contribution as an individual. It's the time that *you* thought of the problem; *you* laid out a solution; *you* presented or tried to come up with that solution with the team. *You* may have encountered problems and had to modify that solution, or *you* may have rolled it out and succeeded. But *you* were the driver behind almost every bit of it. In this era of team building and everything being about the group, it's nice to know that you can do something alone. Don't be afraid to pull together great examples of how you saved the day. It's your superhero moment!

VIDEO 8-01

Make an IMPACT with Your Stories

Manage or Lead

Everyone talks about leadership, and some companies spend the majority of the behavioral interview on this topic. If you have several years of experience and you've managed teams in a work environment, definitely take one of your stories from that time period. Focus on ways you interacted with team members, such as having to evaluate them or deal with difficult personalities. Also emphasize how the team affected you, and how leading or managing them changed your leader-

ship style and the way you approach your work. One way to approach this behavior discussion is to offer your definition of a good leader. If you haven't had any experience managing other people, focus on leadership, using the typical examples of leading a club or some kind of activity. Even in those scenarios, it's important to describe how you were really influenced by the people around you.

Persuasion

Think about the various ways you persuade people in business, and even in daily life. Sometimes you appeal to basic logic; sometimes you bring in convincing facts or data; at other times you use goal alignment or shared passion. We persuade people using different methods for different situations. So as you assemble your persuasion examples, think of how you persuaded people using several distinct techniques. Make certain these different approaches are embedded in your stories. Be sure you also stress your empathy with those you were trying to persuade. Several firms are placing more emphasis on the need to get into the clients' minds or think like a customer. As you prepare your persuasion example, spend time thinking through your customer's perspective. This will show breadth of communication, as well as your ability to be thrown into a new environment and do well at persuading all types of people.

Analytics

The definition of analytics varies according to the situation. In the interviews you'll likely face, focus on analytical examples in which the data told you what to do. This type of example might be a very complicated model or spreadsheet, or a client database which you had to sort through for information and insights. Another good example would be a marketing segmentation study in which you analyzed a data set to find certain customer groups. Your analytical story should not be about complexity, like a major information technology roll-out or a tough logistics problem. Both of those examples are analytical in nature, but to most interviewers they will seem more like an organizational exercise rather than a data-driven one. Keep in mind that you want an example of the data telling you what to do. If you can't pull

an example like that from previous work experience, do your best to gain that kind of experience at work or school. Think about how you can get involved in a project that will require some heavy data analysis.

Challenge or Failure

You will usually be asked about a situation that didn't go well. When you talk about challenge or failure, don't just emphasize how you overcame adversity. Instead, explain how you have been permanently changed. You might describe how you once missed a deadline and consequently now think differently about managing your timelines and projects. That's good news for the interviewer because now if he purchases you (I mean, hires you), he knows that you are "fixed" in that area. You've already improved because of your experience. Don't be afraid to show off skills that have grown because of challenge or failure.

Teamwork

You've been involved in all kinds of team projects; try to pull something from work as well as school experiences, and of course be ready with the ever-important example of how the team did not get along. The interviewer wants to see how you deal with those situations because, no matter where you work, you will eventually be on a team that doesn't get along. Talk about the different roles you have played, and your flexibility and willingness to be a team member in all situations. Don't use team examples in which you always get converted into the team leader. That's not necessarily a good trait, because when you go to work at these new companies, you will not be the team leader. You need to show that you can work under other people with excellence and enthusiasm.

Once you've assembled your IMPACT stories, you will have a set of building blocks: these stories can be combined with one another to make something more complex, and can also be tailored to specific questions your interviewer asks. So if she says, "Tell me about a time you made a difference," you can now take advantage of that vague question by showing off two of your strong traits, and perhaps combining your leadership and persuasion examples. If the interviewer asks,

"How can we trust that you'll be effective at managing clients?", you may describe the time you worked as a good team player by tackling the analytical data set that led to some key insights. Your goal is to show off as many of your great qualities as quickly and effectively as possible.

To help bring your stories to life, try this simple technique: take your finger and point to your eye and say, "What did I see?" Now point to your ear and say, "What did I hear?" and then your temple and say, "What did I think?" Start most of your stories with what you saw, heard and thought. Now take your finger, point to your mouth, and say, "What did I say?" and make a fist and say, "What did I do?" Tapping into these natural observation and action skills will help you prepare stories that sound more real, and you'll also be able to build them out quickly.

Here's an example:

> *"Well, I was new to the group, and our focus was writing quick summaries of AP newswire stories for our financial advice website. I heard a lot of people on our team complaining about how we had too much work and had no direction on what was important. I saw that we were missing deadlines and the overall quality of the summaries was falling. I also noticed that attrition had shrunk our group by 20%, which didn't help. So I started thinking that we would all do better work if we had more prioritization, and that our clients would be happy, too, if they didn't have to read so many summaries. Then I spoke to the team members and my manager about our concerns and the goals of the firm. I also prepared a summary of the team's concerns and developed a method for prioritizing the stories according to key client portfolios. The discussions went well, we developed a process redesign team, and in about 2 months we had a new approach to our work. Overall satisfaction for our team went up by 25% in the next review cycle, and we were getting positive comments from our clients."*

Using this method—"What did I see, hear, and think, and then do and say?"—ensures that the story comes alive with your perspective. I often hear people tell stories that sound very generic, almost like they had no personal part in them. There's never any information that pulls me in or makes me want to know how you resolved the situation. Interviewers do get interested, however, in stories that involve you. Once you get that story flowing properly, draw out the right

VIDEO 8-02

See, Hear, Think, Say & Do

level of detail. For example, adding a simple phrase like "AP news-wires" tells the listener that the team was facing a constant stream of work. It adds some tension and color to an otherwise typical rede-sign-the-workflow story.

It's time to get to work developing your twelve IMPACT stories. Your homework is to create two good stories for each letter of the acronym. Eventually you will add some flexibility to your stories by creating both a 1-minute and a 2-minute version. The 1-minute version (or it could be even shorter) will be the one you might use if you just bump into someone at a cocktail party. The longer one could be used during the interview when the interviewer wants to gain insight into your decision-making or emotions. If he does start drilling for more details, be prepared to simply go down another level. It's not unusual now for certain firms to ask questions like "Tell me what you were feeling when you gave her the feedback," or "When you met with her to tell her your thoughts, what was on your paper?" If you haven't thought deeply about these stories, you'll get caught without anything to say.

Here are some steps to follow for each story you develop:

1 Start by filling out the chart on the right. Make sure you have a well-balanced portfolio of stories that covers work and school, as well as situations where you filled different roles. Try to avoid too many over-lapping themes as you develop your stories.

2 Pick the topic first, and start writing or typing all the bullets that come to mind about that situation. Don't worry about organizing them into a smooth story; you'll do that later. Write down everything from "Didn't like that manager," and "Learned how to manage tough employees," to "Best client and team I ever encountered."

3 Once you get all these facts down, start rearranging them in the order of your story. Have some kind of flow of the main points.

4 Read your story out loud, edit, and correct the obvious problems. Then it's time to involve others.

5 Have a friend ask you the question (e.g., "Tell me about the time you were a strong leader,") and give your story out loud. Ask for feed-back on what was strong or weak. There will usually be one area that is exceptionally strong. Bring that to the top as your tagline. For instance, at the beginning you might now say, "Sure, let me tell you

about the time I had to step up as team leader for an urgent client situation where our work led to a new $1.5M project." Now you are being answer-first and drawing in the interviewer.

6 After hearing the feedback and finding some good material for the front, edit! Ditch anything that does not contribute to a streamlined story.

7 After you have cleaned up your story, prepare a one-minute and a two- to three-minute version. For the one-minute version, eliminate unnecessary details, but keep the results and answer-first tone.

	Story Topics
Individual contribution	1
	2
Manage or Lead	1
	2
Persuasion	1
	2
Analytical	1
	2
Challenge or Failure	1
	2
Team	1
	2

Navigate the Case Interview Dances

Now that you have reviewed your CLASSIC root skills from Section 7, it's time to show off these skills in the interview. I like to compare case interviews to dancing: you're working with a partner, there's a flow and pace that can change, there are some complicated steps, and it's easy to stumble! Part of dancing well is interpreting how your partner will move. During the case you'll also have to do some interpreting. In fact, there's often a lot of complexity that requires quick interpretation.

DANCE 1—SPEAK METHOD FOR MARKET SIZING AND QUICK PROBLEMS

To help with your training, I have categorized case types into two major dances. The first case interview dance type is one in which you have to quickly get to a solution. Your interviewer may present you with a brainteaser or toss out a short scenario that you have to solve, and in a sense, the dance starts immediately. You interpret from his body language, tone and pace that he wants to get into the discussion right away. You'll have to explain your approach while solving at the same time. There's no time for you to ask for a couple of minutes to structure a more complex plan. Instead, you're expected to lead the conversation right from the beginning. To deal with these kinds of case

VIDEO 9-01

Interview Dance Overview

interviews, we're going to use a framework called the SPEAK Method. It's a great methodology for market sizing cases, but it also works well for times when you need to work through something quickly—when you can't take time to think but have to SPEAK right away. And if you are wondering how I came up with the acronym SPEAK, it's because over the years I have seen candidates do everything but speak when the pressure is on. Usually when put on the spot, you want to take a little time to think. But in these case situations, you need to be ready to talk someone through your approach immediately. During the interview you will not write the acronym SPEAK, but it will be a guide for your thinking.

SPEAK

State Your Assumptions

When you're dealing with a market sizing case, or one where the interviewer is demanding your thoughts right away, you'll need to frame up what you are and are not assuming. For instance, you may encounter a straightforward market sizing question: "How many umbrellas are sold in London each year?" You need to state your assumptions to help narrow the analysis, saying something like "I'm assuming that an umbrella lasts only one year," or "Let me assume that the average household has three umbrellas, given my own experience." The main focus should be on getting your assumptions out and making sure your interviewer is following your thinking. You'll often be able to take some basic assumptions from your life experience. When you don't, such as in a case where you have to estimate snowshoes sold in Alaska, try to make reasonable estimates. Remember, you are "dancing" with the interviewer, so he needs to sense where you are taking the discussion, and why, or he'll get frustrated and question your logic. As you practice more market sizing cases and quick questions, you'll improve dramatically in your ability to lay out assumptions, even in situations where you have limited or no life experience.

Pick Your Metric and Approach

Picking your metric means choosing the unit you'll use for counting, like the number of bottles of water. Picking your approach means deciding how you will go about counting it, such as averaging the number of bottles of water consumed by age bracket. Going back to our example of umbrellas sold in London, we know that our metric is the number of individual umbrellas sold. In this situation, the metric is easy to determine. But getting to that number is more complex. You could think of different population brackets, say 35- to 40-year-olds, and how often they buy, use and throw away umbrellas. Or you could consider where umbrellas are sold—department stores, drugstores and train station kiosks, for instance—and estimate how many are sold at each distribution channel. As you can see, there are multiple choices to make and it would be easy to take the discussion in the wrong direction. Here are a few rules to follow:

Pick common-sense metrics: In my *Crack the Case* workshops I have often used the example of counting shampoo usage in a typical downtown hotel. Students usually have no trouble thinking about basic assumptions like number of rooms and usage rates per type of guest, but they often stumble over whether to count ounces or milliliters vs. bottles used. After a little thought, they realize that what the hotel ultimately cares about is their total spending on shampoo, and since they aren't going to recycle shampoo left over in the little bottles once a guest leaves, it's best to count full bottles.

Approach your metric using *population*, cautiously:

As you approach counting the item in question, whether it is umbrellas or snowshoes or hair brushes, it is always tempting to use population. It's easy to think of age groups, like 20- to 30-year-olds, and then make some kind of assumption about how often they use the item. The population approach is great for breaking down users, and when usage rates are consistent, it works quite well. For instance, when counting baby diapers sold, you'd naturally think of the different ages of babies, newborn to two years old, and estimate usage rates. They are consistent so it is very straightforward. How about toothpaste used? We can think of age brackets again and then estimate usage rates, and

since people brush their teeth 2–3 times per day, it's still very straight-forward. But what about counting taxis in NYC? At first you might want to think of New Yorkers and their taxi usage habits, but you soon realize the difficulty of estimating transportation habits when people have so many choices—car, bus or subway. In addition, bad weather can increase usage rates. It seems like using population can require you to make quite a few assumptions that may lead you down the wrong path.

Consider *observation* as your approach:

We know that population will not always work. Let's continue with our taxi question. How about thinking through the number of blocks that are in NYC? Even if you don't know the city well, you can make some solid assumptions. Blocks might work well because you could visualize the number of cabs you see per block and then multiply by your total blocks to calculate your final number.

Let's try another example. Your interviewer asks you to estimate the number of window washers needed to wash all the office windows in Seattle on a regular basis. You also learn the cleaning team won't wash car or house windows and there are no other competitors. So for your metric, what are you really counting? At first you think you're count-ing windows, but then you realize that windows vary in size. Since you need to know the number of workers, it makes sense to think of how much glass a worker can clean per hour or day so that you can calculate how many people to hire.

Now you have your metric figured out, but what about your approach? How will you measure glass cleaned? At first you might be tempted to count the number of workers or business people in the city, but you quickly realize that knowing population won't help you understand the amount of glass or how fast it can be cleaned. Instead, consider using observation. You can think about the size of the city, the den-sity of the buildings per block, and the average height of the build-ings. You could estimate the number of city blocks, multiply by the number of buildings per block, and then multiply by average floors and number of windows per floor. Of course you would have to make some assumptions about the average size of a window and then how fast a window washer can clean one. But you the idea. In this case, observation is a much better approach than population.

Use other complementary approaches:

When population and observation don't quite get you all the way to your metric, consider adding in other approaches.

Geography—different parts of the world have different consumption rates.

Time—breaking down your assumptions by periods of time, whether during a day or throughout a year, can bring you to a more precise number.

Seasons—a variation on time, this approach might help you isolate usage rates more effectively.

Estimate Quickly

VIDEO 9-02

Approach for Market Sizing

Now you need to add some numbers to your assumptions, and fast. If you don't estimate quickly, the interviewer will think that your math skills are weak or that you are hiding from the numbers. You also want to have realistic numbers, so don't round everything too simplistically. For instance, there are 365 days in a year, so round that to 360, not 300. Likewise, don't always work with simple, large numbers like 100,000 or 1,000,000, because your interviewer will note that you're not showing real math skills. S, P and E—stating your assumptions, picking your metric and approach, and estimating quickly— all happen simultaneously. Be prepared to discuss assumptions while structuring an approach and doing math. I wish I could make the activities sequential, but that's not realistic. Over time you'll think of these individual skills as a combined activity and move fluidly from one to the other.

A Note about Notes

We know that firms want their new hires to be productive, so use your notes to show that you can produce neat, organized insights in a very short time. Start with some loose white paper, like what you would put in a printer. Avoid using bound notepads for case interviews; you don't want to be ripping pages out during the interview, and the other option, flipping forward and backward in your notebook, is hard for

VIDEO 9-03

**Using Notes
During Market Sizing**

the interviewer to follow (plus, it makes you look crazy). Position your paper in the horizontal mode as this looks like a PowerPoint slide, the most common output of analytical firms. Remember that for your market sizing cases you will not write the acronym SPEAK, but instead use it to direct your thinking. As you begin stating your assumptions and picking your metric and approach, try laying out some kind of multiple box structure or decision tree. Don't write too much; instead, write like you would if you were in front of a classroom at the whiteboard. In a sense, this piece of paper is your whiteboard. In fact, feel free to position the paper so that your interviewer can see it. As you move into your approach, whether population or some other method, block out groups clearly on your paper by making boxes or bubbles. Add numbers and data below each group when you do the calculations, so that you can adjust your numbers easily during the discussion. For market sizing cases, one piece of paper is usually sufficient. Most people struggle with talking and writing at the same time, so expect some difficulty at first. Remember, this is not the time to fall silent for a few minutes and figure it out on your own. You need to speak and stay engaged. This method of quickly writing out some assumptions while talking will also be useful in the middle of your business cases, when your interviewer puts you on the spot with a question.

Assess Your Approach

Now that you have an estimate for your metric—for instance, 7 million umbrellas—you should assess your approach. Explain to the interviewer why your number might be high or low, and lay out ways you could make it more accurate. For the umbrella example, you may have only included residents of London and their purchase habits, and now want to include tourists. Critiquing your own work is not a bad thing. Interviewers are looking for people who continue to think through a problem and explore alternative ways to reach a solution. This also mimics real-life work, in which you first come up with a rough assumption and then narrow in on the details over time. In addition, you'll be showing off that CLASSIC skill of logic and your ability to think broadly. Your personal critique might sound like this:

"So it looks like my number is about 7 million umbrellas. I think this is a good first number, but I think there are a few ways we could make this more accurate. First off, I only included residents of London and I think it would be important to include visitors to the city. We could calculate that by assuming . . ."

Keep Exceptions in Mind

As you assess your approach you also need to allow for exceptions to the rule. Consider what element you might have forgotten in your analysis, or what situations might make your thinking invalid. In the case of the taxi cabs in NYC, you may want to bring up the fact that some of your blocks could be parks, like Central Park—and in that case there will be no taxis present, so you have to deduct those blocks. Or in the Seattle windows scenario, some of the windows will be very small and take longer to clean, and others will be large enough that the glass can be cleaned faster. Bringing up these points of exception shows the interviewer that you can analyze a topic carefully. It shows your other logic skill: depth of thinking.

VIDEO 9-04

SPEAK Homework

DANCE 1—SPEAK

Now that you understand the SPEAK Method, try it out on the two questions below. You don't need to solve the case fully at this point, but write down a few words for each letter about what comes to mind for assumptions, the different ways to measure your answer, how you would estimate the numbers, and any ways you could approach the problem differently. Also, think about any exceptions to your assumptions that you would want to point out.

For a real market sizing case, you'll use your paper and show the interviewer how you are approaching the problem. It will be important to be neat and organized, use some kind of tree or structure to break down your approach, and be ready to explain your math. Check out this video about using SPEAK during the interview, with some additional tips for your homework.

SPEAK Exercise 1

How many total cups of coffee are consumed in America? How might that vary in European or Asian countries?

Exercise 1	My Initial Thoughts
State Your Assumptions	
Pick Your Metric and Approach	
Estimate Quickly	
Assess Your Approach	
Keep Exceptions in Mind	

SPEAK Exercise 2

The average airline passenger gets heavier each year and it's costing the airlines a lot of money. In fact, the average passenger is 10 lbs. heavier than last year. How would you solve this problem?

Exercise 2	My Initial Thoughts
State Your Assumptions	
Pick Your Metric and Approach	
Estimate Quickly	
Assess Your Approach	
Keep Exceptions in Mind	

VIDEO 9-05

MBACASE Path Overview

DANCE 2—MBACASE PATH FOR BUSINESS CASES

The second case interview dance is one you'll encounter when the case is more complex. There may be more layers to the problem, or more changing variables. There will also likely be several steps to solving the problem. For example:

> "We have a business that's losing money. They just found out that their largest product line has had its best year in terms of sales. Help them figure out what's going on."

This kind of case question is complex and is resolving a real business issue: declining profits. As you solve this case, you'll soon find that the

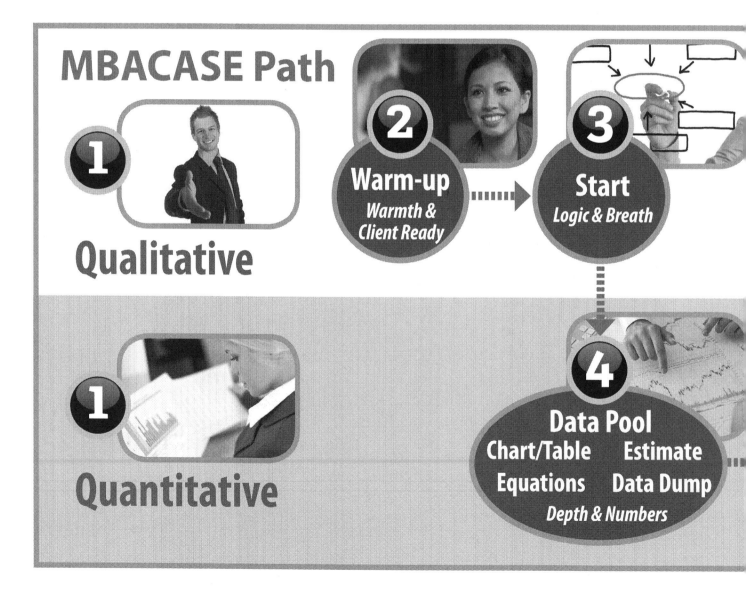

MBACASE Path

1 Qualitative

2 Warm-up *Warmth & Client Ready*

3 Start *Logic & Breath*

1 Quantitative

4 Data Pool Chart/Table Estimate Equations Data Dump *Depth & Numbers*

interviewer has several handouts to review and some data he wants to read to you. Things are about to get very complicated! When a case has several layers or is focused on a business issue, I recommend using the MBACASE Path. Once you fully understand the case path's flow and what is expected of you at every step along the way, you can isolate the steps and build your skills in each area. Doing well in a case interview is not magic, nor is it a form of luck that only a few candidates possess. Instead, it's the result of hard work and careful practice, one step or module at a time. Let's go through each numbered step of the MBACASE Path. Along the way, notice how your CLASSIC root skills are woven throughout the process. I'll highlight some of the skills you need to show and the challenges you'll face, but rest assured that we will cover those in detail in later chapters.

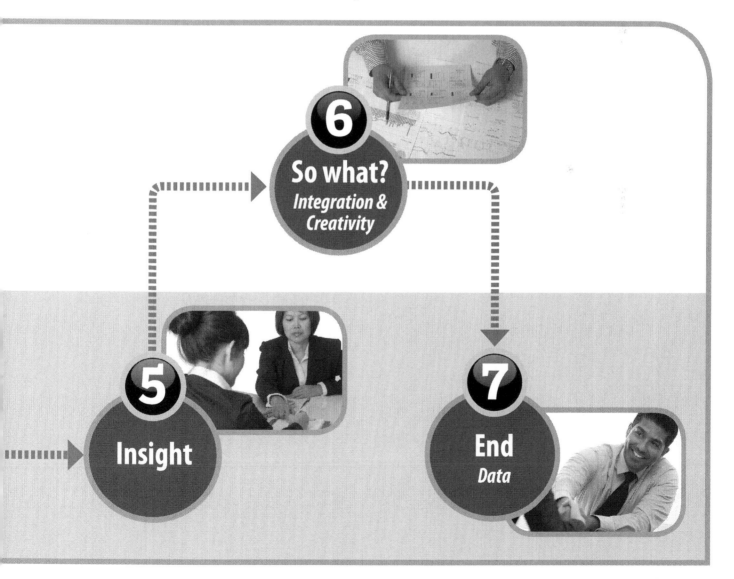

**Qualitative and
Quantitative Zones**

① **Qualitative and Quantitative Zones.** You will move back and forth between these two areas throughout the case. In the chart, they are shown as separate zones on the top and bottom. In the qualitative zone (top half) you'll be expected to use good logic, break concepts and problems into small pieces, and integrate your ideas with the data toward the end of the case. In the quantitative zone (bottom half) you'll be expected to show a high level of comfort with numbers, and a keen ability to estimate the financial impact of a decision. In both zones, the interviewer has similar expectations of you: to communicate clearly what you are doing, and to break down concepts and numbers in a systematic, logical manner.

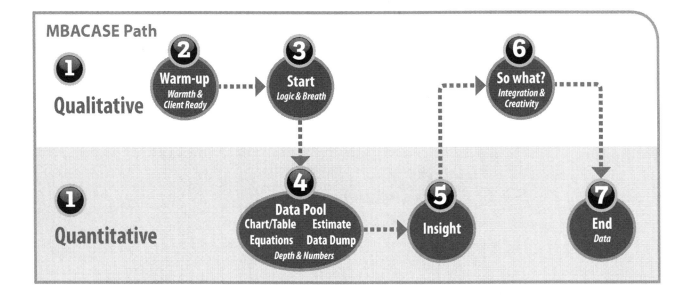

Warm-up

② **Warm-up.** Every case begins with some kind of conversation. Whether it's a quick greeting followed by a brusque "Let's get started on the case," from your interviewer, or a more lengthy 5–10 minute discussion of your background, do your best to warm up the conversation. You are being evaluated from the moment you meet the interviewer. This pre-case discussion often sets the tone for the rest of the interview. He'll be thinking about whether you are client-ready and will be testing your social skills and communication.

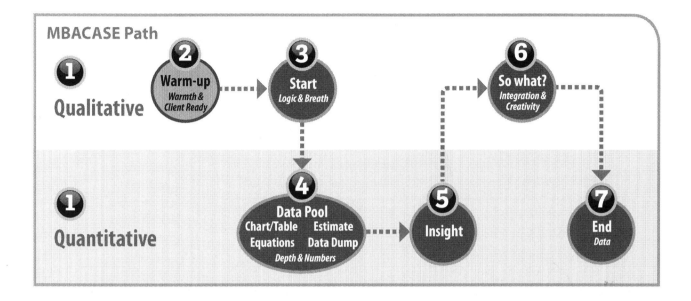

Show Your Interviewer CLASSIC Skills: Social skills and communication are important here. Energy, confidence, and an interest in joining his firm, company or group should be high on your list of skills to show. Guess what? Your interviewer does not care that much about your general career goals (*"I'm so excited about consulting . . ."*). He will be most interested in your desire to join his specific company. He is also very interested in your ability to communicate clearly. As a new hire you'll be expected to communicate across a wide variety of contexts: small internal meetings, client meetings, large client presentations and day-to-day updates. The interviewer will be judging your ability to express your thoughts using clear, prioritized points.

Your challenge: Most interviewers interview 10–12 people in one day. It will be easy for you to blend into the crowd. Also, since your interviewer is looking for flaws (sorry—it's just the nature of the process), you could be setting his mind against you before the case begins. Finally, the length of the warm-up varies, so you need to be ready for a short or extended discussion.

Your advantage: Since you worked on your IMPACT stories, you'll be ready to answer his questions in an impressively answer-first way. Most of the questions are highly predictable; with practice, you can master all of the basic topics and be ready for any curve balls.

VIDEO 9-08

Start the Case

③ Start the Case. Your interviewer will present a situation or problem you need to solve. This is the moment when you need to lay out some kind of structure for solving the case. I'm not a fan of classic, pre-memorized frameworks as I find they make you sound stilted and rigid in your thinking. Interviewers tend to find them off-putting, as well. Instead, think of this as an opportunity to show your careful listening skills and your ability to structure your thoughts in a logical manner. We'll cover how to do that in a natural, integrated way in Chapter 4.

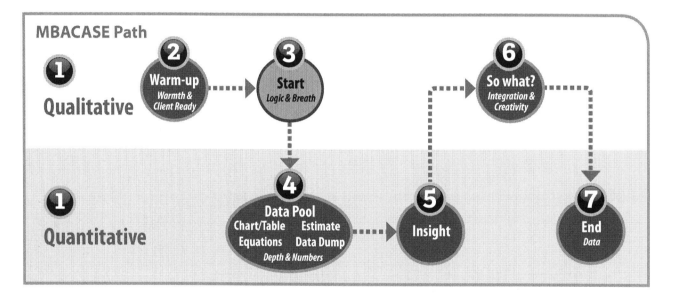

Show Your Interviewer CLASSIC Skills: You need to show logic in the form of structure. This part of the case emphasizes logic, and you'll be demonstrating your breadth and depth of thinking as you lay out your structure. When presenting your structure, expect questions like "What else?" to test your breadth of thinking, and "What do you mean here?" to test your depth of thinking. The interviewer is test-driving your ability to analyze problems, and is evaluating how you would approach an analytical problem on a real case or project with her company. She expects you to be thorough, logical and prioritized as you explain your approach to solving the problem.

Your challenge: There are multiple ways to start any single case, and it's common to never know if you have a complete structure in place or if you missed a critical point. You will feel pressured trying to think strategically while doing detailed, quantitative problems. You also

need to be talking and explaining your thoughts about 90% of the time. Listening, taking notes, structuring, and presenting your ideas constitute a unique challenge.

Your advantage: Most business case problems can be broken down into several large categories—profit improvement, mergers, new product launches, and divestitures, to name a few. Since any business can be analyzed by looking at the revenue and cost drivers, you will become proficient at quickly grasping the root causes of problems. As you practice our 42 cases, you will see many of the same themes repeat, and gain confidence to tackle any new problem.

4 Data Pool. It's time to dive into the data pool! Almost every case will have some type of analytical task. Your new job will likely require you to use your analytical skills often, so your interviewer will want to test those skills to some degree. There is a large variation in the type of analytical problems you'll be expected to solve. After you have presented your plan, explained it, and discussed your priorities and what you'd like to solve first, it's time to get into the analytics. You will either dive into the data pool yourself or be thrown in by your interviewer.

VIDEO 9-09

Dive into the Data Pool

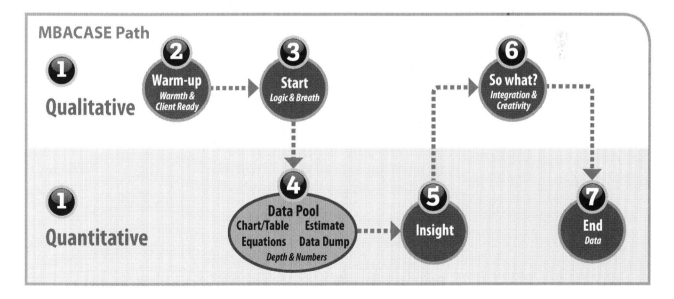

Show Your Interviewer CLASSIC Skills: Your analytics will be on trial here. It's crucial to show comfort with numbers and a strong degree of accuracy. Your interviewer is not likely to ding or reject you

because of a simple math error, but if you continue to confuse scale, make multiple computation errors, or fail at setting up simple equations, your chances of passing to the next round drop significantly. The CLASSIC skill being tested here is clearly analytics, as you'll be expected to show facility with numbers and a strong understanding of how to pull insights from data.

Your challenge: Since you cannot be sure what type of math problem you'll receive, you need to practice a wide variety. One interviewer might expect you to lay out and solve an algebraic equation, and the next might ask you to interpret a slide. Since you will be nervous, it's easy to make mistakes on simple problems. For more complex problems you'll be challenged to do several layers of analysis.

Your advantage: You have already built most of these analytical skills through years of study and math classes. By reviewing basic math concepts and honing in on weak areas, you can sharpen your math skills quickly.

VIDEO 9-10

Go from Insight to So What?

⑤ & **⑥** **From *Insight!* to *So What?*** After you dazzle the interviewer with your quick math and sharp chart-reading skills, you need to have an insight—something about the data that is meaningful and helps you move closer to solving the case. It might be something simple, like "According to this data, 12–15 year old girls are rarely buying our product, but last year they were our largest customer group. That's clearly where the problem is." Or you might say something more involved, like "After reviewing these two charts and the data you read to me, it seems like Italy is going to offer somewhat more growth opportunity than France. Let me show you my calculations." As you do more cases and practice more analysis later in this book, the insights will come more quickly.

Now it's time to climb out of the data pool (was it a leisurely swim, or did you drown?) and show the interviewer your main insight. Every analytical section eventually transitions to a point at which the interviewer wants you to take the data insights to a practical conclusion. In the beginning of the case you were given a problem to solve. At this point you'll be expected to share how the analytical insights you found tie back to the main question of the case. Since your interviewer will likely be a bottom-line-impact kind of person, be ready to answer the "So what?" question. In other words, you discovered

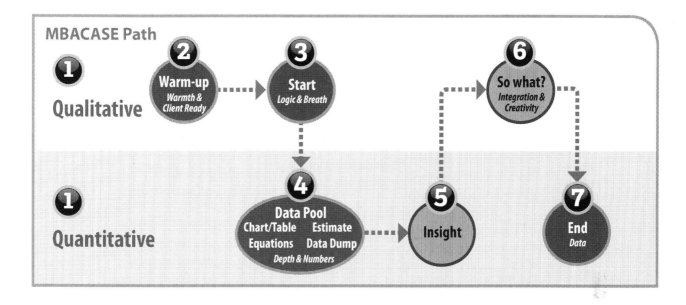

an insight, but how does it bear on the subject at hand? As you do more cases, finding the insight and explaining its meaning will likely become your favorite part of the case. For example, finding out that prices were lowered and that volume for the product didn't go up might indicate that the company made a strategic error. They may now be able to restore prices to their earlier level—or better yet, raise them—without causing volume to suffer.

Show Your Interviewer CLASSIC Skills: Integration and creativity are crucial here. Most interviewers do not plan to hand out job offers to the lucky candidates who guess the main insight of the case. Instead, interviewers want to see your ability to put the different pieces of the puzzle together, and do it with creativity when possible. As you integrate your findings, be as structured as possible. The same interviewer who loved structure at the beginning of the case has not changed his thinking now at the end. Take the time to lay out how the pieces connect, and use your paper to show your thinking whenever possible.

Your challenge: Thinking on your feet mid-case to come up with insights and structure is very challenging. At this point in the case, you'll be expected to integrate several ideas while discussing them with your interviewer.

Your advantage: Since many of the problems you are solving revolve around profit drivers and basic decisions (e.g., expand the business or contract the business), you'll run across repeating themes. As you do

VIDEO 9-11

End the Case

more cases, finding the insight and transitioning to the "So what?" will become easier.

7 **End.** Finally, you get to end your case. Doing well at the close of the case is usually dependent upon doing well during the earlier parts of the case. If you created a strong structure in the beginning, discovered some analytical insights in the middle and developed a well-integrated conclusion, ending the case is quite simple.

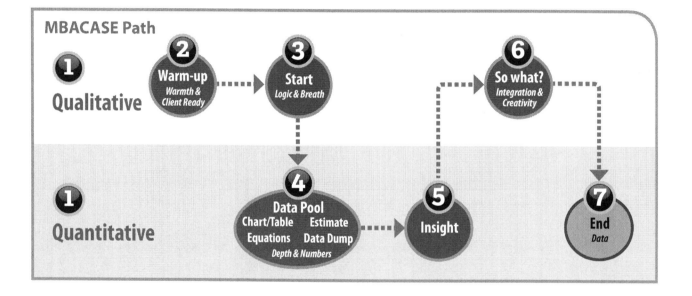

Show Your Interviewer CLASSIC Skills: Always end your case with solid logic and supporting data. Your interviewer will want to hear you use the facts and data from the case to reach your conclusion, and will want them presented in a logical fashion. She will also want to hear some form of an "elevator pitch". In other words, "The CEO will be here in a minute; what do you want to tell him?" Speaking in a succinct, structured, answer-first manner will be critical to making your points and doing well. After the case wraps up, you may quickly transition to a discussion about your background, the company, or the real case you just solved. Your social skills will be needed here, as you may face unexpected questions like "Why do you really want to move to Dubai?"

Your challenge: Your head will probably be spinning by the time you reach the end of the case. Good cases typically have lots of layers and analytical challenges which can be tough to pull together. If the earlier parts of the case did not go well, it's difficult to close well. Also, if you feel you performed poorly on the case, it can be hard to fake a smile and enjoy your closing chat with the interviewer.

Your advantage: Since you are building skills that will help you with the earlier parts of the case, your close will be a natural continuation of those parts. The more you practice your starts and your analytical skills, the easier it will be to end your cases. As for ending on a high note, keep in mind that you can never fully predict how you are being evaluated. Instead, focus on staying positive and use the final discussion to find out more from the interviewer whenever possible.

DANCE 2—MBACASE PATH

For your homework, it's time to think through the acronyms. We have covered quite a few: CLASSIC Skills, IMPACT Stories, the SPEAK Method for market sizing, and the MBACASE Path. Take the following quiz to see if you have everything straight before you move on. If there is something that is not clear to you at this point, take the time to re-read the material before moving to Chapter 4.

MBACASE | **Acronym Quiz**

C	L	A	SS	I	C

I	
M	
P	
A	
C	
T	

S	
P	
E	
A	
K	

MBACASE Path

1 Q → **2** W → **3** S → **4** DP CT E   E DD → **5** I → **6** S → **7** D

1 Q

CHAPTER 4

Use FRAME, MVM, and SAVED to Build Integrated Skills

Use FRAME to Diagnose and Build Skills

In Section 9 we covered the general flows of the case interview "dances"; now we want to focus on the business case and how to flow through it with ease. Top companies will expect a lot from you: a great smile, engaging conversation and succinct answers. And this is before you even get to the case! Once the case is underway, your nerves are in high gear. At that point, your success will depend on the amount of "muscle memory" you've built in your preparation. If you have practiced methodically, then you'll be in good shape. If you haven't, you will probably fall into a well-worn pothole. Candidates tend to stumble in a few areas:

- Riding, not driving—they approach the interview passively, leaving the interviewer in charge.
- Getting started—they don't even know where to begin or how to set a solid plan.
- Reading me, the audience—they don't listen well or follow my pace when presenting.
- Staying focused on the data—they tend to talk about the non-quantitative elements first.
- Wandering around the answer—they have no hypothesis, so they don't know where to go.

"The shrewd guess, the fertile hypothesis, the courageous leap to a tentative conclusion—these are the most valuable coins of the thinker at work. But in most schools guessing is heavily penalized and is associated somehow with laziness."

—C. R. Smith

- Ending the case—they are afraid to finish, thinking that adding one more idea will help.

I developed the FRAME Method™ to help you avoid these hazards during your business cases. It is a simple five-step approach to consistently setting up the problem and then moving through the case. You won't need to worry about missing a major part of the case or forgetting to end on time. You will have a dependable method for successfully solving your cases. And since it lies directly on the MBACASE Path, you'll have a reliable way to navigate through your cases.

F R A M E

Form a Plan   *Read the Audience*   *Anchor a Hypothesis*   *Mine for an Answer*   *End the Case*

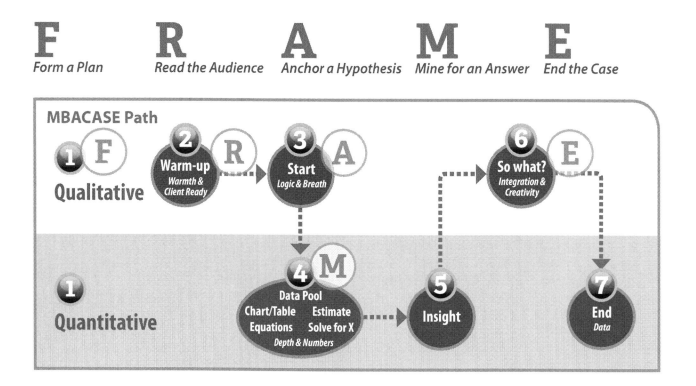

STEP 1: FORM A PLAN (F)

The first step in the FRAME Method™ is Form a Plan. In Section 11 we'll talk about how to think through the profit levers of a business using the Maximum Value Model MVM™ as your mental roadmap, and in Section 13 you'll practice planning in much greater detail with our case-specific roadmaps. But for now, we'll use some common business sense you already have as we work through your plan at a high level. Your goal is to highlight for the interviewer where you'll start the

discussion and the areas you plan to explore. In this step, you should aim to create a unique framework for the case, using your own words.

Beginning this way accomplishes two things: it shows the interviewer where you are taking the case and that you have some depth of thinking. You already practiced this method in your homework 7B. When you look at the MBACASE Path, we are going deeper into area number 3, the Start.

Let's bring in a real case question to help you walk through FRAME. Your interviewer presents the following question:

> Plushy Petz, maker of dolls and soft toys, has a successful line of miniature plush animals called Wild Critters. They are sold only in North America. Recently, sales have been successful in the US and Mexico, but the same products have not sold well in Canada. Management has reviewed a few obvious potential problem areas, but they do not have an answer for the weak sales. They want to understand what is going wrong. What would you advise?

So what do you do? How do you start this case dance?

1 **Recap**. After you hear the question you should first recap out loud. Basically, you'll want *briefly* to highlight what you heard, using the format of situation, complication and the task at hand. This is a good opportunity to use your answer-first communication skills. Keep it brief!

"Plushy Petz is doing well in North America and Mexico, but facing some sales issues in Canada. My job is to help management understand the issues and to recommend some solutions. At this point I don't have any additional questions, so do you mind if I take a quick minute to put together an approach?"

2 **Take some time.** It's normal at this point to say something like "Do you mind if I take a minute to collect my thoughts?" or "Let me map out an approach," or "I'd like to take a little time to plan my structure." It doesn't matter what you say, but please ask for a little time. Business cases require more thought and planning, so you do not want to speak immediately like you would with the SPEAK method. Over time you'll be very fast at mapping out a plan, but for now you need a little time to think.

3 **Think, Plan, Present.** Now that you have asked for a little time and you are alone with your thoughts, you have to think through how to approach this problem.

Think: For now we'll use some common-sense business ideas, but soon you'll be able to draw from the MVM and other analytical structures that will help you think more deeply.

Plan: While you are thinking, you'll want to lay out your ideas in some kind of basic structure you can share with your interviewers. Usually that will be a simple profit tree:

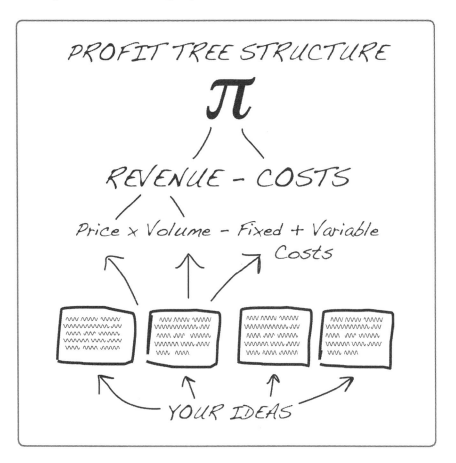

Or it might be a broad set of buckets or categories, like you laid out in Section 7 as you worked on breadth and depth of thinking (see right).

Present: Finally, you'll need to present your ideas out loud. You need to explain how you are thinking through your plan to solve the case and how each part supports your approach. At this point, the

interviewer begins to hear how you communicate in a business situation. It's a good chance to see your client skills up close. He'll also begin to evaluate your logic and general thinking skills and will judge whether or not you have a good structure.

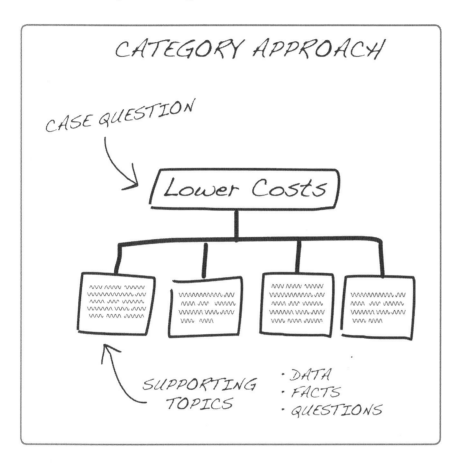

So let's try this approach out by thinking through the Plushy Petz problem and what we know. First, we know that this is not a broad strategic question, since we are not making any major changes to the business. We also know that this is probably not a financial question about cash flow or the balance of debt and equity. Most likely this problem will relate to something we are doing as a company with our operations, our people, or our sales process. It could also relate to something unusual about the Canadian market, since it would be strange for an interviewer to bring this fact up for no reason. You would first lay out a path for the interviewer that will wind through these areas in a logical manner.

Here's one approach with your voice-over:

"Since Plushy Petz sales are strong in the US and Mexico but not in Canada, I'd like to talk about some potential unique aspects of the Canadian market. I would also like to explore operations to find out whether there is something different about how we get our product to market in Canada or how our sales process works."

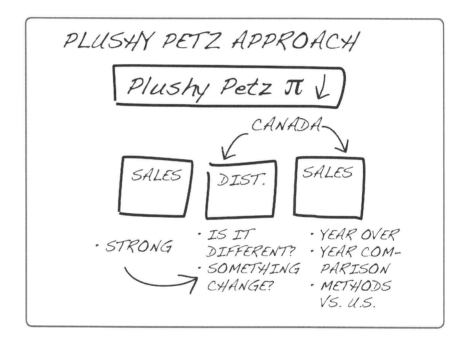

That's all there is to it. You'll be able to develop more sophisticated starts to your cases over time; but for now, you've launched the discussion by outlining, in your own words, the path you intend to explore. In a sense, you have created your own custom framework. Using this roadmap, you will be able to navigate smoothly through each section, discussing how best to maximize Plushy Petz' value. And the roadmap will be easy to remember—because you just developed it.

Making Your Plan MECE

After you become comfortable starting different types of cases, you need to begin presenting your material in a MECE format. MECE (pronounced "me see") stands for mutually exclusive, collectively

exhaustive. You want all of the elements of your plan to be separate and distinct (mutually exclusive), and together all the elements should solve the problem at hand (collectively exhaustive). But you will face several challenges when trying to develop a MECE plan:

Time: you should take only about one minute of quiet thinking time to collect your thoughts at the beginning of the case. Developing a tight MECE format in less than a minute is difficult.

Variety: the ultimate MECE plan is Revenue Minus Costs = Profit. It is at the core of every business and provides a very clean structure. But, as discussed earlier, using the same formula for every case would not showcase your creative thinking.

Audience: every interviewer has a different take on MECE. Even firms who tout MECE as the key to good structure produce practice cases that are not quite MECE.

So, how do you meet the MECE standard when faced with the above issues? First, focus on setting the right tone. When you speak about each element of your plan, be sure to emphasize how it does not overlap with other parts of the plan (mutually exclusive) and how it fits with the other parts of the plan to solve the problem (collectively exhaustive). For example, let's say you have a market entry case and competitors are especially protective according to the initial case facts. It would be natural to want to explore what the competitors are doing and how their actions may impact your client. But be sure to mention how these actions will impact revenue and may even cause the client to incur more costs to compete.

It's also important to know your audience. Certain firms are more interested in seeing a MECE format than others. If necessary, consider showing your plan in an issue tree format that shows how each piece links back to revenue and cost. In each MVM Practice Roadmap in Section 13 I have included a section called "MECE Mode!". These sections will help you understand how to tie most of your analysis back to revenue and costs. With a little adjustment you can present your plan in the most MECE way possible.

VIDEO 10-01

Form a Plan

STEP 2: READ THE AUDIENCE (R)

The second step is Read the Audience. By now you should have formed an overall impression of your interviewer. That's right; you aren't the only person being judged! As you shook hands, walked to the interview room, and made small talk, you formed a good idea of your interviewer's style. Reading your interviewer is critical to every step in the case. (I could have put it first in the acronym, but the RFAME Method wasn't as catchy. As a result it will stay in second place, even though you are "reading the audience" throughout the interview.)

Reading your audience consists of listening carefully to what your interviewer says and watching closely how he responds to you throughout the case.

Reading your audience consists of listening carefully to what your interviewer says and watching closely how he responds to you throughout the case. Small changes in tone, pace or body language can give you big clues on how to proceed with the case. For instance, when I was an interviewer I tried to be warm and friendly during the first couple of minutes, but then shifted to a more businesslike "show me the answer" tone throughout the case. I found that I could better read someone's skills if I gave him focused questions and created a more serious tone for the interview. When I'm serious, I tend to show little emotion. Even though I tried to remain poker-faced regardless of a candidate's answers, I'm sure changes in my body language, the pace of the conversation, and my tone of voice gave clues to what I thought of her analysis.

It's fairly common for each person who interviews you to have an equal say about your fate, however, so don't get hung up on your interviewer's rank in the company.

My approach to giving cases is one style among many. During your interviews you will meet a variety of personalities. You also will encounter a variety of experience levels, from third-year consultants to very senior partners. It's fairly common for each person who interviews you to have an equal say about your fate, however, so don't get hung up on your interviewer's rank in the company. If just one of them doesn't like you or thinks you didn't do well on the case, you'll probably be dinged. To give you an idea of the types of interviewers you might encounter, I would like to introduce you to some common characters. Of course, no two people are exactly alike, but in the business world there are a few basic categories. Let's meet these folks and talk about the best way to respond to their various styles.

Silent Partner

He is congenial and polite, but he doesn't say much. You comment on the weather, and he just nods and looks at you. You wonder if you

rubbed him the wrong way because he just doesn't try to be particularly pleasant. It's impossible to tell what he is thinking. His complete neutrality throws you off balance.

He is the Silent Partner. You're not sure whether he is calmly accepting your answers to the case, or hiding an extreme desire to laugh out loud; unfortunately, you won't find out the answer until you get either the congratulatory offer or the sympathetic ding later that evening.

The best way to handle the Silent Partner is to keep the discussion moving in a logical flow from one topic to the next. If you are a rapid talker or a little louder than most, you may need to calm it down. Stay focused on the data. He won't give you much guidance as you move through the case, so you'll need to be confident in your analysis. Make sure you stick to the facts, and whatever you do, don't try to schmooze.

Chatty Cathy (or Charlie)

You get the creepy feeling that Cathy is just as nervous as you are. For some reason, she really wants you to like her. Is she interviewing for a firm or a sorority? She spends a good deal of time talking about her clients, her work/life balance, and her last good meal at a restaurant.

The truth is, she may have a short case and wants to spend 50% of the time getting to know you. Her interview partner is probably a Data Ma'am, so a little extra talk isn't going to hurt. Play along, but keep the conversation professional. If you are enthusiastic and friendly, Chatty Cathy will make you feel like you're a part of the team already.

But don't be lulled into a false sense of security. The Chatty Cathys and Charlies may treat you like gold, but they will judge your performance as critically as any other interviewer.

Data Man (or Ma'am)

"Just the facts, ma'am," is this person's mantra. Don't expect a lot of chitchat with a Data Man. He'll greet you with a forced smile, but you can tell that his mind is elsewhere. His mission is to push you through the case as quickly as possible and put a score by your name. So don't go crazy trying to bond before the case begins.

Throughout the interview, be pleasant but stay focused on the data. Ask specific questions and give specific answers. Remember that a

VIDEO 10-02

Read Your Audience

Data Man is only interested in seeing you solidly crack the case. He is asking himself: do I want you on my project team? Do you have enough horsepower? Will you be low-maintenance?

STEP 3: ANCHOR A HYPOTHESIS (A)

How do you prove that you are a savvy business advisor in less than 20 minutes? The key is to Anchor a Hypothesis. In my experience, when you execute this step in the FRAME™ Method, you will distinguish yourself from 90% of your peers.

Your hypothesis is your educated mental guess or hunch about where the solution and the value of the case lie. It answers the core question at the heart of most cases: where is the value? You should use your hypothesis as an internal guide to help you focus your questions as you try to find the "so what?" of a case quickly. You do not need to explicitly state your hypothesis to your interviewer.

You may be wondering how this step is different from Step 1: Form a Plan. The short answer is that your plan is your roadmap, guiding you to all the necessary locations to look for value (revenue, costs, competitors, etc.), and the hypothesis is your thought about where you'll find the value as you follow the plan. Let me offer you a simple example.

The Golden Egg Hunt

Let's say you and I meet in a school building on the campus where you are now a student. The building is about ten floors high and each floor has a variety of classrooms and study rooms. One floor has a café and another floor is dedicated to lounges and lockers.

We meet in the lobby, and when I arrive, I say, "Guess what? I have a special challenge for you today. Somewhere inside this building I have hidden a golden egg. Now if you find that egg in the next 30 minutes, I will give you 1 million US dollars." Of course you accept the challenge and are about to race off when I say, "Wait! I almost forgot to tell you. I hid the egg in a space about 1 foot high by 1 foot wide by 2 feet long. Good luck." This last piece of information really gets your mind racing. It could be in a trash can, or locker, or desk drawer, or maybe a spot you haven't even thought of yet. A trash can seems odd, though, since someone might empty the trash can before you can find it. Lockers may be a good idea, but many of them are locked. A desk

drawer seems like a great idea as there are many desks throughout the building, which would make the million-dollar search difficult.

Meanwhile, you plan to start on the 10th floor and then run down the stairs to the 9th. Both floors have a lot of classrooms and plenty of desk drawers. You'll then go to the 3rd floor because it is the lounge and locker floor. You can't completely eliminate lockers, even though your hunch is that the egg is in a desk drawer. After a quick look through most of the lockers, you'll finish on the 2nd floor. It is close to the lobby where you have to meet me in 30 minutes, and is full of classrooms and desk drawers.

Do you see the connection between the plan and the hypothesis here? Of course, there is a logical plan you want to use to find the egg. You know that you can't limit yourself to just one floor, so you lay out a path you will take. But, as you move through the building, you have a hunch. You think the egg is in a desk drawer and secondarily, you're willing to look at some lockers. This approach is the only way you can cover this huge building in a logical but focused manner. Think of Forming a Plan as a path you want to take, similar to taking yourself through the building to find the golden egg. You tell the interviewer where you plan to go so that you all understand the path you're taking. Anchoring a Hypothesis is the quick process of locking down where you think you'll find insights and value. It serves as a mental anchor, providing focus as you move through the case. But you will need to prove it with data from the case. If your hypothesis proves to be wrong, its inverse is usually the answer.

I'll give you an example of hypothesis generation using Plushy Petz. But first, let's look at two advantages of using a hypothesis.

A Hypothesis Saves Time

Case interviews are short and fast: you don't have much time to get to the bottom of the problem and recommend a solution. Remember, you must establish the direction of the case within a very short period of time. Chances are that your first exposure to the interviewer's case question inspired an initial gut reaction to it. Don't be afraid to follow your gut. A hypothesis merely gives you direction as you investigate the data and arrive at a solution. If your hypothesis proves to be wrong, that's fine. The important thing is to determine whether the data supports the hypothesis or not.

When consultants at top firms begin a case, they typically develop a hypothesis. It is especially important if they are digging into an unfamiliar area or industry. Since most consulting engagements are between four and six months long with solid insights expected around the three-month mark, there is little time to chase ideas not directly related to the client's problem. Consultants develop a hypothesis to focus their project team's efforts on a finite set of issues. If the data disproves the hypothesis, the team has still arrived at an answer.

"Theory can leave questions unanswered, but practice has to come up with something."
—Mason Cooley

A Hypothesis Puts a Stake in the Ground

Firms are looking for confident leaders, people who can take charge of a difficult situation and resolve it. Interviewers will evaluate your confidence as you solve your case problem. If you amble about, asking lots of interesting but poorly-focused questions, they will think you're weak-minded and disorganized. But if you show laser focus and systematically solve the problem, they will think you're a star. Forming a mental anchor for your questions will give you this focus.

To State or Not to State?

For most candidates, I recommend not stating your hypothesis. When presented in the wrong way, it can come off sounding presumptive and not data-driven. However, I have interviewed some candidates who have definite views on where the core value lies in a case. These individuals were typically very good communicators. Stating their hypothesis at the outset worked to their advantage, giving the impression that they were quick-thinking leaders. But in all cases they quickly followed their hypothesis with the statement: "I'll have to see if the data proves my thoughts."

Many (if not most) candidates are not sure about where the "golden egg" is hidden as they begin to work on cases. They do have a hunch, but it is not a particularly strong one. If you are in this situation, I would suggest using your hypothesis as a gentle guide, allowing it to provide direction to your analysis and questions. You do not have to state it to the interviewer, but try to develop one for every case. As you begin to exercise this hypothesis-development "muscle", you'll grow your intuition about how to quickly get to an answer.

Case Example

Let's go back to our Plushy Petz case. Here's the case question again:

> Plushy Petz, maker of dolls and soft toys, has a successful line of miniature plush animals called Wild Critters. They are sold only in North America. Recently, sales have been successful in the US and Mexico, but the same products have not sold well in Canada. Management has reviewed a few obvious potential problem areas, but they do not have an answer for the weak sales. They want to understand what is going wrong. What would you advise?

As you recall, in our first step, Form a Plan, we decided to focus on the company's internal areas, specifically distribution and the sales process. We also knew that external forces might be contributing to the problem. To develop a hypothesis about why sales are weak in Canada, let's review what you already know and eliminate some obviously wrong paths. During an interview you will naturally think through these elements quickly, ask your interviewer questions, and select which you want to pursue. Let's go through them one by one.

Ideas You Can Eliminate Quickly

Customers: "Kids or parents are different in Canada." It could be that Canadians do not buy stuffed animals for their kids, but that's not likely.

Product: "Our products offend Canadians." We know from the intro that the product itself is a line of animals, meaning that there is a variety and, as a result, little likelihood that every animal is offensive. On the whole we'd expect similar sales.

Quality: "Our products are considered poor quality." We know that the products sell well elsewhere, so that's probably not it.

We've now eliminated some issues that are probably not applicable in this case. What are some likely reasons for the poor sales figures in Canada?

Ideas You Should Consider Carefully

Price: "Our prices are too high." This could be a good reason, especially if the US dollar is stronger than the Canadian dollar. But that seems too obvious for management to miss.

Volume: "We're selling too few." We know that is true because of the case question. Maybe we're just not getting them enough product, or maybe our salespeople in Canada stink.

Salespeople: "Our representation in Canada is low." This also seems obvious and one that management should have caught.

Distribution: "Our processes of getting product into Canada are ineffective." Well, we know that we can get product to Mexico with no problem. Perhaps the product is made in Mexico. Or if it's made in the US, maybe it's easier to ship to Mexico. It can be shipped by land to both countries, so that seems odd. But let's keep this one in mind.

Competitors: "Maybe we're a small player in Canada." This could be a possibility. Maybe we're not getting shelf space or any push by our retailers? Have competitors introduced a cool new line of products that is stealing our sales?

Legislation: "Something is blocking our access to the customer." Are there costly tariffs to enter the country, or some other legal holdup?

The next step is to pull these hunches together and anchor them as your hypothesis. Layer them on top of your plan; it's easier than you think.

In the golden egg hunt, you had a methodical way of searching for the egg, but you *also* had a hunch about where the egg was likely to be. In a similar manner, you now have a plan for thinking through why profit is down. You want to look in both the distribution and sales areas. Simultaneously, you have a hunch about where the answer is. You'll start there.

Keep in mind that these are your thoughts and do not have to be stated out loud. Here are some hunches you might have for Plushy Petz:

Hypothesis #1: *"I think the biggest problem area will be distribution. We'll probably need to restructure Plushy Petz' distribution channels to ensure that a sufficient volume of product is arriving at the retail sites."*

Hypothesis #2: *"My hunch is that Plushy Petz has a hard time getting good shelf space since they are a small player in the Canadian toy market. There may be a few big companies that dominate the stores and get prime positioning."*

Hypothesis #3: *"I think we'll find that Plushy Petz' sales force isn't being properly motivated to get the product into enough retail venues, most likely because their bonus and commission structures don't provide the right incentives."*

Let's lay these ideas on top of your previous structure.

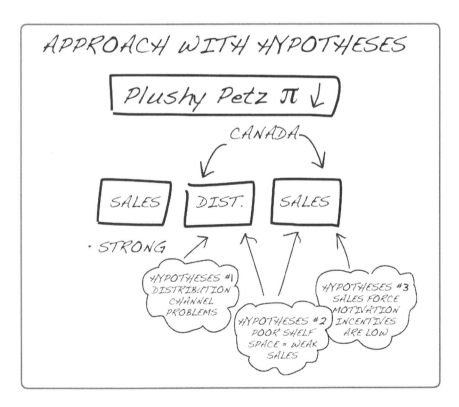

You don't need to write these into your structure during the case, but you may want to put a check mark or star next to the category where

VIDEO 10-03

Anchor a Hypothesis

You'll know you've mined deep enough when you can synthesize your findings into an answer that is backed up with facts and financial data.

you'd like to start. We have them as bubbles because they represent your thoughts. As part of your training it's important to think ahead and "work out" this hypothesis muscle for every case.

As you can see, creating a hypothesis involves eliminating unnecessary lines of investigation and quickly narrowing in on the relevant ones. In some case interviews this process will be more difficult than in others, but if you start training your mind to think ahead and anchor a hypothesis, you'll begin to see more focus in your cases and you'll move through the material more quickly.

If you are completely stuck and do not have any kind of hunch, just think about where you want to start first. If you think about why you want to start in that area, it will usually uncover your hunch.

STEP 4: MINE FOR AN ANSWER (M)

After you have laid out your plan and created a hypothesis, it's time to find the answer. That's right: an answer. Despite all the talk about cases not having one right answer, there is usually only a small range of acceptable responses. If you "solve" a case with a crazy (albeit logical) solution, you won't succeed.

You can mine for an answer by drilling into areas that follow your plan and also align with your mental hunch. With almost any case you could always mine for answers in the categories of revenue and costs. But that approach may be unnecessarily broad in many case interviews. Instead, it may be clear from the beginning that you need to ask questions in a couple of focused areas. You mine by asking focused questions aimed at proving or disproving your hypothesis. I'll give you some examples:

Formulating these focused questions is easy because you have already broken the problem into a few buckets to investigate, and you have some hypotheses by area. As you ask these questions you will find yourself engaging in the case and enjoying the discussion. It will begin to feel more like the kind of conversation you might have with a friend over a drink as you wonder, "What parts of Apple are the most profitable?" or "What makes BMW so successful?" You'll be asking very focused questions, and as a result, your interviewer will be able to interact with you and guide you more effectively.

Distribution Channels	Shelf Space	Sales Team Compensation
■ How do we get product to our Canadian retail store customers? ▸ *We ship it to them.* ■ What is different about this distribution? ▸ *Since we do not have a warehouse or hub-like distribution center, we send each shipment separately. Oftentimes, shipments are held up in customs. Toy lines look incomplete as they arrive piecemeal.* ■ Are there other channels we could use? ▸ *We could set up a distribution hub (like we do in Mexico) and deliver product to retail stores as well as other outlets.*	■ What portion of shelf space do we have today? ▸ *On average, we have about 75% as much shelf space as our competitors.* ■ What has caused us to lose shelf space? ▸ *We need to increase our delivery time dependability with our customers. Our product delays have led many to give some of our shelf space to competitors.* ■ What can we do to increase our shelf space? What are the issues with pursuing more and better shelf space? ▸ *Purchasing shelf space requires large promotional fees which we want to avoid.*	■ What is each team member's compensation today? How does this compensation compare to what our competitors pay their sales staff? ▸ *On average, team members make about 80% of what they could make at a competitor. The real difference is in the commission structure. Most commission structures pay for themselves since the increase in sales covers the additional payments to team members.* ■ What do our sales team members think? ▸ *Most team members have been asking for a new commission structure for a long time.*

Once you reach specific answers to your questions and have reviewed any data at hand, you need to tie your conclusions together to form an answer. You will find either that your original hypothesis is wrong, or that you nailed the case question from the beginning. In either case, you'll know you've mined deep enough when you can synthesize your findings into an answer that is backed up by facts and financial data.

Mine for Data

STEP 5: END THE CASE (E)

Now comes the best part of every case interview: ending it. Unfortunately, few candidates end a case properly. It is almost as if they are afraid to "close their blue book" and say, "That's it. That's my

best shot." Instead they tend to meander about until the interviewer forces them to wrap it up.

To succeed, you need to end the case each and every time without prompting. Occasionally, I got into a great discussion with a star candidate and had to prompt him to wrap it up, but in general, you should be tracking the time and know when to bring the discussion to a close.

Ending a case well means summarizing your thoughts in a form that answers the original question. Even if the case lacks a very specific question, your final thoughts should bring conclusion to your analysis in a synthesized manner. To do this, return to the answers you found while mining the data. Let's go again to our Plushy Petz example. Here's a solid ending:

> *"Plushy Petz is facing a distribution and sales force compensation problem in their Canadian operations. Products are consistently arriving late to stores due to customs hold-ups and general delays. Shelf space has eroded to 75% of our competitors' as retailers trust us less. Our sales force is also making 20% less than they could at competitors due to our lack of a commission structure. I recommend that we look into setting up a hub distribution center in Canada to make delivery faster and more reliable. We should implement a new compensation model immediately as it will cost us very little and prevent the exit of our best people."*

You have now finished your trial run of the FRAME Method™. We will use this method for solving each of the Case Packs in this book. As you practice with a partner, you will become adept at forming a plan, anchoring a hypothesis and determining where to begin your questioning. Along the way, you will learn to focus your questions and responses on the quantitative data and key value levers of each case.

As with any new habit, it will take practice to become second nature. In Section 13 we'll practice with the MBACASE Roadmaps that will help reinforce the FRAME Method™ as you work through the most common types of business cases.

VIDEO 10-05

End the Case

Practice going through the FRAME Method™ by doing the Plushy Petz case again. You'll need to practice out loud in order to learn how you sound during these interviews, and to build better communication skills for your partner practice. Follow these tips:

1 Read the problem out loud just like an interviewer would.

2 Play the role of the candidate now. Start by recapping the question and asking for a minute.

3 Develop your plan on your paper. Add different categories than we had before. Your goal is to get comfortable thinking through an approach. Put down common-sense categories where you think you'll find data to help solve the case.

4 Present your ideas out loud. Go through each category, mentioning the main idea and what you are seeking to find.

5 Now look at the Mining for Data chart. Pretend that the interviewer just gave you these answers to your questions about Plushy Petz. Discuss what the findings might mean and how they help you come to a conclusion.

6 Present a final answer and your recommendations for going forward.

Good job! You just worked through a very fundamental drill: repeating a case you already know. By speaking out loud, you are practicing your transitions between sections and helping your brain anticipate where to go next. You can use this on any case you find, and it's an especially helpful exercise after you have done a case with a partner.

Integrate Your Thinking with the Maximum Value Model (MVM)

The Maximum Value Model, or MVM™, is the heart of Crack the Case's approach to solving business cases. This model captures the basic elements or zones of a business, and presents them in a graphic format that is easy to understand and remember. I designed this model to directly address three pervasive problems I observed in the candidates I interviewed:

- Heavy reliance on well-known, yet inflexible, business frameworks
- The inability to stay calm under pressure
- The lack of an integrated, holistic view of how businesses work

Before I introduce you to the Maximum Value Model™, I want to share some thoughts on these issues.

THE CASE AGAINST FRAMEWORKS

Instead of helping you land your dream job, using a well-known business framework can actually hurt your chances of succeeding on your case interviews. There are three major reasons to avoid them.

Everyone knows them

Do you think your interviewers are familiar with Porter's 5 forces, the Seven S's and the 4 P's? Of course they are. They are also familiar with Relative Market Share analysis, Experience Curves, High Road/Low Road analysis, and several other concepts that you may have learned in B-school. These frameworks are like a consultant's hammer and saw: familiar tools used on a daily basis. Don't expect to dazzle an interviewer with a recitation of a basic framework. He has heard it all before.

I often interviewed candidates who didn't know how to get started. After hearing my case question, they panicked and slapped a formulaic framework onto the case. (I call this the "throw it out there and see if it sticks" approach.) This random selection didn't produce much confidence in them or in me. I immediately questioned their logic, depth of thought, and creativity. I am not alone in my view. Consider what a few of the top firms have to say:

> "Some Common Mistakes: . . . Force-fitting familiar business frameworks to every case question, whether they are relevant or not, or misapplying a relevant business framework that you do not really understand, rather than simply using common sense."
>
> —McKinsey & Co website

> "A good case interview should be an enjoyable and thoughtful discussion of business issues and problem-solving techniques. We are not looking for a 'right answer' or asking you to spit back memorized business terms, current events or well-known frameworks. Rather, we hope to see a good dose of problem-solving skills, creativity and common sense."
>
> —Bain & Company website

They are too narrow

One framework never quite does the job of hitting all the relevant issues of the case. Like most real business problems, cases are complicated. It is difficult to pick a framework that will exhaust all the ave-

nues of a case question. Interviewers expect you to handle the twists and turns of the case without getting lost. One basic framework will not help you shift gears when the case changes direction.

You need a holistic framework that gives you flexibility as the case proceeds. For example, if you select the 4 P's (price, product, position and promotion) for a new product launch case, you might not remember to consider issues around the organization's internal capabilities or launch financing. Before long, most interviewers will move you off the framework and into areas where you no longer have a road map. Bored interviewers especially love to shake you up.

They make you sound robotic

As an interviewer, one of my favorite cases was the operational question, "How can my client improve its profit?" Along with this question, I gave the candidate a slide with several bullets on industry conditions and some specifics about the company (similar to the DuraMed slide from Chapter 1). I expected successful candidates to lay out an approach for evaluating revenue and cost, the two major levers of profitability. I wanted them to give me a roadmap of where they were taking the discussion. Whether it was nerves, the information on the slide, or just my intimidating presence, I'd say that about 20% of the candidates could not formulate this basic framework. These were students from the MBA and undergraduate programs of Wharton, Harvard, Northwestern, Michigan and the University of Chicago.

Of the remaining candidates who made an attempt at framing the discussion, most sounded like this: "Ummm . . . profit . . . well revenue minus costs equals profit so . . . I would like to talk about each of these . . . do you have any more information about revenue?" It sounded robotic and shallow. I wondered if they had been cramming frameworks on flashcards the night before and were now reading them off the backs of their eyelids.

The candidates who caught my attention said something like this:

> *"Since we're focusing on profit, I'd naturally like to understand what's happening with your client in the areas of revenue and costs. My hunch is that competitors in this industry tend to differentiate more on price and less on costs, so I'd like to start with revenue. I would also like to talk a little more about the industry barriers and*

competitor landscape. To get started, do you have any information on total sales for the last couple of years?"

Wow! Not only is this person relaxed and confident, but she sounds like a business advisor. She made a great first impression.

THE POWER OF NERVES

Memorizing is one thing—keeping it all straight is another matter entirely. To really take advantage of your memorized material, you need to recall the right information at the right time. But how? If you're a framework junkie trying to assess a company's competitive environment, when should you use the 4 C's versus SWOT analysis? If you are trying to launch a new product in an unfamiliar industry, do you start off with the 4 P's or Porter's 5 Forces? Picking just the right framework at the right time is difficult, especially when you're in the hot seat.

Few people fully anticipate the power of nervous energy during an interview. The same adrenaline rush that gives you laser focus one day can cause you to say all kinds of illogical things the next day. And no matter what you try to do to harness this energy, it's a force that is difficult to control.

This is the time when the carefully memorized information in your head turns into a big pot of framework soup. Structures blend together; questions flash in your mind, then disappear; insights cloud over. When you're nervous, you'll cling to what you know best.

Unfortunately, this will be only a portion of what you memorized. But by studying the MVM™ and using the practice cases in this book, you can build a knowledge base solid enough to beat your nerves every time.

GAINING A LARGER VIEW

All the memorization in the world will not help you if you don't understand the topics you are discussing. Sometimes candidates go through the motions of solving a case without really knowing what they are talking about. They worked hard to memorize a bunch of formulas. They reviewed the various types of case questions. They practiced with a partner. But at the end of it all, they didn't grasp the bigger picture.

Let's say you intend to memorize a list of questions for every type of case. How do you ask them in a manner that helps move your analysis forward? What happens when your interviewer throws you a curve ball? Can you jump off of your mental check-list and quickly take the case in a new direction?

I have heard some candidates take a relaxed view: "Don't worry about it. The main thing is to get the case discussion started and then let it evolve. If you're smart, you'll get to the right answer eventually." That's much like saying, "For open heart surgery, don't worry about where you make that first incision; you'll find the heart eventually." Like heart surgery, this way of solving cases is messy. Ideally, you want to pinpoint what the case is about, start the dialogue in the optimal area, and bring to bear a full set of questions and analysis to solve the problem. To do this, you will need an integrated and holistic framework that keeps the big picture in view.

UNDERSTAND HOW IT ALL CONNECTS—MAXIMUM VALUE MODEL

Your ultimate objective in a case interview is to figure out how to maximize the company's value. Your analysis will be misdirected unless it answers that basic question. Whether the case centers on an operations issue, an organizational problem, or a change in strategy, your goal is to increase the bottom line.

The Maximum Value Model—Zone by Zone
(Burger Heaven Revenue)

You were exposed to part of the MVM™ when you read through the types of business cases in Section 6. That list reflects the simple truth that a company's value levers can be grouped into additive parts. To understand this additive approach visually, review the chart at right. What you're looking at is a simple waterfall or cascade chart. This type of chart shows how various parts add up to a whole. Basically, one plus one equals two when it comes to company value.

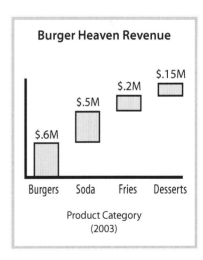

Burger Heaven Revenue

$.6M Burgers
$.5M Soda
$.2M Fries
$.15M Desserts

Product Category
(2003)

First, let's spend some time reviewing how each zone contributes to the company's overall value. These explanations are free of unnecessary business jargon because, in a case interview, you should be able to explain each topic in common-sense language. Next to each value lever is a simple picture, a small memory aid that will help you pull your knowledge together.

ZONE 1—STRATEGY

In the Strategy Zone, all but one of the four levers requires that something be done to or with the company or a major portion of the company. The four levers are:

- Expand Scope
- Reduce Scope
- Change Direction
- Do Nothing

Think of these as the dramatic actions you can take to effect a major change. These activities fall under the classic definition of corporate strategy.

VIDEO 11-01

MVM Zone 1—Strategy

EXPAND SCOPE

- **Merge** with another company and gain access to their resources, like smart executives, well-connected salespeople, efficient processes and new customers. These new pieces of the business pie, if properly integrated with your business, can help you sell more products and services and/or cut costs, the two ultimate levers of profit.

- **Acquire** another company and get the benefits of merging without the hassle of compromise. You can shut down plants, eliminate divisions or redirect resources into more important areas. With any acquisition there should be some clear facts around what you are buying and its potential value.

- **Joint venture** with another company and gain some new opportunities without the risks of merging and acquiring. Joint ventures usually bring something new to the market, like a hybrid product. JV partners use each other's technological resources to develop new products and then use each other's customer base to sell the products. It is important to negotiate properly and understand the limits of the agreement to ensure that the new deal generates additional value.

REDUCE SCOPE

- **Divest** a part of the business or a subsidiary. Eliminating a "dog" of a division can free up personnel and dollars to focus on more important products (to sell more), or it can eliminate costs that may not be paying for themselves. Since businesses are like the human body, with myriad connections among all parts, cutting off one part affects more parts of the business than you may expect.

CHANGE DIRECTION

- **Enter a new market** with your present product line or a new line of products. Consider what share of the market you will be able to capture and how much it will cost in terms of research & development (R&D), marketing, and distribution. External Forces (Zone 5) like competitor strength, government restrictions and patented technology may come into play. Your method of entering the new market may result in additional costs (see Strategy, Expand Scope) that affect the bottom line.

- **Exit a market** and potentially reduce costs. Since you will no longer be selling to this market, your value lever is cost savings. Removing sales force personnel, administrative labor, manufacturing lines and raw materials will cut your costs. Keep in mind that you may lose sales when you exit a market. Customers may become disenchanted, or your company's image may be diminished. Your absence in one market could strengthen a competitor, which ultimately could hurt you in another market.

- **Develop and sell new products and services.** This lever is an opportunity to gain more revenue; the questions are where and how. Your product must differ from your competitors' and must provide the customer with some benefit. It would be ideal to protect the new product from imitation using patents or copyrights, but such legal protection is not always available. Also, you want the new product to complement your current offerings without cannibalization (customers switching from one of your products to another), unless it's a planned replacement. Distributing the product to your customers may involve new channels and overcoming external factors like competitor response and government regulation.

- **Reposition the company's brand, focus or image.** This may mean an entire upgrade of the brand or a plan to shut down low-performing product lines. In any case the repositioning is likely to increase costs in the short term as you spend more on advertising, sales initiatives or research. You must be reasonably sure that customers will respond by buying more or paying more.

MAINTAIN THE STATUS QUO

- **Do nothing** to the present strategy after careful assessment of all of your strategic options. To make sure you didn't miss any strategic opportunities, review the levers of the strategy zone. If you are sure that entering or exiting markets, making new products or repositioning the company will not increase the bottom line, then taking no action makes the most sense. Your company may need to direct its energy internally to Zone 2 (Operations) or Zone 3 (Organization).

ZONE 2—OPERATIONS

When you think of operations, think about the internal activities of the company. How can we change our day-to-day practices to increase our profits? This is the meat and potatoes of running a company—managing revenue and costs. This is the basic formula that we all know well:

Basic Profit = Revenue (Price x Volume)–Costs (Fixed + Variable)

Here's how you can think about the levers of profit using common sense.

VIDEO 11-02

MVM Zone 2—Operations

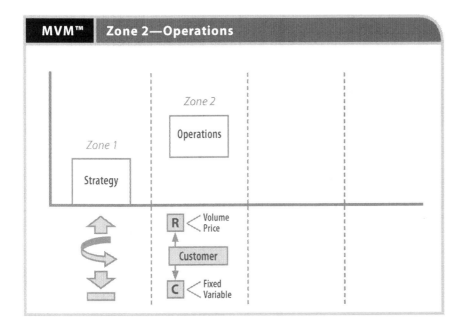

INCREASE PRICE

- **Raise prices**, and you may or may not see the bottom line increase. Revenue will go up if you sell the same amount of goods, or go down if customers buy less or switch to your competitors' products. Competitors may quickly match your price, which would mean everyone in the industry is giving himself a raise. Your suppliers might raise the price of raw materials, negating the effect of your price hike.

- **Change your pricing matrix.** This is more complex than a simple price bump. The pricing matrix, grid, or table (or whatever you want to call it) refers to how prices are structured for the product line. Market pricing reflects true market demand (i.e., what people will pay). Simplistic cost-based pricing is the cost to produce the item plus a standard margin. Changing this matrix may involve repositioning some products with a price increase to reflect their high demand and lowering the price of others to dominate a category. This is called a pricing strategy because it is complex and considers the impact of various pricing actions. Changing the pricing matrix may either increase or decrease profits, depending on its effect on sales volume.

INCREASE VOLUME OR CHANGE VOLUME MIX

- **Keep customers** at their present purchase levels by encouraging loyalty. Customer retention is one of the most powerful levers for maintaining revenue, as many companies experience significant customer attrition each year. The effort to retain customers may be costly. Retention programs may include additional hand-holding from the sales force, marketing literature, or advertising and coupon offers, to name a few examples. Measure the impact of the program by the difference between revenue maintained and the cost to sustain it.

- **Increase share of wallet** with present customers by enticing them to buy more. One way to increase the share of wallet is by taking sales from your competitors. This approach may or may not increase costs. In some cases, it can be accomplished by evaluating your sales force and changing its approach. A more expensive option would involve

INCREASE VOLUME OR CHANGE VOLUME MIX *(continued)*

spending more time with customers. Net out the increase in revenue with the additional costs, and you have your bottom line impact.

- **Change the mix of the volume sold**, thereby boosting revenue and profit. By promoting products that are higher-margin or that bring in more revenue per transaction, both the top line and bottom line may increase. Examples of taking action to change sales mix are upgrading the customer (e.g., buy a high-end car vs. a mid-range car) or giving the sales force incentives for selling higher-margin products.

- **Acquire new customers** through increased selling effort. This approach may involve bulking up the sales force or changing their tactics to reach a broader portion of the market. In conjunction with their efforts, the company may spend more on advertising, marketing materials and administrative support. Sometimes new customers are attracted by your reduced prices. You should carefully evaluate the cost/benefit of price reductions to avoid a loss of profit.

- **Develop new channels or better utilize existing channels** to increase sales. This is a straightforward means of gaining access to new customers and is a part of almost any effort to increase volume. New channels may include Internet commerce or direct marketing. Keep in mind the trade-off between increased selling costs and increased revenue.

V

REDUCE COSTS

- **Assess fixed vs. variable costs** and determine which ones can be reduced to their minimum operating level. Most cutbacks focus on reducing variable costs or substituting fixed costs with cheaper alternatives. Product quality, delivery time and other service standards must be monitored carefully, or cost savings will be offset by revenue losses.

- **Examine internal vs. external costs** to find savings opportunities. For instance, it might be cheaper to outsource production.

UNDERSTAND THE CUSTOMERS

- **Understand the customer** to best measure the true impact on volume, price and costs. If the customers are demanding a better quality product, then costs may rise to meet those demands. If customers become infatuated with a brand, they may buy more volume or you may be able to charge them a higher price. Customers are closely linked to the revenue and operating costs of the business, since the business is typically designed to please customers. Incorporate customer needs, demands and expectations into your revenue and cost discussions.

ZONE 3—ORGANIZATION

VIDEO 11-03

MVM Zone 3—Organization

This zone includes the qualitative elements that make a company work well or poorly: people, processes, technology and measurement. The impact of these areas on the bottom line is relatively difficult to quantify. People are tied together through roles, responsibilities, departments and hierarchies. Information technology systems function as the nervous system of a company, linking parts together with information critical for success. Processes are the rules for keeping everything working smoothly. And measurement, a consistently hot topic in companies today, tracks how everything is progressing. Pulling

Now we can add Zone 3 (Organization) to our MVM™ waterfall chart. Notice how the box representing Zone 3 is smaller than the first two zones' boxes. The Organization zone, while important, does not contribute as much toward the overall value of the company as the first two zones.

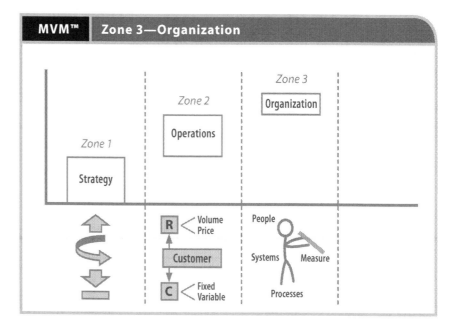

these Organization Zone value levers requires that you identify how each of the four elements relates to the bottom line, and that you develop measurement systems to determine whether they are having the expected impact.

OPTIMIZE PEOPLE

- **Build skills** throughout the ranks, and you will (theoretically) have a stronger team and a more profitable business. Some skills can be "imported" with the talent you hire, but most employee capabilities must be built through training programs. More skilled employees may help you sell more or cut costs, but there are no guarantees that training investments will pay off.

- **Optimize compensation** by trying to spend your wage dollars on the most valuable people. An optimized compensation system brings the most value to the bottom line, whether through a highly-paid management team or an aggressive sales force. A compensation scheme needs to provide the right incentives and minimize turnover of valuable employees.

- **Simplify the organization** by creating the right roles, responsibilities and relationships. Over time organizations tend to become unnecessarily complex, with layer upon layer of bureaucracy that bogs down the company and limits its performance. Simplification may involve restructuring, firing, hiring, and redefining roles and responsibilities. When changes are made, you must manage employee morale to stem attrition and avoid increased hiring and training costs.

Head =
People

STREAMLINE PROCESSES

- **Improve quality** by reviewing everything from raw material handling to the R&D process. Ensuring that quality stays high keeps customers happy—but it comes at a price.

- **Focus on internal efficiency and supply** to ensure that products are moving through the company quickly and getting to the customer as promised.

- **Focus on capabilities** to determine whether the correct processes are in place.

Legs =
Processes

OPTIMIZE INFORMATION SYSTEMS

■ **Upgrade information systems** and gain better control over the data that drives the company's results. Most large companies migrate to some form of an ERP (Enterprise Resource Planning) package that ensures that everything from customer orders to manufacturing to accounting is tightly integrated. New systems, however, have a way of sucking up massive amounts of people's time in getting them customized and installed. And once they're in place, there's no guarantee that they will house or integrate actionable information. To truly impact the bottom line, a close eye needs to be cast upon what kind of data goes into the system and what is the purpose of collecting it. At best these systems will track data that will help management understand the status of the business and enable them to make data-driven, strategic decisions.

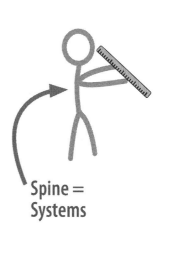

Spine =
Systems

■ **Simplify and integrate information systems** and free up people from the drudgery and confusion that comes from duplicate data entry points. By taking away redundancy in data collection, there should be more time to focus on the important aspects of the business.

■ **Automate non-value-added activities** through new information systems and enable people to focus on what is truly important to the business. Information systems will never directly impact the bottom line through revenue generation, but they can free up people to concentrate on maximizing the company value.

MEASURE RESULTS

■ **Create metrics** to track the most important activities and results of the business. To be actionable, these metrics should be narrowed down to a reasonable set (15–20 maximum), be consistent throughout the company, and be gathered and reviewed often. Most companies have enough KPIs (key performance indicators) and reports to wallpaper the company cafeteria. Despite all the talk about measuring results, most companies are very weak in this area. Once a team does pull together a good set of metrics, however, they can begin to affect the bottom line by making better decisions.

Ruler =
Measure

MEASURE RESULTS *(continued)*

- **Compare metrics** from year to year to understand how the company is performing, and to better understand parts of the business that are not being measured. Use these insights to make changes that increase company value.

ZONE 4—FINANCE

These items show up on your balance sheet and directly impact both your bottom line and the overall potential value of the company. For example, reducing inventory levels can free up investment dollars to expand the business. Even though these levers show up on the balance sheet, fixing them often touches back to operational and organizational actions.

MVM Zone 4—Finance

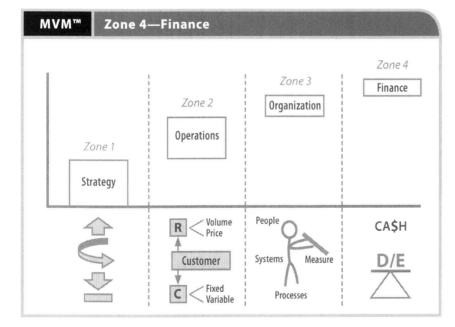

Zone 4 (Finance) is the last column of the MVM™ waterfall chart. Like Zone 3, it makes a relatively small contribution to the bottom line.

KEEP CASH KING

- **Reduce inventory** and you may be able to shave costs in a couple of ways. Think of inventory as a cost item necessary to run the business. You need to have stock in the production cycle, reserve stock in case of shutdowns, and seasonal stock. Many companies also have inventory that is being shipped or is located at customer sites. Your goal is to reduce these amounts as much as possible while balancing the needs of customers and the costs of late shipments. Tighten up too much, and you may see revenue drop off as customers become dissatisfied.

- **Reduce receivables** to put cash in your hands. Credit sales are a fact of business. It's important to determine the best balance between giving acceptable credit terms and collecting payments promptly. If your terms are too tight (e.g., <30 days of credit), customers may be turned off. If they are too loose, your cash flow will decrease and eventually restrict other business activities.

- **Increase payables** by working closely with your suppliers to secure the most favorable credit terms. This frees up cash which can be used to meet more pressing needs like payroll, taxes, operational costs and dividends. Securing favorable payment terms may be more important than getting goods at a discount, as angering key suppliers can put production and shipments in jeopardy and potentially cause customer service problems.

CA$H

BALANCE DEBT & EQUITY

- **Balance debt and equity** to maximize the company's value in the eyes of investors. Starting with the extremes, 100% equity (amounts paid in by original owners and profits over the years) implies that the company has not taken advantage of debt, both for expansion and for tax shields. On the other hand, taking on extreme amounts of debt increases the company's chance of default and reduces their borrowing power, as investors will require a higher rate of return on such a risky investment. You must find the right balance between the benefits

D/E

BALANCE DEBT & EQUITY *(continued)*

of debt and the curse of default risk. In terms of bottom-line impact, debt can provide money for expanding the business, developing new products or financing a sales campaign. But it is certainly unwise to put the company at risk by assuming too much debt, and depending upon the economic climate, debt may or may not be readily available.

ZONE 5—EXTERNAL FORCES

Now that we have moved through the primary levers of company value, let's address external forces. These items have an overarching effect on your business and can affect any of the first four zones. They are rarely the main drivers of a case but are still very important.

Here's a way to remember the eight external forces. The first letter of each word spells out "SPECIAL-T", as in: "Cracking cases is my SPECIAL-T." Corny, but memorable!

VIDEO 11-05

MVM Zone 5 - External Forces

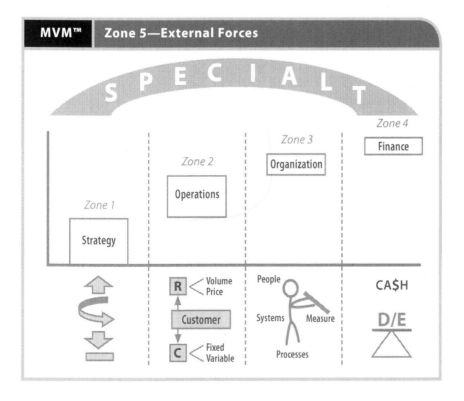

SUPPLIERS

■ **Supplies** are vital, and nothing brings a business to its knees faster than having its supplies cut off. A supplier's strength increases with the uniqueness of its product offerings. Likewise, its strength decreases if its product is considered a commodity. Suppliers feel the heat when purchasing agents expect price reductions year after year (Zone 2). Sometimes a company strategically acquires a supplier in order to capture savings and ensure the availability of supplies (Zone 1).

S

PEOPLE

■ **Public reaction,** not necessarily identical to customer response, can greatly influence management decision-making. Think about the bad press that oil companies get for damaging the environment, or the recent trend among consumer packaged foods companies to "green" their products and packaging. In both cases customers have not necessarily reduced their consumption of the products, but the public as a whole has disapproved of the company's actions. To avoid public censure, companies may make changes in one or more of the first four zones.

P

■ **Shareholders** impact the decisions a company makes, depending on their level of power. When there are few shareholders and their relative strength is concentrated, they may have significant influence over the management team. They may become involved in strategic decisions like acquisitions or joint ventures (Zone 1), or they may want to influence the makeup of the management team (Zone 3). The reverse is naturally true when the power is spread across a larger number of shareholders.

ECONOMY

■ **The economy** affects every one of the four zones (e.g., whether or not it's a good time to acquire a small competitor [Zone 1], how important it is to reduce costs [Zone 2], how difficult or easy it is to find top talent [Zone 3], or the availability of financing [Zone 4]). Forecasting the company's performance becomes increasingly difficult as the economic forecast becomes more variable.

COMPETITORS

- **Competitors** are a topic every management team would like to know more about for one simple reason: the competition can force their response in almost every area of the business. The obvious area is revenue, within Zone 2, since competitors market products and services that compete directly with your own. However, Zone 1 is also a target, as competitors can take away potential acquisitions or joint ventures. Back in Zone 2, if competitors decide to drastically cut costs, then your company must do the same. They can also wreak havoc in Zone 3 by outshining you in the eyes of customers, through the use of systems and measurement or by employing a better management team. Finally, their efficient use of cash and debt may give them leverage difficult to match (Zone 4).

INDUSTRY

- **The playing field, the industry**, can determine several elements of the business. The first and perhaps most obvious is the nature of profit in the industry (Zone 2). Grocery sales are not likely to ever provide the same margins as computer sales. Varying segments within the industry can exhibit varying profitability. Growth rates can also vary widely.

AUDITORS

- **Auditors** can be any external body that might dig into your company's finances and its ethical behavior. Serving as watchdogs, they can influence the management team by requiring greater accountability to shareholders. However, additional checks and balances may increase costs in the areas of people and systems (Zone 3).

LEGISLATION

- **Following the rules** can require a company to understand legislation covering the environment, trade unions and national concerns. The business must comply with and is naturally restricted by these laws.

TECHNOLOGY

- **Technology** wields tremendous power for change. It can transform industries or products to such a degree that acquisitions, joint ventures and mergers become necessary in order to compete (Zone 1). Technology improvements in raw materials can result in better products or significant cost reductions (Zone 2). Processes that used to be time-intensive can be streamlined through technical improvements and systems changes (Zone 3). Finally, dramatic technology change can result in the need for additional funds to invest in new plants and equipment (Zone 4).

VIDEO 11-06

MVM Topic Drills—Explaining Your Thinking

You have just finished building the MVM™. You should now have a basic understanding of how each lever can impact the bottom line, either through direct control (like cost reduction), or through a secondary influence (like hiring a new CEO).

At this point, don't worry about memorizing every point I made in each section. You already know most of this information from your business experience, class work, and common sense. You will have plenty of time to make this knowledge rock-solid as you practice navigating through the MVM™. To help you prepare, Section 13 contains ten Practice Roadmaps for the most common case types, and the second half of the book has over 40 tough practice cases. Both sections are designed to reinforce the concepts presented here.

Let's take some of your head knowledge and get it to come out of your mouth. Clients always tell me that they are surprised at how hard it is to explain what they are thinking. To warm up for your cases please do the following drills:

1 Pick a zone in the MVM, like Zone 5—External Forces.

2 Pick a sub-topic in the zone, like Technology.

3 Read through the explanation.

4 Now, without looking, explain out loud what the term means. You should pretend you are in a real case and you are explaining how this

works with your approach to solve the case. For example, you could think about a situation where costs are out of control at a grocery chain and a new technology system has been installed. You might say,

"Next I'd like to focus on the technology roll-out. I'd like to understand the total budget and what portions may have gone over budget. If we had a delay in rolling out the new bar code scanners, there may have been more service fees. Also, if the hardware or software was not working correctly, there may have been more expense for repair or customization."

You get the idea. Try this with several topics and you'll quickly learn which ones you understand and which ones would require a little more study.

Use SAVED for Finance Interviews

Sometimes you know when it's time to bring in an expert. Although I was fortunate enough to work with about thirty different clients during my nine years in consulting, I never got a chance to go deep in the area of financial analysis. And over the years as I've seen a growing need for good training designed to help answer strategic questions with a finance bent, I knew I needed to add to my team someone with strong finance skills.

I'm proud to introduce a very talented guy, Michael Katz. In addition to knowing the finance world cold, he's a very charismatic and engaging trainer. In my travels to schools all over the world, I get to meet many very smart people. Michael always stood out to me as someone who not only knew finance well but could also explain it in common-sense terms. Work through his SAVED model to better understand how you can approach your finance-oriented cases, and check out the five finance-specific cases in the back of the book. These skills, in addition to what we've covered so far, will greatly expand the types of cases you can solve and make your thinking even more flexible.

INTRODUCTION BY MICHAEL KATZ

Greetings! This chapter was born out of my day job: coaching MBA students to find summer internships and jobs upon graduation. I have spent roughly four years in top MBA career services departments—

VIDEO 12-01

Meet Michael Katz

first at UT McCombs and now NYU Stern. And I've learned what hiring managers and recruiters across the financial services industry, and the banking and corporate finance functions, see in their top job candidates. Enter the SAVED™ method. The method builds not only on my research about recruiting, but also on my experience leading hundreds of hours of interview training, working as a consultant to the financial services industry (at First Manhattan Consulting Group and kasina, LLC) and as an Assistant Vice President of Corporate Planning at Merrill Lynch. I also studied at Stern and Emory, giving me an excellent foundation in all areas of finance.

The SAVED™ method helps you build a conversation from a technical question while navigating industry and market questions, even if you lack key facts about the underlying issue. This is crucial for nailing your interviews. Top job candidates display their hypotheses and logic during their finance interviews, just like you are learning with FRAME and the MVM. You might give your opinion on a merger for investment bankers, a new line of business for corporate finance managers, financial market conditions or client profiles for private bankers, or where you would go long and short for traders. But in every case, you must present an opinion and walk your interviewer through your supporting logic. And you do all of this while showcasing your personality!

Ideally, your interview should feel conversational. This style gives the interviewer a taste of your personality and really allows him to see how you think. Yet if you are like many other students, you treat a finance interview less like a conversation and more like a quiz. Preparing for questions like "What is DCF? What is WACC? What is IRR?" certainly makes finance interviews feel quiz-like. But quizzes usually are not the best venue for showing your personality or how you think.

Let's say you get hit with an interview question like this:

> "What do you think about
> Providence Capital buying Hasbro?"

You might think this is an easy question if you have read about that specific deal. But what if you haven't? I asked my coaching client this same question one morning. That day he hadn't read the cover of the Wall Street Journal; I could tell because I could hear a pin drop in the room! But I don't think just knowing the facts of the deal would have

helped him anyway. Like studying technical questions, scanning and memorizing deals takes you to Quiz Land and away from improvising a natural conversation.

The secret to transforming an interview, with its technical and non-technical questions, into a conversation is to treat these questions as mini-consulting cases. I developed SAVED™ precisely to serve this purpose. SAVED™ will help you construct a hypothesis and its underlying logic as you engage in conversation with your interviewer. It will enable you to show structure, polish, and creativity when discussing both technical and non-technical knowledge. Additionally, it will allow you to discuss industries without direct knowledge of those areas, just as you would during any other analytical case interview.

Take a look at this diagram to see where SAVED™ fits into your overall interview preparation.

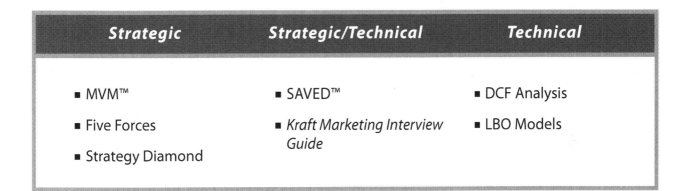

Strategic	*Strategic/Technical*	*Technical*
■ MVM™	■ SAVED™	■ DCF Analysis
■ Five Forces	■ *Kraft Marketing Interview Guide*	■ LBO Models
■ Strategy Diamond		

I recommend using it as a complement to your technical prep as well as a stand-alone approach for discussing non-technical finance questions. It will build on your knowledge and help make your answers more fluid. Over time, you will find yourself directly relying on the method less and less, because you will have developed your intuition for framing and answering finance questions.

In the following sections, we will cover the SAVED™ method, discuss how to apply it in typical situations, and then practice it using five different cases. Keep in mind that these cases are more thorough than most interview questions. They serve to build your skills so you can answer interview questions smoothly and comprehensively in any setting.

The SAVED™ Method

Similar to SPEAK and FRAME, SAVED™ is an acronym for the steps in your thought process. When you answer a question using SAVED™, you walk through the issues in order. We will first review the full method, which is most useful for answering non-technical finance questions. We will then cover the partial method, which is better suited for answering technical finance questions.

SAVED Full Method

VIDEO 12-02

SAVED Method—Full

Strategy

State whether the organization in question seeks to increase or decrease its overall presence in a market. This will frame the rest of your answer or discussion around one particular issue. You can focus in on that further by clarifying what the organization is doing. Drawing from the MVM, you will find the organization is undertaking a merger or acquisition, a restructuring or divestiture, a product launch or cull, or a joint venture or alliance. Since these activities are intended to improve overall performance—as measured by market share, revenue, profitability, or return on investment (ROI)—you should also pick a performance measure that you think is relevant to the issue. In the case of valuation or technical finance questions, your performance measure would focus on ratios involving enterprise value, EBITDA, stock price, earnings, or sales, among others.

What would an answer sound like in a conversation? We will review the example from earlier: "What do you think about Providence Capital buying Hasbro?" Without knowing anything about Providence, we know that they probably want to increase their presence in Hasbro's markets: toys and movies. With that in mind, a sample opening statement from you might sound like this:

"With the recent blockbuster successes of movies based on Hasbro properties, I think Providence wants to increase its return on investment by growing that business even further and potentially reigniting Hasbro's toy business as well."

From there, you can begin explaining what the scenario would look like and whether it makes sense for Providence to do the deal.

Assets

The next step involves naming the assets that the organization uses to execute its strategy. Doing so allows you to explain *why* the organization would improve its performance by executing this strategy. Assets fall into four major categories:

1 Physical: Property, plant, and equipment, inventories, and infrastructure owned or used by the organization.

2 Intellectual: Patents, licenses, trademarks, brands, and proprietary design or distribution processes.

3 Social: Individual and group-level knowledge, skills, and abilities, such as experienced CEOs or salespeople, a high-performing team of employees, a training program, a corporate culture, etc.

4 Financial: Specific classes such as cash and foreign exchange, equity and fixed income investments, and commodity and real estate investments.

Make sure you discuss only the key assets involved. Depending on the issue, you might also discuss assets that exist in more than one organization. In our example, the next comment might look like this:

> *"Providence likely has a network of managers with experience in the movie and toy industries to increase the cash flow from Hasbro's businesses, as well as access to enough capital to drive those businesses. Hasbro, on the other hand, owns the intellectual property for a number of toys that have, or will, become movies. They also have the infrastructure to produce toys associated with the success of those movies."*

Value

Discussing value means explaining *how* the assets in question will improve performance. Here, you walk the interviewer through the main components of your performance measure and discuss how the assets will affect those components. The table below shows examples of common performance measures and their main components. You can expand this list to include virtually every measure on a Profit & Loss Statement.

Performance Measure	Components
▪ Revenue	▪ Market size, market share ▪ Price, volume (including product mix, # of customers, and # of purchases per customer)
▪ Profit	▪ Revenue, fixed costs, variable costs
▪ ROI	▪ Cash flows, terminal value, initial investment

As you walk through the components, whenever possible take a position on where the business is trending. This will show the interviewer that you can develop your own hypothesis on business performance. You can prepare by studying the industries that interest you and developing a sense of the growth rates within them.

Continuing with our example, discussing value might sound like:

"Since Hasbro already owns the IP for these movies, Providence could increase Hasbro's ROI by generating cash from more licensing deals with film producers. They might also increase cash flows by reorganizing toy production to lower costs."

Expectations

When you discuss expectations, you begin showing creativity in addition to your analytical skills. Highlight the key assumptions that make value possible. This means stating that: 1) the assets in question do what you expect of them and 2) outside stakeholders (e.g., customers, investors, alliance partners, etc.) behave as anticipated.

"This deal makes sense so long as Providence knows how to generate licensing deals, film producers license more IP from Hasbro, and consumer demand for those films increases. Reorganizing toy production will help, but I would not rely on efficiency gains alone to do this deal."

Delivery

Although you can end by stating your expectations, you can also go one step further and frame an action plan for reviewing the business issue and implementing the strategy. This extra step is especially useful for showing your creativity with research, your expertise within a given industry, and your knowledge about particular organizations.

If you have little or no knowledge of this deal, the industry, or the organizations, you can still move forward:

"To feel comfortable with the buyout, I would first confirm that Providence knows how to generate a greater number of licensing deals than Hasbro would on its own. I would also confirm whether film producers want to license more IP from Hasbro and find out if consumers are willing to pay for those films. Finally, I would want to

know if Hasbro can produce toys more efficiently without compromising quality."

On the other hand, if you happen to know something about the industries or organizations in question, then you can offer insights based on your own knowledge or experience. This is your chance to show your unique expertise.

SAVED PARTIAL METHOD

While many finance questions lack a technical component, virtually all interviews involve answering at least one technical finance question. The most common approach to answering a technical question is to recite one or more formulas and calculate numbers when appropriate. While this approach does the job, it wastes an opportunity for you to show the interviewer that you understand the logic behind finance concepts. If you come from a field outside of finance, then this is an opportunity that you do not want to miss.

The partial SAVED™ method will help you structure an answer that shows you understand the logic behind a technical finance question. Typically, a technical question starts at the "V" in SAVED™. For example, your interviewer might ask, "How would you value Hasbro?"[1] Rather than jumping right into a list of valuation methods*, you can start one level higher, discussing the key assets, moving to how to value them, and then closing with expectations, or the key assumptions behind each valuation method.

Your answer might look something like this:

VIDEO 12-03

SAVED Method—partial

*We will not discuss valuation methods in detail in this chapter. For an excellent reference on these methods, I recommend reading "Investment Banking: Valuation, Leveraged Buyouts, and Mergers and Acquisitions" by J. Rosenbaum and J. Pearl

A *"To value Hasbro, we want to ensure that we account for its key assets, which are its IP for toys and its infrastructure for producing toys.*

V *"I think a discounted cash flow analysis (DCF) would capture the intrinsic value of its IP portfolio, including licensing revenues from film producers and sales from movie-related toys. I would also look at multiples from precedent transactions, focusing on companies that had similar IP portfolios. Also, I would see where similar companies are trading right now.*

E *"It's important to keep in mind that not all IP portfolios are created equal. Hasbro's portfolio might generate significantly greater returns than comparable companies, especially if the blockbuster movie trend continues. The DCF approach would most accurately capture this, while the other methods would show the range of how the market currently values companies with this type of IP."*

For an answer that takes about one minute to deliver, it conveys significantly more structure, polish, and creativity than the typical answer.

Other technical questions will start with the "E" in SAVED™. In similar fashion, you can answer the question by starting one level higher, at "V," and closing one level lower, at "D." For example, an interviewer might ask, "What are the pros and cons of a DCF analysis?"

To answer this question, start with value and work your way down.

V *"A DCF analysis captures the net present value of a company by projecting out its cash flows based on a growth rate and then discounting those cash flows based on a required rate of return."*

E *"Its key advantage is that it captures the intrinsic value of the firm by relying on the time value of money as a principle and detailed information from the industry, the firm, and capital markets to arrive at a growth rate as well as discount rate. Its key disadvantage is that it also relies on the accuracy of these rates to calculate a value. Small errors in assumptions can produce larger errors in measuring value."*

D *"To capture the benefits of a DCF while mitigating some of its disadvantages, I would also engage in a rigorous analysis of industry dynamics. In addition, looking at the firm's performance over time would strengthen the analysis."*

SAVED Method Homework

To help these concepts go deeper, work through Roadmaps 10 and 11 in the next section (13). After you work through the rest of this book, you'll be ready to start training with cases. Check out five cases (403, 407, 504, 203, and 508) for practicing the SAVED™ method. They align with Roadmaps 10 and 11 and should reinforce your ability to go deeper in a finance discussion. These cases range in complexity and difficulty. Some of them demand financial calculations while others test only for your logic. Remember that it often takes a few tries before these concepts become a natural part of your thinking, so be sure to do each case several times and in a different order. I'm excited about the new skills you are going to build!

Drill Your Skills

Learn the Roadmaps and Practice Your Starts

Keep in mind that interviewers today are looking for a healthy dose of common sense and everyday language.

Now it's time to buckle down and learn how to start your case. In this section you can learn how to approach almost any business case with the MVM™ and SAVED™ Practice Roadmaps. You will need to cement the concepts in your mind and practice discussing them. Do this by reading through the supporting text for each value lever (Sections 11 and 12) and thinking carefully about how you would describe each lever. Keep in mind that interviewers today are looking for a healthy dose of common sense and everyday language. These are communication interviews, so our goal with this practice is to learn to comfortably discuss business concepts. Don't allow too much unnecessary jargon to creep into your conversation. Take the concepts in Sections 11 and 12 and put them in your own words. Practice speaking about these topics out loud, as this will help you to gauge how fluid you sound.

Before you begin, review the FRAME Method™ in Section 10. FRAME lends structure to your interview, and keeps the discussion moving forward in a logical manner. Pay attention to each part as you practice, as different interviewers prioritize different parts of the case flow. The most challenging concept to practice is your hypothesis development. You may find this step to be difficult at first, but as you practice, you'll become faster at creating a hypothesis or hunch and more succinct in explaining it. Not every interviewer will ask you to state it, but having a hypothesis anchored in your mind will help you

Get to Know Your Roadmaps

to focus and to anticipate analysis and data. Every time you plot your course through the MVM™ and SAVED™, you'll learn new connection points between value levers. By being thoroughly familiar with the FRAME Method™, you will avoid losing your way during the discussion—or, worse, freezing up at the crucial moment.

CASE PACKS BY ZONE AND MENTAL ROADMAP

101 START ★☆☆
- Track your progress
- Know your region
- Study by type
- Practice by difficulty

ZONE 1 — Strategy

Case Number and Type

ROADMAP 1 — Merge, Acquire, Joint Venture
- 401 START ★☆☆
- 506 MINI ★★☆

ROADMAP 2 — Growth Strategy
- 201 START ★☆☆
- 501 START ★☆☆
- 602 START ★☆☆
- 613 MINI ★★☆

ROADMAP 3 — New Business or Product
- 510 FULL ★★★
- 604 MINI ★★★
- 609 START ★★☆

ROADMAP 4 — Enter a New Geography or Market
- 408 START ★★☆
- 603 FULL ★★★

ROADMAP 5 — Exit a Business or Market
- 102 START ★★☆
- 606 FULL ★★☆

ZONE 2 — Operations

ROADMAP 6 — Maximize Profit
- 101 START ★☆☆
- 404 FULL ★★☆
- 601 FULL ★★★
- 607 MINI ★★☆

ROADMAP 7 — Change Price
- 507 FULL ★★☆
- 605 MINI ★★★
- 611 START ★★☆

ZONE 3 — Organization

ROADMAP 8 — Streamline a Process
- 302 FULL ★★★
- 612 START ★★★

ROADMAP 9 — Restructure the Team
- 202 MINI ★★★
- 701 START ★★☆

ZONE 4 — Finance

ROADMAP 10 — Valuation
- 403 FULL ★★★
- 407 FULL ★★☆
- 504 MINI ★★★

ROADMAP 11 — Risk Management
- 203 START ★★☆
- 508 START ★★☆

ZONE 5 — External Forces

ROADMAP 12 — Competitor Attack
- 402 MINI ★★★
- 405 START ★☆☆
- 702 FULL ★★★

ROADMAP 13 — Market Shift
- 509 START ★★☆
- 608 FULL ★★★

Market Sizing Cases
- 204 SIZING ★★☆
- 301 SIZING ★★☆
- 406 SIZING ★★★
- 502 SIZING ★☆☆
- 503 SIZING ★☆☆
- 505 SIZING ★★☆
- 610 SIZING ★☆☆
- 614 SIZING ★☆☆

Merge, Acquire, Joint Venture

TYPICAL QUESTIONS

"ABC Co. and XYZ Co. are merging; help me think through the major issues."

"My client is thinking about acquiring a competitor. Tell me if it's a good idea."

"It seems that a joint venture would really help us grab more market share. Do you think that's a good approach and who should we pursue?"

SIGN POSTS
Listen for These Key Terms

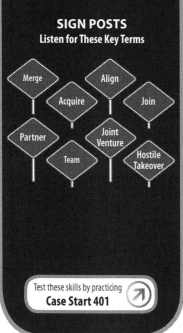

Test these skills by practicing
Case Start 401

F | **Form a Plan**

1 Think It

MVM™ Roadmap

There's a lot to discuss with an expansion case.

1. **Expand**—scope kind of case.
   Economy—Environment right for this?
   Competitors—Are they responding?
   Industry—Is this common right now?

2. **Operations**—How big are new sales? What will the customers expect?

3. **People**—How will we handle integration?

4. **Finance**—How will we finance this?

2 Plan It

Merger—what to consider?

Strategy
- We're growing through acquisitions so . . .

Industry / Competition
- What are the trends? Other acquis. and mergers going on?
- Why would comp. be doing this?

Rev/Cost Synergies
- Revenue growth?
- Volume up through new prods?
- Prices up via new customers?
- Cost reductions? How combine? How save?

Practical
- Systems—consolidate
- People—align
- Financing—where?

3 Present It

"I'd like to consider several areas. First, I would like to look at the industry trends and competitor actions. Is this merger the result of a shift in the business environment and will other companies also be merging? Second, I'd like to review revenue and cost streams to see where we may benefit and understand how we plan to make those synergies happen. A third area that links to the cost analysis will be the organization. How will we integrate the systems and people in an efficient manner? Lastly, if we have time I'd like to explore the financing of the deal. Do you have a preference for where we begin?"

R Read Your Audience

Look!	Listen!	MECE Mode!

• **Boredom**—You may go down the wrong path and talk too long. Look for broken eye contact, a glazed stare or scribbling and drawing.
• **Agitation**—Interviewer may want to move you to another area. Look for squinting, a furrowed brow, crossed arms or restlessness.
• **Interest**—Interviewer may want to see you go deep in one area. Look for wide eyes, steady nodding or leaning forward.
	• **Curiosity**—"What else would you consider?" Move to your next topic.
	• **Skepticism**—"Why is that important ('so what')?" Explain your thinking by tying back to your hypothesis or your overall plan.
	• **Interest**—"Let's talk about that some more." Be prepared to go deep.
	• **Frustration**—"Let's move on." Begin to pick up the pace.
		• If you are pushed to be more MECE, emphasize these points:
		• **Revenue**
		  ▸ Establish value of company using current revenue streams
		  ▸ Estimate new value with new streams
		  ▸ Consider synergies and cannibalization
		• **Costs**
		  ▸ Develop baseline costs
		  ▸ Outline cost shifts: e.g., employee cost reductions

A Anchor a Hypothesis

A basic approach will be a "good idea" or "bad idea" hypothesis. The bottom row here shows some variations on that theme:

Merging is a good idea and will be net positive in terms of market share and sales.	Merging is a bad idea. There will be minimal synergies between the two entities.	This acquisition will expand the company's reach and product offerings.	This acquisition will leave the company heavily leveraged and may be a drain on human capital.	This JV will successfully combine diverse skills and areas of technical expertise.

M Mine for an Answer

Areas to explore include, but are not limited to, the following:

Sales	Organization	Costs	Customer Expectations	Deal Mechanics	Your Notes
• To what degree will they increase? • What do we stand to lose as a result of this action?	• How will our two organizations work together? • Where are the potential biggest problems in bringing them together? • Are there any deal-breakers?	• Are there cost categories that will decrease immediately? • To what degree can we reduce them? • Will we risk our business with these cuts?	• How will the combined entity or partnership meet the needs of the customers? • How will customers respond to the merger (JV or acquisition)?	• How will the deal roll out? • What is the timeline, and what are the expected costs and potential delays? • Who is required to make the deal happen?	• • • •

E End the Case

• Be prepared to give a go/no go decision.	• Be concise with your reasons, reflecting on your hypothesis tree and the facts you found in your discussion.	• Deals involve egos, so don't forget about the strong human desire to make the deal happen even if the data is not convincingly positive.

Growth Strategy

F | Form a Plan

❶ Think It

MVM™ Roadmap

Look for connections to revenue and costs.

1. **External Forces**—Assess the state of the industry and where growth opportunities may be. Are competitors changing their strategies? Has the industry landscape changed? Are there any legislative consequences that are being introduced? How do we fit into this scene?

2. **Assess Growth Options**—Change directions through new products, new marketing or a new focus. Push volume through more channels. Grab share through acquisitions. Estimate the value of each option.

3. **Review Funding and Cash Flow**—Ensure feasibility of growth strategy by checking sources of funds.

❷ Plan It

Growth—how should we grow?

Suppliers/ Industry/ Comp.
- *Competitor strategies? How growing?*
- *What supply chain/ inputs do we need to grow?*
- *Tech changes?*
- *Industry trends—growth areas? How are we aligned?*

Growth Options
- *Current revenue streams:*
  - *—Volume?*
  - *—Price?*
  - *—Baseline numbers?*

Funding
- *Where will it come from?*
- *How will we maintain it?*

❸ Present It

"As we consider growth options, I would first like to understand several factors that could have an impact on our decisions, like competitor strategies, supply of critical products and overall shifts in technology and industry. Since any one of these could affect our ability to grow revenue, I also would like to know about our current revenue streams, broken down by volume and price. I can then estimate the potential growth that we would gain from our growth strategy. Lastly, it will be important to ensure that we have the funds to grow."

ROADMAP 2

TYPICAL QUESTIONS

"Axlo's divisional strategy has been weak and they are looking for help. Two divisions are in desperate need of a growth strategy. What would you develop for them?"

"XYZ is looking to boost growth in their Japan subsidiary. How would you assess where growth opportunities are?"

SIGN POSTS
Listen for These Key Terms

- Growth
- Available Cash
- Competitor Strategy
- Growth Trajectory
- Strategy
- Dog and Star
- Channel Strategy
- Slow Growth

Test these skills by practicing
Case Starts 201, 501, and 602

R   Read Your Audience

Look!	Listen!	MECE Mode!

• **Boredom**—You may go down the wrong path and talk too long. Look for broken eye contact, a glazed stare or scribbling and drawing.
• **Agitation**—Interviewer may want to move you to another area. Look for squinting, a furrowed brow, crossed arms or restlessness.
• **Interest**—Interviewer may want to see you go deep in one area. Look for wide eyes, steady nodding or leaning forward.
	• **Curiosity**—"What else would you consider?" Move to your next topic.
	• **Skepticism**—"Why is that important ('so what')?" Explain your thinking by tying back to your hypothesis or your overall plan.
	• **Interest**—"Let's talk about that some more." Be prepared to go deep.
	• **Frustration**—"Let's move on." Begin to pick up the pace.
		• If you are pushed to be more MECE, emphasize these points:
		• **Growth implies revenue increase**
		  ‣ Pure volume increase, customers demand more or we find new outlets.
		  ‣ Price increase on present sales.
		  ‣ Mix shift, sell more high-priced items.
		• **Cost reduction = profit growth**
		  ‣ Per-unit cost reduction will boost profit.

A   Anchor a Hypothesis

Here are some possible hunches:

Division X can increase profit next year through strategic growth (e.g., market segmentation, niche opportunities for existing products).	Axlo's core business is becoming obsolete. They will not grow without significant innovation.	Division X should be divested. The company's resources are better spent on other thriving divisions.	XYZ should consider acquiring Company Y to gain access to its new technology.

M   Mine for an Answer

Areas to explore include, but are not limited to, the following:

Segmentation	"Buy" Market Share	Innovation	Invest in Growth	Cost Reduction	Your Notes
• How big is our market? • What's our market share? What niches exist that we do not cover today? • Can our product line work in this space?	• Is Company Y for sale? • Why are they selling? • How would their product line fit into ours? What level of return do we expect over what time period?	• Can we adopt newer technologies? • Do we have R&D people who can develop new/better products?	• Are there divisions where we could invest more funds to seed growth? • Which product lines are growing the fastest and could use additional investment?	• Will cost management play a role in boosting profit? • How can changes in our product variable costs quickly bump up profit? Can this profit be used for growth?	• • • •

E   End the Case

• Be prepared to offer a specific growth strategy and support it.

• Be concise with your reasons, reflecting on your hypothesis tree and the facts you found in your discussion.

New Business or Product

F Form a Plan

1 Think It

MVM™ Roadmap

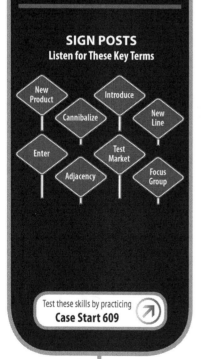

This is a full-blown tour of the model.

1. **Strategy**—Change direction, new product

2. **Volume/ Customers**—How much demand is there?
   Price—how much can we charge?
   Volume—What do we need to do to build it?

3. **Suppliers**—Any raw material problems?
   Competitors—Does our product compare?
   Industry—Barriers to our new product? Patents?
   Technology—How does this help us?

4. **People**—Do we have the right people?

5. **Processes**—How will we distribute?

6. **Finance**—How will we finance this?

2 Plan It

New Product—how succeed?

Strategy
- We're changing direction—new prod

Revenue
- Who wants this product?
- How much can we price it for?
- Will pricing change on current products?

External Forces
- Competitors—same product offered?
- Industry—overall trends. Is our timing good?

Internal Factors
- Team—who will head this up?
- Can we use same distribution channels?
- Fund normally? Or investors or banks?

3 Present It

"This client would like to introduce a new product, so my initial thoughts are around demand and pricing. Basically, do customers want this item? I would also like to explore external forces like competitors and the industry landscape, as well as internal issues like our team, distribution and financing. Do you have a preference of where we begin?"

TYPICAL QUESTIONS

"My client is interested in launching a new product internationally; what would you do?"

"Our client, Paper Shaper, Inc., wants to get into 'post-it' type notes; how would you assess if this is a good idea?"

"Tubby Tubs wants to launch a new two-person tub; what do you think?"

SIGN POSTS
Listen for These Key Terms

New Product · Introduce · Cannibalize · New Line · Enter · Test Market · Adjacency · Focus Group

Test these skills by practicing
Case Start 609

R | Read Your Audience

Look!	Listen!	MECE Mode!

• **Boredom**—You may go down the wrong path and talk too long. Look for broken eye contact, a glazed stare or scribbling and drawing.
 	
• **Agitation**—Interviewer may want to move you to another area. Look for squinting, a furrowed brow, crossed arms or restlessness.
 	
• **Interest**—Interviewer may want to see you go deep in one area. Look for wide eyes, steady nodding or leaning forward.
	• **Curiosity**—"What else would you consider?" Move to your next topic.
	
	• **Skepticism**—"Why is that important ('so what')?" Explain your thinking by tying back to your hypothesis or your overall plan.
	
	• **Interest**—"Let's talk about that some more." Be prepared to go deep.
	
	• **Frustration**—"Let's move on." Begin to pick up the pace.
		• If you are pushed to be more MECE, emphasize these points:
		• **Revenue assessment**
		  ‣ Estimate the total revenue for a time period.
		  ‣ Review risks that could hinder revenue.
		• **Cost management**
		  ‣ Estimate total costs of the venture.
		• **Organization and Funds**
		  ‣ Outline what kind of effort and support it will take to launch the business or product.

A | Anchor a Hypothesis

In this type of case, the bottom line is a red light or green light.

Introducing this product is a good idea and it will succeed.	The company should not put its resources behind this new product. It will not succeed.

M | Mine for an Answer

Areas to explore include, but are not limited to, the following:

Demand	Product	Internal Support	Competitors	Costs	Your Notes
• Do we have evidence that people want this product? • Can we estimate demand? How about price? • Where do we see demand to be highest?	• What is unique about our product? How long do we expect our unique advantage to last?	• Is the team in place? Do we have the right skills? • How will we sell and distribute the product? • Is our financing in place?	• How will competitors respond? • Are they developing any new products or strategies?	• Do we have a good estimate of the total costs? • How will these costs be broken down? • What are some risks associated with these costs?	• • • • •

E | End the Case

• Be prepared to give a go/no go decision.	• Be concise with your reasons, reflecting on your hypothesis tree and the facts you found in your discussion.	• Remember, expanding the business will require resources in terms of money and people's time. Count the costs carefully across all aspects of the organization.

Enter a New Geography or Market

F | Form a Plan

❶ Think It

MVM™ Roadmap

Similar path to introducing a new product.

1. **Strategy, Change Direction**—Our client is starting something in a new location.

2. **Operations**—What's the demand? What can we charge? How do we build awareness?

3. **External Forces**—Will suppliers have enough raw materials? How does our product compare to the competitors? How does our market share compare? Are there barriers to this industry in our new countries?

4. **People**—How good are our people?

5. **Distribution**—How will we distribute?

6. **Financing**—What will happen with the company's debt/ equity?

❷ Plan It

How do we enter a new market?

Strategy	Revenue	External Forces	Internal Factors
• Expanding so how do we pick the market? What attributes do we need?	• Which customer will pay the most? • Which country is easiest to enter?	• Suppliers—do we have the chain we need? • Will other competitors rise up? • What industry or country walls exist?	• Team—who will head this up? • Will we market the same? • Can we use same distribution channels? • Fund internally? Or investors or banks?

❸ Present It

"Our goal is to enter a new country, so I want to determine which countries offer the best revenue and ease of entry. Issues like suppliers, competitor response and industry barriers will be important. Time permitting, I also would like to discuss internal support issues like our team, marketing, distribution and financing. Before I go down this path, does management have any specific goals for our team? For instance, the number of countries or revenue or profit targets?"

ROADMAP → 4

TYPICAL QUESTIONS

"My client wants to start selling their product line in Asia. Is that a good idea?"

"ABC Co. is ready to open seven new retail locations in Texas. What kind of issues do you think they'll face?"

"I have a construction company client that wants to begin opening restaurants. How would you advise them?"

SIGN POSTS
Listen for These Key Terms

Core Business
Expand
Enter
New Market
Star Selling
Distribution
Channels
Barriers to Entry

Test these skills by practicing
Case Start 408

R Read Your Audience

Look!	Listen!	MECE Mode!

• **Boredom**—You may go down the wrong path and talk too long. Look for broken eye contact, a glazed stare or scribbling and drawing.
• **Agitation**—Interviewer may want to move you to another area. Look for squinting, a furrowed brow, crossed arms or restlessness.
• **Interest**—Interviewer may want to see you go deep in one area. Look for wide eyes, steady nodding or leaning forward.
	• **Curiosity**—"What else would you consider?" Move to your next topic.
	• **Skepticism**—"Why is that important ('so what')?" Explain your thinking by tying back to your hypothesis or your overall plan.
	• **Interest**—"Let's talk about that some more." Be prepared to go deep.
	• **Frustration**—"Let's move on." Begin to pick up the pace.
		• If you are pushed to be more MECE, emphasize these points:
		• **Revenue assessment**
		  ‣ Estimate the total revenue by time and geography (or market).
		  ‣ Outline risks that could limit revenue.
		• **Cost management**
		  ‣ Estimate total costs of the venture.
		• **Organization and Funds**
		  ‣ Discuss unique aspects of the venture.

A Anchor a Hypothesis

In addition to the fallback "go/no go" approach, here are some more specific hunches:

The Asian marketplace will be receptive to this product line.	The competitor landscape will determine the success/failure of the new retail stores.	Without domain experience, the construction company should not open restaurants.

M Mine for an Answer

Areas to explore include, but are not limited to, the following:

Demand	Product	Internal Support	Competitors	Geography Challenges	Your Notes
• Do we have evidence that people want this product? • Can we estimate demand? How about price? • Where (geography/ market) do we see the highest demand?	• How will the product attributes fit the geography? • How will the product need to be modified to best fit the new market?	• What are the distribution and sales plans by geography? • Does our team have international experience? • Is our financing in place?	• How will competitors respond? • Are they developing any new products or strategies that will beat us in terms of timing, price or design?	• How different is this new geography or market from the areas we serve today? • What items do we need to respond to in the near term (e.g., language barriers)?	• • • •

E End the Case

• Be prepared to give a go/no go decision.	• Be concise with your reasons, reflecting on your hypothesis tree and the facts you found in your discussion.	• Do not underestimate the hidden challenges with a new country or market that your team may not understand.

Exit a Business or Market

TYPICAL QUESTIONS

"Looking over the restaurant portfolio, Papa Burgers should be spun off. How would you help their parent company think this through?"

"Forever Young wants to exit the teen market and focus only on mother-of-the-bride and bridesmaid dresses. Does it make sense?"

"XYZ is thinking that fax machines are finished. Are they right?"

SIGN POSTS
Listen for These Key Terms

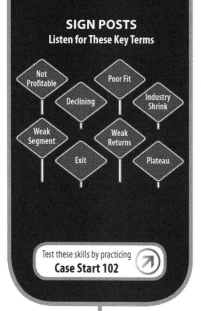

Not Profitable · Poor Fit · Declining · Industry Shrink · Weak Segment · Weak Returns · Exit · Plateau

Test these skills by practicing
Case Start 102

F Form a Plan

❶ Think It

MVM™ Roadmap

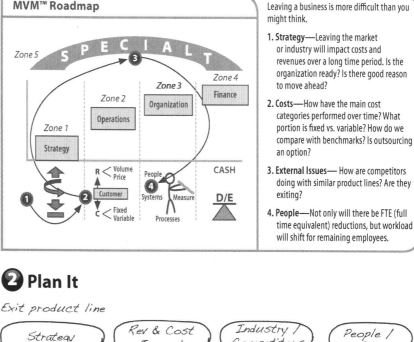

Leaving a business is more difficult than you might think.

1. **Strategy**—Leaving the market or industry will impact costs and revenues over a long time period. Is the organization ready? Is there good reason to move ahead?

2. **Costs**—How have the main cost categories performed over time? What portion is fixed vs. variable? How do we compare with benchmarks? Is outsourcing an option?

3. **External Issues**— How are competitors doing with similar product lines? Are they exiting?

4. **People**—Not only will there be FTE (full time equivalent) reductions, but workload will shift for remaining employees.

❷ Plan It

Exit product line

Strategy	Rev & Cost Impact	Industry / Competitors	People / R&D
· Why do we need to exit this product line? · How will this change affect our remaining company?	· Total drop in revenue? · Will customers buy other products? · Savings overall in costs? · Eliminate some fixed costs?	· How will competitors respond? New prods? · Are other players leaving? · How will this industry shift make new opps?	· Who in the organization need to go? Repositio some? · How will workload shift to current employees? · Will R&D suffer with fewer people?

❸ Present It

"Since we are evaluating whether or not to leave this product line, I want to keep checking in on two strategic questions: first, why are we doing this; and then, if we do this, what is the total impact on the remaining company? To answer these questions, some useful analysis would be to first assess the total anticipated drop in revenue and the potential savings on costs. We might find that certain fixed costs can be eliminated, which would lead to significant savings; or there may new ones, like severance or paying off vendors. As for competitors, we need to forecast how they might respond and whether other players are also exiting. Finally, how will we manage our team? Who should be let go, and how will we shift the remaining workload?"

R | Read Your Audience

Look!	Listen!	MECE Mode!

• **Boredom**—You may go down the wrong path and talk too long. Look for broken eye contact, a glazed stare or scribbling and drawing.
• **Agitation**—Interviewer may want to move you to another area. Look for squinting, a furrowed brow, crossed arms or restlessness.
• **Interest**—Interviewer may want to see you go deep in one area. Look for wide eyes, steady nodding or leaning forward.
	• **Curiosity**—"What else would you consider?" Move to your next topic.
	• **Skepticism**—"Why is that important ('so what')?" Explain your thinking by tying back to your hypothesis or your overall plan.
	• **Interest**—"Let's talk about that some more." Be prepared to go deep.
	• **Frustration**—"Let's move on." Begin to pick up the pace.
		• If you are pushed to be more MECE, emphasize these points:
		• **Revenue assessment**
		  ‣ Calculate the revenue loss, breaking down the volume and price.
		• **Cost assessment**
		  ‣ Calculate the total costs saved, breaking out the variable costs and the fixed costs.
		• **Other factors**
		  ‣ Emphasize how the revenue will go to zero with the exit, but not all costs may disappear.

> Exiting a business or market will typically present unexpected challenges with the organization and hidden costs that appear over time.

A | Anchor a Hypothesis

Exiting will help us focus on other divisions and product lines.	Exiting will help us streamline our operations and remove extra costs.	Exiting will hurt our business by weakening our offering and economies of scale.

M | Mine for an Answer

> Areas to explore include, but are not limited to, the following:

Volume	Prices	Innovation / Team	Competition	Customer Reaction	Your Notes
• How much will the volume drop after exiting the product line? • Will other products in our portfolio suffer related volume losses?	• If we exit, will there be any impact on our current pricing? • Will this exit shift the image of our company (e.g., remove low value line), allowing for higher pricing?	• Are there niche markets where we undersell or do not sell? • Do we have the skills to reach these customers? • How will our team suffer the most?	• What is our competitor's offering in relation to the one we are exiting? • Will they modify their products or capture new share due to our absence?	• Will customers continue to buy our other products? • Will this exit prompt them to try other brands, leading to additional losses? • How will their perceptions change?	• • • •

E | End the Case

• Answer the main question directly: "I would assess the market exit by . . ."	• Be concise with your reasons, reflecting on your plan and the facts you found in your discussion.	• Market or business exit problems can be very broad-based as they often involve shifts in the industry or customer habits. If pushed to be very MECE, just stick to revenue and costs.

Maximize Profit (increase revenue, reduce costs)

F | Form a Plan

① Think It

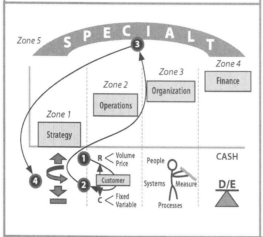

MVM™ Roadmap

Zone 5

S P E C I A L T

Zone 1 — Strategy
Zone 2 — Operations
Zone 3 — Organization
Zone 4 — Finance

R < Volume / Price
Customer
C < Fixed / Variable

People
Systems
Processes
Measure

CASH
D/E

Look for additional layers in a basic profit case.

1. **Revenue**—How do we make money (break it down across product, geography)? What's our market share? How have we been trying to increase revenue (price, volume, new stuff)?

2. **Costs**—How have the main cost categories performed over time? What portion is fixed vs. variable? How do we compare with benchmarks? Is outsourcing an option?

3. **External Issues**—How do we compare to competitors on revenue and costs?

4. **Strategy**—Are there any significant actions we need to take to increase revenue and reduce costs? What is the best mix of V, P and C?

② Plan It

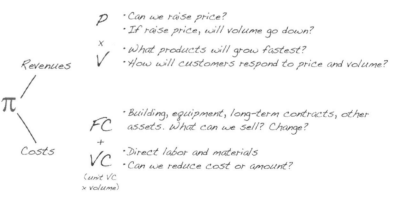

Profit—how do we maximize?

π

Revenues

P
- Can we raise price?
- If raise price, will volume go down?

× V
- What products will grow fastest?
- How will customers respond to price and volume?

Costs

FC
- Building, equipment, long-term contracts, other assets. What can we sell? Change?

+ VC
(unit VC × volume)
- Direct labor and materials
- Can we reduce cost or amount?

③ Present It

"We are trying to maximize profit, so I would like to spend most of my time focused on the operations of the business. It will first be important to understand how we make money and whether or not volume or price can be increased. There will be a trade-off between the two. Secondly, costs also may be reduced to maximize the profit. Lastly, I would like to review how competitors are performing and whether or not there is some kind of strategic action we need to take to increase profit. I would like to start with revenue unless you prefer we begin elsewhere."

ROADMAP → 6

TYPICAL QUESTIONS

"The San Francisco Opera is losing money. Tell me why."

"My client is looking for ways to increase revenue in hopes of increasing profit. I think that reducing costs is the only way to impact profit in this case. Can you break the tie?"

"External investors are trying to make my client as profitable as possible so they can sell them off. What would you suggest the investors do?"

SIGN POSTS
Listen for These Key Terms

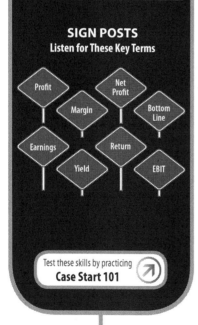

Profit
Net Profit
Margin
Bottom Line
Earnings
Return
Yield
EBIT

Test these skills by practicing
Case Start 101

R Read Your Audience

Look!	Listen!	MECE Mode!

• **Boredom**—You may go down the wrong path and talk too long. Look for broken eye contact, a glazed stare or scribbling and drawing.
• **Agitation**—Interviewer may want to move you to another area. Look for squinting, a furrowed brow, crossed arms or restlessness.
• **Interest**—Interviewer may want to see you go deep in one area. Look for wide eyes, steady nodding or leaning forward.
	• **Curiosity**—"What else would you consider?" Move to your next topic.
	• **Skepticism**—"Why is that important ('so what')?" Explain your thinking by tying back to your hypothesis or your overall plan.
	• **Interest**—"Let's talk about that some more." Be prepared to go deep.
	• **Frustration**—"Let's move on." Begin to pick up the pace.
		• If you are pushed to be more MECE, emphasize these points:
		• **Revenue assessment**
		  ‣ Calculate the revenue estimates, breaking down the volume and price.
		• **Cost assessment**
		  ‣ Calculate the total costs, breaking out the variable costs and the fixed costs.
		• **Other factors**
		  ‣ Group additional items like competitors and industry trends to focus your actions.

In a profit maximization case, keep in mind price elasticity, the competitor landscape, and market share and size.

A Anchor a Hypothesis

Profit can be maximized by cutting costs.	Profit can be maximized by increasing volume.	Profit can be maximized by raising prices modestly.

Areas to explore include, but are not limited to, the following:

M Mine for an Answer

Volume	Prices	Niche Markets	Variable Costs	Fixed Costs	Your Notes
• What has volume been over time? Do we have it by product line or sub-category? • What are the reasons for the change?	• How have prices changed over time? Why are they constant? • What are the risks of price changes? • What are the expected trade-offs between volume and price?	• Are there niche markets where we undersell or do not sell? • Do we have the skills to reach these customers? • How long will it take to mobilize and begin selling?	• Are there obvious variable costs that can be reduced? • Which variable costs will be harder to reduce? • What variable cost reductions have been made thus far?	• Are there any fixed costs (e.g., lease) where the contract is almost complete? • Are there any fixed costs that we can slow (e.g., replacing equipement) or eliminate?	• • • •

E End the Case

• Answer the main question directly: "I would increase profit by . . ."	• Be concise with your reasons, reflecting on your hypothesis tree and the facts you found in your discussion.	• Profit maximization cases tend to seem basic but have several layers you'll need to tie together. If pushed to be very MECE, just stick to revenue and costs.

Change Price

① Think It

MVM™ Roadmap

Tracking the changes is critical to understanding impact.

1. **Price**—How do we price our product today? Is it based on costs or the market? What is our pricing trend line? How have customers responded (volume) when price changes?

2. **External Forces**—How are competitors pricing? How do our prices compare to the industry overall? Are supplier actions affecting our pricing?

3. **Price**—How should we change our pricing going forward? What will this do to volume?

4. **Measure**—What will we do to track prices going forward?

② Plan It

Pricing—how do we price to our advantage?

Internal—Price Basis
- Are we using a cost plus system?
- Does the market demand a price?
- How often do we review this approach?

External Review
- Pressure from competitors
- Industry overall—how is it trending?
- Have input supplier costs forced us to raise prices?

Measurement
- What is market response to new pricing?
- How do we measure the impact on volume?

③ Present It

"To set prices at a level that is both competitive and advantageous to our client, we'll need to review both internal practices and external forces. Internally, I would like to understand our pricing basis, either cost- or market-driven, and how it has changed over time. Externally, I want to explore the market pressure from competitors, the industry and suppliers that may be affecting our prices. With these facts in place, we can determine how to set and measure them going forward. Could we start with the pricing that has been done to date? Do you have any data or background information I could review?"

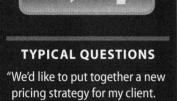

ROADMAP 7

TYPICAL QUESTIONS

"We'd like to put together a new pricing strategy for my client. Where should we start?"

"Company XYZ is complaining about their transfer prices being too high and the fact that they lose out on too many bids. How would you get to the bottom of this problem?"

"How would we determine if there is an opportunity to increase price at my client?"

SIGN POSTS
Listen for These Key Terms

Price Increase
Price Matrix
Market-based
Equilibrium
Discipline
Cost-based
Private Label
Discount

Test these skills by practicing
Case Start 611

R | Read Your Audience

Look!	Listen!	MECE Mode!

• **Boredom**—You may go down the wrong path and talk too long. Look for broken eye contact, a glazed stare or scribbling and drawing.
 	
• **Agitation**—Interviewer may want to move you to another area. Look for squinting, a furrowed brow, crossed arms or restlessness.
 	
• **Interest**—Interviewer may want to see you go deep in one area. Look for wide eyes, steady nodding or leaning forward.
	• **Curiosity**—"What else would you consider?" Move to your next topic.
	
	• **Skepticism**—"Why is that important ('so what')?" Explain your thinking by tying back to your hypothesis or your overall plan.
	
	• **Interest**—"Let's talk about that some more." Be prepared to go deep.
	
	• **Frustration**—"Let's move on." Begin to pick up the pace.
		• If you are pushed to be more MECE, emphasize these points:
		• **Revenue assessment**
		  ‣ Review price within the revenue equation (R = price x volume) to best understand to what degree prices can impact revenue.
		  ‣ Tie all price discussion (increase or decrease) back to impact on revenue and how the price change is linked to volume (go up?).
		• **Cost assessment**
		  ‣ Review variable cost decreases to see if price may be lowered with little resulting profit loss.

It is easy to have a belief about what to do with prices. Be sure to back yours up with data from the case:

A | Anchor a Hypothesis

We can raise price and gain the full value of the price increase.	There is no price elasticity in our industry. If we raise prices, volume will fall.	Our current pricing strategy (cost plus margin) is inappropriate, as our product is perceived as "premium."	Our transfer pricing model shifts too much profit to offshore subsidiaries.

M | Mine for an Answer

Areas to explore include, but are not limited to, the following:

Prices Too Low	Prices Too High	Customer Response	Variable Costs	Pricing Mechanics	Your Notes
• When was the last time we performed a price increase? • How have competitors been pricing? Have we missed an increase? To what degree are we lower?	• What happened to sales volume when we raised prices? • What evidence do we have that competitors have had the same experience?	• How have customers responded in the past to both increases and decreases? • Is there evidence that they will respond in a similar manner going forward?	• How can our pricing changes be assisted with reductions in costs? • Can we hold off on any pricing changes for a while by reducing costs?	• How will we roll out the new pricing? • What will our sales people say for business-to-business sales? • For retail sales, how will we advertise the change (if at all)?	• • • • •

E | End the Case

• Answer yes or no to the price increase; if yes, give a range as to how much.	• Be concise with your reasons, reflecting on your hypothesis tree and the facts you found in your discussion. Try to show profit and volume trade-off.	• Pricing cases tend to have a simple solution at the core, but they become complex quickly when applied to large product lines or several markets.

Streamline a Process

F Form a Plan

1 Think It

MVM™ Roadmap

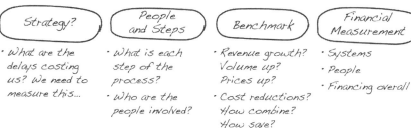

Look for connections to revenue and costs.

1. **Organization**—How is the process being used today? How long does it take? How consistent is the output? This process vs. other internal ones?

2. **Competitors/ Industry** —What can we learn from external benchmarks? What is the gap between us and competitors? Industry standard vs. us?

3. **Revenue/ Cost**—Which steps in the process are the most value-added, in terms of reducing costs and increasing revenue? How do we affect those first?

4. **Measurement**—How do we quantify/ track the value?

2 Plan It

Process—how do we streamline it?

Strategy?	People and Steps	Benchmark	Financial Measurement
· What are the delays costing us? We need to measure this...	· What is each step of the process? · Who are the people involved?	· Revenue growth? Volume up? Prices up? · Cost reductions? How combine? How save?	· Systems · People · Financing overall

3 Present It

"Our goal with this process redesign should be to focus on what will increase our bottom line. To do that, I would like to understand its present state and how its performance is affecting the company; in other words, cost out how much delays and ineffectiveness cost us as a company. Collecting the data to understand this would give us insights on how to fix the process. After putting in a new approach I would measure its effectiveness."

ROADMAP → 8

TYPICAL QUESTIONS

"My client's order-to-cash process is 50% slower than their competitors'. How would you go about tearing apart this process?"

"Quill and Company would like you to review their back office processes to determine where we can generate the most value. Where would you start?"

SIGN POSTS
Listen for These Key Terms

- Best Practices
- Streamline
- Process Redesign
- Speed
- Bottleneck
- Inefficient
- Redundant
- Cycle Time

Test these skills by practicing
Case Start 612

R Read Your Audience

Look!	Listen!	MECE Mode!

• **Boredom**—You may go down the wrong path and talk too long. Look for broken eye contact, a glazed stare or scribbling and drawing.
• **Agitation**—Interviewer may want to move you to another area. Look for squinting, a furrowed brow, crossed arms or restlessness.
• **Interest**—Interviewer may want to see you go deep in one area. Look for wide eyes, steady nodding or leaning forward.
	• **Curiosity**—"What else would you consider?" Move to your next topic.
	• **Skepticism**—"Why is that important ('so what')?" Explain your thinking by tying back to your hypothesis or your overall plan.
	• **Interest**—"Let's talk about that some more." Be prepared to go deep.
	• **Frustration**—"Let's move on." Begin to pick up the pace.
		• If you are pushed to be more MECE, emphasize these points:
		• **Revenue assessment**
		  ▸ How will improvements in the process result in additional revenue?
		  ▸ Can we assess additional volume that can be processed, and will customers buy this volume?
		• **Cost assessment**
		  ▸ How much money do we need to invest in this process improvement?
		  ▸ How long until we pay back this investment?

Process improvement cases are among the hardest for forming a hypothesis. Think of the core areas of Zone 3—Organization: People, Systems, Measurement, and Processes.

A Anchor a Hypothesis

Streamlining the Order-to-Cash process will reduce costs and increase revenue.	New IT systems will improve speed and quality.

Areas to explore include, but are not limited to, the following:

M Mine for an Answer

"Broken" Process	Wait Times	Customer Response	Variable Costs	Competitors	Your Notes
• What problems have we seen with the process? • How have these processes hurt the bottom line? • What are the worst parts of the process?	• What are the wait times today? • What portions of the process will change? • What is the expected wait time after the process is complete?	• How many customers left due to the slow OTC process? • How many of them were satisfied with other aspects of our service? • What % are estimated to return?	• How much money do we need to invest to change the process? • Aside from investments, what specific costs in the process will go up or down?	• How do we expect to beat the competition with our process changes? • What specific change will give us the greatest advantage?	• • • • •

E End the Case

• Give a recommendation for how the new process will work and what the savings will be.	• Be concise with your reasons, reflecting on your hypothesis tree and the facts you found in your discussion.	• Process improvement cases can be strategic if you tie them to the value levers.

Restructure the Team

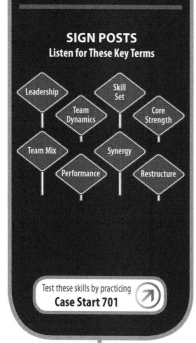
F Form a Plan

1 Think It

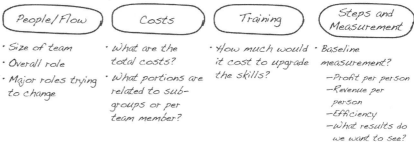

MVM™ Roadmap

SPECIALT

Zone 5

Zone 4 — Finance
Zone 3 — Organization
Zone 2 — Operations
Zone 1 — Strategy

Volume / Price
People
Customer — Systems — Measure
Fixed / Variable
Processes
CASH
D/E

Look for connections to revenue and costs.

1. **People**—What is the organization in question? How big is it and should we change it?

2. **Costs**—What are the costs associated with the team? What are current costs? How will they change as we restructure?

3. **Revenue**—What do we need to have this team increase the revenue line? Bottom line?

4. **Processes**—How do people work together today? Are these processes effective or should they be changed as well?

2 Plan It

How should we optimize the team?

People/Flow
- Size of team
- Overall role
- Major roles trying to change

Costs
- What are the total costs?
- What portions are related to sub-groups or per team member?

Training
- How much would it cost to upgrade the skills?

Steps and Measurement
- Baseline measurement?
  - Profit per person
  - Revenue per person
  - Efficiency
  - What results do we want to see?

3 Present It

"Our goal is to make this team more effective, so I need to understand the fact base first. After reviewing a snapshot of their size, role and cost today, I would like to think about our goals for them and how much it will cost to upgrade the skill set. Additionally, the way that this improved team will interact with the organization is going to change. All of their day-to-day work processes need to be created with the bottom line in mind."

R Read Your Audience

Look!	Listen!	MECE Mode!

• **Boredom**—You may go down the wrong path and talk too long. Look for broken eye contact, a glazed stare or scribbling and drawing.
• **Agitation**—Interviewer may want to move you to another area. Look for squinting, a furrowed brow, crossed arms or restlessness.
• **Interest**—Interviewer may want to see you go deep in one area. Look for wide eyes, steady nodding or leaning forward.
	• **Curiosity**—"What else would you consider?" Move to your next topic.
	• **Skepticism**—"Why is that important ('so what')?" Explain your thinking by tying back to your hypothesis or your overall plan.
	• **Interest**—"Let's talk about that some more." Be prepared to go deep.
	• **Frustration**—"Let's move on." Begin to pick up the pace.
		• If you are pushed to be more MECE, emphasize these points:
		• **Revenue assessment**
		  ▸ How will changes to our people result in boosting revenue?
		  ▸ Will the volume of sales or price we procure from the market change as we restructure?
		• **Cost assessment**
		  ▸ Will the restructuring save us money or cost us more?
		  ▸ How long would it take pay back any increases in salary or overall people costs?

Keep in mind that when dealing with people, everything takes longer than you expect. It takes a long time for people to understand their new roles and be able to perform well. Here are two example hunches:

A Anchor a Hypothesis

Too many layers of personnel in finance/accounting are slowing down processes and resulting in duplicative workstreams.	A successful product launch team requires people with experience in the marketplace, both geographically and with the industry.

Areas to explore include, but are not limited to, the following:

M Mine for an Answer

Overpaying	Internal Results	Revenue Increase	Team Structure	Roles	Your Notes
• How much are we paying today? • How does this compare to the marketplace? • Where can we cut costs and still maintain or improve the skill sets?	• Where are there problems between our team and other internal groups? • How does that need to change going forward? • What do we need to do first?	• Can we reallocate people to more value-added activities? • Are the sales people over-burdened with administration and not making enough time to generate new business?	• What kind of structure are we proposing? • How will people report to one another? • In what ways will the work be completed differently?	• How will roles specifically change? • What kind of response do we expect from those people whose roles have changed?	• • • • •

E End the Case

• Give specifics about how you would change the team and how it could impact the bottom line.	• Be concise with your reasons, reflecting on your hypothesis tree and the facts you found in your discussion.	• People are everything in terms of making the business concept work, so do not get distracted from the bottom line when trying to restructure the organization.

Valuation

TYPICAL QUESTIONS

"Tell me about a recent deal that interests you."

"Walk me through how to value a firm."

"What is WACC and how is it used?"

SIGN POSTS
Listen for These Key Terms

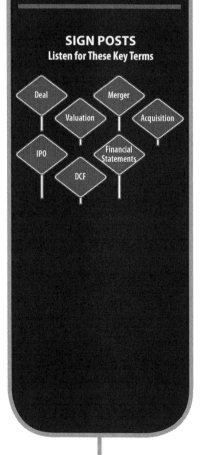

Deal

Merger

Valuation

Acquisition

IPO

Financial Statements

DCF

F Form a Plan

Sample Question: "What are some issues involved with valuing a pharmaceutical firm?"

1 Think It

Listen for the central point of the question. Typically you'll need to:

- Discuss issues for a company, industry, or deal (A)
- Value a company (V), or
- Comment on valuation methods (E)

2 Plan It

You can frame the central point of the question by moving up one letter in SAVED™ from where the question is located. Moving up one letter allows you to put the question in a useful context. After you frame your answer, move down one letter to answer the question. Finally, close your answer by moving down one more letter to discuss next steps you would take if you had to address the question in practice.

3 Present It

Discuss at least three letters from SAVED™ and be sure to cover:

- your starting point
- your central point
- your closing point (For non-technical questions, aim to use the full SAVED™ method.)

"A DCF is useful for measuring the intrinsic value of a firm rather than the market's perceptions of value. That means we would need to rely on assumptions for growth and risk that may produce valuations at odds with market perceptions. To take advantage of a DCF analysis, we would need to research the validity of our assumptions and also use comparables and precedent transactions analysis to get a full picture of firm valuation."

R Read Your Audience

Look for:

- ‣ Agreement: the interviewer may want you to continue your discussion of the issues.
- ‣ Disagreement: the interviewer may dispute your claims and want you to explain or revise them.
- ‣ Boredom/Agitation: the interviewer wants to hear a shorter starting point and longer central point.

Standard approaches cover opportunities and risks while taking a position on the issue when possible.

A Anchor a Hypothesis

An acquisition would increase the firm's set of unique assets and increase its competitiveness in that market. The question, however, is what should they pay to acquire these assets.	When valuing unique assets of the firm, we want to ensure we capture the intrinsic value of that whole portfolio while also measuring the comparable value of both its strategic and non-strategic assets relative to its peers.	Since growth rates and discount rates are developed from a set of assumptions about the firm and its markets, let's discuss those assumptions.

You have satisfied the category and can move to the next one when you have discussed:

M Mine for an Answer

Strategy	Assets	Value	Expectations
• A reason for the M&A or IPO.	• Which assets are unique and which ones are not.	• The different valuation methods and how they apply to the different assets. • The components of these valuation methods.	• The assumptions behind each component of the valuation methods.

E End the Case

- • Sum up your analysis of the issue.
- • Walk through a set of next steps to show the interviewer your action plan.

Risk Management

TYPICAL QUESTIONS

"What would you look for in your due diligence of this company?"

"Evaluate whether we should launch this product."

"What are the risks of executing this business?"

SIGN POSTS
Listen for These Key Terms

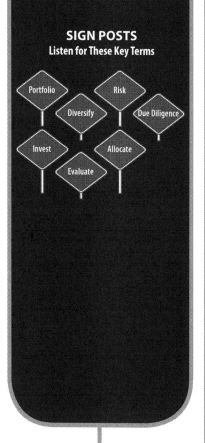

Portfolio · Risk · Diversify · Due Diligence · Invest · Allocate · Evaluate

F Form a Plan

"Under what circumstances should we invest venture capital in this new social networking startup?"

① Think It

Listen for the central point of the question. You'll typically need to identify:

- The assets the company will use to improve performance (A)
- Risks that would prevent the company from generating value (V)
- Factors that would enable the company to mitigate these risks (E)

② Plan It

You can frame the central point of the question by moving up one letter in SAVED™ from where the question is located. Moving up one letter allows you to put the question in a useful context. After you frame your answer, move down one letter to answer the question. Finally, close your answer by moving down one more letter to discuss next steps you would take if you had to address the question in practice.

③ Present It

Discuss at least three letters from SAVED™ and be sure to cover:

- your starting point
- your central point
- your closing point (For non-technical questions, aim to use the full SAVED™ method.)

"A social networking startup relies on core intellectual property and the abilities of its key employees. In addition to obtaining an appropriate valuation, we should only invest in this startup if we can ensure its intellectual and social assets remain with the firm, so we would first need to conduct due diligence on its patent portfolio as well as ensure that key man risk is mitigated through employment contracts."

R Read Your Audience

Look for:

- ‣ Agreement: the interviewer may want you to continue your discussion of the issues.
- ‣ Disagreement: the interviewer may dispute your claims and want you to explain or revise them.
- ‣ Boredom/Agitation: the interviewer wants to hear a shorter starting point and longer central point.

Standard approaches cover opportunities and risks while taking a position on the issue when possible.

A Anchor a Hypothesis

The investment capital could help the startup grow, but we will need to evaluate 1) whether the intellectual property is unique enough to qualify as a strategic asset and 2) if the key employees have the acumen to grow the company successfully.	When valuing the unique assets of the firm, we want to identify the risks associated with those assets that would prevent the firm from generating cash flows.	Since these risks manifest under specific conditions, we need to discuss those conditions and how they can be avoided.

You have satisfied the category and can move to the next one when you have discussed:

M Mine for an Answer

Strategy	Assets	Value	Expectations
• The business objective and/or financial goal of the firm.	• Which assets are unique and which ones are not.	• What risks would prevent assets from generating value	• Necessary conditions under which risks to assets will be mitigated.

E End the Case

- • Sum up your analysis of the issue.
- • Walk through a set of next steps to show the interviewer your action plan.

Competitor Attack

F Form a Plan

1 Think It

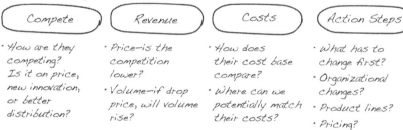

MVM™ Roadmap

Use common sense to figure out what's going on.

1. **Competitor**—What has changed recently in their behavior? What are the bottom line results (for them) of their change? How would we describe their new products or services?

2. **Revenue and Cost**—What has been the impact to our revenue and cost?

3. **Strategy, Change Direction**—What kind of action do we need to take to respond? Should we introduce a new product? Change our pricing? Match their changes? Look for talent?

2 Plan It

How do we fight off a competitor attack?

Compete	Revenue	Costs	Action Steps
· How are they competing? Is it on price, new innovation, or better distribution?	· Price—is the competition lower? · Volume—if drop price, will volume rise?	· How does their cost base compare? · Where can we potentially match their costs?	· What has to change first? · Organizational changes? · Product lines? · Pricing?

3 Present It

"XYZ appears to be coming on strong with their new product line, but I also want to understand if there is more depth to this threat. They may have built some new relationships with suppliers or retailers that we cannot see. I also want to clearly understand the impact on our revenue and costs and separate out anything that is not related to the effect. With this clear picture in place we can determine our next steps."

ROADMAP 12

TYPICAL QUESTIONS

"Amco was just dealt a terrible blow—their main competitor lowered prices 15% across the board because of a new deal with their main suppliers. What would you do?"

"My client is worried that their competition is developing a new line of technology that will make our products obsolete. How would you figure out what's going on?"

"Spiffy Stuff's new clothing line is leaving us in the dust. How do we respond?"

SIGN POSTS
Listen for These Key Terms

Introduce — Shift in Dynamics — Competitive Response — Market Share — Landscape — Aggressive — Play Hardball — Attack/Poach

Test these skills by practicing
Case Start 405

R Read Your Audience

Look!	Listen!	MECE Mode!

• **Boredom**—You may go down the wrong path and talk too long. Look for broken eye contact, a glazed stare or scribbling and drawing.
• **Agitation**—Interviewer may want to move you to another area. Look for squinting, a furrowed brow, crossed arms or restlessness.
• **Interest**—Interviewer may want to see you go deep in one area. Look for wide eyes, steady nodding or leaning forward.
	• **Curiosity**—"What else would you consider?" Move to your next topic.
	• **Skepticism**—"Why is that important ('so what')?" Explain your thinking by tying back to your hypothesis or your overall plan.
	• **Interest**—"Let's talk about that some more." Be prepared to go deep.
	• **Frustration**—"Let's move on." Begin to pick up the pace.
		• If you are pushed to be more MECE, emphasize these points:
		• **Revenue assessment**
		  ▸ Outline ways in which the competitor's actions will be cutting into our revenue.
		  ▸ Determine whether volume will decrease or we will have to lower prices to match an attack.
		• **Cost assessment**
		  ▸ Estimate the impact on costs due to competitor actions.

A Anchor a Hypothesis

Make sure your initial hypothesis is where you think the value is found.

Competitor threats seem strong. We need to defend our market share aggressively.	We can respond to this threat with a better product line and stop the revenue decline.	We need to change our product line to keep up with the competition.

M Mine for an Answer

Areas to explore include, but are not limited to, the following:

Competitor Products	Revenue Impact	Innovation	Product Cost	Customer Reaction	Your Notes
• What is the technology that our competitor is offering? • Can we match it? • Of the products that are in our pipeline, how soon can we get them out?	• What else is happening in the industry? • Are these new entrants offering the same products? • Even though their quality is lower, are they taking revenue?	• After launching these new products, will they have others? • Will our output of new products match the competitor's? • How long can we sustain this innovation?	• Have competitor actions caused us to spend more on product innovation? • What specific costs will go up (services, product parts, etc.) that may hurt our business?	• How have customers responded overall to what the competitor is doing? • Do we sense any shifts in customer loyalty?	• • • • •

E End the Case

• Respond to a competitor threat with a specific plan. Outline savings, new revenue opportunities and "stop the bleeding" plans.	• Be concise with your reasons, reflecting on your hypothesis tree and the facts you found in your discussion.	• This is a common case, so practice several scenarios within the MVM™.

Market Shift (industry, technology, suppliers)

F Form a Plan

❶ Think It

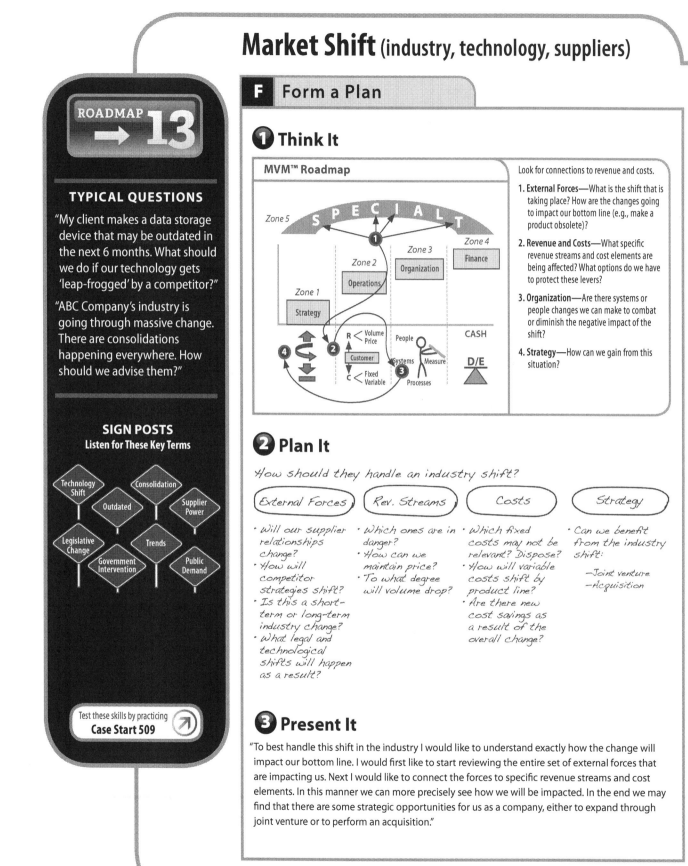

MVM™ Roadmap

Look for connections to revenue and costs.

1. **External Forces**—What is the shift that is taking place? How are the changes going to impact our bottom line (e.g., make a product obsolete)?

2. **Revenue and Costs**—What specific revenue streams and cost elements are being affected? What options do we have to protect these levers?

3. **Organization**—Are there systems or people changes we can make to combat or diminish the negative impact of the shift?

4. **Strategy**—How can we gain from this situation?

❷ Plan It

How should they handle an industry shift?

(External Forces)   **(Rev. Streams)**   **(Costs)**   **(Strategy)**

- Will our supplier relationships change?
- How will competitor strategies shift?
- Is this a short-term or long-term industry change?
- What legal and technological shifts will happen as a result?

- Which ones are in danger?
- How can we maintain price?
- To what degree will volume drop?

- Which fixed costs may not be relevant? Dispose?
- How will variable costs shift by product line?
- Are there new cost savings as a result of the overall change?

- Can we benefit from the industry shift:
  —Joint venture
  —Acquisition

❸ Present It

"To best handle this shift in the industry I would like to understand exactly how the change will impact our bottom line. I would first like to start reviewing the entire set of external forces that are impacting us. Next I would like to connect the forces to specific revenue streams and cost elements. In this manner we can more precisely see how we will be impacted. In the end we may find that there are some strategic opportunities for us as a company, either to expand through joint venture or to perform an acquisition."

ROADMAP → 13

TYPICAL QUESTIONS

"My client makes a data storage device that may be outdated in the next 6 months. What should we do if our technology gets 'leap-frogged' by a competitor?"

"ABC Company's industry is going through massive change. There are consolidations happening everywhere. How should we advise them?"

SIGN POSTS
Listen for These Key Terms

- Technology Shift
- Consolidation
- Outdated
- Supplier Power
- Legislative Change
- Trends
- Government Intervention
- Public Demand

Test these skills by practicing
Case Start 509

R | Read Your Audience

Look!	Listen!	MECE Mode!

• **Boredom**—You may go down the wrong path and talk too long. Look for broken eye contact, a glazed stare or scribbling and drawing.
• **Agitation**—Interviewer may want to move you to another area. Look for squinting, a furrowed brow, crossed arms or restlessness.
• **Interest**—Interviewer may want to see you go deep in one area. Look for wide eyes, steady nodding or leaning forward.
	• **Curiosity**—"What else would you consider?" Move to your next topic.
	• **Skepticism**—"Why is that important ('so what')?" Explain your thinking by tying back to your hypothesis or your overall plan.
	• **Interest**—"Let's talk about that some more." Be prepared to go deep.
	• **Frustration**—"Let's move on." Begin to pick up the pace.
		• If you are pushed to be more MECE, emphasize these points:
		• **Revenue**
		  ▸ Determine if the shift will enhance or hurt our revenue streams.
		  ▸ Be specific about finding out the impact on volume or price.
		• **Cost assessment**
		  ▸ Determine the ways in which this shift will cause us to increase costs on products or services.

A | Anchor a Hypothesis

Here are a few ideas to get you started:

This industry shift will mean the end of our company. We have neither the product line nor the talent to keep up with this change.	An industry shift can create new opportunities for companies that are nimble.

M | Mine for an Answer

Areas to explore include, but are not limited to, the following:

Obsolete Products	Customer Shift	Innovation	Product Costs	Competitor Shift (Attack)	Your Notes
• Will our technology still be valued in the market? • Is there an opportunity to use our products in a different manner?	• What percent of our customers is interested in the new technology? • How quickly will they defect? • Is there anything we can do in the short term?	• What technology do we have in the pipeline that can match this innovation? • Can we acquire a smaller player to gain knowledge and build products?	• How will the shift impact variable costs in particular? • Will any change in the product features or method of production cause costs to increase?	• See Roadmap #9.	• • • • •

E | End the Case

• Industry shifts can strand your client, so be ready to come up with alternatives in these cases.	• Be concise with your reasons, reflecting on your hypothesis tree and the facts you found in your discussion. Back up your new ideas with data or plans to get data as a next step.	• Most cases should have a "can do" hypothesis, but do not be afraid to paint a negative picture when the facts support it.

VIDEO 13-02

Roadmap Homework

HOMEWORK 13

The roadmaps represent the largest homework assignment in the book. If you want to be good at solving cases you need to spend a lot of time practicing (out loud), making sure you are very comfortable with all the basic business case types and that you can discuss all of the value drivers. Over time the drivers will come to you naturally, and you will begin intuitively asking questions and looking for data. You should probably dedicate at least one hour to reading each roadmap, talking through the different elements and practicing asking questions about data. I can't emphasize enough how important it is to be speaking aloud. Ultimately you will be interviewing with another person and have to share your thoughts out loud, so practice this skill a lot. You will never regret over-investing in Section 13.

Revive Your Math

SECTION **14**

Revive Your Math

Everywhere I go I hear one consistent question about case interviewing; 'How do I improve my math skills?" It's a constant refrain when I do my Crack the Case workshops and I hear it all the time from my private clients. Most candidates who practice diligently become very good at structuring a start to a case question, but when it comes to the math, many find that their skills plateau or remain inconsistent. Usually they try to get better by doing more cases, but they don't see any overall progress with their math skills. To revive your skills, you must refresh your mastery of math concepts layer by layer, beginning with basic facts and building toward greater complexity.

The MBACASE Math Pyramid is a systematic approach to help you rebuild skills that you had when you were younger, but also reinforce new skills that are more complex. You'll see that most of our cases deal with Numbers levels 1 and 2 because I want you to be very comfortable with multiplying, estimating, using equations and thinking through the scale of the issue. Those skills tend to be the most important and show up in almost all cases. After you've mastered these skills, levels 3 to 5 will be quite easy. You can quickly learn new things about balance sheets, calculating present values and reading more difficult slides.

MBACASE
Math Pyramid™

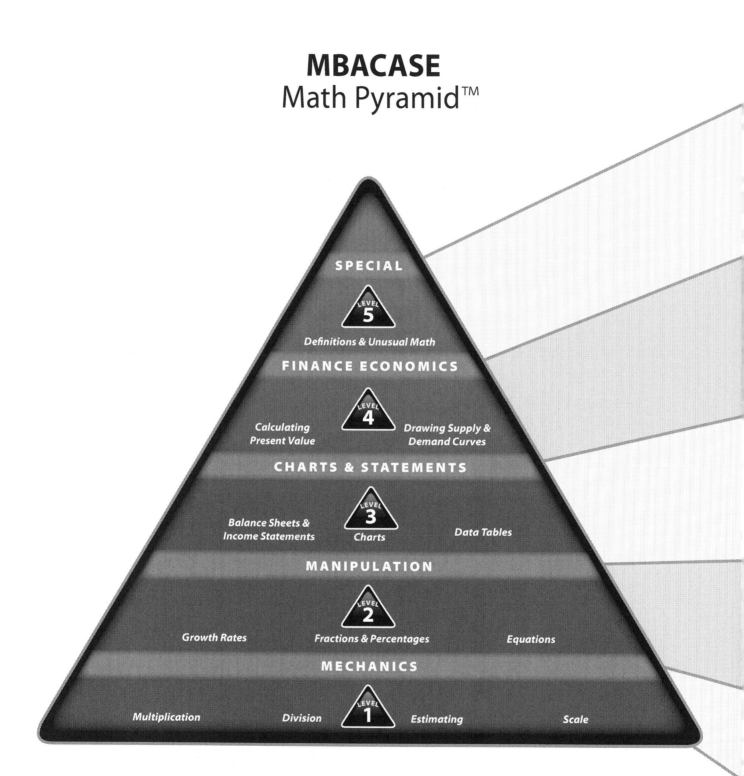

SPECIAL

LEVEL 5

Definitions & Unusual Math

FINANCE ECONOMICS

LEVEL 4

Calculating Present Value   *Drawing Supply & Demand Curves*

CHARTS & STATEMENTS

LEVEL 3

Balance Sheets & Income Statements   *Charts*   *Data Tables*

MANIPULATION

LEVEL 2

Growth Rates   *Fractions & Percentages*   *Equations*

MECHANICS

LEVEL 1

Multiplication   *Division*   *Estimating*   *Scale*

LEVEL (5) Definitions & Unusual Math

THIS FINAL ZONE holds the smallest portion of the MBACASE Math Pyramid because these activities do not occur often. For instance, you might tackle unusual conversions—like converting kilowatts to megawatts in Case 613, Windy Island—but never encounter that challenge again.

When you come across something unusual, like a new equation or math concept, make sure you fully understand it. But don't try to comb thought hundreds of cases in search of highly unusual math problems unless your foundational skills are very solid. It's not a good use of your time, since the case

interview is testing more than just math concepts. One set of conversions that you should master is your English-to-metric calculations. These math definitions come up often and it's important to know how to convert easily to your preferred system.

LEVEL (4) Finance & Economics

IN THIS LEVEL you should fully understand basic economic concepts and present value calculations. You'll need to memorize simple economic activity (like how a supply curve shifts) and also be able to apply the concepts to case questions. I have a particularly painful memory of not being able to explain shifting supply and

demand curves in a final round interview. This was rather embarrassing for someone who graduated from the Wharton School twice, but nerves have a way of exposing your weak spots. I often see this kind of confusion with present value calculations, as well. Be sure to review the basics and then understand a few tricks for estimating

payback periods so that you can avoid the long math. As you practice these present value calculations, they'll become much easier. Be sure to memorize some common discount patterns using discount factors like 5%, 8%, and 10%.

LEVEL (3) Charts & Statements

IN THIS STAGE it's important to be very comfortable with tables and charts, as many of your interviewers will give you handouts to analyze. You'll see a lot of these charts and graphs in the Crack the Case mini and full cases. As for balance sheet and income statements, these

documents are less common. It would be helpful to study a couple of cases that have balance sheets and income statements and be ready to write those out in a simplified form. There are quite a variety of charts that could show up on your cases; to see a full set, check out www.mekkographics.

com. This is a great wizard tool for making charts that many consulting firms and analytical "shops" use. They have a free tool that explains how each chart is used and the type of data it is illustrating.

LEVEL (2) Manipulation

AS YOU BUILD Level 2 skills you'll want to focus on setup and memorization. Setup means you are very comfortable selecting the right equation, defining the variables properly and testing the assumptions behind each variable. You'll use these equation set-up skills for break-

even problems, growth rate calculations, and basic "solve for x" problems. Not only should you memorize the most common equations, but more importantly, you should be able to recognize the type of case situation where you'll use each equation. Fractions and percentages are

best learned though repetition. Be sure to memorize the most common fraction-to-decimal conversions (e.g., $1/8 = .125$) and be comfortable multiplying and dividing in quarters (25, 50, 75) to speed up your estimates.

LEVEL (1) Mechanics

IT'S TIME TO GO BACK to 5th Grade and regain the fast math skills you once had. You'll need to refresh basic multiplication and division skills so that you can do quick estimates and more precise math when asked. It's also important to become very

comfortable working in different scales, like thousands, millions and billions. Your goal with Level 1 training should first be to revive your basic skills and then to pick up the speed of your calculations. Practice using "close to" numbers. Those are quick

estimates that get you close to the right answer and in the right scale ("I meant $500 million, not billion"). Almost every case in Crack the Case System includes some Level 1 math.

MATH TYPES

In my experience people's math skills fall into three general categories:

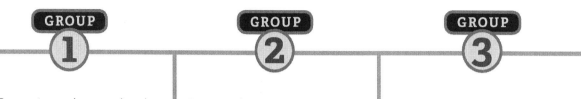

GROUP 1	GROUP 2	GROUP 3
In Group 1 are the people who like to "play" with math. What I mean by "play" is that they like to talk with numbers, they do math quickly in their head and they have no problem roughing out quick estimates. They consistently get the right answer with little effort and are very comfortable with new math challenges. Case interview math is easy for them.	For people in Group 2, doing math is somewhat of a chore, but they can usually perform well with practice. They are adept at laying out equations and doing long division. If they can structure the problem properly they typically get it right. They score high on standardized multiple choice tests because of their diligence and their ability to memorize patterns, but math is not as intuitive to them. Case interview math tends to show the cracks in their skill set, as the problems vary greatly and are given with time constraints.	Group 3 is the "I don't like math" crowd. To them any kind of math problem—whether standardized multiple choice tests or, worse, high-pressure case interview math—routinely panics them. In the past they have done fairly well on math tests thanks only to lots of hard work and a little luck. They consistently make mistakes and are not quick to see mathematical connections. Case interview math seems random and difficult and is their biggest worry about the case interview process.

Whichever category you fall into, you can do well on the math portion of your case interview! If you are reading this book, you have likely already obtained degrees that show you understand math well enough to do well on cases. You just need to put in time practicing and drilling systematically so that you are prepared for a variety of analytical challenges. Even if you fall into Group Three, you can build your skills to the point where you can succeed consistently. It comes down to how badly you want the job and how willing you are to put in consistent practice.

HOMEWORK

As you think about how to quickly build your math skills, repetition and drilling are your best tools. For your homework, go online and look for different places where you can build your Level 1 and Level 2 skills. There are plenty of math websites for young kids that are excellent for rebuilding forgotten skills through math sheets and online games (look for 4th–6th grade). There are also a variety of math books with methods that can help strengthen your mental math as well as teach you how to estimate with some simple tricks. Keep your practice sessions short and focused, and be sure to spend the majority of your time rebuilding multiplication, division and basic equation skills. After you are comfortable with Level 1 and 2, then move to the other areas. Finally, don't forget to keep a list of your soft spots. Write down analytical weaknesses that you see as you do your cases. This list will help guide your study sessions.

Math Skills Homework

Find 2nd Level Insights Using Your Notes and Mid-case Structures

After you've mastered the basics of solving cases, you'll need to show your interviewers that you can drive to deeper insights. These are sometimes referred to as second level insights, because they go beyond a simple understanding of what the answer is or what the data chart says. Most candidates think that have to already know a lot about the industry or have amazing intuition to find these second level insights. That would be great if you had those skills but in reality, there are a few basic techniques you can learn that will help you consistently take the discussion deeper. Let's review those techniques and then you can start practicing them on your cases.

GREEN CLEAN CASE

Imagine you are solving a case about Green Clean, a dry cleaning franchise that has been successful to date and wants to roll out a new hanger to all their locations. About half of the customers complain about wire hangers, saying they are hard to handle and recycle; Green Clean wants to roll out an innovative cardboard hanger. They think it will be easier for people to recycle, and it has a lighter impact on the environment, which is one of their goals with all of their products. In addition, they like the idea that customers won't have to hassle with bundling and bringing back the used wire hangers to the store. They have been testing this new product in a few markets. At the end of the

case, after you've gone through customer feedback as well as cost data, you're asked to pull your conclusion together. What do you find?

Your analysis shows that the new hangers will be cheaper to produce, but only half of the customers like them. They have 27 stores in total but only 6 were used as test markets. In this case, a second level insight would be to talk about whether or not the test market data reflects all of the markets. You would also want to ask if the wire hangers could be rolled out to all the different locations in a consistent manner, whether there would be additional shipping and handling costs in some markets, and whether some regions care less about environmental issues. Another deeper thought would be whether having the customers return the hangers to the store leads to additional dry cleaning sales. Since half the customers are not complaining, maybe customers don't find the wire hanger process to be a hassle. And perhaps it encourages them to do more dry cleaning on a consistent basis, since they are going back to the store. By bringing up these second level insights you are showing your depth of thinking and your desire to discuss the business problem in detail. But how do you come up with these insights?

NEW JOB DEPOT CASE

Let's look at another short case and find some second level insights. New Job Depot is an outsourcing company that helps people who were displaced (fired, laid off or "right-sized") and matches them with new organizations. They have grown rapidly by acquiring a variety of similar mom-and-pop organizations around the United States. They have also grown organically by finding new markets and opening up offices. Now they're trying to get lean by reducing costs and systemizing their organization. They are wondering if there's a better way to streamline their locations, develop the right employee mix and still remain effective. They are also open to growth options. After reviewing cost data and some organizational structures, you find that there are too many people at the senior levels and they seem to be overpaid compared to the market. What second level insights would you explore?

A natural progression of second level thought would be this: if we can save money with these senior folks, why not try to save money with the lower level people? Perhaps acquisitions brought in too many new people at all levels. Another place to look would be consolidation.

Can certain offices be combined to cut costs, or can some functions be shared to save money? At the same time, what about service risks? Perhaps these higher level people were critical to landing large contracts or accelerating the placement of outsourced senior executives. What kind of revenue risk does reducing these senior levels represent?

Green Clean and New Job Depot reflect case questions that I have given to hundreds of people in my private case interview practice. And I can tell you that very few people push the discussion to a deeper level. Why is it that some people naturally move to second level insights and others do not? I think the main reason candidates can't take the discussion deeper is that they do not manage their notes well. I'd like to share with you several note management skills that you can incorporate into your case performance. As a part of that skill set you'll need to develop mid-case structures, which we'll review later in this section. We'll start with the basics of taking great notes that track your case data but also lead you to insights.

TAKING GREAT NOTES—THE KEY TO FINDING INSIGHTS

By now you've mastered the ability to create a first page of notes where you probably write down all the facts and numbers that you hear early in the case. You've also figured out where you like to put your plan so that you can structure and show your approach to the case. This first page is something you can show and explain to other people. But even though you have that first page of note-taking under control, I'm sure you can still make some improvements. By taking the time to have neat, organized and accurate notes early in the case, you are increasing your odds of finding the insights that will help you crack it. Let's expand your basic skills now and incorporate some best practices for every page.

YOUR NOTES—PAGE ONE

For your fist page, I strongly recommend that you have clearly marked areas where you keep your information. I travel a lot for my *Crack the Case* workshops and have to pack and unpack often. One of the few very organized things in my life is my dresser. When I'm in a rush and have to pack in 15 minutes, I need to find things quickly. So I try to put everything, from socks to t-shirts, in exactly the same spot every time.

4 Pages of Notes

Put your paper in landscape mode.

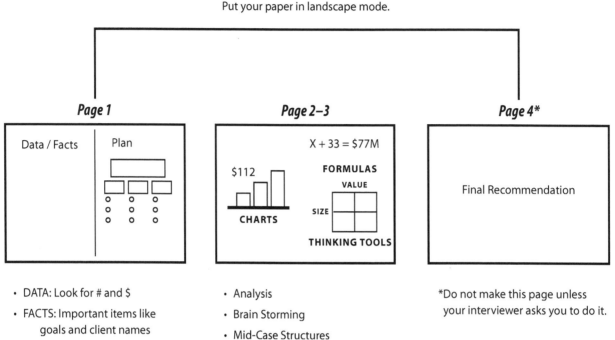

- DATA: Look for # and $
- FACTS: Important items like goals and client names
- PLAN: Show your structure clearly

- Analysis
- Brain Storming
- Mid-Case Structures

*Do not make this page unless your interviewer asks you to do it.

Likewise, you will be in a rush during the case interview! You will need to find data and numbers quickly, and you'll need to be organized. To avoid inconsistencies from case to case, put your data and facts in the same place every time. I like to mark off 1/3 of my first page for these basic items, but create a method that works best for you. I know this sounds basic, but you'd be surprised at how many people scribble facts and numbers all over their page and hope to find what they need later. Nerves can hurt your performance in the case interview, so it's important to make sure you have a consistent approach to coding your notes. I recommend you try different methods of laying out your notes over your first 5–10 cases, and then pick one and stick to it from then on. As you get additional information throughout the case, you add it to this first page. You should keep interacting with this page as the case goes along. After you write out your plan for solving the case, plan to go back to it and and use it. You might point at it or write notes on

it. As your interviewer makes comments about your approach or gives you new information, you can go back to your plan and adjust it. Feel free to write on it or cross out parts or, of course, even add a section to your plan as you go along. Simply looking back at your plan more often as the case progresses makes you more likely to remember some of the important facts that you heard at the beginning of the case. Another great approach is to put check marks by facts and numbers that sound important or might be used later. These simple actions will help you find information quickly later on.

YOUR NOTES—PAGES TWO TO THREE

After you have presented your initial structure and are into the details of the case, you'll eventually have to do some math. As you transition to your second sheet of notes, keep your first page close by. I call this my "left hand page", because it's always under my left hand, ready for me to look at whenever I need it. To help your analysis, you'll want to be very systematic in how you handle your second page. This page is for doing math or writing down more detailed data. It can also be used for laying out a qualitative topic, like how we should change the steps in the proposal development process. Check out some of the best practices below for this page.

Taking Great Notes

As you go, it's helpful to put check marks next to comments or numbers that might be useful when you end the discussion. That way, when the interviewer pushes you and says, "Let's wrap it up," or "What's your final recommendation?" or "Can we be finished now?" (which is never a good thing, by the way), you can scan the page and see some clear check marks. You can then refer back to earlier data and integrate everything together. This also helps your interviewer see that you haven't forgotten anything.

YOUR NOTES—FINAL PAGE

Some people recommend that you create a final page (or slide) for your interviewer with your final recommendations. I'm not a fan of that method, as I find it impractical: it's time-consuming, your page looks messy, and it wrecks the rhythm of the case. By the time the interview is almost over you'll be hyped up, and also typically feeling pressure from your interviewer to wrap it up. It's not easy at that point to stop the flow, ask for a minute and make a final slide. That's not a

good use of your time. If you've been taking good notes along the way, you should just verbally sum up the key points. If you marked your important facts and data with check marks, look for those and sum up. I find it more compelling when the candidate can deliver a quick executive summary verbally, rather than taking another minute to write things down. Besides, taking another moment of silence towards the end tends to lose the momentum of the case, and as a result I don't think it creates a powerful ending or good final impression. If the interviewer wants you to create a final slide, you should certainly do so, but try to keep it simple and succinct.

To help yourself bring all of the insights of a case together, it's important that you lay out your notes neatly. It's much easier to find things when they are clean, and it's also easy to show the interviewer. There has been an increasing trend of interviewers asking for the candidate's notes at the end of the case. They may do this to review them later, or to ensure that the case facts are not leaking out to the masses. In either case, it's another reason to keep your notes neat and view them as a tool for explaining your approach. Two practices that can improve your neatness are printing and simply writing less. A third habit I encourage my private clients to form is to keep all of their case notes in a folder and date them. After practicing for a few weeks, take the notes out and lay them out in chronological order. Have you seen them improve in neatness and organization and content? Do they seem more sophisticated and succinct? Could someone else read them? If your notes are getting better on these dimensions, then you are probably getting better at cases.

SECOND PAGE GOOD HABITS = EASY-TO-FIND INSIGHTS

In order to integrate and come to second level insights, you need to not just take good notes, but actually read and use them during the case. One way to integrate everything well in a case is to have your notes spread out in front of you and keep the main case question top of mind. Especially as you do analysis during the middle of the case, you'll want to compare your findings to the main question and think through the "So what?" of everything you find. As you ponder how your findings matter to the company at hand, you can use the following techniques to pull insights from your analysis.

BLOCK AND BREAK

There are several techniques for improving your second page; the first is the very basic discussion technique called Block and Break. You need to be a pro at taking any topic and blocking it out into different parts. For instance, if your interviewer is talking about jet engines and wants to have a deeper discussion about why certain sub-components may be going up in price, this might be a good time for you to use your second sheet to create a small structure and talk through the issue. I call this a mid-case structure; it can be as simple you drawing 3–4 boxes below a header. It's easy to write down "Component Costs Up" and start talking and drawing boxes as you discuss it.

Block & Break (part 1)

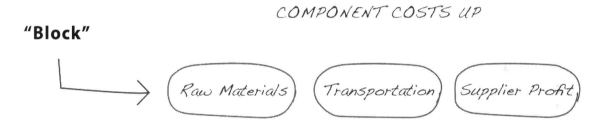

"Block"

"Well, component costs could be increasing for a couple of reasons. Let me block these out so we can talk about them . . . one thought is that the raw materials that go into the sub-assemblies could be increasing . . . or transportation costs that are bundled in with the price could be going up . . . or maybe the supplier of the product just raised prices because they want to make more money. Now of course there are additional reasons, but I think these three are a good start."

You don't have to use the word "block", but be sure you have something on your paper that shows your interviewer that you're thinking carefully about the topic and not randomly throwing out ideas.

Now we come to the concept of "break" in the phrase "block and break". To show your depth of thinking and ability to discuss a topic to a sufficient degree, you should break every block into at least two parts. When your interviewer pushes on a block and asks you what you are thinking, if you have sub-divided it into two parts then you'll be able to have a more in-depth discussion. Going back to our engine sub-components example, we have three blocks. Now let's break them down into sub-components.

Block & Break (part 2)

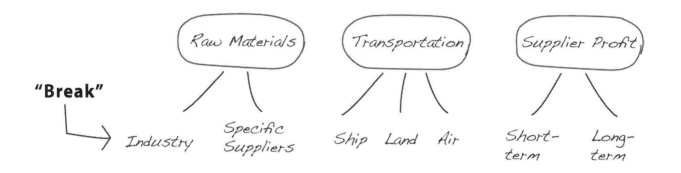

As you can see, by breaking these sub-components, you now have more to discuss and have shown more depth of thinking. Going back to your earlier voiceover, it would have sounded like this with the breaks layered in:

"Well, component costs could be increasing for a couple of reasons. Let me block these out so we can talk about them . . . one thought is that raw materials that go in to the sub-assemblies could be increasing, and that could be driven by an industry-wide trend or specific suppliers . . . or transportation and costs bundled in with the price could be going up, and I'll split those between ship, land and air . . . or maybe the supplier of the product just raised prices because they want to make more money, and we'll have to look into whether this is a short-term or long-term increase. Now, of course there are additional reasons, but I think these three are a good start for our discussion."

VIDEO 15-02

Power of Block and Break

That structure was easy to lay out for your interviewer while talking, and it provided a solid starting point for the discussion. Block and Break is a very basic technique to use during the middle of the case, and it's a good way to make sure that you stay on point and show your interviewer you can think on your feet. Master this technique and you'll use it frequently at different points during the case.

CREATING INSTANT TABLES

Block and Break was helpful for dealing with a qualitative discussion, but your second page will usually be focused on dealing with numbers and calculations. You'll be given some data and asked to do a fast calculation, or to write down some numbers and rattle off your impressions on what they mean. To accelerate your learning, you need to turn data into tables and charts quickly. The key to creating these helpful charts and tables is the ability to anticipate what kind of numbers you'll be discussing.

For instance, if your case is about a tire store with three different categories of tires—High Performance, Winter-Safe and All Year—and there have been problems with overall sales, the interviewer may likely give you data related to each category for the last 12 months. Your mind immediately moves to price point changes or volume drops by category. Or you might think about profit per category. If your interviewer reads you data that you have to interpret, you would expect to put down columns with each tire type as the headers. You would basically make a data table.

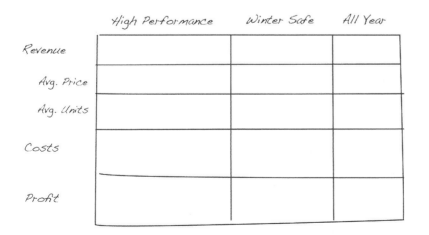

VIDEO 15-03

Creating Instant Tables

By anticipating the analytics and data in the case, you can better predict what the interviewer will give you and how to best lay out your table. The earlier you anticipate your data and the more cleanly you lay it out, the better your chances of understanding the key insights in the case. I've given many cases over the years that have tables of data, and sometimes, rather than hand the data table to the candidate, I'll just read the data out loud. I'm amazed at how much a candidate's performance weakens when he has to write out the data himself as opposed to having the table in front of him. We all respond well to clean visuals like tables, charts and graphs. The better you learn how to create that kind of clean visual for yourself, the better you'll do in the case.

Developing Mid-Case Structures

Finding second level insights during a case is all about creating small structures that help you think, explore, and describe your logic. Learning how to create these small structures during the case is one of the most important skills you can build as you practice. The best way to learn this is to keep trying to create them for every case and to be on the lookout for structures you can add to your arsenal. Since you'll typically have to create them quickly while talking, keeping them simple is vital. Here are a few tips for starting to think about and design them. To keep these basic categories straight, we'll use a picture of the human body as our memory tool.

VIDEO 15-04

Using Mid-Case Structures to Succeed

Human Body Memory Tool

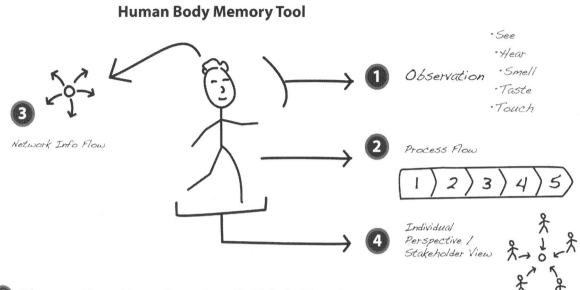

① Observation: Hear, See, Smell, Think, Touch

When you are pushed to discuss something you may not know much about, like a typical mom-and-pop diamond store or a pet shop, you might want use mental observation as your tool. Think about the scene and consider what you might see, hear, smell, taste or touch. Of course, there's not much to taste in the diamond store and you may want to avoid the smells in the pet shop, but these mental observations can trigger topics to discuss with your interviewer. Here's an example:

> **Interviewer (about 7 minutes into the case):** "I think you've fully covered the initial structure. Well, let's take a few minutes and discuss one of Totally Hip Fashion's five stores. They want to improve the customer experience and make the store more efficient. How would you help them?"

> **You:** "I've spent a limited amount of time in women's clothing stores, but let me talk through the different areas we might see in a typical store and ways to improve them. First, the customer walks in and I'm sure she sees a sea of clothes and racks. I know from looking into the stores at the mall that nothing seems to be very clearly marked. You have to know what you want and where you are going. Improving the signage could really help. Second, since they are supposed to be hip and current, the right kind of music will be important . . ."

As you work your way through an observation discussion, feel free to write down key words and circle or box them. You can put notes around them to keep yourself on track.

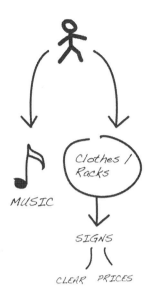

② Process Flow

The next thing you should think about is how something flows. There are many flows throughout the body: blood, digestion and oxygen come to mind quickly. Businesses are also full of flows: data to insight, raw materials to product, and inventory to sales. A flow chart, or some kind of sequential chart, is a very common way to think through a business problem. If you're interested in working for a company that does a lot of operations work, you'll particularly want to be ready to create flow charts during your discussion. When you have to create a flow on the spot, try to think of the basic steps first and then add in more detail later.

One example might be getting approval for a home mortgage. Can you think through the most basic steps? First you have to fill out forms about your financial status, next you need to submit the forms, the bank then reviews them and evaluates your risk, and then you are finally approved for the mortgage. As you discuss this process with the interviewer, you might add in a due diligence step where the bank

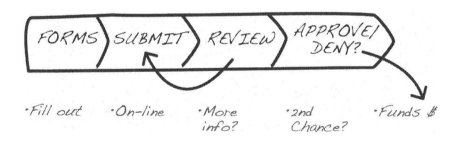

keeps asking for more information, or the final step of receiving funds. But don't hold out for perfection. It's best that you start working on your paper *while* talking to the interviewer. As you look at businesses around you, think about the flows that make them work.

③ Network Information Flow

Another great mid-case structure is one that maps out how information might flow. But since that is not always sequential, it might be better to think about how one hub sends out multiple messages, just like your brain sends different messages to the body: *pump the blood*, *eat the food*, and *walk across the street*. Since many cases now deal with information flow and technology, considering how a piece of information or data might flow through an organization could be very helpful.

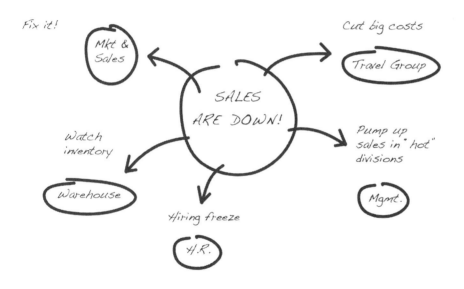

④ Individual Perspective or Stakeholder View

Another way to create a small structure is to go back to the human body again—but this time, think of multiple humans. Consider how different people may view a situation or have an interest in a certain outcome. Stakeholder analysis is an excellent way to gain different perspectives. Basically, you lay out how different people might be involved in a decision and talk about how they might view it.

For instance, you could think about the decision to roll out a new inventory management system. You might think of the employees who have to enter the data, management who want to manage costs

better, people within the plant who need more accurate data, the Chief Information Officer who's worried about the cost, and finally, the customers, who won't experience as many stock outs. I'm sure you can think of more people and their concerns. Building your ability to incorporate multiple perspectives will help you both during the cases and also on the job.

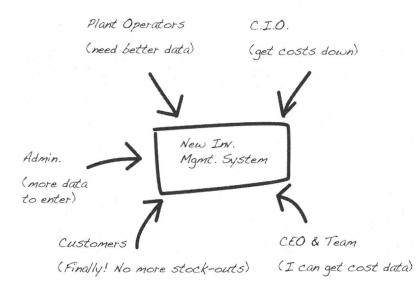

How to Make Mid-Case Structures: Review

1. Can I observe something in my mind? For this topic, is there something unique about the look, sound, feel, smell, taste or touch?

2. Does this discussion lend itself to a process? Is there a clear input and output?

3. Should I be thinking about a flow of information?

4. Am I considering several perspectives? How does everyone view the problem at hand?

CREATING CHARTS AND GRAPHS

No discussion of small structures and second level insights would be complete without addressing charts and graphs. You may think of these as only something to review when the interviewer hands you one. But there are some basic ones you can create during your mid-case discussions that will help you quickly organize your data, show off your analytical skills, and pinpoint insights.

VIDEO 15-05

Creating Charts & Graphs

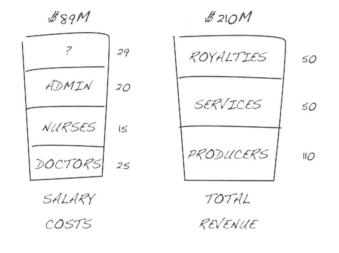

BAR CHARTS

$89M — ? 29, ADMIN 20, NURSES 15, DOCTORS 25 — SALARY COSTS

$210M — ROYALTIES 50, SERVICES 50, PRODUCERS 110 — TOTAL REVENUE

Bar Charts

The bar chart is my favorite, as it is easy to create quickly and is effective at keeping your numbers all together. It's simple: just draw a stack bar, put your number at the top and then fill in what you know. You can lay out for the interviewer what you understand and what you need to find. Stack bars work well for both cost reduction and revenue growth discussions.

Data Over Time

Another thing to consider is data over time. Simply drawing a chart plotting your data over multiple years can show you some insights. You are also letting the interviewer know that graphs are second nature to you.

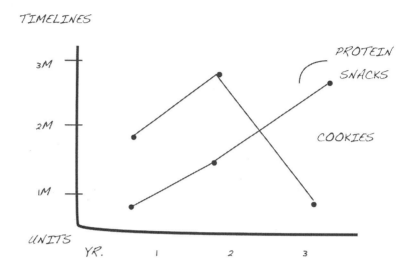

2 x 2s

When you want to bring in several perspectives, using a 2 x 2 can be very helpful. Just try not to become a 2 x 2 addict who attempts to turn every discussion into two dimensions and four boxes. A common situation that lends itself to a 2 x 2 is that of a company deciding which projects to roll out. On one dimension you put the pay-off. How much value will these projects bring to the company? The other dimension is the cost or difficulty of rolling out the project. Either dimension can be low or high. If you arrange the chart properly you'll have your easy-to-roll-out, high-impact projects in the upper right hand corner. This set of projects would be your high priority list.

As we've discussed, being effective in the middle of the case is power-fully driven by using neat, well-organized notes and being structured, just like in the beginning of the case. So think about ways you can use these simple structures as you practice various cases. The best way to master simple structures is to go back and do old cases a second time. The more you use small structures, the easier it will be to drive to second level insights.

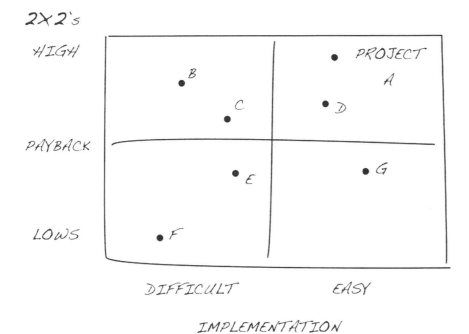

HOMEWORK 15

Review all of the sample drawings and methods for organizing your thoughts. Practice drawing each one individually and then choose 2–3 that are easy for you to remember and use. Try using these small structures in your next few cases. Look to add more mid-case structures to your skill set over time.

CHAPTER

6

Be Smart with Insider Tips & Tricks

Look Over My Shoulder— Interviewer and Case Coach Tips

As you aim to be fully prepared for your interviews, you need to know what you are up against, how you'll be judged, and how you should prepare. I've been fortunate to experience the interview process on multiple sides: as a candidate preparing for my big interviews years ago; as an interviewer at top-tier undergraduate and MBA programs while a consultant and manager at Bain & Company; and now as a case interview coach working with over a hundred private clients a year. In this chapter I'll share with you the perspectives of the interviewer and coach, and help you gain some insights into how the process works and how you can reach your full potential. Let's build new insights together; then you can do your best to work on the things that you can control, and relax about the things that you can't.

MY VIEW AS AN INTERVIEWER

Students often wonder how firms make their final hiring decisions. They tend to have the mistaken notion that since so many candidates crack their cases, the final decision must be somewhat arbitrary. In reality, very few people crack all of their cases. Sometimes a candidate shines in one interview and bombs another. Here is an overview of how the firms sort everything out.

"We must believe in luck. For how else can we explain the success of those we don't like?"

—Jean Cocteau

The Matching System: Hashing it Out with Your Partner

During first-round interviews, each interviewer has a partner who will see the same dozen or so candidates. Each interviewer has been with the firm for at least two years, though the two are not necessarily of equal rank. At the end of the day, they need to agree on which candidates to pass to the final round. To avoid confusion and potential mistakes, most interviewers try to check in with their partners around lunchtime to make sure they are assigning similar rankings to the candidates. They then meet again at the end of the day to make the final cut. Here's an example of how it works. Marcos, a second-year manager, and Nora, a third-year consultant, are comparing notes on the six people they've seen this morning:

> **MARCOS:** How's it going? Any superstars?
>
> **NORA:** Hardly, but I did have one bright spot. What did you think of Henry?
>
> **MARCOS:** Ugh, I was afraid of that. He was doing great but cratered at the end.
>
> **NORA:** How bad was it?
>
> **MARCOS:** His logic fell apart, and he really couldn't pull a recommendation together. He just seemed to get super nervous. It's a shame, because I really liked him.
>
> **NORA:** That's too bad, because he crushed my case. What about Serena?
>
> **MARCOS:** I liked her. I thought she was a great fit, and definitely bright, but she didn't get off to a good start. Her framework was a little weak. I'd say give her another year.
>
> **NORA:** Let's be sure to let her know that when we call her.
>
> **MARCOS:** I hope the afternoon crowd is better.

At this point, no one will be passed on to the next round. Even if the afternoon candidates are worse than the morning, Marcos and Nora will not change their decisions. They have given their cases at other schools and have watched star candidates solve them.

No one's rank ever rises throughout the day. I've interviewed people who seemed pretty good in the morning but ended up squarely in the middle of the pack by the end of the day. To succeed you must absolutely crack every case you receive, period. Let's revisit Marcos and Nora at the end of the day. They've seen seven more people in the afternoon.

MARCOS: What a difference from the morning! Could you believe that group?

NORA: Finally! I was worried about this place. So, who are your top three?

MARCOS: Katarina's one, Pierce's two and Spencer's three. How about you?

NORA: We're pretty close. Pierce's first, Katarina's second, Sundeep's third and Spencer's fourth. Any concerns about the first two?

MARCOS: No. Basically, Katarina crushed the case and definitely had a lot more poise than Pierce. There's no doubt that guy is smart, and I'd take him in a heartbeat; I just think he's a little on the quiet side. We may have to push him to be more confident if he makes it through.

NORA: I'm surprised you say that about Pierce because he really came alive for me. He burned through the case and even handled a few curve balls I made up on the spot to push him. He was a lot more creative than I expected, but I think he knew quite a bit about the industry. We also had time to talk a little about the start-up he was involved in before he came to school. He seemed to show a lot of leadership. Katarina was smart; I would just like to see her put a stake in the ground more forcefully.

MARCOS: What about Spencer?

NORA: I don't know . . . he did fine on the case, but he wasn't spectacular. I don't see him making it all the way. I thought Sundeep was better.

MARCOS: Yeah, let's go with just two. Sundeep bombed my case, and Spencer was solid—but not great. Also, there's no way Sandra [Recruiting Manager] will let us bring in three from this list unless they're amazing.

Good luck to Katarina and Pierce. Maybe one will make it through the final round. How about Spencer? It's interesting that neither interviewer said he failed the case. He was "fine" and "solid" but not amazing. He cracked the cases but, on the continuum of performance, paled in comparison with the first two. Why? Because of subtle differences in the way he solved the problem and presented the solution. If he's a first-year MBA going for a summer position, he might improve and get an offer next year.

Final Calibration–Dings and Passes

Next, the interviewers meet with the recruiting team. You may have talked with this team a few times at a firm-sponsored event or when you scheduled your interview. Its members sometimes have a few favorites among the candidates, but naturally they must defer to the interviewers' final decisions.

After the last candidate is ushered to the door, everyone meets in some kind of "war room" at the hotel or recruiting center. Depending on the recruiting manager's personal style, the room may be plastered with flip chart pages listing the names and a few notes—or the recruiting manager might simply note everything in her master book.

With so few full-time positions available, it doesn't make sense to send borderline candidates to see the partners; they almost never make it.

The purpose of the meeting is to ensure that everyone understands who is being passed to the next round and who is not. The decisions are usually very straightforward. During one session, my partner and I wanted to pass three or four candidates to the final round and had to vigorously defend our picks. With so few full-time positions available, it doesn't make sense to send borderline candidates to see the partners; they almost never make it. In general, two or (maybe) three candidates from each pair's schedule make the cut.

After giving the recruiting manager his decisions, an interviewer's final task is to call everyone on the ding list and break the bad news. The interview process moves very quickly on most campuses (especially for summer positions), so students can expect a call the evening of the day they interviewed.

The two interview partners usually split the ding list according to which partner gave each candidate the lower ranking. They use this method because it's easier to ding someone who melted down on your case. Imagine how awkward it would be to say, "Honestly, John, I

liked you, but the other interviewer thought you choked. Hey, good luck on the rest of your interviews."

DING CALLS AND FEEDBACK

Unfortunately, in my years of interviewing I never got to make the happy calls. Our office policy was to streamline all interaction with the candidates through the recruiting staff. They made all of the congratulatory calls and booked the next round of interviews; this approach reduced the number of missed calls and scheduling complications. After the candidates heard the good news, we (the interviewers) were allowed to call and congratulate them.

If you are tempted to think that interviewers enjoy making ding calls, think again. It is painful to disappoint someone's hope of working for your firm, no matter how wildly unsuited for the job he is. We managed the conversation like this:

> **INTERVIEWER:** Hello; this is David Ohrvall from the Firm. Is this Serena?
>
> **SERENA**: Yes; hi, David. How are you?
>
> **INTERVIEWER:** Fine, thanks. Unfortunately, Serena [this is the key word in the conversation, letting them know right away that it's bad news], we will not be passing you on to the next round.
>
> **SERENA:** [Awkward silence.] Oh, um, as you can imagine, I'm disappointed. Is there any feedback you could give me on my performance?

Ah, yes, the feedback question. This is the moment a candidate believes will be magical. Everyone, from the career services staff to the firms' own recruiting people, recommends asking your interviewer for feedback. After all, this is a real live interviewer. This person saw you perform under actual stress. Surely the feedback will be incredibly insightful.

I hate to disappoint you again. The sad truth is that the interviewer probably doesn't have time to go into the details. You're probably one of six calls he is making that night. Or worse, he doesn't really remem-

*The sad truth is
that the interviewer
probably doesn't have
time to go into the
details.*

ber the specifics about your case performance. A dozen mediocre cases tend to run together, and without photos, it's sometimes difficult to remember your face.

Unless the interviewer has perfect notes and a mental picture of each candidate, he isn't sure whether the person on the other line is the one who said random things at the wrong time, or the one who had a really weak hypothesis. It would be incredibly mean to tell someone that he failed the Pizza Test, or that her habit of rocking back and forth as she talked drove you up the wall. So the feedback will almost always be focused on the case.

Here are some vague refrains along with a good follow-up question for digging out the useful information:

- **You could have structured the problem better.**

  Take this one at face value. Most people fail the case because they don't know how to attack the problem or how to structure the analysis.

  Try to pull out some more meaningful feedback by asking one question (there probably won't be time for more). For example: "Was there a part of the case that I missed due to my structure?"

- **I didn't really see the depth of thinking I was seeking.**

  You can classify this one as a framework problem. You may have appeared shallow because you didn't drill down to enough detail or open enough "doors."

  Try asking the following: "Does a specific part of the case where I could have gone deeper come to mind?"

- **I think you lost your focus about halfway through the case.**

  This statement is the vaguest of the vague. It could mean anything from going down a tangent to being distracted by the interviewer's curve-ball question.

  Ask: "Where should I have taken the analysis and discussion?"

You may be surprised at one time or another (let's face it, you will get ding calls) by the interviewer's concern for you. If she is willing to provide specific feedback, milk it for all it's worth. Her insights far outweigh anything your practice partners tell you. Drill down with specific questions about your analysis, your framework, your communication style, your logic and your solution. One of the best ways to improve is, when possible, to gather specific feedback from your real case interviews.

If she is willing to provide specific feedback, milk it for all it's worth.

OTHER BEHIND-THE-SCENES QUESTIONS

- Timing—Should I Interview in the Morning or Afternoon?

    Honestly, timing doesn't matter that much. What's most important is when you're at your best. If you are most alert in the morning, then by all means take an a.m. slot. If you need the morning hours to gather your thoughts, then shoot for the afternoon slots. It is more important to feel confident in your ability to perform than to try to game the system.

    There are too many variables to control, like what time the superstar candidate is interviewing (let's hope that person is you), or what mood your interviewer will be in after he gets an angry voicemail from a client. That said, a few time slots are riskier than others:

    8:00 a.m. High Risk. Interviewer may be running late or still waking up.

    8:30 a.m. Mild Risk. Still waking up.

    9–11:30 a.m. PRIME ZONE. Awake and full of caffeine.

    11:30 a.m. High Risk. Your interviewer is thinking about lunch and which texts and emails to send on his break.

    1:00 p.m. Risk. She may be less focused due to post-lunch low blood sugar.

    1:30 p.m. Mild Risk. See above.

    1:30–4:00 p.m. PRIME ZONE. Awake and full of caffeine again.

Final Time Slot: High Risk. He is wrapping up, is probably rushed, and may have picked a favorite already.

- **Are there really quotas or limits for the number of new hires?**

Yes and no. When I was in business school, I attended a presentation given by a top-tier strategy firm. The presenting partner told the crowd of hopeful candidates that his firm wanted to hire a lot more people, but just couldn't find enough candidates who met their standards. That comment didn't sit well with the audience and didn't make sense to me, either. I thought, "Here is a crowd of about 500 top-tier MBA students, and he's telling us that they can't find enough good people? What a joke."

With so many cases to crack, the quota takes care of itself; it is rare for firms to turn away great candidates.

Now that I've been on the other side of the situation, I can understand what he meant (although it was still a poorly-timed and arrogant comment). With so many cases to crack, the quota takes care of itself; it is rare for firms to turn away great candidates. There are times when the selection is tighter than normal: perhaps extra offers were extended at another school, or chargeable hours in the office are down. In those situations, it is easy to narrow the field by adding a few more curve balls to the cases or being pickier about non-case elements like presentation and pedigree.

- **Scores, GPA, Work Experience and Undergrad Degree. Do they really matter?**

Once you make the interview schedule, these other factors should no longer matter. The only time I've seen a candidate's scores evaluated, the person in question was an undergraduate. She was a borderline choice in the final round and had a 1360 SAT (out of 1600 total), while all of the other candidates' scores were in the 1400s and 1500s. Since her job at the firm would involve a good deal of heavy analytical work, a few interviewers were concerned about whether she could handle it—so they checked her scores. As for MBA candidates: scores and grades never came up. Once you meet an acceptable threshold, firms weigh the case interviews over all else.

In terms of securing an interview slot, your scores, GPA, work experience and undergraduate degree are everything. Here are a few things that get noticed:

GMAT score over 700 (This is fairly common now, thanks to prep courses and obsessive studying.)

Ivy League undergrad and/or other top-tier programs (Snobby, but true.)

GPA of at least 3.8 (The tougher the school, the better.)

Engineers (Strong math skills are supposed to be a given.)

Consulting experience (They know you can deliver consistent output and are client-ready.)

Investment banking (You've proven you can put in the hours.)

Business unit or product line responsibility (You can manage people and profit.)

Very significant non-business achievement (Anything you won in sports, music or academics.)

Living abroad and speaking a foreign language (Both are almost a basic requirement now.)

The "I'd like to meet you" factor (e.g., fashion model, writer for MTV, or the President's limo driver.)

Past residency in a particular city (For example, the London office likes people who have lived in London.)

Once you meet an acceptable threshold, firms weigh the case interviews over all else.

No candidate has all of the above items, but you should do your best to highlight your strongest features. Some resumes contain so much junk that the best parts become lost in the review process. Most resumes get a ten-second review at best; only the most salient features stand out. The employees assigned to review resumes basically have carte blanche in their decision-making: some scan the cover letters for a few unique factors; others focus only on past residency in the city of choice; still others like to bring in candidates who have specific work experience. These practices vary widely by office.

If you don't find yourself on the interview list, you should call the recruiting coordinator and plead your case. It's now very difficult to get through, given the on-line submission process—but remember, no firm wants to lose a top candidate to a competitor. If you have secured interviews with the competition, let the firm know. All you have to do is introduce yourself, remind them of your strong desire to work for them, and then bring up your problem: you have interviews with all of the firms except them. They usually try to find a slot for you.

- ### What if I'm waitlisted?

    If you are waitlisted, it's time to go face-to-face. But before you do anything, remember to be nice, nice and nice again. If you anger or annoy one of the recruiting team (full-time recruiters as well as on-campus reps), it's all over: let's just say that you will remain waitlisted. With that in mind, try to meet with any of the company's reps on campus, or at least call one of them. Again, remind him or her of your marked interest in working for the firm and of the problem that you face—an interview with everyone but them. Cancellations do occur, and openings are sometimes made for those who connect well enough.

    Though it seems arbitrary, decisions sometimes come down to simple human connection. Some people just stand out in your mind, and others don't. No recruiting team member wants to keep a stellar candidate out of the firm, though. If you can build enough rapport with one of them, you'll get your slot.

    As for being treated like a second-class candidate, don't worry about it. Your interviewers are unlikely to know that you made the list at the last minute. You'll have as fair a shot as anyone else.

    In fact, I know a man who wasn't on the original interview list with Bain & Company. He called the recruiting team and squeaked into a last-minute slot, and then went on to fill one of the firm's few summer associate positions. He later became a manager with the firm. That, of course, is my story. Persistence definitely pays off.

VIDEO 16-01

**David Ohrvall,
Interviewer's Perspective**

MY VIEW AS A CASE INTERVIEW COACH

As a coach at MBACASE since 2003, I have privately trained over 700 clients, many of whom have gone on to successfully land the job they jobs they wanted. Of course, not everyone does as well as they would like—and I have noticed that the people who do succeed tend to have some common practice habits that I want share with you. Compare yourself (as much as you can at this point) to this list of best practices, and then plan to return to this list after you have practiced a few cases.

1 Remember, It's an Oral Test

I'm sure you are good at taking tests. You're analytical, you enjoy problem-solving and you find it fun to get the answer right! In fact, you are probably a pro at getting ready for tests as you have done it so often. But this case interview "test" is different. It's an oral exam, in a sense, and it's not likely you've taken many spoken tests before. Successful candidates quickly recognize that preparing for this test will be different. They start to practice everything out loud, even when rehearsing by themselves. They also use technology to get a new perspective, using webcams to film the cases they do with their practice partners. Interviewers will be judging you on how you present because it is such a big part of your future job. They know that you'll be presenting to all types of clients, as well as leading teams. So learning to see yourself as they see you will accelerate your improvement. Your oral skills will set you apart or doom you, so the more you practice out loud, the better-prepared you will be.

2 Take It Seriously, Over a Longer Period (When Possible)

The top performers have taken their case interview prep seriously by planning out practice times, working on specific skills, and seeking feedback on how to improve. They tend to do these activities over a longer period, ensuring there is enough time to let the material sink in. I know some of you reading this are in a "cram" situation, and I assure you that it is possible to get a lot done in a short period of time. In fact, I have helped people succeed with their interviews in as little as 2–3 days. But that is the rare situation and should be avoided when possible. Building

strong case interview skills takes a while; you must allow time for the material to go deep. Give yourself a minimum of 6–8 weeks to prepare.

3 Build Your Skills in Layers

Successful people also tend to build their skills in layers. They first create a good foundation of understanding by using basic cases. After they've mastered simple cases, they move on to the next level of difficulty, progressing through a variety of business problems and tackling new analytical and logic skills. When they encounter a case or type of question that does not go well, they repeat the process of solving it several times until they have fully mastered it. Much like a musician who practices a few bars until she can play them perfectly, these individuals break a case into portions and make sure they can "perform" each part. This layer-by-layer approach improves their odds of doing well during the important interview, because they have carefully built deep skills that will hold up under pressure.

4 Take Your Structures Deeper

Another key to faster success is going beyond the initial structure. I would estimate that the majority of people who get dinged failed to do two things: present a compelling plan that lays out enough topics (breadth), and thoroughly investigate each of those topics to find a solution for the problem (depth). But I must also say that the people who go all the way to getting an offer are those who can move beyond the structure. They can think about second level insights, and can go a little deeper with mini structures for qualitative discussions, or another piece of analysis for quantitative work. Some people train themselves to only develop the first level structure, and then when they get a case that doesn't fit neatly into one of their pre-planned, fully-memorized approaches, they don't know what to do. Interviewers are looking for people who are savvy and flexible. And making certain you build those skills is extremely important. Be sure to review the concepts in Section 15 and find ways to consistently take the discussion deeper.

5 Be Excited about the Numbers

When you talk about numbers, show the interviewer that you're not afraid to discuss them. You might be shaking in your boots on the inside, but on the outside you should look very calm and excited to be digging into the data. It's almost impossible to get one of these jobs if you don't do well on the math portion, so be sure to strengthen your analytical skills whenever you practice. It's really important that you build your skills to the point of feeling confident with almost any piece of analysis.

Do you like to play with numbers? That shows you are comfortable with math. What I mean by that statement is that average performers don't want to discuss the numbers until they have their final answer. They look at the math problem in the case as an equation requiring an exact solution. But people who are comfortable with numbers (the "naturals") start estimating and talking about their estimate right away. If I tell a natural there's a 19% savings on 3 billion, he'll say, "Oh, that's about 20% so that would be 600 million. I could be more precise if you'd like . . ." This shows that he is using the data as a tool and effortlessly weaving it into his discussion.

In my coaching, I can always tell who's afraid of the math. After I give them the numbers, there's a bit of an extra pause, and even some formality in their manner. It's almost as if they are saying, "OK, this is my big analytical moment! Let me take my time and not mess up." They try to calm themselves down, lay out an equation with every zero written out (usually a sign of a novice) and then don't talk to me until they've finished all their calculations. They lack the comfort and confidence to use the numbers immediately to help solve the case.

To become more like a natural and show your comfort with numbers, you need to start with the foundational skills: practicing your multiplication, division, and growth rates skills and estimating quickly. I notice the importance of this foundational practice when I see people take the time to truly conquer the math. They break things down into basic multiplication and division, learn how to deal with growth rates, improve at using percentages, and become very good at managing scale (thousands vs. millions vs. billions). As a result, in their interviews, they don't make the mistakes that trip other

Average performers look at the math problem in the case as an equation requiring an exact solution. But people who are comfortable with numbers (the "naturals") start estimating and talking about their estimate right away.

candidates up and that would betray the fact that they have a weakness in math. Reviving these skills and using them to your advantage will help you do significantly better in your interviews.

6 Embrace Feedback from the Right Team

Successful candidates embrace feedback. I've had to give coaching clients hard feedback about everything from their appearance (get rid of glasses, change haircuts, stop touching your hair), to communication (look me in the eye more, eliminate your sing-song tone, be more answer-first), to logic (use numbers for your points, eliminate your overlapping thoughts, stop thinking in circles). I give this advice because people come to me for it. They signed up for coaching because they want specific feedback, and they always say, "Tell it like it is; be tough on me; I really want to know the truth." I think one reason they come to me for this is because no one else tells them the truth.

You need to find people who will tell you the truth about your case skills and overall interviewing style. Most of you begin practicing with your friends or family—people who care about you. While doing solo study and completing your CTCS homework, you should think about whom you want to put on your case prep team. Beginning with like-minded friends and family is a good place to start building basic skills, but it's not typically a good place to receive honest feedback. It's often too difficult for these people to tell you the truth about how you're performing, because they don't want to risk the relationship. So after you build your basic skills with that first group of people, it's time to seek out people who can honestly tell you how you're doing. You'll want to set up regular practice sessions, ask for their feedback, embrace it, and be ready to change. Top performers make a point of working with a variety of study partners; these may include alumni, other students who don't know you well, people familiar with your target firm's interview style, and even professional coaches.

7 Own the Problem

A final mark of successful candidates is how they enthusiastically invest their minds and energy into the problem. It feels like the problem at hand is one they are actually trying to solve. Star candidates work really hard to understand the business situation and get excited about it. I can always tell when people are thinking about the problem at hand because they use case-specific language. If we're talking about a hamburger chain, they are thinking about the speed of deep fryers, how hot the food is, and whether or not the menu items are tasty and appeal to the customers. If we're involved in a landscaping business, they are thinking about gardens, grass and water usage. Interviewers look for candidates who are curious, and who are willing to think hard about a problem and engage in the matter right away. Interviewers also want candidates to take ownership very early in the case and, in a sense, act like the CEO as well as the analyst. You can build this skill by genuinely trying to solve the problem and to think about the specific challenges the business will face. The more you do this during your practice sessions, the more likely it is that you'll be able to do it during a high-pressure interview.

VIDEO 16-02

David Ohrvall, Case Interview Coach's Perspective

This chapter is one you want to return to after you have done several cases. Mark the list of coach's tips with a post-it for future reference. Return to it several times throughout your preparation period to see how you are improving. Now review your resume and list a few items that you think make you stand out. It could be an achievement or interesting experience. Ask others familiar with the interview process to give input. You should be ready to highlight your special features as a candidate during a discussion, but also know how to redirect the conversation to other areas. Remember, the case interviewer can become too interested in one part of your profile and miss other parts, or burn interview time you'll need to solve your case.

Avoid the Ding—Patterns that Kill During the Interview

COMMON REASONS FOR BEING DINGED

Remember Derek and Bindu from Section 4? They were given a very simple case. But the mistakes Derek made are more common than you might imagine. So why do the Dereks of this world fall apart while the Bindus sail into the stratosphere? Setting aside true differences in raw intelligence, I believe there are six key reasons why some candidates find themselves in the ding pile. Consider these your "watch out" list as you begin your more intense training.

1 Not Knowing When to Drive and When to Follow

When you're solving a case, you're supposed to be in charge. You set the plan. You ask the questions. You make the assertions. You synthesize the conclusions. You end the case. Let's face it: it's all about you. But many of the candidates I have interviewed prefer to sit in the passenger seat. Instead of confidence I see timidity, fear and half-heartedness. Don't be afraid to drive.

You may ask, "But what about when the interviewer is clearly driving, and hitting me with a barrage of questions?" Good question. There is a new trend among many companies toward using a "Command & Control" style in the early round interviews, followed by a more open-ended style in the final rounds. In a "Command & Control" interview, you might be

The bottom line is that you need to respond to whatever approach comes your way and be ready to drive the interview when given the opportunity.

asked to explain one part of your plan in great detail, solve a specific equation, or respond to detailed questions. It can feel like you are not in control at all.

The bottom line is that you need to respond to whatever approach comes your way and be ready to drive the interview when given the opportunity. Successful candidates adjust to the style of the interview when necessary, and push the analysis ahead whenever possible.

2 Limiting Your Insights with a Standard Framework

Porter's Five Forces; The Four P's; The Seven S's; Supply Chain Analysis: you are probably very familiar with these and other business frameworks. They have stood the test of time as convenient tools for examining specific aspects of business. For example, the Four P's (product, price, promotion and placement) apply primarily to marketing issues. Their narrow focus can make them unsuitable for use in many case interviews, though; they may lead you to a dead end too quickly. Most case questions offer several "doors" to open. For example, a merger case might include a discussion of the industry, the economy, market sizing, organizational management, and financing. A great candidate distinguishes himself from a mediocre candidate by opening all—not just one or two—of the case's doors. A canned framework may get you through door 1 and door 2, but you will probably bypass doors 3, 4 and 5.

While basic business models can be useful in structuring your thoughts, they may end up limiting your creativity as the case progresses. Instead, consider building skills that will give you the most agility and mental creativity possible. To an interviewer who has heard the same answers all day long, your second level insights will set you apart.

3 Listening and Presenting Poorly

Despite a selective screening process to ensure that only the best candidates actually sit for an interview, the communication skills of some candidates are sorely lacking. Typically, the bottom third of my interview list bombed the case because they suffered a fatal flaw in their ability to listen or present. Their nerves overcame them and their communication skills unraveled. Why? They did

not encounter enough tough mock interviewers while preparing for their case interviews, and as a result the intensity of the real case overwhelmed them.

Sweating, hunching, shaking, avoiding eye contact, stuttering and staring like a deer in headlights do not enhance your chances. The solution: practice, out loud, with a great set of interviewers. Remember, it's fine to start practicing with your friends, but eventually you'll need to upgrade to more difficult and honest partners. If you are careful about the people you select and make sure to practice with several tough mock interviewers in the most realistic setting you can find, your consistency at solving cases will increase rapidly.

Typically, the bottom third of my interviewee list bombed the case because they suffered a fatal flaw in their ability to listen or present. Their nerves overcame them and their communication skills unraveled.

4 Showing Incomplete or Non-MECE Logic

To crack a case, you must build a logical path for solving the problem and then support your thinking with the facts of the case. In Chapter 4 I showed you how to flow through the steps of a business case with the FRAME Method, and how to think holistically with the MVM. You also learned how to formulate a basic hypothesis and how to develop MECE (mutually exclusive and collectively exhaustive) logic to prove it out. There isn't enough time to lay out a perfect logic tree during every case, but you can and should prove a few basic assertions. When discussing candidates, interviewers will almost always lead with their opinion of the candidate's structure and logic. It's one of the most basic thresholds that every new hire must pass. Organized thinking and well-supported logic will provide a solid roadmap for an entire case, and will help show the interviewer your thoroughness.

5 Being "Data-Light" and Making Simple Math Errors

Almost every company that gives cases during interviews makes the claim of being "data-driven." This basically means that their employees tenaciously root out the facts and then let the facts determine the answers. If this approach seems obvious to you, consider that some strategists rely on an experience-based model. They work on similar business problems for various clients within the same industry and then transfer insights from one client to the next. This kind of experienced advisory work is fine

During case interviews, it's easy to rely on your experience rather than the data at hand. This is a disastrous approach to case interviews.

With practice, you can learn how to pace yourself to consistently end the case with a solid answer and still have five to ten minutes to spare.

VIDEO 17-01

Avoid the Ding

17

HOMEWORK →

as long as it is backed up with data. The best problem solvers do not let their past experience overwhelm the present facts.

During case interviews, it's easy to rely on your experience rather than the data at hand. Candidates may know a little about the industry, or the problem may sound similar to one they've solved before, and as a result they shoot from the hip instead of analyzing the data of the case at hand. This is a disastrous approach to case interviews. Follow that up with a few simple calculation errors and the candidate is quickly pegged as "data-light." Interviewers may worry that he won't be able to handle the analytical work of the firm and will instead want to reuse models that worked in the past.

6 Not Synthesizing Well

Most candidates lose track of time. They naturally get sucked into the guts of the problem and forget the fact that they are 22 minutes into the interview and not even close to a conclusion. With practice, you can learn how to pace yourself to consistently end the case with a solid answer and still have five to ten minutes to spare. You do not want the interviewer to interrupt you with something like: "Let's imagine that the CEO walked into the room right now. What answer would you give to this problem?" This ability to quickly synthesize the analysis covered during the case, and turn it into a recommendation, will be tested at every interview.

As you now dive deeper into your training plan, be sure to return to the preparation tips in Section 16 and this ding list in Section 17. New habits, both good and bad, often spring up after you practice more cases; you should regularly assess whether you are developing in the right direction.

One of the best ways to prevent something is to plan for it. Let's prepare to avoid showing the ding patterns listed in the table to the right. Think through the weakness being shown by that pattern and fill in some specifics. Now think through how you'll address each weakness. Work through all six even if you don't see yourself having a particular struggle with one of them.

DING PREVENTION WORKSHEET

Common Reasons for Being Dinged	Specific Weaknesses (review Section 17 and fill out)	Practical Ideas to Help Prevent This Ding Reason
1 Not Knowing When to Drive and When to Follow	Example: - not responding to the interviewer - talking over the interviewer - not taking charge when appropriate	Example: - practice with different types of interviews - have my partner switch styles - know key phrases that indicate I should drive (e.g., "what are some of your ideas?")
2 Limiting Your Insights with a Standard Framework		
3 Listening and Presently Poorly		
4 Showing Incomplete or Non-MECE Logic		
5 Being "Data-Light" and Making Simple Math Errors		
6 Not Synthesizing Well		

How to Best Use Each Type of Case Material

There are a lot of different case interview resources on the market. You can divide your choices into five broad categories:

1 Single-author content

2 School- or club-developed guides

3 Compilation guides written by career-oriented websites like Wet Feet

4 Consulting firm or industry websites

5 Websites with case interview links and downloads

Using a variety of materials is helpful, as you want to get several viewpoints on how to prepare and you need to expose yourself to a variety of cases. But you only have a limited amount of time to prepare, so you'll need to select high-quality materials and be sure to use them fully. It makes sense to spend some time investigating all the materials that are on the market and then determining which ones you want to acquire and which ones you'll skip.

Once you have your full set of materials in front of you, I recommend that you look at all of them together and develop an overarching approach for how to use them. *Crack the Case System* will be a great foundation for any resource you use, as we focus on the balanced approach of communication, thinking, analytics and presentation. We are reinforcing the most important skills that you'll need for all of your cases and for your future career. Some of you will be focusing on a very specific type of interview. Whether it's a high-tech interview or one with a certain consulting firm you really want to work for, it makes most sense for you to first build your foundation, and then narrow your approach and practice schedule accordingly. I'll help you put this all together—and rather than naming specific resources that may come and go, I'll teach you how to evaluate whether or not the resources you find will help you.

Warning!

Be warned: there are a lot of products out there that over-simplify the process of learning how to think and communicate through a business problem. Here's the typical faulty approach:

1. "Memorize these frameworks and questions."
2. "Identify the type of case you are solving."
3. "Apply the best-fitting framework."
4. "Do the math right and don't make any mistakes."
5. "Oh, yeah, don't forget to be decisive."

"Do these things and you'll get the job."

You and I know that the above recipe typically won't get you the job. More preparation is necessary than simply memorizing a few formulas and applying them. Recruiters are looking for you to think on the spot, tear apart unique problems, and clearly communicate your thoughts. They also want to find someone who will be effective at communicating and influencing people in a lot of different environments. Since our system addresses these foundational skills, I think you've made a good investment of your time by using *Crack the Case System,* and I know the skills you build here will last you your entire career. But let's think though how you can find some additional materials, and the different ways to use them effectively. I've noted the benefits of each

resource and how to best leverage them. Also, I think it's important to note the "watch-outs" for each type of resource. These concerns may not be true for every resource by category, but you need to be on the look-out as you review them.

1 Single-author Content

Some of the best case interview materials (including books, articles, videos and audio files) are written by case interview pros who either went through case interviews themselves or train others professionally. *Crack the Case System*, of course, lands squarely in this category. These types of resources typically have a couple of well-thought-out overriding themes and are packaged with practice tips and cases. They come in the form of e-books, paperbacks, on-line text-based quizzes, audio files and videos. Over time these authors tend to create several revisions as they fine-tune their perspective through candidate feedback and experience. In my situation, I noticed that I was using a lot of great insights and techniques in my *Crack the Case* workshops and in my private coaching that were not covered in my book. So I knew it was important to create *Crack the Case System* by overhauling the content and adding exercises and videos to make it more effective. When you review a book, be sure to look for updated content that reflects the author's own growing experience.

BENEFITS

- **Single-author Perspective.** Because one person or small team developed and designed the content, the material is usually very consistent. Typically, you'll find well-thought-out ideas, smart tips on framework analysis, good questions to ask, and a variety of cases.

- **Training Approach.** Most single-author-driven content has a training tone. There are usually exercises, or questions to answer, that will reinforce the concepts and help the material go deeper. The cases tend to have some continuity or theme.

- **Varied Analytical and Case-solving Style**. Another great benefit to using a variety of materials is that you get to face varied analytical and

case-solving styles. Having worked at Bain & Company, I'm inclined more towards slides with detailed data. I also like "aha!" business insights when designing cases. I think it makes them interesting and reflects the kind of work I did at Bain. Other authors may be more interested in setting up and solving equations. And still others lean toward industry overviews and market studies. You'll benefit from working through a variety of cases that push your thinking in different directions.

WATCH-OUTS

- **Superstar Authors.** If someone claims to have succeeded at every case interview he ever tried to solve, or says he got almost every offer, we know that person is an extreme outlier. In my experience it's very unusual to have a person get offers from "all the top firms". In reality a solid performer may get one or two offers, and be really close or just make final rounds with a few others. Even for candidates who have practiced quite a bit and have very strong skills, there are too many variables—like interviewer style, the candidate's performance that day, and the level of competition—that make it unlikely a person will snag every offer.

  So as you look at single-author material, ask whether you are about to receive good information and training, or just war stories of how the outlier author did so well. Amazing performers don't always make good coaches. Your goal is to learn how to consistently solve cases well, so make sure the material helps with that.

- **Limited Training Materials.** Over the years, almost every one of my private clients who went on to succeed at a top company started out with at least one or two soft spots that needed special attention, whether those were communication, logic or organizational skills. The only effective way to build those skills is to understand your weaknesses and then practice with drills to eliminate them. Look for exercises and drills as you review resources. You must train in order to get better.

- **Limited Experience.** The best coach is someone who understands all aspects of the challenge. This is someone who had to practice, train, and overcome challenges similar to the ones you'll face. It's also vital that their approach has been tested with feedback and then

reworked. Sometimes highly successful people attribute their success to a few techniques when in reality, they succeeded because they were naturally smart and every part of the process was easy. For me personally, there were several things I had to develop when I practiced cases, like thinking more broadly and getting faster at setting up mid-case structures and equations. I also know what it feels like to get dinged by many top firms. I had to sweat it out like each of you, and still remember my spreadsheet of thirteen firms that I hoped to work for over the summer. And I know what it's like to have a poor performance (I can't forget the time I choked during an interview and couldn't draw a supply and demand curve). So look carefully at the skills this coach can help you develop, and the kind of experience he or she had.

■ **Overestimate Your Skill Set.** When I first wrote *Crack the Case* I had very little experience as an interview coach. I had mainly served as an interviewer. I really only had one perspective on the process. As a result, my first book overestimated the average candidate's skill set. It's taken years of coaching and training for me to understand what it takes to build consistent case interview skills, and so I've developed a system that builds those skills step by step. I believe many of the materials out there make the same mistake I initially did. You can't tell a reader, "Don't mess up your math," without addressing the issue of why they make mistakes in the first place. You shouldn't say, "Be sure to capture their attention," without analyzing how to be more answer-first. Look for materials that address your true abilities and then help you build the skills to be a top performer.

LEVERAGE POINTS

■ **Structure.** In these books you'll really start to learn how to map a structure for a problem. I lean very heavily away from memorized approaches, but I do know that they can come in handy when you are in a jam. I think learning to put an anchor in one direction, while also thinking broadly, is the best approach. But your brain might respond better to another approach. I had a very successful client who, after reading several single-author books, developed a structure that worked best for him and that he used for most of his interviews. I appreciated how he took the time to understand several approaches and then worked with the one he liked best.

- **Practice and Planning.** These resources will provide the best methods of preparing over time and will help you sketch out a plan. You should be able to find a combination of study materials that will help you the most.

- **Case Starts.** Many of the cases in these books are not easy to use for partner study, as they follow a strict script; if you don't follow that line of thinking, or say the right thing, it's difficult to know where to go next when practicing.

2 School- or Club-developed Guides

Over the years I've probably seen over 12 different case interview guides and thumbed through quite a few. Basically, a consulting club at a school like Wharton, Kellogg, or McCombs decides that they want to create a case interview guide for their members. The approach tends to go like this:

How to Build a Case Guide

1) Give forms to club members for cases they took during an interview.

2) Club member fills out the form to the best of his ability, trying to remember the case question and any accompanying charts and graphs.

3) Club officers (in charge of the case book) try to clean up the case and then think of a structure that would approach the problem best. If possible, they'll create an answer or closing set of comments.

BENEFITS

- **Real Live Cases!** A long time ago when I was prepping for cases, the materials available for study were limited. I think Wet Feet and Vault had developed some resources and that was about it. But now, when you get your hands on one of these consulting club case interview books, you may think you have struck gold! You get to see the tone

and type of cases recently given in interviews, and that can be very helpful when prepping. But there is a downside to these case books, which I cover in the "Watch-outs" section.

- **Variety of Cases.** Usually these books give you a wide variety of case types, from profit and acquisitions to cost cutting and operational improvement. Using these resources will quickly uncover topics you don't quite understand. And since they delineate by firm or company, you do start to get a feel for how different companies give cases. I caution you, though, that two or three samples from a firm do not necessarily give you a full representation of all the cases you might get from a company.

WATCH-OUTS

- **Ethics—Stop Stealing Cases.** Most of the companies giving cases explicitly say, "Please don't pass the information or material from this case to other people." Yet the clubs still do it. I realize that I can't stop you from reading these books, and it's hard to know what has been done historically that is not in compliance with the firms' requests. Some clubs may have changed the case names, content and data. But going forward, I would encourage you to say, "No thanks," the next time anyone asks you to pass along information directly from an interview. People send me information all the time that I try to ignore as it's not my information to pass along.

- **Faulty Facts and Perspective.** A lot of these consolidated books are built from pieces of information gathered during a very stressful moment. Keep in mind that at the end of a real interview, the interviewer does not explain to you how you should have solved the case, nor does he give you charts and graphs to take home. Thus candidates trying to recall all that happened during the interview may have a hard time. It's easy to leave some important facts out. It's like being in a car crash: you have a perspective and you know some bad things happened, but you don't have the full picture or all the details. For the candidate, this case interview was one of the most stressful environments of his life. He may only remember pieces of the case—most of the analysis, perhaps, but very little of the interviewer's thoughts. It would be very difficult for a candidate to notice subtleties in the interview that may have been important to solving the case.

- **Limited or No Answers.** These consolidated case books often do not contain answers to the cases. They are great for giving you an interesting problem to solve, but not so good at closing out the case with a crisp answer. If you are new to cases, or trying hard to firm up your analytical skills, this situation can be frustrating.

- **Simplistic, Framework-driven Approach.** Occasionally answers are included, but since the students editing the cases for the book are not likely to know the full case situation or what the interviewer really wanted, these answers are often simplistic or entirely framework-based. By following the answer key to the letter, you may be training yourself to think about problems in the wrong way. Most likely the real interviewer was looking for a blend of approaches. Many cases are based on real work at the company or firm, so it makes sense that the real answer would be a combination of structure, analysis and data—and too complex to fit a simple framework. But writing up the multiple approaches one could take would be very time-consuming and difficult for someone new to cases (like the club officers), so the simple framework explanation usually wins out. As a result, you are not being challenged to take your thinking to the next level.

LEVERAGE POINTS

- Analytical Variety. Some of the school books I have seen have a fantastic array of math, charts and analytical problems. Even if the case context is poorly put together, it's great to come up against a problem you haven't seen before.

- **Case Variety.** Because these cases were often based on real projects, you get a glimpse of the kinds of problems the firm or company may have been facing. You also get the benefit of so many different types of cases in one book.

- **Drilling.** One of the greatest values of the school books is the additional material they provide for doing drills. If you want to practice reading slides for an hour, you'll have lots of examples. Or if you want new material to practice your starts (the first 7 minutes of the case), you'll have quite a few examples. They can also be helpful for working on your closing recommendation. Whatever the weak spot you want to address, these case books will offer you a lot of opportunity for practice.

3 Compilation Guides by Career-oriented Websites like Wet Feet

Compilation guides can be found on a variety of career-oriented websites and are generally written by a team of people. The companies that sell them present the product as their take on case interviews; although they can be a good place to start your preparation, they often lack the insightful training and unique perspective of the single-author materials. They also tend to be dated, containing old cases rather than ones that reflect more recent interview styles.

BENEFITS

- **Quick Overview.** It's great to know what you are up against, and these guides will give you that perspective. You'll understand case basics and get a broad perspective on the process. You'll also learn how you can structure your thinking and approach for different case types.

- **Confidence-builder.** Most of my clients who started with these books have told me that they thought cases were going to be relatively easy and straightforward. These materials gave them an initial mental boost, helping them think that they could conquer their case interviews. Reality set in when they started reading other materials and trying tougher cases, but in the short term their confidence went up.

WATCH-OUTS

- **No Strong Opinion or Direction.** Since the book has been written by a group of people, it can sometimes feel like a few friends searched around the internet, read up on case interviews in general, and are telling you what they found. But none of them knows enough to give you firm advice on how to train, what to practice, and which skills to build first.

- **Random Frameworks, Out-of-date Cases**. Because these types of guides tend to be compilations of many facts on case interviewing, the frameworks and tools they recommend to use can seem random and out of date. They often lay out suggestions of what you could do

rather than what you should do. Be sure to cross-check structuring ideas with what you find in more recent publications.

- **Assume Your Skill Set is Strong.** Like the single-author material, these books tend to assume you have all the basic communication and analytical skills in place.

LEVERAGE POINTS

- **Gain an Overview.** These are the types of books that you want to borrow from the library and skim through. I would save your money for more up-to-date materials that will challenge you and put you on a path to building skills.

4 Consulting Firm or Industry Websites

Candidates pose specific questions about the case interview process and how to best prepare, and the consulting firms and some companies have developed more sophisticated responses. In addition to providing more answers to basic questions about the process and their new case material, some have posted videos and interactive, text-based training questions. All of this information sharing has been a forcing function, requiring the firms to be more open about their process and making them more consistent with their interviews.

BENEFITS

- **Straight from the Firm's Mouth.** You can trust the source of the information and begin to understand how one company might have different requirements from another. This information is especially valuable as you near your interview date, once you have already built a solid set of basic skills.

- **Learn the Firm's Culture.** The interview process reflects what the company values. By fully understanding their approach to interviews, you'll better evaluate your fit with the culture, day-to-day work and skill development.

- **No Surprises.** You don't want any surprises on interview day, so take advantage of these sites and work through them carefully. They are a great way to take away any fears of the unknown and to help you with your overall confidence.

- **False Sense of Security.** Because these companies have taken the time to lay out their process of evaluating candidates, it's easy to get a false sense of security about how it will work. Keep in mind that what is posted on the website is not necessarily how the process will go. Ultimately the evaluation process is completely dependent upon the team making the decision, which can vary by region or local office. The website information is a great guide, but keep in mind that you may be thrown some curve balls during the real process.

- **Over-simplification.** "Be sure to write down important facts the interviewer is telling you," says the spokesmodel for one of the firm videos. Really? Wow, thanks for the insight. It's easy to see that if this is the level of content some of the companies are providing, they really are not offering great insights. "Stay relaxed," or "Just carry on a business conversation," or "You may be required to do some math," are not the kinds of insights that can help you improve. For a period of time, I had several clients complain that they had been "duped" by the McKinsey sample written test. They were shocked at how the real test was longer and harder than the sample on the website. For those candidates who also had their in-person interviews that same day, the test shook their confidence. So be sure to avoid surprises by training harder than you think. I love hearing from clients that their interview was "so easy compared to the cases I did with you, David!"

LEVERAGE POINTS

- **Great Starting Point.** Getting to know the company's approach to interviewing is a great place to start as you begin your training.

- **Company-specific Logic.** Every company values certain skills more than others. By carefully studying their interview materials you can begin to understand what skills they <u>may</u> emphasize more than others. For instance, some firms love data-heavy handouts while others look for subtlety in your reasoning. If you see a skill set that

seems to be emphasized more than others, take note and look for that pattern in other materials from that company.

5 Websites with Case Interview Links and Downloads

In recent years, several websites have cropped up offering links to companies that provide cases, quick tips, white papers, short cases and places to network and comment. It can almost feel like there is an endless supply of new information on case interviews. Your biggest challenge with these sites is finding the ones to invest your time in without feeling overwhelmed.

BENEFITS

- **Lots of Information.** You'll see quite a few categories that are interesting and that answer your questions about case interviews. Current case interview issues (e.g., "McKinsey Written Exam") are highlighted, which is great for getting you ready for interview mode.

- **Lots of Links.** It's the fastest way to find what you need with links to firms and resources that you would want. That can be helpful when looking for company applications and contact names.

- **Variety of Case Problems.** There will be a large variety of case problems that you can use to test yourself, and to gauge which areas of the case and which skills will be easier or more difficult for you.

WATCH-OUTS

- **Too Many Bits of Information.** Be careful if you start to feel overwhelmed. A lot of these sites specialize in giving you every perspective possible; at times that can be too much information. It's normal to be like a kid in a candy store, wanting to read everything you find, but be sure to gauge how you are feeling. I have found that once your foundational skills have been built and you are consistently solving cases, it might be time to ease up on looking at everything you find. One more site may offer diminishing returns.

- **Pet Theories Gone Crazy.** Since many of the writers of these articles have limited experience of what it takes to do well in case interviews, some of their theories are untested. They might write about how certain firms like certain things, or advise that "This is one thing you should never do" for this company. The best use of your time is to stick to what you know to be true and keep working on your fundamental skills.

LEVERAGE POINTS

- **Final 20%.** Use these sites as a way to find some missing information after you have determined your training plan, target skills to improve, practice partners and study cases. Once you have built a solid foundation of skills and can get through the basic pieces of most cases, these sites are helpful to find out if you missed anything. Use them as your last 20% of study time and general preparation, and you'll avoid being overwhelmed and confused.

VIDEO 18-01

Gather Your Materials

It's time to assess your portfolio of materials. Using the categories listed in this section, determine if you need to add any new resources. Review the ones you do have and determine which will be your high-priority resources, to be used for serious training and skill building, and which ones you'll read for general awareness. Plan to gather all of your resources at one time and develop a study plan with those materials. If you do your research now, you'll reduce the odds of encountering a new resource at the last minute.

Now that we've worked through different ways to be savvy, it's time to begin training methodically. Chapter 7 will quickly outline for you some ways to use our TRAIN case methodology effectively, and will highlight common pitfalls. After you build basic skills, you may want to prep for specific companies and case styles in Section 20. Section 21 will serve as a reference guide for all of the case packs in the back half of the book.

CHAPTER 7

You're Ready to TRAIN with Cases

Skip These Training Mistakes

As you begin training with cases, it's essential that you practice well. One of my brothers used to say, "Practice doesn't make you perfect; but perfect practice makes perfect." Your goal should be to create both solo sessions that build your foundational skills, and partner practice sessions that replicate a real interview. But before you speed down one path or another, let me alert you to a few potential wrong turns and dead ends. In this chapter I'll address the three most common mistakes that waste your time and build the wrong skills.

MISTAKE 1 : STUDY ONLY BY YOURSELF

Preparing for the interview on your own is a must. You'll need to put in hours of drilling and make sure that you practice each case piece by piece. However, self-study is not sufficient. You must practice with a partner who will challenge you, just like a real interviewer would, and will give you honest feedback. Studying with a buddy allows you to hear yourself talk through a case. And with a partner, you can also practice basic interview elements like giving a solid handshake, making good eye contact, and managing small talk.

Most people go awry when they practice alone because they mistakenly assume that reading about cases will help them solve cases. It's not quite that simple. Think about the last mystery or suspense novel you read. (Or think of a movie if you don't read fiction.) Did

VIDEO 19-01

Self-Study Tips

With self-study, it's easy to delude yourself into thinking you did okay on the case, when in reality you bombed it.

you get to the end of the story and realize that you had pegged the wrong person as the murderer? When the plot revealed the real perpetrator, it suddenly made perfect sense. The light bulbs went on; you saw connections and clues that you had missed along the way. But let's not forget one basic fact: you failed to solve the mystery. You picked the wrong person. Although you thought you were close to the answer, you bombed the case.

Solving case problems by yourself is similar. You read through the problem, try to solve it on your own for a while, and then flip to the answer page. Many times you discover your answers are completely different from the case guide's. As you read through the solution, you say to yourself, "Of course it was the labor issue!" or "I knew price was the driver of the problem." With self-study, it's easy to delude yourself into thinking you did okay on the case, when in reality you bombed it.

I'm not saying there is only one right answer for every case. After all, case interviews are not murder mysteries. And your solution may be just as valid as the answer key's. But without another person there to listen to you, how do you know if your analysis was logical and data-driven? How do you know if your communication style was effective? Can you really evaluate yourself accurately? Unfortunately, you cannot.

Use self-study for building your skill base: review the building blocks of business, become familiar with how to frame a problem, and practice saying your answers out loud. But don't use self-study as your only preparation tool. Be sure to include lots of partner practice as you prepare. You need another set of eyes and ears to give you input that is important for your success.

MISTAKE 2: BOIL THE OCEAN

Some of you out there are studying machines. You know who you are; your friends probably call you a grind and constantly pester you to ease up a little. No matter how huge the workload, you can always tough it out with long hours of study. Memorize twenty Italian verbs and all their conjugations for tomorrow's quiz? No problem! Read three Harvard Business School cases and pull together your insights in an afternoon? No problem! Despite incredible pressure, you almost

always succeed with flying colors. Naturally, you plan to approach case preparation the same way. "Why not just memorize everything?" you ask. "There can only be so many case types and so many case questions and so many frameworks. If I just cram everything into my head, I'm sure I'll do well."

Interviewers like to call this approach "boiling the ocean." It means learning everything there is to know instead of targeting your efforts on several key areas. To the few who are gifted with photographic memories: get out the flash cards and go for it! For the rest of us, there are several problems with this approach. First, you are relying on your memory to withstand the nervousness that inevitably comes with every interview. Second, you must recall exactly the right piece of information at just the right time. Third, you jeopardize your ability to view the problem in its larger context. That is, reliance on lists of memorized material can obscure the big picture, and turn your focus instead to discrete bits of data and isolated issues. Remember, you are not preparing for a multiple-choice test, but an oral interview.

Being open to feedback is just the first step. How do you know whether the feedback is thoughtful and valuable? Feedback that recommends no action or lacks honesty (or "teeth") is worthless. Actually, it is worse than worthless, because overly rosy feedback can convince you that you're more prepared than you really are.

MISTAKE 3: AVOID HONEST FEEDBACK

Feedback and your future go hand in hand. Most top companies create feedback mechanisms for almost everything they do. As a new consultant, I was shocked when I received feedback and input on seemingly minor items, like presenting new data to teammates or meeting clients for the first time. At times I felt that it was unnecessary and just too much to absorb and apply. For instance, I once worked for a manager who chewed me out for giving a client a document with some minor speck marks left by the *client's* copier (he suggested I roam the halls until I found a better one). Every top company will have standards they want you to meet, so get used to giving and receiving feedback— a lot of feedback.

There can be two common problems with feedback from your study partner.

VIDEO 19-02

Don't Boil the Ocean

How do you know whether the feedback is thoughtful and valuable? Feedback that recommends no action or lacks honesty (or "teeth") is worthless. Actually, it is worse than worthless, because overly rosy feedback can convince you that you're more prepared than you really are.

VIDEO 19-03

David's Feedback on Feedback

It's Not Actionable

Flawed feedback sounds something like this:

"I like the way you ask questions."

"You had a pretty good structure."

"You did a good job of responding to my redirection."

These comments sound like they are providing you with valuable insights, but they are not. It does little to help you understand specifically what you are doing well (or not doing well). Even when the feedback is negative, it can be too general, and therefore not actionable. For instance, if your buddy says to you, "I feel like the pace of the interview was off," or "We never really connected," how will you change your style in the future? With the "pace" comment, you are left wondering if you should speed up or slow down. With the "we never connected" comment, you're not sure if you should have made more small talk, asked more questions during the case, or tried to elicit more conversation. Neither comment gives you many clues on how to change.

It's Not Honest

Study partners tend to be overly positive when it comes to giving feedback. Who wants to hurt a friend's feelings? Even if you don't know the interviewee well, giving honest feedback can be a little painful. We all want people to like us, and telling the truth doesn't always endear us to others. But let's face it: most of us stink when we try to do cases. It's hard to get started, the problem is unfamiliar, and we sound like a know-it-all when we hear ourselves speak. The whole thing is very awkward.

When you are doing a mock interview with someone and they really flub, how honest are you? There's the standard platitude: "This one was tough." Or the very mild: "You may want to work on your structuring." Or the general affirmation: "I like the way you drill down with questions—you should continue to do more of that." It is difficult to improve when you get feedback that doesn't paint an honest picture.

Wouldn't it be great to hear this instead?

"You are talking too fast; it makes you seem nervous."

"The way you sit makes you look lazy. You were slumped in the back of your chair the entire interview."

"Your framework was illogical. I got lost when you brought in the discussion on pricing."

"You asked questions about the organizational structure when the important issue was declining revenue."

Well, it might not actually feel great to receive this kind of direct feedback. But these comments are certainly more specific and more actionable than the platitudes we usually tell each other. Ask your study partners to be brutally honest. When you get your first offer, you will thank them all the way to the bank.

LEARN TO GIVE GREAT FEEDBACK

Since giving and receiving detailed feedback is critical to your success, it's time to learn how to do it better. The first step is to understand your natural tendencies in the feedback process. Think through the last time you received it. Did you ask for more details or did you just fill in the gaps with your own thoughts? How about when you gave it? Did you shy away from giving the detail necessary for your partner to improve? Work through the homework below by filling out the table on the next page. As your case interview skills improve, continue to ask for the detailed feedback that will make you better.

Review the Feedback Training table with general vs. specific comments. Put the specific ones to use during your case interview practice sessions. In the table you'll see some common ones to get you thinking, but be sure to develop your own. When receiving feedback on your case performance, ask for comments that help you take action. When giving feedback, be a good case interview partner and center your comments on skills that can be improved.

VIDEO 19-04

Case Interview Coach's Perspective

19

HOMEWORK

FEEDBACK TRAINING

General	Specific
1 Your pace felt a little off.	1 You were talking too quickly (or slowly). That makes you seem nervous (or dull).
2 I had a little trouble following your thinking.	2 You sometimes used poor logic. Be sure to number out your comments (first, second, etc.) and make sure they follow some kind of logical flow.
3 Your questions could be a little more on point.	3 Your questions seemed to have no purpose. Be sure to ask for specific data and make it clear to me why you are asking for something.
4 You should continue to work on your structure.	4 Your approach seemed unstructured because the ideas were overlapping (give examples) and you didn't cover all the important points (give examples).
5 Your analysis could have been stronger.	5 Your math was slow and you got the wrong answer. About 75% of the people I've given this case to get the math right, so this is a serious issue. Consider estimating first and then trying to solve for the more specific answer. You should practice drilling on these types of equations.
6	6
7	7
8	8
9	9
10	10

Fine-tune for Specific Companies and Situations

One of the hottest topics at my workshops and in private coaching sessions is the question of differing company interview styles. I hear these questions all the time:

> "Aren't Company A's cases different from Company B's? How should I get ready for their case style?"

Or it might sound more like this:

> "I heard that Capital One (or your favorite company) likes their people to be super-analytical (insert 'numbers-oriented,' 'creative,' 'structured,' etc.). How can I get better at that?"

Many candidates want to package their performance in a way that will appeal to a certain company. I understand this desire and often help my private clients "fine-tune" before a specific interview. However, I must caution you before we embark on this topic: trying to adapt your case-solving methods to a specific company before you build some basic skills will often backfire. The reason it seldom works is that no company has one single style of case interviewing. The interview style can vary by level, interviewer personality, and office location.

However, to find out the general case style a firm uses, you can talk to people who have gone through the process recently, meet with alumni who are inside the firm, attend company presentations and read fresh resources like blogs and articles. Be savvy and evaluate the source, and don't forget that there are no rules to the interview process. Anyone can change the interview style at any time!

In addition to style changes, the format can vary quite a bit as well, and we'll cover that topic later.

DIFFERENT STROKES FOR DIFFERENT COMPANIES

Once you're competent with a wide variety of cases, it's time to consider the distinctive flavor of the individual companies. For instance, some companies love the "Aha!" case. You know the type: you're moving through the case, trying to keep things on track, when out of the blue the interviewer presents you with a new data set. After reviewing the data, you recognize a connection or thread throughout the case that you hadn't seen before. You found the "Aha!" When you present it to the interviewer, he goes crazy with excitement: "Exactly! So now that you know the spa tubs are so heavy, do you think they charged enough for shipping . . . ?" Because you found the "Aha!", the rest of the case unfolds nicely and you are in the interviewer's good graces.

**Pros and Cons of
Fine Tuning**

This style contrasts sharply with a company that is interested in testing your breadth of thinking. They want to see logic and the ability to generate lots of crisp, carefully-defined ideas. Rather than pushing you for an insight in a particular area, the interviewer may ask you to generate a list of ideas. You are expected to continue to respond to the "What else?" question over and over again, each time making sure your ideas are not redundant and that they fit logically together.

Depending upon your natural thinking style, one of the two examples above may feel like a better fit. Of course, it's best to prepare to handle all types of cases and expectations, but let's be savvy and think about what the companies are trying to evaluate with their differing methods. If you understand what skills they value, you will be better equipped to crack their cases.

RETURN TO CLASSIC SKILLS

Let's go back to the CLASSIC Skills diagram that we used in Section 7. We'll focus on understanding how your interviews may vary across the following skills: Logic (Breadth and Depth), Analytics, Integration and Creativity.

BREADTH

Every time you start a case by sharing your plan with the interviewer, you are presenting your breadth of thinking. As we learned in Section 7, a typical case "start" or plan will consist of three to five areas that you think are worth exploring to solve the problem. By laying those areas out for your interviewer, you are stating, "These are the areas that I think are important, and together they provide a relatively complete picture of how to solve this problem." But what if the interviewer thinks your "complete picture" isn't quite broad enough? Perhaps he wants to see how your mind can be stretched, or find out if you can explore additional areas without becoming confused. When you get comments like "Are those all the areas you'd like to explore?", you are likely being tested on your breadth of thinking.

What you'll hear

"Tell me more . . . what else do you think you should explore?"

"Give me three more ideas" (may be repeated often).

"Is that all you would look at?"

What you should keep in mind

■ You are not failing the interview. Your interviewer will ask you questions like "What else?" in order to push your thinking and to better compare you to other candidates.

■ Keep your answers MECE (mutually exclusive, collectively exhaustive). You'll need to show that additional requests don't confuse you, nor do they make you nervous.

McKinsey & Company is famous for these kinds of "What else?" questions. Pushing you to think broadly and show your ability to keep the ideas MECE is their hallmark approach.

- Your interviewer is helping you arrive at a better answer. By pushing you to think more broadly, the interviewer is likely guiding you into the area he wants to explore next.

Where to expect it

McKinsey & Company is famous for these kinds of "What else?" questions. Pushing you to think broadly and show your ability to keep the ideas MECE is their hallmark approach. In addition, many of their cases have answer keys which naturally drive the interviewer to ask, "What else?" Expect a lot of these types of questions during your first-round interviews, especially if the interviewer is comparing your answers to an answer key. This approach is true for any company using an answer key.

How to prepare

You'll likely encounter breadth questions earlier in the case. I recommend that you practice your starts. See Section 13.

- Start your case like normal, with a well-thought-out plan and MECE topics you would like to explore.

- After you present your approach, pretend that your interviewer asks, "What else would you look into?" Put down two more areas, explain them, and then pretend you are again asked, "What else would you explore?"

- Keep going with this method 3–4 times. Now stop and review your notes. Where did you overlap in your thinking? Where did your approach become confusing?

- Now that you have a broad perspective on the case (thanks to your own great thinking), restart the case from the beginning. Use a broader structure that incorporates the full set of ideas you developed.

VIDEO 20-02

Interviewers Pushing on Breadth and Depth

DEPTH

Just when you thought you had your "What else?" answers under control, your interviewer starts drilling deep. Before you can gently move the conversation to your topic of choice, she hits you with this: "Wait. Why don't we go back to your plan and talk about competitors [or interviewer's favorite topic] for a little bit." That's right—it's time to start drilling. Your interviewer wants to know whether, when she scratches the surface of your discussion, there will be anything of value below. Don't worry; depth questions have a high repeat rate. In other words, once you've figured out how to explain how you would research competitor revenue or what you would look for in fixed cost trends (to name a few examples), you'll know how to explain such topics for all of your cases.

What you'll hear

"Tell me more about this topic [e.g., short term costs]."

"Can you break this down for me? What would you do first?"

"How would you get this data? I don't think it's that easy. Please clarify."

What you should keep in mind

Your responses need to be data-driven. Imagine you are breaking each topic into multiple parts. Calmly explain each part and why it's important to the main topic.

Your interviewer is a pro at finding data, solving problems, and structuring analysis. It's her day-to-day job and she knows the answers to the case. It would be unusual for you to out-think her on the topic, so expect to see a furrowed brow and some skepticism. It's all part of the evaluation process.

Where to expect it

Among the top companies, expect all of them to test you on depth at some point. Your interviewers often want to know—in detail—how

Your interviewer is a pro at finding data, solving problems, and structuring analysis. It's her day-to-day job and she knows the answers to the case.

you would go about the work. Be especially alert for companies that do their own primary research. Employees of these companies pride themselves in knowing how to analyze and dig deep into the data. Your interviewer will probably want to know if you have similar skills.

How to prepare

As with breadth questions, expect to encounter most depth questions early in the case. You will likely have to explain what kind of data you need and how you would solve a particular problem. Be prepared to drill down on any basic subject, like industry or competitors. Here's a way to practice:

- Start your case as usual, with a well-thought-out plan and MECE topics you would like to explore.

- Present your approach out loud, and then pretend you were asked to explain one of the topics in your plan.

- Referring to your plan, describe that topic in more detail (e.g., revenue data). Outline data you would request (e.g., volume, price and mix), how you would find it (e.g., company historical data), and what you would do with it (e.g., find out which products are not performing well).

- Practice this drill with several cases.

ANALYTICS

Your facility with numbers will be viewed as an indicator—perhaps the main indicator—of your intelligence.

Good case interviews will always include a set of data that is helping guide your answer. Whether it's the first-round interview with a second-year consultant who hands you two slides and an algebra problem, or the final round with a senior partner who grunts, "How much do you think the idea is worth?", you need to use the numbers to successfully crack your case. Your facility with numbers will be viewed as an indicator—perhaps the main indicator—of your intelligence. We can argue that such a test doesn't give a fair representation of your skills, but the reality is that your interviewers will judge you on how well you work with the data.

What you'll hear

"Could you quickly calculate profit (total revenue, gross margin, etc.)?"

"Now that you've reviewed the numbers, what's the cost impact of this decision?"

"Here's the formula. Can you solve for the break-even amount?"

"For this part, rough estimates are fine."

What you should keep in mind

Try to gauge how comfortable your interviewer is with estimates versus exact math. Many interviewers are fine with rough estimates. You should start with one whenever possible in order to speed up your calculations.

Be sure to use the numbers you've calculated throughout the case to support your recommendations.

Where to expect it

It is the rare company that doesn't expect you to use numbers quickly and accurately. Almost all of your cases will have a lot of data in the early rounds. As the rounds progress and you interview with more senior partners, you may run into fewer number-intense cases. But there is no set formula. You should expect to have to run the numbers for every case you solve. It's not unusual for a partner or senior manager to have a favorite math question or trick. Be prepared!

How to prepare

- Make it a habit to quantify any business situation:

    ▸ Practice quantifying throughout the case. Ask, "How much is this action worth?" or "What kind of financial impact will this event have?"

Being Data Hungry

▸ Estimate using lots of high-level cases that involve total revenue or cost, growth projections, and return on investment decisions.

■ In everyday life, practice quick, simple math throughout the day to sharpen your math skills. Classic market sizing questions are a good warm-up: "How many coffee cups does a typical Starbucks use each day?, "How much money does a toll-taker recieve each day?", or "How much money does that shoe store make?""

■ Become familiar with calculating large numbers, i.e., in the millions and billions. Use rounding and rough estimates to get to your answers more quickly (for example, 10% of 2B is 200M or .2B). Consider using flash cards to practice your estimating skills.

INTEGRATION

As I mentioned earlier in the chapter, sometimes cases have an "Aha!" moment. As you are moving through the case, there comes a point when several disparate facts come together magically, and you find yourself staring at the solution. It's a great feeling. Of course, if you've done enough cases, you also know the sinking sensation of looking at several disjointed pieces, having no idea how they relate. All of your interviewers will want you to solve their cases, but some will put more weight than others on your ability to quickly integrate the case facts and find a connection. As you practice more cases, your ability to see connections and integrate these facts will increase.

What you'll hear

"Now that you know 'x', do you have a different perspective on 'y'?"

"What do you see when you look at this data?" (Hint: Don't say, 'Just a bunch of numbers!')

"Let's go back to our earlier discussion. Any new thoughts?"

What you should keep in mind

It's normal to feel like you've been put on the spot when you are asked questions like these. Your interviewer is expecting you to integrate several items at once. Take your time and explain how you are thinking through the problem.

If you fail to integrate the pieces and find the "Aha!", it does not mean you have bombed the case. You probably showed strong skills in several areas. Even if you don't have the complete answer, explain the connections that you do understand.

Where to expect it

All companies love to see a candidate integrate information quickly. I don't think there's enough of a pattern to predict which companies emphasize these types of questions and which ones do not. But I can say that you will likely encounter them sooner or later. Expect your interviewer at some point to say, "Let's pull it all together."

How to prepare

- Putting pieces of the case puzzle together quickly is ultimately a matter of experience. Do lots of practice cases across several problem types (e.g., profit case, pricing case) and several industries.

- After solving a practice case with an "Aha!" moment, draw a simple logic tree (see diagram on next page) that would have gotten you to the answer more quickly. By seeing the connections laid out, you will build a deeper understanding of how to work through this type of case in the future. You can use these flows during the interview as well.

CREATIVITY

Given the heavy emphasis on analytics during the case interview, it may be hard to believe that the companies are also judging your creativity. In fact, you may even hear some companies talk about it during campus visits, or see it in writing on their website. The mantra is, "We're looking for creative thinkers." But don't be fooled into expect-

VIDEO 20-04

Improving Your Integration

The mantra is, "We're looking for creative thinkers." But don't be fooled into expecting your interviewer to whip out a sheet of paper and ask you to do a little origami.

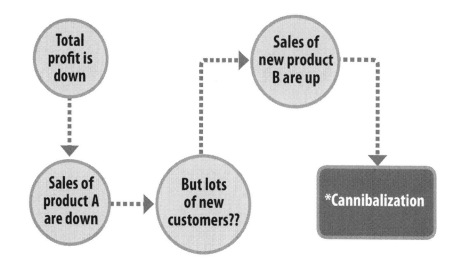

ing your interviewer to whip out a sheet of paper and ask you to do a little origami. He will, however, expect you to think of an innovative solution, or develop a novel approach to a problem his client is facing. It can be tough to be creative on the spot. Sometimes you'll have great thoughts and other times you won't. Regardless of whether inspiration strikes, you can push yourself during your practice cases. With practice, the bright ideas will come more frequently.

What you'll hear

"So what are some creative ideas for our client in this particular situation?"

"How would you solve this problem differently?"

"Do you have any unique ideas you would like to see the client explore?"

"Let's get creative. How would you change this business?"

What you should keep in mind

Earn the right to give creative solutions. Don't start the case with something unique and different just to prove you are being creative. First show the interviewer that you can systematically solve the problem, and then reveal your creativity toward the end of the case.

Don't start the case with something unique and different just to prove you are being creative.

Interviewers tend to enjoy creativity within a narrow set of parameters. Don't worry if you can't think of something wildly unique. For instance, ideas for product line extensions will display your ingenuity, even if you don't invent a brand-new product line.

Where to expect it

Which company expects you to be the most creative? Of the five dimensions we've discussed in this chapter, this is the one that varies the most from company to company and interviewer to interviewer. It's best to be prepared. Plan to offer creative solutions for every case you solve—after you have proven your analytical skills.

How to prepare

Solve cases two or three different ways. After you are finished with a case, go back and try to solve it with a different start. Also see if you can conclude with a different emphasis or direction for the company. By practicing in this manner, you'll train your mind to be nimble when pressed for alternate options.

Feed your creativity by reading about a wide variety of businesses and industries. A great way to gain exposure to a broad range of business problems is to read magazines like *Business Week* and *Forbes*.

Develop some "mental mentors." Think about how some of your personal business associates or classmates might solve the problem. Your mental mentor could even be a well-known business personality. For instance, how would Warren Buffett or Steve Jobs solve this problem?

BUSINESS CASE VARIANTS

Just like interviewers have different personalities and test different CLASSIC skills, companies also now vary the interview across several dimensions in order to test you more thoroughly. They typically set some guidelines on the interviewer's style, pre-determine the format of the interview, and guide the content of the case. Take a look at the Business Case Variants chart and let's walk through each part so that you can fine-tune according to your target company.

Business Case Variants

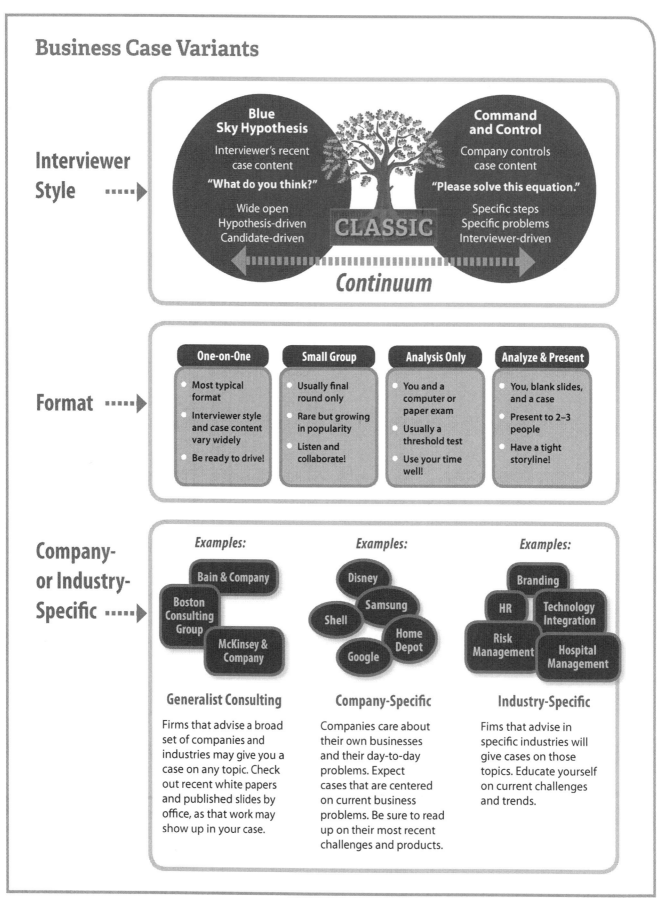

Interviewer Style ·····▶

Blue Sky Hypothesis

Interviewer's recent case content

"What do you think?"

Wide open
Hypothesis-driven
Candidate-driven

CLASSIC

Command and Control

Company controls case content

"Please solve this equation."

Specific steps
Specific problems
Interviewer-driven

Continuum

Format ·····▶

One-on-One
- Most typical format
- Interviewer style and case content vary widely
- Be ready to drive!

Small Group
- Usually final round only
- Rare but growing in popularity
- Listen and collaborate!

Analysis Only
- You and a computer or paper exam
- Usually a threshold test
- Use your time well!

Analyze & Present
- You, blank slides, and a case
- Present to 2–3 people
- Have a tight storyline!

Company- or Industry- Specific ·····▶

Examples:

Bain & Company
Boston Consulting Group
McKinsey & Company

Generalist Consulting

Firms that advise a broad set of companies and industries may give you a case on any topic. Check out recent white papers and published slides by office, as that work may show up in your case.

Examples:

Disney
Samsung
Shell
Home Depot
Google

Company-Specific

Companies care about their own businesses and their day-to-day problems. Expect cases that are centered on current business problems. Be sure to read up on their most recent challenges and products.

Examples:

Branding
HR
Technology Integration
Risk Management
Hospital Management

Industry-Specific

Fims that advise in specific industries will give cases on those topics. Educate yourself on current challenges and trends.

Interviewer Style

Most companies vary between two extreme points on the interviewer style continuum: Blue Sky Hypothesis cases vs. Command and Control cases. Keep in mind that all interviews will fall some place on this continuum, and many will offer a mix of broad and narrow questions.

Blue Sky Hypothesis

In the Blue Sky Hypothesis cases the interviewer allows you to drive the interview by asking open-ended (big and broad like the blue sky) questions, like "What do you think?", "How would you approach this?" or "What's your hunch?". It often feels like the interviewer has no specific agenda and will not help guide you much at all. You might hear similar questions during a Command and Control case, but the interviewer's response will be very different. In the Blue Sky Hypothesis format the interviewer leaves it to you to drive the discussion forward. You are well trained for these types of cases, as the Crack the Case System approach teaches you to lay out a plan and solve it piece by piece. If you struggle with structuring broadly, thinking through a hypothesis, or driving a conversation with your own thoughts, you will probably not like this case style.

Command and Control

In sharp contrast, Command and Control cases have a different tone than Blue Sky Hypothesis cases. The interviewer will spend more time asking you to answer particular questions or to solve specific equations. He or she will ask questions like "What two other things should you consider?" or "Please solve this equation to the second decimal." You also might catch your interviewer checking off items you need to answer to make sure that you've covered all the topics. Some people like these kinds of cases because the interviewer requires only that you answer the direct question rather than drive the case forward. Command and Control cases are very much like an oral GMAT, where you are tested on specific questions and there are right and wrong answers. In my opinion, it's much better to train for Blue Sky-Hypothesis cases and then, when

VIDEO 20-05

Blue Sky Hypothesis vs. Command & Control

you encounter a Command and Control interviewer, alter your style to answer his questions directly. It's much easier to back off and just answer questions than to learn to drive a case when you are not used to doing that. Both case styles are prevalent and you should practice both types.

FORMAT

Another variant is the format of the interview itself. Recently companies have tried to mix it up by offering different approaches to test their candidates. Focus on building strong foundational skills and you won't be thrown off-guard by their new challenges.

One-on-One

Most of your interviews will be one-on-one: you will face one interviewer who will present her case question and guide you through the discussion. This format is the most common style of interview you'll face, and the interviewer's personal style and case content can vary wildly, even within the same company.

Small Group

You might find yourself in a final-round interview with other candidates. These people are competing for the same job you want, so it is a very awkward situation. Typically you'll be asked to solve a case as a group, so be sure to listen carefully to each person as you participate. Several people might be observing you in the room or watching through a two-way glass wall. Their focus is on seeing how you interact and solve problems in a group exercise. Use the same great skills you would apply to a one-on-one interview, but avoid dominating the conversation or trying to lead everyone. You should focus on collaborating and showing good team skills.

Analysis Only

Some very analytical companies are now requiring the computer- or paper-based test. One approach is to have you read a case scenario and then answer multiple choice questions. Another one is to have you use a computer to build basic

Excel models and solve some analytical problems. This format is nerve-racking as it is easy to make mistakes and you have no feedback on how you are doing. But don't worry; many of these tests are threshold-oriented and designed to weed out those whose analytical skills are weak. If you have above-average analytical skills, you'll likely pass. Do not worry if you cannot answer all the questions, but be sure to manage your time well. You will feel rushed!

Analyze & Present

The fastest-growing trend in case interviews is probably the Analyze & Present approach. Typically you'll be given one hour to do the following:

- Read through a paper case (there's always too much information).

- Design a short slide deck with either given slides (there will be unnecessary ones in the pile) or those you make yourself.

- Present to a team of people for about 15 minutes.

The secret to doing well on these cases is to manage your time well and to develop a clean storyline. Since you will be sorting through quite a bit of information, having a concise and logical storyline is very important. As you read through the case and sort through slides, develop the tag lines you'll put on each slide. When you string those tag lines (or headlines) together, they should make a sensible story. Also, practice your presentation out loud one time before the reviewers come into the room; it's the best way to make sure you catch logic errors.

Company- or Industry-Specific

Generalist Consulting

Generalist consulting firms like Bain & Company, Boston Consulting Group, and McKinsey & Company, to name a few, tend to give a wide variety of case questions. Since these firms advise a broad set of companies and industries, you can expect to receive a case on any topic. Different offices of large firms often have specializations (e.g., a NYC office may focus

VIDEO 20-06

Dealing with Unexpected Interview Situations

Expect most non-consulting companies that give cases to present questions that center on their recent work or trends in the industry.

on banks and insurance). So be sure to check out recent white papers and published slides from that office, since that work may show up in your case.

Company-Specific

When a company like Home Depot, Amazon or Disney gives a case, they naturally want to see how you'll think through their most common problems. Expect most non-consulting companies that give cases to present questions that center on their recent work or trends in the industry. Such questions are great for you, as you can prepare in advance and show your interest in what they do. Also, since many of these companies are public, their most important projects are in the news. The main risk here is not being well-read, so don't forget to do your homework.

Industry-Specific

Specialist firms that focus on a specific industry are similar to the company-specific cases, in that, they care the most about their own industry. Their cases will tend to stay in their chosen industry, and it's common for them to want to test your overall industry knowledge. In addition to prepping for the case, be sure to know the industry terms well and read up on expected trends.

TEST-DRIVING YOUR SKILLS

Now that you have built solid case interview skills and have fine-tuned them for a specific company, it's time to test the waters. You'll want to seek out interviewer partners who can honestly tell you where your style or case interview strengths align or do not align with a specific company's approach. As mentioned earlier in the chapter, the style of the interview can vary broadly from person to person within a company, but certain patterns do exist. The insiders who are knowledgeable about the company's case interview style can help you fine-tune your skills.

Here are some tips on how to meet these people, secure interviews with them and use their knowledge to the fullest.

Second-year MBAs

If you are a first-year MBA, your best and most easily accessible interview partners are the second-year MBAs. Unfortunately, the students who worked at well-known companies before graduate school will be swamped with requests to practice cases. But don't ignore the ex-summer associates at a wide range of companies, or those who just received full-time offers. All of those students will be familiar with the companies' interview styles.

Personal network

Through friends and other connections, you may know a few people who are presently working at your target company. Ask them to do a case with you, even if it's over the phone. Keep in mind that this approach carries some risk, as your interviewer might note your performance or talk about you to other company representatives. It's best to have some case experience under your belt before you meet with them.

Company mock interviews

Attend all the mock interview workshops or interview training sessions offered by the companies. These events are designed to help you, but don't let your guard down. Prepare ahead of time and take the interview seriously. The company representatives will be taking note of your abilities. Despite the risk of doing poorly, this type of practice is well worthwhile.

Company information sessions

Attend all the "meet and greets" offered by the companies. The interview process is a common topic at these events, and you'll learn more about their interview approach.

Career center mock interviews

Many career center representatives are very tuned into the companies and can offer you the latest information on the interview process.

Some of the personnel are experienced with cases. Be sure to take advantage of their mock interview sessions.

Review the What You'll Hear sections for each of the five skills we reviewed and highlight the examples. Now think about other phrases or words that might clue you into the skills the interviewer wants to test. Write those in your book and keep track of what you hear or don't hear during practice interviews. Learning to gauge what matters most to your interviewer is an important fine tuning skill.

Use TRAIN to Create Strong Case Skills

Now it's time to build long-lasting case interview skills with the MBACASE *TRAIN* Method. Each case pack is designed to complement the other cases and present a breadth of challenges. Because case elements are modular, you get exciting case topics that keep you interested and get you up to speed fast. With each case you'll know what you are learning and easily identify soft spots in your skill set. You will be thoroughly tested and interview-ready!

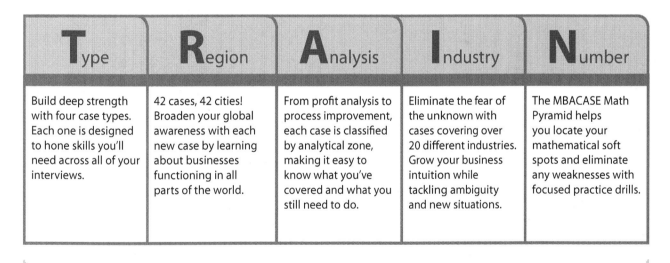

Type	**R**egion	**A**nalysis	**I**ndustry	**N**umber
Build deep strength with four case types. Each one is designed to hone skills you'll need across all of your interviews.	42 cases, 42 cities! Broaden your global awareness with each new case by learning about businesses functioning in all parts of the world.	From profit analysis to process improvement, each case is classified by analytical zone, making it easy to know what you've covered and what you still need to do.	Eliminate the fear of the unknown with cases covering over 20 different industries. Grow your business intuition while tackling ambiguity and new situations.	The MBACASE Math Pyramid helps you locate your mathematical soft spots and eliminate any weaknesses with focused practice drills.

OVER 40 CASE PACKS

Type

TYPES OF CASES

Case interview practice should be focused on consistently building skills. To do that you need to start with the basics and then progress to more advanced materials. Our four case types take you through this progression so that you can consistently solve tough, fully integrated business cases. After building these skills you can fine-tune them by focusing on variants that may appear in your specific interviews.

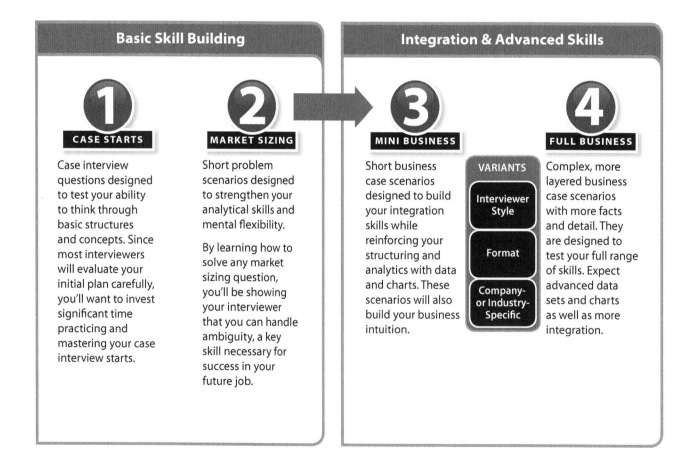

Basic Skill Building

1 CASE STARTS

Case interview questions designed to test your ability to think through basic structures and concepts. Since most interviewers will evaluate your initial plan carefully, you'll want to invest significant time practicing and mastering your case interview starts.

2 MARKET SIZING

Short problem scenarios designed to strengthen your analytical skills and mental flexibility.

By learning how to solve any market sizing question, you'll be showing your interviewer that you can handle ambiguity, a key skill necessary for success in your future job.

Integration & Advanced Skills

3 MINI BUSINESS

Short business case scenarios designed to build your integration skills while reinforcing your structuring and analytics with data and charts. These scenarios will also build your business intuition.

VARIANTS

Interviewer Style

Format

Company- or Industry- Specific

4 FULL BUSINESS

Complex, more layered business case scenarios with more facts and detail. They are designed to test your full range of skills. Expect advanced data sets and charts as well as more integration.

SKILLS BY TYPE

Each case type emphasizes a different set of skills. Case Starts and Market Sizing are great for building your structural and analytical thinking, while Mini and Full Business cases require you to step it up with more analysis, integration and insights. All case types work together to make you consistent and well-prepared. Each case pack will have a section for your interviewer to evaluate the appropriate skills. Tracking skills across cases will accelerate your progress.

	Warm Up and Drill		Apply and Test	
	CASE STARTS 15 case packs 10 minutes	**MARKET SIZING** 8 case packs 15 minutes	**MINI BUSINESS** 8 case packs 20 minutes	**FULL BUSINESS** 11 case packs 30+ minutes
PHYSICAL SKILLS				
Body Language	✓	✓	✓	✓
Verbal	✓	✓	✓	✓
Listening	✓	✓	✓	✓
THINKING SKILLS				
Hypothesis Generation	✓		✓	✓
Comfort with Ambiguity		✓ (emphasis)		
Initial Structure & Output	✓ (emphasis)	✓	✓	✓
Data Gathering		✓	✓ (emphasis)	✓
Data Analysis		✓	✓	✓ (emphasis)
Conceptual Thinking	✓		✓	✓
Integration			✓	✓ (emphasis)
Basic Business Intuition	✓	✓	✓	✓
2nd Level Insights			✓	✓ (emphasis)
Creativity			✓	✓
Recommendation			✓	✓ (emphasis)

✓ Additional emphasis

Region

Building a global business perspective takes time and exposure. Our case packs give you the added benefit of different locales and business practices built into each scenario.

AFRICA

101 Cape Town, South Africa
102 Lagos, Nigeria

MIDDLE EAST

201 Cairo, Egypt
202 Riyadh, Saudi Arabia
203 Tel Aviv, Israel
204 Dubai, United Arab Emirates

OCEANIA

301 Christchurch, New Zealand
302 Melbourne, Australia

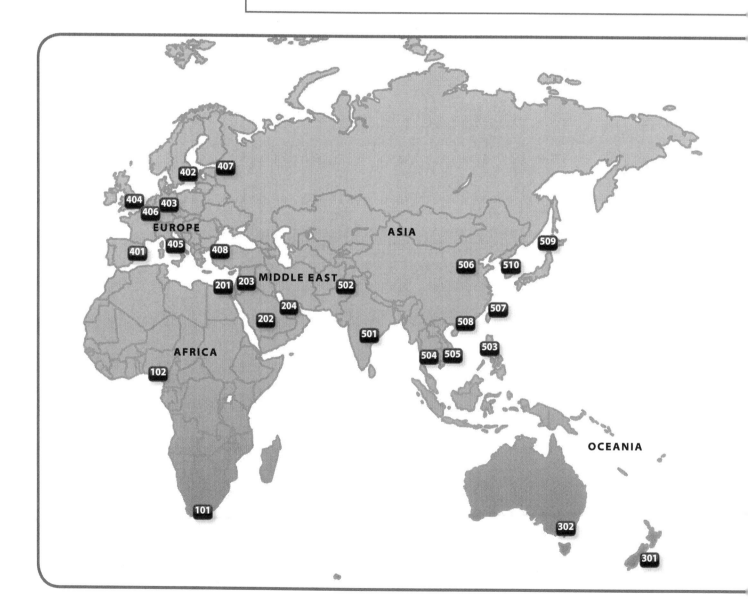

EUROPE	ASIA	NORTH AMERICA	SOUTH AMERICA
401 Barcelona, Spain	**501** Hyderabad, India	**601** Naperville, Illinois, US	**701** Bogota, Colombia
402 Stockholm, Sweden	**502** Punjab, Pakistan	**602** Muncie, Indiana, US	**702** Santiago, Chile
403 Frankfurt, Germany	**503** Manila, Philippines	**603** San Francisco, California, US	
404 London, England	**504** Bangkok, Thailand	**604** Cape Cod, Massachusetts, US	
405 Rome, Italy	**505** Ho Chi Minh City, Vietnam	**605** Panama City, Florida, US	
406 Brussels, Belgium	**506** Beijing, China	**606** New York, New York, US	
407 St. Petersburg, Russia	**507** Taipei, Taiwan	**607** Dallas, Texas, US	
408 Istanbul, Turkey	**508** Hong Kong, China	**608** Newark, New Jersey, US	
	509 Sapporo, Japan	**609** Bismarck, North Dakota, US	
	510 Seoul, South Korea	**610** Princeville, Kauai, US	
		611 Los Angeles, California, US	
		612 Mexico City, Mexico	
		613 Toronto, Ontario, Canada	
		614 Kingston, Ontario, Canada	

By testing your business skills on problems based in different regions of the world, you'll reduce the chance of being surprised in the real interview. You'll also begin to build regional factors like language, infrastructure and cultural norms into your analysis.

Analysis

ANALYSIS BY ZONE

You learned about the Maximum Value Model in Section 11. Our Case Packs will leverage that knowledge by teaching you to think in an integrated way. By using five zones to categorize business problems and navigate through potential solutions and integration points, you build a lifelong mental model for solving problems. Our case packs will help you understand what to think about in each zone as well as how to move your thoughts and discussion between zones. You'll strengthen your breadth and depth of thinking.

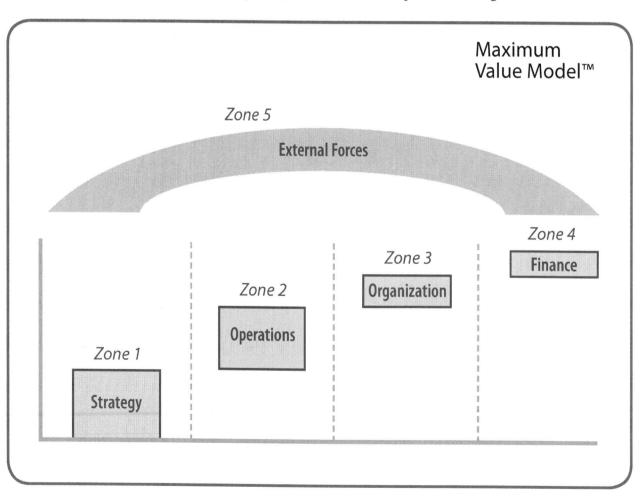

CASE PACKS BY ZONE
AND MENTAL ROADMAP

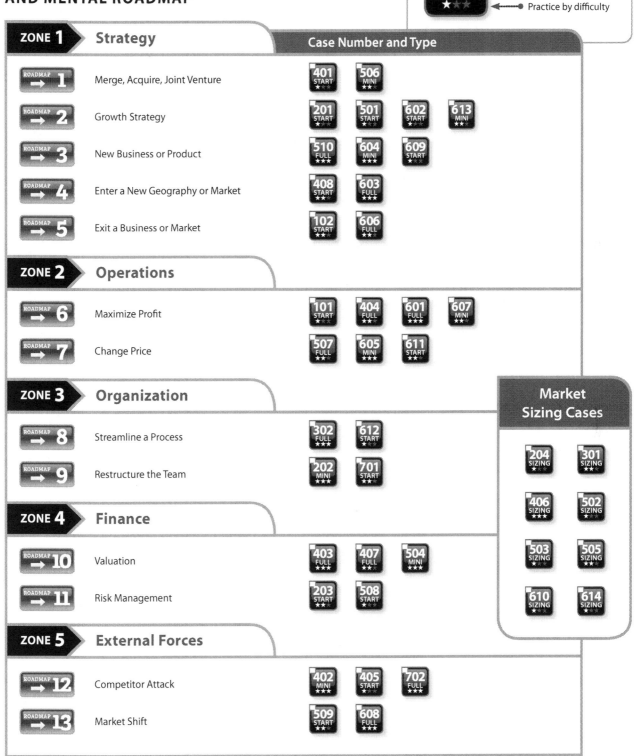

101 START ★★★
- Track your progress
- Know your region
- Study by type
- Practice by difficulty

ZONE 1 Strategy

Case Number and Type

ROADMAP 1 — Merge, Acquire, Joint Venture
401 START ★★★ | 506 MINI ★★

ROADMAP 2 — Growth Strategy
201 START ★★★ | 501 START ★★★ | 602 START ★★★ | 613 MINI ★★

ROADMAP 3 — New Business or Product
510 FULL ★★★ | 604 MINI ★★★ | 609 START ★★★

ROADMAP 4 — Enter a New Geography or Market
408 START ★★ | 603 FULL ★★★

ROADMAP 5 — Exit a Business or Market
102 START ★★ | 606 FULL ★★

ZONE 2 Operations

ROADMAP 6 — Maximize Profit
101 START ★ | 404 FULL ★★★ | 601 FULL ★★★ | 607 MINI ★★

ROADMAP 7 — Change Price
507 FULL ★★ | 605 MINI ★★★ | 611 START ★★

ZONE 3 Organization

ROADMAP 8 — Streamline a Process
302 FULL ★★★ | 612 START ★★

ROADMAP 9 — Restructure the Team
202 MINI ★★★ | 701 START ★★

ZONE 4 Finance

ROADMAP 10 — Valuation
403 FULL ★★★ | 407 FULL ★★★ | 504 MINI ★★★

ROADMAP 11 — Risk Management
203 START ★★ | 508 START ★★

ZONE 5 External Forces

ROADMAP 12 — Competitor Attack
402 MINI ★★★ | 405 START ★ | 702 FULL ★★★

ROADMAP 13 — Market Shift
509 START ★★★ | 608 FULL ★★★

Market Sizing Cases

204 SIZING ★★ | 301 SIZING ★★
406 SIZING ★★★ | 502 SIZING ★★
503 SIZING ★★ | 505 SIZING ★★
610 SIZING ★★ | 614 SIZING ★

Industry

INDUSTRY GRID

Worry no more about new industry shock during your big interview. Our Case Packs will continually test your knowledge across 34 industries. Build specific skills by doing cases related to a few industries, or stretch your learning by doing them all. Go deeper into any industry by using our online resources at mbacase.com.

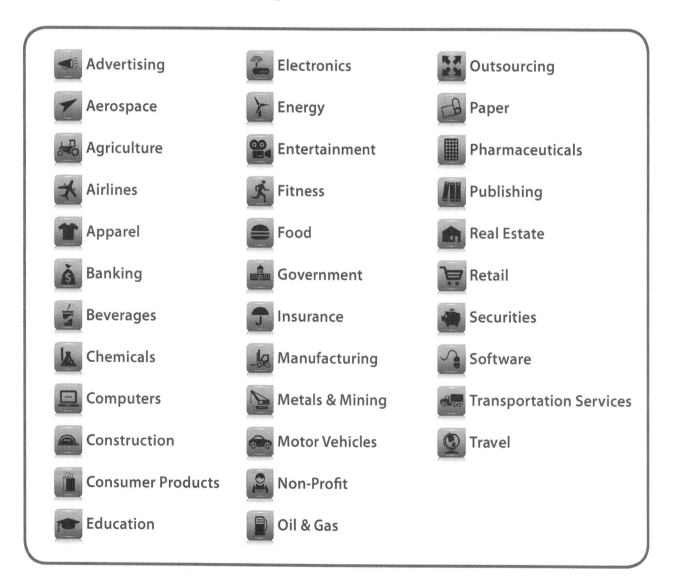

Advertising	Electronics	Outsourcing
Aerospace	Energy	Paper
Agriculture	Entertainment	Pharmaceuticals
Airlines	Fitness	Publishing
Apparel	Food	Real Estate
Banking	Government	Retail
Beverages	Insurance	Securities
Chemicals	Manufacturing	Software
Computers	Metals & Mining	Transportation Services
Construction	Motor Vehicles	Travel
Consumer Products	Non-Profit	
Education	Oil & Gas	

Numbers

"You need to work on your math," is feedback no one wants to hear, but what does it really mean? We created the MBACASE Math Pyramid as a systematic approach to building number skills. With heavy concentration on Levels 1 and 2, our cases will refresh your skills through a broad set of problems. After doing several cases you'll understand your weakest areas. The fastest way to improve your numbers skills is to do drills and more cases that test those areas.

MBACASE
Math Pyramid™

Perfect Practice Plans

As I said in section 19, I don't agree that "practice makes perfect"; I think it's better to remember that "perfect practice makes perfect." It's definitely best to approach your case interview practice sessions with purpose and a clear plan, rather than hurrying through a lot of cases. Use these Perfect Practice Plans as a starting point and modify them to fit your schedule. Also refer to your homework in Section 3 as you refine your study plan.

	Rocket	Sprinter	Steady Ready
Your Situation	**VERY DIFFICULT** **< 1 week**	**CHALLENGING** **< 2 weeks**	**IDEAL** **3–10 weeks**
Your Advantage	Your deadline will help you focus, but this time period is very difficult since you can focus on only a few basic skills. It's normal to feel frustrated and wish you had more time.	You have enough time to complete Crack the Case System, but limited partner practice time will hinder reinforcement of the knowledge. It's tempting to try to cram in more than you can handle.	You have ample time to do CTCS in depth, focus on weak spots, practice with partners, and use other case materials to be fully ready. In this situation it's easy to think you have more time than you do.
Your Focus	■ Be able to start any type of case ■ Refresh math and chart-reading skills ■ Know how to close a case with 2–3 points	■ Be able to start and end any case type ■ Spend extra time on Math Levels 1–3 ■ Communicate well in every case part	■ Be able to start and end any case type ■ Improve math; tackle Math Levels 3–5 ■ Learn how to use mid-case structures
Phase I	■ Focus on Sections 7–12 ■ Review Roadmaps; do all Case Starts ■ Refresh math with Market Sizing cases	■ Work through Chapters 1–7 in order; do all the homework and drills ■ Follow Rocket Phase I plan	■ Follow Sprinter Phase I plan ■ Drill math skills with additional cases and math materials ■ Follow Sprinter Phase II plan
Phase II	■ Do all Mini Cases and focus on integration ■ Practice closing each Mini case several times ■ Review handouts only in the Full cases	■ Do all Mini cases; find math weaknesses ■ Do several Full cases with handouts ■ Practice your close for each case several times ■ Repeat old cases to reinforce connections	■ Work on developing your own mid-case structures (Section 15) ■ In addition to CTCS, do 30 or more cases
Watch-outs & Cures	■ STRESS! > focus on executing your plan ■ The unknown > master the basics	■ Thinking you can do it all > limit yourself ■ New is better > it's not; repeat old cases	■ Over-confidence > work hard to the end ■ Peaking too soon > plan to accelerate

Using the Crack the Case System Videos

As you practice, you'll want to recreate the real interview experience as much as possible. You should also find good mentors to learn from and imitate. The MBACASE videos will help you start to meet both of those goals. We have videos placed throughout Crack the Case System to help you at just the right point, providing insights, tips and good role models. You'll face over 40 case questions from an interviewer and then see how a top candidate would approach the problem. At the end of each case I will help you understand the second level insights.

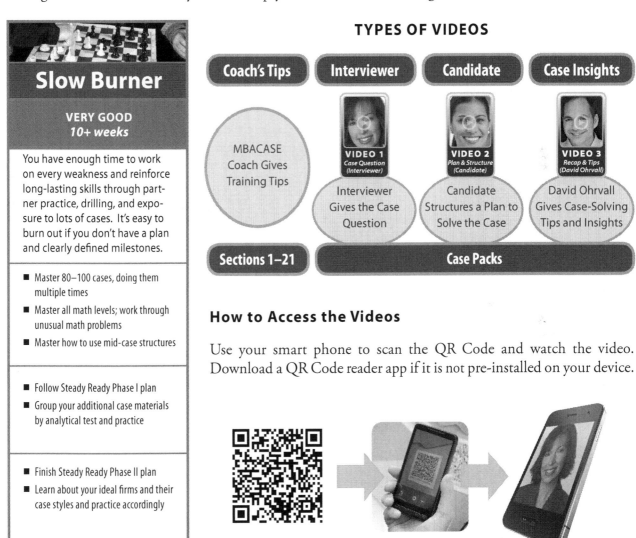

Slow Burner

VERY GOOD
10+ weeks

You have enough time to work on every weakness and reinforce long-lasting skills through partner practice, drilling, and exposure to lots of cases. It's easy to burn out if you don't have a plan and clearly defined milestones.

- Master 80–100 cases, doing them multiple times
- Master all math levels; work through unusual math problems
- Master how to use mid-case structures

- Follow Steady Ready Phase I plan
- Group your additional case materials by analytical test and practice

- Finish Steady Ready Phase II plan
- Learn about your ideal firms and their case styles and practice accordingly

- Burn out > at first, study a few hours a week
- Overload > after 100 cases, limit new material

TYPES OF VIDEOS

Coach's Tips — **Interviewer** — **Candidate** — **Case Insights**

MBACASE Coach Gives Training Tips

VIDEO 1
Case Question (Interviewer)
Interviewer Gives the Case Question

VIDEO 2
Plan & Structure (Candidate)
Candidate Structures a Plan to Solve the Case

VIDEO 3
Recap & Tips (David Ohrvall)
David Ohrvall Gives Case-Solving Tips and Insights

Sections 1–21 — **Case Packs**

How to Access the Videos

Use your smart phone to scan the QR Code and watch the video. Download a QR Code reader app if it is not pre-installed on your device.

You can also visit www.mbacase.com
and scroll through our easy-to-use video library.

VIDEO 21-01

Solo vs. Partner Practice

Let's Get Started

Solo Practice with Video Assist

1. **Find your videos**—Go to MBACASE.com and find all videos with this case pack's same case number or scan the QR code.

2. **Set up**—Turn to the My Initial Plan and Output page. Avoid reading the case question ahead of time; wait for the video. Flatten your book so you can write on the blank page. If you cannot use the video interviewer, turn to page 2 and read the case question aloud; then turn to My Initial Plan and Output.

3. **Present question**—Play the video and take a few notes while the interviewer talks. If you are not using the video, read the question out loud.

4. **Recap**—Respond as a candidate in a real case interview. Briefly restate the problem (situation, complication and your task). Ask 1–2 clarifying questions if you have them. Ask for a minute. If you are new to cases, take as much time as you need.

5. **Create your plan**—Fill in the sections of the My Initial Plan and Output page.

6. **Present your plan**—Explain the structure piece by piece, mentioning questions you have and data you want to find.

7. **Stop and study**—Refer to the roadmap listed on page 1. Look for any topics you missed. Write the additional topics on your My Initial Plan and Output page. Mark it up! Working in this way will help the ideas stick in your mind and will help you correct bad habits.

8. **Reinforce**—After you are finished with all the videos, practice this case again. Grab a stack of white paper, put it in the landscape mode and do the same case again. You'll now be able to customize the paper layout to your liking.

Partner Practice

Note: Case Start cases are designed mainly for self-study, to help you learn how to create and present an initial structure. If you choose to use a live partner for case starts, have your partner interact with you and your plan and ask for feedback on your communication and structure.

1. **Set up**—Find a table where you can sit directly across from your practice "interviewer". Have 1–2 pieces of white paper in landscape mode and a dark pen. Act like it's a real interview: shake hands, sit down, chit chat and begin. Your interviewer may take on a certain personality, like friendly, firm or foe.

2. **Present the case question**—The interviewer should read the question.

3. **Recap**—Briefly restate the problem (situation, complication and your task). Ask 1–2 clarifying questions if you have them. Ask for a minute. If you are new to cases, take as much time as you need.

4. **Create your plan**—Write out your structure on your paper.

5. **Present your plan**—Explain the structure piece by piece, mentioning questions you have and data you want to find.

6. **Stop and study**—Refer to the roadmap listed on page 1. Look for any topics you missed. Copy your original plan on your My Initial Plan and Output page for your records. Mark it up with new ideas! Working in this way will help the ideas stick in your mind and will help you correct bad habits.

7. **Reinforce**—Practice this case again with a partner or by yourself.

Krause Aerospace

Cape Town, South Africa

Krause's profit has hit some turbulence. Can you determine what's keeping this company from soaring?

101 START ★★★

CAPE TOWN CITY FACTS

▸ Famous harbor: the Port of Cape Town

▸ Known for Cape Dutch style architecture

▸ Metered taxis are not allowed to drive around the city to solicit fares

▸ Home to oldest wine-making region in the southern hemisphere

TRAIN Profile

Type	**R**egion	**A**nalysis	**I**ndustry	**N**umber
1 CASE START	CAPE TOWN, S. AFRICA Population: 3.5M Currency: Rand, ZAR, R	ROADMAP → **6** **M**aximize Profit	✈ Aerospace	LEVEL **1**

Solo Practice with Video Assist

1. Find your videos
2. Set up
3. Present question
4. Recap
5. Create your plan
6. Present your plan
7. Stop and study
8. Reinforce

10 minutes

Partner Practice

1. Set up
2. Present the case question
3. Recap
4. Create your plan
5. Present your plan
6. Stop and study
7. Reinforce

CRACK THE CASE SYSTEM

101 START ★★★

Krause Aerospace
Cape Town, South Africa

Interview Guide

Case Situation & Question

Krause Aerospace has built a thriving business in Cape Town over the last 12 years. Over the last six months gross profits have fallen quite a bit and they need you to determine what's happening.

How would you approach this problem?

Case Twist

Redo your start now with the information that Krause saw a 30% decline in profits just last month.

How would this change your plan?

VIDEO 1
Case Question
(Interviewer)

Feedback

Physical Skills	Weak		Strong
Body Language	①	②	③
Verbal	①	②	③
Listening	①	②	③

Thinking Skills			
Hypothesis Generation	①	②	③
Initial Plan & Output	①	②	③
Data Gathering	①	②	③
Basic Business Intuition	①	②	③

Total Score _____ / 21

Case Start Self Study Reminders

Present Question	Recap & Ask for a Minute	Create Your Plan	Present Plan	Stop & Study	Reinforce
Read the question out loud like an interviewer or watch the MBACASE video interviewer.	Briefly recap the situation, the complication, and your task. Speak out loud just like you would in an interview.	Using the paper below, fill in the sections.	Turn your plan toward the interviewer (or mirror or webcam) and present it piece by piece.	Review the roadmaps and the Post Case Review page to see what you missed. Mark up your plan to make it better.	Do the start again with the video interviewer, or find a live partner and get some feedback. Incorporate what you learned the first time.

101
START ★★★

Krause Aerospace
Cape Town, South Africa

My Initial Plan and Output

Today's date:

Questions I'm thinking about:

Topics I know to cover:

Profit Tree Approach:

Topic Bucket Approach:

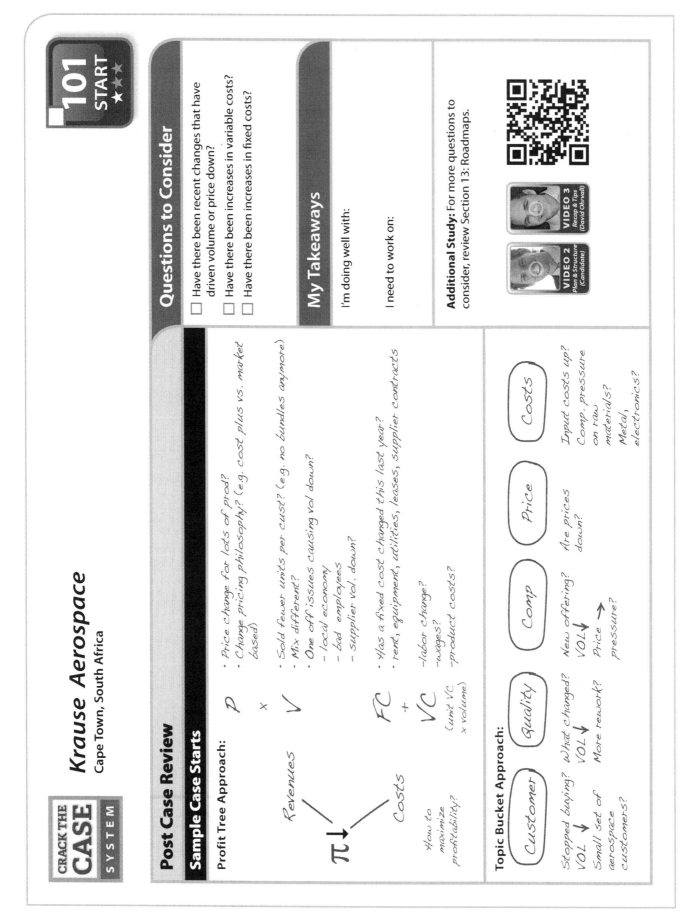

Krause Aerospace
Cape Town, South Africa

101
START
★ ★ ★

CRACK THE CASE SYSTEM

Post Case Review

Sample Case Starts

Profit Tree Approach:

$$\pi \rightarrow$$

Revenues

Costs

How to maximize profitability?

P

×

V

FC
+
VC

(unit VC × volume)

- Price change for lots of prod?
- Change pricing philosophy? (e.g. cost plus vs. market based)

- Sold fewer units per cust? (e.g. no bundles anymore)
- Mix different?
- One off issues causing vol down?
  - local economy
  - bad employees
  - supplier vol. down?

- Has a fixed cost changed this last year?
- rent, equipment, utilities, leases, supplier contracts

- labor change?
- wages?
- product costs?

Topic Bucket Approach:

(Customer)   (Quality)   (Comp)   (Price)   (Costs)

Stopped buying? VOL ↓

Small set of aerospace customers?

What changed? VOL ↓

More rework?

New offering? VOL ↓

Price → pressure?

Are prices down?

Input costs up? Comp. pressure on raw materials? Metal, electronics?

Questions to Consider

☐ Have there been recent changes that have driven volume or price down?
☐ Have there been increases in variable costs?
☐ Have there been increases in fixed costs?

My Takeaways

I'm doing well with:

I need to work on:

Additional Study: For more questions to consider, review Section 13: Roadmaps.

VIDEO 2
Plan & Structure
(Candidate)

VIDEO 3
Recap & Tips
(David Ohrvall)

United Standard

Lagos, Nigeria

Is United strong enough to deal with this business blow?

LAGOS CITY FACTS

▸ Explosive growth has been fueled by Nigeria's oil industry

▸ Center of the Nigerian movie industry, known as "Nollywood"

▸ Predicted to be one of world's 10 largest cities by 2010

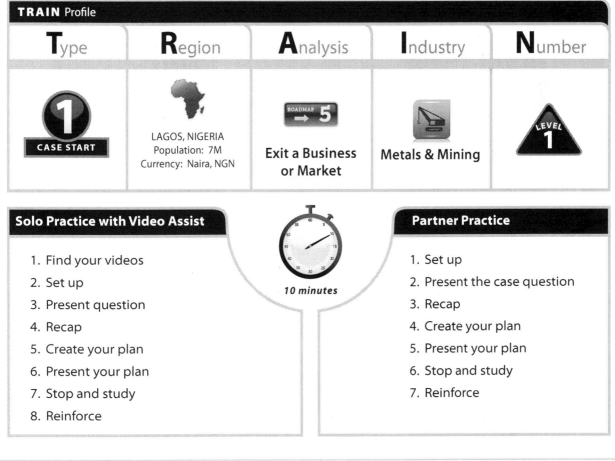

TRAIN Profile

Type	**R**egion	**A**nalysis	**I**ndustry	**N**umber
1 CASE START	LAGOS, NIGERIA Population: 7M Currency: Naira, NGN	ROADMAP **5** Exit a Business or Market	Metals & Mining	LEVEL **1**

Solo Practice with Video Assist	*10 minutes*	**Partner Practice**
1. Find your videos		1. Set up
2. Set up		2. Present the case question
3. Present question		3. Recap
4. Recap		4. Create your plan
5. Create your plan		5. Present your plan
6. Present your plan		6. Stop and study
7. Stop and study		7. Reinforce
8. Reinforce		

www.mbacase.com

287

102 START ★★☆

United Standard
Lagos, Nigeria

Interview Guide

Case Situation & Question

United Standard is a European metal fabricator. They produce metal beams for the booming Nigerian construction market. One of their production facilities in Lagos has continued to struggle to produce high-quality metal. Due to several poor grades during inspection reports, the Nigerian government is now demanding that United shut the facility down. They say the tensile strength of the metal is not the proper quality for construction.

What should United do?

Case Twist

Local labor unions have rallied community support to keep the plant open.

How does this affect your approach?

VIDEO 1
Case Question
(Interviewer)

Feedback

Physical Skills

	Weak		Strong
Body Language	①	②	③
Verbal	①	②	③
Listening	①	②	③

Thinking Skills

Hypothesis Generation	①	②	③
Initial Plan & Output	①	②	③
Data Gathering	①	②	③
Basic Business Intuition	①	②	③

Total Score _____ / 21

Case Start Self Study Reminders

Present Question	Recap & Ask for a Minute	Create Your Plan	Present Plan	Stop & Study	Reinforce
Read the question out loud like an interviewer or watch the MBACASE video interviewer.	Briefly recap the situation, the complication, and your task. Speak out loud just like you would in an interview.	Using the paper below, fill in the sections.	Turn your plan toward the interviewer (or mirror or webcam) and present it piece by piece.	Review the roadmaps and the Post Case Review page to see what you missed. Mark up your plan to make it better.	Do the start again with the video interviewer, or find a live partner and get some feedback. Incorporate what you learned the first time.

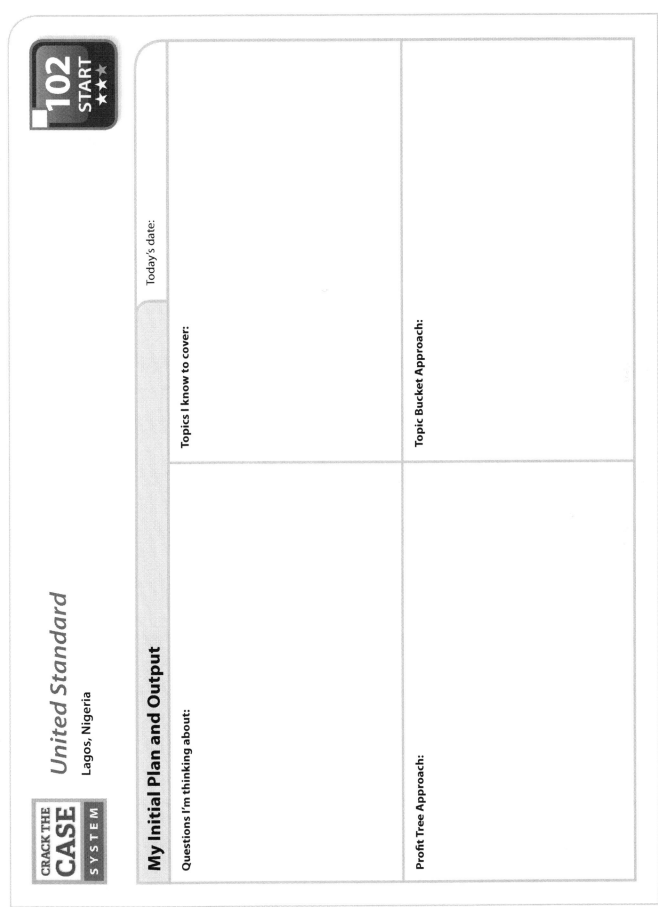

CRACK THE CASE SYSTEM

United Standard

Lagos, Nigeria

102 START ★★★

My Initial Plan and Output

Today's date:

Questions I'm thinking about:

Topics I know to cover:

Profit Tree Approach:

Topic Bucket Approach:

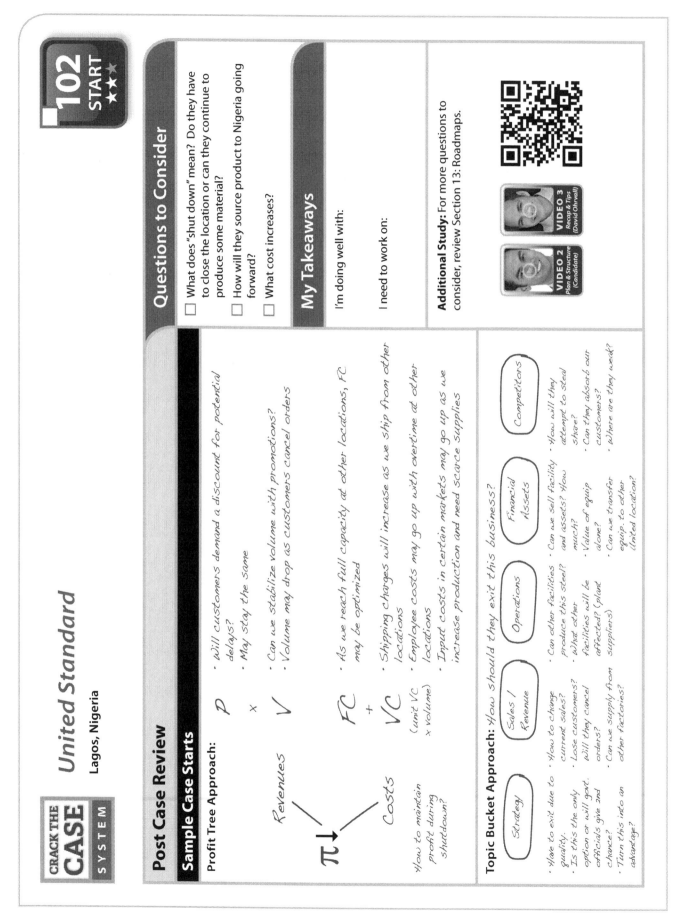

Post Case Review

Sample Case Starts

Profit Tree Approach:

$$\pi \rightarrow \begin{cases} Revenues \rightarrow P \times V \\ Costs \rightarrow FC + VC \\ (unit\ VC \times volume) \end{cases}$$

How to maintain profit during shutdown?

P
- Will customers demand a discount for potential delays?
- May stay the same

V
- Can we stabilize volume with promotions?
- Volume may drop as customers cancel orders

FC
- As we reach full capacity at other locations, FC may be optimized

VC
- Shipping charges will increase as we ship from other locations
- Employee costs may go up with overtime at other locations
- Input costs in certain markets may go up as we increase production and need scarce supplies

Topic Bucket Approach: How should they exit this business?

(Strategy)
- Have to exit due to quality.
- Is this the only option or will govt. officials give 2nd chance?
- Turn this into an advantage?

(Sales / Revenue)
- How to change current sales?
- Lose customers? Will they cancel orders?
- Can we supply from other factories?

(Operations)
- Can other facilities produce this steel?
- What other facilities will be affected? (plant suppliers)

(Financial Assets)
- Can we sell facility and assets? How much?
- Value of equip alone?
- Can we transfer equip. to other United location?

(Competitors)
- How will they attempt to steal share?
- Can they absorb our customers?
- Where are they weak?

United Standard

Lagos, Nigeria

Questions to Consider

☐ What does "shut down" mean? Do they have to close the location or can they continue to produce some material?

☐ How will they source product to Nigeria going forward?

☐ What cost increases?

My Takeaways

I'm doing well with:

I need to work on:

VIDEO 2
Plan & Structure
(Candidate)

VIDEO 3
Recap & Tips
(David Ohrvall)

Additional Study: For more questions to consider, review Section 13: Roadmaps.

Khepri Transportation

Cairo, Egypt

Can Khepri shift gears and put their company on the road to higher growth?

201
START
★★★

CAIRO CITY FACTS

▸ Largest city in Africa & the Arab world

▸ Only metro system in Africa with 700 million rides a year

▸ Over 2M cars on the streets; 60% are over 10 years old

TRAIN Profile

Type	**R**egion	**A**nalysis	**I**ndustry	**N**umber
1 CASE START	CAIRO, EGYPT Population: 6.8M Currency: Egyptian pound, EGP	ROADMAP → **2** Growth Strategy	Transportation Services	LEVEL **1**

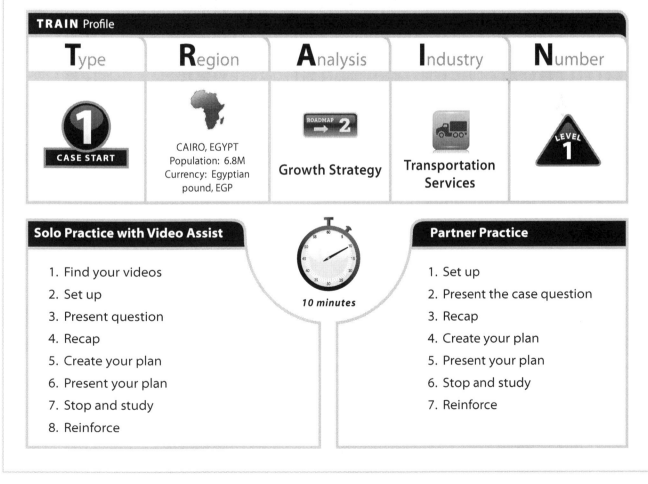

Solo Practice with Video Assist	*10 minutes*	**Partner Practice**
1. Find your videos		1. Set up
2. Set up		2. Present the case question
3. Present question		3. Recap
4. Recap		4. Create your plan
5. Create your plan		5. Present your plan
6. Present your plan		6. Stop and study
7. Stop and study		7. Reinforce
8. Reinforce		

CRACK THE CASE SYSTEM

201 START ★★★

Khepri Transportation

Cairo, Egypt

Interview Guide

Case Situation & Question

The Egyptian government is about to invest heavily in new public transportation buses, and Khepri believes they are well positioned to grow. With a strong customer base and consistent manufacturing processes, this transportation company has been asked to bid on the manufacturing of several hundred buses for the city of Cairo.

Assuming Khepri wins the bid, what do they need to consider as they prepare for growth?

Case Twist

The government has announced that they are going to limit bids to only natural gas buses. These buses save fuel and run cleaner. Khepri has no experience with this kind of bus.

How does this affect your plan?

Feedback

Physical Skills

	Weak		Strong
Body Language	①	②	③
Verbal	①	②	③
Listening	①	②	③

Thinking Skills

Hypothesis Generation	①	②	③
Initial Plan & Output	①	②	③
Data Gathering	①	②	③
Basic Business Intuition	①	②	③

Total Score _____ / 21

VIDEO 1
Case Question (Interviewer)

Case Start Self Study Reminders

Present Question	Recap & Ask for a Minute	Create Your Plan	Present Plan	Stop & Study	Reinforce
Read the question out loud like an interviewer or watch the MBACASE video interviewer.	Briefly recap the situation, the complication, and your task. Speak out loud just like you would in an interview.	Using the paper below, fill in the sections.	Turn your plan toward the interviewer (or mirror or webcam) and present it piece by piece.	Review the roadmaps and the Post Case Review page to see what you missed. Mark up your plan to make it better.	Do the start again with the video interviewer, or find a live partner and get some feedback. Incorporate what you learned the first time.

CRACK THE CASE SYSTEM

Khepri Transportation
Cairo, Egypt

201 START ★★★

Today's date:

My Initial Plan and Output

Questions I'm thinking about:

Topics I know to cover:

Profit Tree Approach:

Topic Bucket Approach:

Khepri Transportation

Cairo, Egypt

201 START ★★★ ★

Questions to Consider

☐ What capacity is in place to produce new demand?

☐ At what point does Khepri need to make major investments in new production and inputs?

☐ Do they produce what the government wants?

My Takeaways

I'm doing well with:

I need to work on:

Additional Study: For more questions to consider, review Section 13: Roadmaps.

VIDEO 2
Plan & Structure
(Candidate)

VIDEO 3
Recap & Tips
(David Ohrvall)

Post Case Review

Sample Case Starts

Profit Tree Approach:

$$\pi \rightarrow \begin{array}{c} Revenues \\ \\ Costs \end{array}$$

$$Revenues \rightarrow \begin{array}{c} P \\ \times \\ V \end{array}$$

P
- Will price increase? Not likely due to govt. contracts?
- Will volume make up price decrease?

V
- Will the government order a large number?
- Will the sales be even over time or cyclical?
- Risk of contract dropping suddenly?

$$Costs \rightarrow \begin{array}{c} FC \\ + \\ VC \end{array}$$

(unit VC x volume)

FC
- What capacity do we have today?
- What needs to be built? Can we do it in stages?

VC
- Employee related costs (mechanics, production, warehouse)
- Are supplier inputs in place? Can they keep up with new demand?

How to grow profitably?

Topic Bucket Approach: How should Khepri prep for growth?

(Industry / Competition)   (Growth Options)   (Funding)   (Costs)

Industry / Competition
Which bus competitors want bids?
What supplier relationships does Khepri need?
What's charging with govt. push: new tech, suppliers, legislation, infrastructure?

Growth Options
Products - buses, parts, hybrid buses?
Channels - just public transport? Other?
Marketing to other countries?
Lower price because of govt.?

Funding
Reduced rate funding from govt.?
Cash demands for new production?
Support new debt payments?

Costs
New factory or use current capacity?
Training & inventory
Equipment and variable costs: new labor, materials
Will some costs/unit go down?

Saudi Major Group

Riyadh, Saudi Arabia

Your friend Jasper is offering you a sweet deal . . . or is it?
Should you bite?

RIYADH CITY FACTS

▶ Riyadh is Arabic for "the gardens"

▶ The traditional lunch meal in Riyadh is a spiced rice and meat dish called Nejdi Kabsa

▶ The distribution and consumption of alcohol is illegal in Riyadh, as in the rest of Saudi Arabia

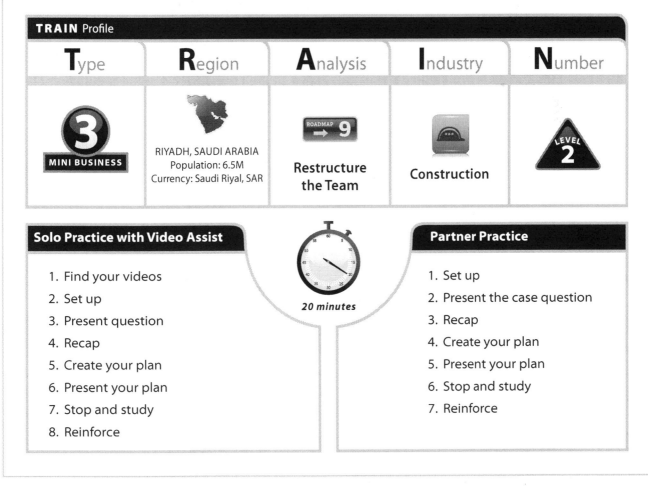

TRAIN Profile

Type	**R**egion	**A**nalysis	**I**ndustry	**N**umber
3 MINI BUSINESS	RIYADH, SAUDI ARABIA Population: 6.5M Currency: Saudi Riyal, SAR	ROADMAP **9** Restructure the Team	Construction	LEVEL **2**

Solo Practice with Video Assist

1. Find your videos
2. Set up
3. Present question
4. Recap
5. Create your plan
6. Present your plan
7. Stop and study
8. Reinforce

20 minutes

Partner Practice

1. Set up
2. Present the case question
3. Recap
4. Create your plan
5. Present your plan
6. Stop and study
7. Reinforce

CRACK THE CASE SYSTEM

Saudi Major Group
Riyadh, Saudi Arabia

202 MINI ★★★

Interview Guide

Case Situation and Question

You are a Director at the Saudi Major Group, a major construction company that builds everything from housing projects to fast food franchises, hotels and public works like bridges and government buildings.

A slowdown in the local Riyadh economy is forcing you to evaluate FTE reductions. You are most concerned about the proposal team. Creating winning bids is the lifeblood of the company. You are not sure you have the right team to produce proposals quickly and effectively.

At lunch your friend (you were analysts together years ago) proposes that his proposal writing team leave your rival and join Saudi Major. He guarantees bigger proposals, faster output and a higher hit rate. But you must decide by the end of lunch or he'll go to another competitor.

You quickly excuse yourself and call the office. What questions would you ask? What data do you need? What calculations will you make? What's your answer to your friend?

Case Twist

It turns out that your current team has a severance package that averages to $100k per team member. Does this change your decision? Check out the Crack the Case System videos on mbacase.com or scan the Video 3 QR code on the Post Case Review page to hear more insights.

VIDEO 1
Case Question (Interviewer)

Feedback

Physical Skills
	Weak		Strong
Body Language	①	②	③
Verbal	①	②	③
Listening	①	②	③

Thinking Skills
Hypothesis Generation	①	②	③
Comfort with Ambiguity	①	②	③
Initial Plan & Output	①	②	③
Data Gathering	①	②	③
Data Analysis	①	②	③
Basic Business Intuition	①	②	③
Integration	①	②	③
2nd Level Insights	①	②	③
Creativity	①	②	③
Recommendation	①	②	③

Total Score _____ / 39

Intro Facts (Tell the Candidate if Asked)

Cost Reductions: Management wants to focus on FTE (Full Time Equivalent) reductions. Other cost categories were considered but are not a part of today's discussion.

Your Role: You have the power to hire and fire. If you want to take Jasper's offer on the spot, you can.

Key Insights (Do Not Tell the Candidate)

Think High Level: Successful candidates discuss the pieces to test: new team cost and performance, old team severance and implementation.

Measure Impact: Candidates should lay out a form of cost (salaries, severance) and benefit analysis (hit rate, bigger proposals and more throughputs).

Mid-case Data (Tell Only at Appropriate Time)

Develop Options: Candidates that lay out clean options early in the discussion do well. If the candidate is struggling with how to approach the discussion and numbers, prompt with questions, data and directions. Use the Interviewer's Data Guide.

Case Flow and Milestones

1 Prep and Review
For this case the Candidate needs to interpret data from one chart and take notes on some additional facts. There may be a few questions before you get to the slide.

2 Present Main Question
Take on a personality (friendly, firm or foe). Ask one or two background questions. Present the question. Candidate will take notes and ask for time to think or begin talking.

3 Answer & Ask
This is an ambiguous problem. Try to help the candidate by offering ideas if he is stuck. Continue to ask why he is thinking a certain way.

4 Guide Discussion
Give any missing data if necessary and the Mid-case Data tips. Review the answer on page 4 of the case pack and offer suggestions if the candidate needs help.

GIVE CLUE

5 Get Recommendation
Be firm and expect a final number. To see if the candidate is thinking about broader business issues ask what he would do with this information.

Saudi Major Group

Riyadh, Saudi Arabia

Interviewer's Data Guide

Step 1 – Give Key Facts and Data

- Test the candidate's ability to lay out the options and do the math quickly.
- Say: "What data would you need to test Jasper's proposal?"
- **Key Facts to Give (prompt any that the candidate misses)**

		Current Method			Proposed Approach		
1	Average Bid Size	$10 million USD			$11 million USD		
2	Hit Rate	15%			16%		
3	Throughput	7 per month			8 per month		
		#	Salary	Total by Type	#	Salary	Total by Type
4	Director	1	$175,000	$175,000	2	$218,750	$437,500
5	Managers	2	$95,000	$190,000	3	$118,750	$356,250
6	Associates	4	$65,000	$260,000	2	$281,250	$162,500
				$625,000			**$956,250**
7	Hit Rate Bonus	0			If hit 16%, flat $5M		
					If >16%, flat $20M payment		
8	Severance (<12 months)	No severance package			$50k per person		

*may be fired for poor performance

Say: "Now that you have the data, what calculations would you perform to compare the options?"

Step 2 – Check Candidate's Options and Calculations

Your Calculations

	Current Method		Proposed Approach	
Monthly Revenue Comparison (1x2x3)	$10.50	million USD	$14.08	million USD
Estimated Annual Rev (Mo. Revenue x 12)	$126	million USD	$169	million USD
Monthly Revenue Upside in millions ($14.08 -$10.50) =	$3.58			
Annual Revenue Upside (12 x $3.58) =	$42.96			

Additional Thoughts

Biggest downside is if the new team fails. If they underperform, the original team would have likely been better.

You have to either find a new team or train them.

Upside to Saudi Group for Option 2 or 3 is huge. The potential for large gain outweighs the risks of Option 1.

To make this essentially risk free, negotiate the salaries down to current levels and eliminate the severance.

Argue that the new team needs no "safety net" and that both sides need to bear risk.

Option 1	**Option 2**	**Option 3**
New team misses target	Team hits target goal, 16% hit rate	Team exceeds target goal
Fire them for poor performance		
Salary $(331,250)	Salary $(331,250)	Salary $(331,250)
No severance	Rev upside (in M) $43	Rev upside (in M) $43 plus
	Bonus (in M) $(5)	Bonus (in M) $(20)
Saudi Group net $(331,250)	Saudi Group net Over $35M	Saudi Group net Over $20M
Will need to find a new team	Huge upside to Saudi Group	Huge upside to Saudi Group
May be tough to do quickly		
May need to train them more		

Step 3 – Ask for an Interpretation of Analysis and a Final Recommendation

- Ask: "What does your analysis say at this point?"
- Look for the candidate to concisely sum up the options. Here are the three most common options, but expect variations:
- **Option 0:** Do nothing. Use Jasper's offer as an idea to train your own team and get their performance higher. If age and experience are important, hire 1–2 people but don't swap out the whole team.
- **Option 1:** If the team does not work out for performance reasons, there will be no severance. However, there will be the extra salary expenses (estimated at about $330k per year) and, if the team is let go, Saudi Major will not have a revenue machine until the team is replaced.
- **Option 2 and 3:** Under either scenario, Saudi Major makes significant upside. Under scenario 2, the net gain of $35M is about 25% of the current revenue ($140M). Under scenario 3, the net gain of at least $20M is about 14% of the current revenue.

Saudi Major Group

Riyadh, Saudi Arabia

202
MINI
★★★

Post Case Review

Case Insights & Takeaways

- This is a good deal. If the team performs as promised the revenue increase to Saudi Major could be $20M or more.
- But if the team doesn't work out, Saudi Major will have burned its bridges. They will have lost their first team, upset company morale, and potentially provoked additional employee departure.
- Ask yourself, "How much is this worth in its simplest form?" After you have a rough estimate, layer in the complications.
- Additional concerns relate to Jasper. He seems like an agitator. If his team members are like him, this team could be volatile.

Math Tips

- For cases like this where you can develop clear options, consider making ranges quickly. Think about the potential upside and what rough range it would fall into.
- Don't expect to calculate all the specific numbers before making a decision. As soon as you calculated the expected new monthly revenue, it should have been clear that seven new salaried employees wouldn't exceed that upside.
- Practice laying out the math comparison table. Be neat and organized.

What to Expect with Cases Like These

- When you have to make a quick decision, try to lay out outcomes or options. Having a few clear "points" on which to lay your recommendation will make you sound more supported and confident.
- You will be HDDM (head down doing math) for a large part of this case. Keep connected to the interviewer by explaining what you'll do, and then doing it quickly.
- Be confident with your closing statement. You don't know how your competition performed that day. Everyone may have gotten it wrong, but your analysis may be the strongest and other factors could weigh in your favor.

My Takeaways

To build skills and improve, you must apply what you learned to future cases. Take a few moments and review the interviewer feedback and jot down some key insights about your performance in the space below.

Thinking Skills

My top 2 strengths are:

My top 2 soft spots are:

To address these problems I'll begin to:

VIDEO 3
Recap & Tips
(David Ohrvall)

My Performance During the Case

Add up your points. ➡ Total Score: _____ /15

F Form A Plan	**R** Read My Audience	**A** Anchor a Hypothesis	**M** Mine for Answers	**E** End the Case
points	points	points	points	points
③ Structured, clean	③ Good back & forth, caught clues	③ Solid hunch, pursued clue	③ Specific questions, solid analysis	③ Used facts and data, connected the dots
② Somewhat organized and logical	② Awkward, trouble with interviewer style	② Partial direction	② Missed some questions, some math mistakes	② Some data, mostly understood connections
① Messy, overlapping ideas	① Interviewer not interested, couldn't follow	① No hypothesis at all	① Vague questions, weak math, no linkages	① No data, no passion, no connections

CRACK THE CASE SYSTEM

WORKSHEET

Saudi Major Group

Riyadh, Saudi Arabia

202 MINI ★★★

SAUDI MAJOR GROUP

My Initial Plan and Output

Today's date:

2. Be original with your data

4. Leave ample room for a structure and additional notes as the case progresses

1. Zone out your paper

3. Take clean and simple notes

299

WORKSHEET

Saudi Major Group
Riyadh, Saudi Arabia

Potential Plan and Output

SAUDI MAJOR GROUP

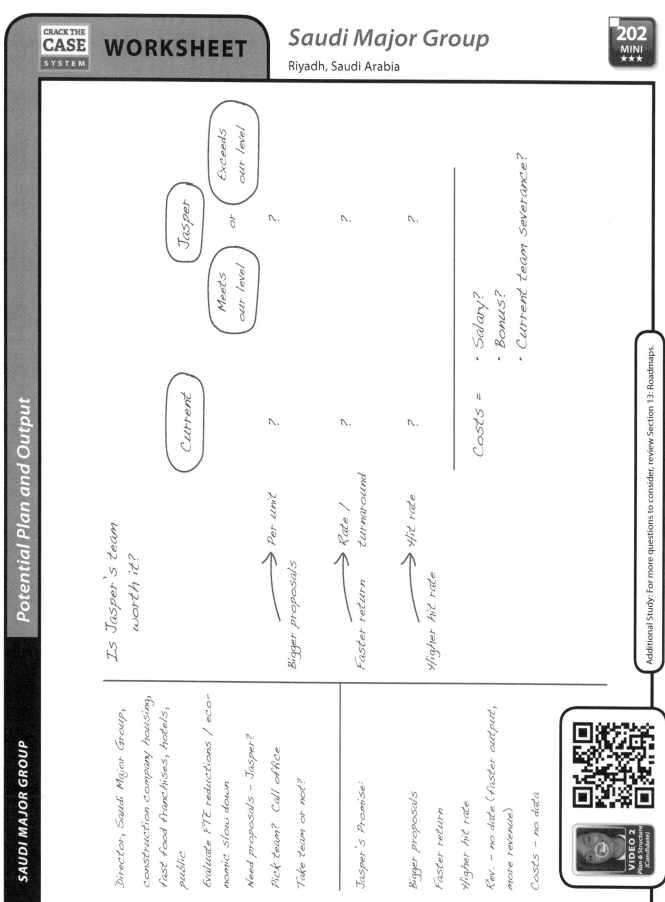

Is Jasper's team worth it?

Current — ?   Jasper   Meets our level   or   Exceeds our level

Bigger proposals ↗ Per unit   ?   ?   ?

Faster return ↗ Rate / turnaround   ?   ?   ?

Higher hit rate ↗ Hit rate   ?   ?   ?

Costs = • Salary?
       • Bonus?
       • Current team severance?

Director, Saudi Major Group,
construction company housing,
fast food franchises, hotels,
public

Evaluate FTE reductions / economic slow down

Need proposals – Jasper?

Pick team? Call office

Take team or not?

Jasper's Promise:

Bigger proposals
Faster return
Higher hit rate
Rev. – no date (faster output,
more revenue)
Costs – no data

Additional Study: For more questions to consider, review Section 13: Roadmaps.

VIDEO 2
Plan & Structure
(Candidate)

Shavit Technologies

Tel Aviv, Israel

Shavit's success has it flying high. But what will it take to get it to the moon?

TEL AVIV CITY FACTS

- ▸ One of the world's high-tech centers
- ▸ Has the world's largest concentration of buildings in the Bauhaus style
- ▸ Growth was revived by waves of immigrants from the former Soviet Union in the early 90s
- ▸ Has over 100 sushi restaurants

TRAIN Profile

Type	**R**egion	**A**nalysis	**I**ndustry	**N**umber
1 CASE START	TEL AVIV, ISRAEL Population: 394,000 Currency: New Israeli Shekels, ₪	ROADMAP **11** **Risk Management**	**Software**	LEVEL **1**

Solo Practice with Video Assist		**Partner Practice**
1. Find your videos		1. Set up
2. Set up	**10 minutes**	2. Present the case question
3. Present question		3. Recap
4. Recap		4. Create your plan
5. Create your plan		5. Present your plan
6. Present your plan		6. Stop and study
7. Stop and study		7. Reinforce
8. Reinforce		

www.mbacase.com

START 203
★★

Interview Guide

Case Situation & Question

Shavit is a new software company that developed a cutting-edge database management system. Their founder, Yael Vardi, is considered a genius in the software engineering community. Using software from the Israeli Defense Forces that tracks soldiers' performance, she developed an IT system that creates profiles of consumer and product profitability for insurance companies. She wants to have an IPO next year so Shavit can grow internationally.

Shavit wants to present a case to their VCs for going public next year instead of in 3 years as advised.

They have hired you to identify and evaluate key concerns that potential investors might have about their business.

Case Twist

After meeting with the VCs, you learn that Shavit will likely be sold to a major IT consulting firm. How would your concerns change as a result of this discovery?

Shavit Technologies
Tel Aviv, Israel

Feedback

Physical Skills

	Weak		Strong
Body Language	①	②	③
Verbal	①	②	③
Listening	①	②	③

Thinking Skills

Hypothesis Generation	①	②	③
Initial Plan & Output	①	②	③
Data Gathering	①	②	③
Basic Business Intuition	①	②	③

Total Score _____ / 21

VIDEO 1 Case Question (Interviewer)

Case Start Self Study Reminders

Present Question	Recap & Ask for a Minute	Create Your Plan	Present Plan	Stop & Study	Reinforce
Read the question out loud like an interviewer or watch the MBACASE video interviewer.	Briefly recap the situation, the complication, and your task. Speak out loud just like you would in an interview.	Using the paper below, fill in the sections.	Turn your plan toward the interviewer (or mirror or webcam) and present it piece by piece.	Review the roadmaps and the Post Case Review page to see what you missed. Mark up your plan to make it better.	Do the start again with the video interviewer, or find a live partner and get some feedback. Incorporate what you learned the first time.

302

Shavit Technologies

Tel Aviv, Israel

My Initial Plan and Output

Today's date:

Questions I'm thinking about:

Topics I know to cover:

Profit Tree Approach:

Topic Bucket Approach:

CRACK THE CASE SYSTEM

CRACK THE CASE SYSTEM
WORKSHEET

Shavit Technologies
Tel Aviv, Israel

203 START ★★☆

SHAVIT TECHNOLOGIES

Post Case Review

Questions I'm Thinking About

Expansion possible?
Founder critical?
IPO successful?
Competitors?

Topics I Know To Cover

Hiring process
Key investors and relationships to customers
Incentive comp
Golden handcuffs   key man risk
Hardware   technology risk

Topic Bucket Approach

Strategy	Assets	Value	Expectations	Delivery
↑ # of customers	Salespeople	Growth rate	Salespeople can sell	Assess quality of salespeople Research customer needs
↑ # of products/customer	Founder Tech talent Hardware	Growth rate	Founder stays Tech talent stays Best tech available	Examine ways to reduce key move risk Talent leaves Competitor analysis on existing tech

VIDEO 2 Plan & Structure (Candidate)

VIDEO 3 Recap & Tips (David Ohrvall)

Additional Study: For more questions to consider, review Section 13: Roadmaps.

Cop Cars in Dubai

Dubai, United Arab Emirates

How big is the market for police cars?

DUBAI CITY FACTS

▸ Only 17 % of residents are UAE nationals

▸ Burj Khalifa, the world's tallest building: 828 m (2717 ft)

▸ Port Jebel Ali is the world's largest man-made harbour, the biggest port in the Middle East, and the 7th-busiest port in the world

▸ Most popular sports are soccer (football) and cricket

TRAIN Profile

Type	**R**egion	**A**nalysis	**I**ndustry	**N**umber
2 MARKET SIZING	DUBAI, UAE Population: 2.2M Currency: Arab Emirate Dirham, AED	**Extrapolate**	Motor Vehicles	LEVEL 1

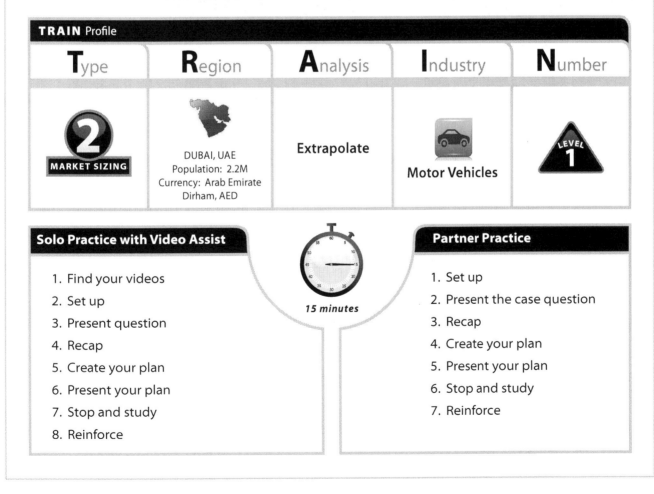

Solo Practice with Video Assist

1. Find your videos
2. Set up
3. Present question
4. Recap
5. Create your plan
6. Present your plan
7. Stop and study
8. Reinforce

15 minutes

Partner Practice

1. Set up
2. Present the case question
3. Recap
4. Create your plan
5. Present your plan
6. Stop and study
7. Reinforce

Cop Cars in Dubai

Dubai, United Arab Emirates

204
SIZING
★★★

Interview Guide

Initial Question

Audi is trying to win the police car contract for Dubai, which is currently held by BMW. It would like to determine how many cars are sold annually by BMW to the Government of Dubai.

How many cars do they need?

VIDEO 1
Case Question
(Interviewer)

Feedback

Physical Skills	Weak		Strong
Body Language	①	②	③
Verbal	①	②	③
Listening	①	②	③

Thinking Skills			
Initial Plan & Output	①	②	③
Data Gathering	①	②	③
Data Analysis	①	②	③

Total Score _____ / 18

Intro Facts (Tell the Candidate if Asked)	**Key Insights** (Do Not Tell the Candidate)	**Mid-case Data** (Tell Only at Appropriate Time)
There are 8000 police vehicles used in London. New York City uses 9000 police vehicles. The population of Dubai is 2.2M, New York City is 17M, and London, 14M. The average BMW car life is 5 years.	Candidate will need to extrapolate from the number of police vehicles in the other two cities and find a comparable estimate.	If the Candidate is stuck suggest that they may compare Dubai with other cities and the police fleets in those cities.

Case Flow and Milestones

1 Prep and Review

Read all the notes in the Interviewer Guide. Understand when to ask certain questions and when to give data and clues.

2 Present Main Question

Take on a personality (friendly, firm or foe). Ask one or two background questions. Present the question. Candidate will take notes and ask for time to think or begin talking. Discourage silence as market sizing cases are meant to be interactive.

3 Answer & Ask

This is an ambiguous problem. Try to help the candidate by offering ideas if he is stuck. Continue to ask why he is thinking a certain way.

4 Guide Discussion

Give any missing data if necessary and the Mid-case Data tips. Review the answer on page 4 of the case pack and offer suggestions if the candidate needs help.

GIVE CLUE

5 Get Recommendation

Be firm and expect a final number. To see if the candidate is thinking about broader business issues ask what he would do with this information.

CRACK THE CASE SYSTEM

204 SIGNING

Cop Cars in Dubai

Dubai, United Arab Emirates

My Initial Plan and Output   Use the space below to write your thoughts.

State your assumptions

Pick your main metrics and approach

Estimate quickly and with round numbers

Assess your approach and answer

Keep exceptions and next steps in mind.

My Numbers

What are some simple estimates for getting started?

How might you refine these numbers?

Cop Cars in Dubai

Dubai, United Arab Emirates

204 SIZING ★★★

Post Case Review	**My Score**		
Potential Solution & Output	**Weak**		**Strong**
State your assumptions • Dubai requirement for police cars is roughly similar to that of New York or London with similar police vigilance.	①	②	③
Pick your main metrics and approach • Extrapolation is based on the amount of police cars in London and New York.	①	②	③
Estimate quickly and with round numbers • Cars per capita in New York are 9000 / 17M = ~1 per 2,000 people. • Cars per capita in London are 8000 / 15M = ~1 per 2,000 people. • Assuming the same proportion of cars, Dubai may have around 11,000 police cars. • Annual sales are 11,000 / 5 years life = 2,200 per year.	①	②	③
Assess your approach and answer • 2K cars * 50K price estimate = $10M per year for an automotive contract. This seems high but possible for an oil-rich nation.	①	②	③
Keep exceptions and next steps in mind • Harsher criminal sentencing may mean fewer police cars. • BMW average life may be more (or less) which will alter the number of cars needed.	①	②	③
Total:			

Different Approaches to Consider

• Determine the total car : police car ratio from other cities. Estimate the total cars in Dubai based on population and compare to the ratio from other cities.

Tips and Takeaways

• When using division, use whole numbers to keep the overall case moving (ie 9K/17M = roughly 1 per 2000).

VIDEO 2 Plan & Structure (Candidate)

VIDEO 3 Recap & Tips (David Ohrvall)

School Daze

Christchurch, New Zealand

Little Kiwis have been missing school too much and it's a bit of a worry. Can you help the government suss out what's going on?

301
SIZING
★★☆

CHRISTCHURCH CITY FACTS

▸ One of the purest water supplies in the world, sourced from natural aquifers in the Southern Alps mountain range

▸ Has pioneered a zero-fare hybrid bus service

▸ Cathedral Square in the central city has a famous speaker's corner where the Official Wizard performs

TRAIN Profile

Type	**R**egion	**A**nalysis	**I**ndustry	**N**umber
2 MARKET SIZING	CHRISTCHURCH, NZ Population: 373,000 Currency: New Zealand Dollar, NZD	**Funnel, Observe**	**Education**	LEVEL 1

Solo Practice with Video Assist	**Partner Practice**
1. Find your videos	1. Set up
2. Set up	2. Present the case question
3. Present question	3. Recap
4. Recap	4. Create your plan
5. Create your plan	5. Present your plan
6. Present your plan	6. Stop and study
7. Stop and study	7. Reinforce
8. Reinforce	

15 minutes

School Daze
Christchurch, New Zealand

301
SIZING
★★☆

Interview Guide

Initial Question

The Education Ministry of New Zealand is worried about the high levels of truancy in primary and secondary schools in Christchurch compared to the rest of the country. They are keen to understand why this is happening and how they can address the problem. First, they need to quantify the magnitude of the problem.

How many students are 'un-justified absent' from primary and secondary schools every week in Christchurch?

VIDEO 1
Case Question
(Interviewer)

Feedback

Physical Skills	Weak		Strong
Body Language	①	②	③
Verbal	①	②	③
Listening	①	②	③

Thinking Skills			
Initial Plan & Output	①	②	③
Data Gathering	①	②	③
Data Analysis	①	②	③

Total Score _____ / 18

Intro Facts (Tell the Candidate if Asked)	**Key Insights** (Do Not Tell the Candidate)	**Mid-case Data** (Tell Only at Appropriate Time)
The total population of New Zealand is 5M. The 4 key cities in New Zealand (including Christchurch) account for 50% of the population Usually there is 1 school for every 1,500 people in the country.	The candidate may use his own mental observation of size and absenteeism in typical primary and secondary school classrooms. Combining that with the intro facts will help support a reasonable estimate.	If the candidate is stuck, suggest that he might think about classroom size and absenteeism in his own country's primary and secondary schools and use that as a benchmark for New Zealand. Also, let him know that the justified absence rate is 4%.

Case Flow and Milestones

1 Prep and Review	**2** Present Main Question	**3** Answer & Ask	**4** Guide Discussion	**5** Get Recommendation
Read all the notes in the Interviewer Guide. Understand when to ask certain questions and when to give data and clues.	Take on a personality (friendly, firm or foe). Ask one or two background questions. Present the question. The candidate will take notes and ask for time to think or begin talking. Discourage silence as market sizing cases are meant to be interactive (remember the SPEAK Method).	This is an ambiguous problem. Try to help the candidate by offering ideas if he is stuck. Continue to ask why he is thinking a certain way.	Give any missing data, if necessary, and the Mid-case Data tips. Review the answer on page 4 of the case pack and offer suggestions if the candidate needs help.	Be firm and expect a final number. To see if the candidate is thinking about broader business issues, ask what he would do with this information.

GIVE CLUE

CRACK THE CASE SYSTEM

301
SIZING ★★★

School Daze

Christchurch, New Zealand

My Initial Plan and Output   Use the space below to write your thoughts.

State your assumptions

Pick your main metrics and approach

Estimate quickly and with round numbers

Assess your approach and answer

Keep exceptions and next steps in mind.

My Numbers

What are some simple estimates for getting started?

How might you refine these numbers?

School Daze
Christchurch, New Zealand

301 SIZING ★★★

Post Case Review	My Score	
Potential Solution & Output	**Weak**	**Strong**
State your assumptions	①	② ③
• Total Population of New Zealand is about 5 M. 4 key cities in New Zealand (like Christchurch) account for 50% of the population. • Typically there is one school per 1,500 residents.		
Pick your main metrics and approach	①	② ③
• Observe class size and absenteeism per week in your country's primary/secondar schools and use that number as a guide for Christchurch.		
Estimate quickly and with round numbers	①	② ③
• Students per class: 25 / Classes per school: 12. • Christchurch population: (50% × 5M)/4 = 625,000. • Number of primary and secondary schools: 650,000/1,500 = 400. • Total students: 400 × 25 × 12 = 120,000. • Assuming 2 students absent per class per week: 2 × 12 × 400 = 9,600. • Truancy rate: 9,600/120,000 = 8% (high, compared to justified absence rate of 4%).		
Assess your approach and answer	①	② ③
• E120k students in Christchurch is about 1/8 the total number of students in NZ. This means the total number of students in NZ is 120k × 8 = 960k. (Actual student pop. is 800k) • Therefore the total justified absence per week in NZ to 4% × 800k = 32k (actual justified student absence per week in NZ is about 30k)		
Keep exceptions and next steps in mind	①	② ③
• Outside the 4 key cities, school attendance rates might be significantly different because of socio-economic factors		
Total:		

Different Approaches to Consider

Estimate the truancy rate from usually accepted norms of 4-5% and assume that for Christchurch it would be double the country average (8–10%).

Tips and Takeaways

Try to keep all numeric assumptions to the nearest 5s/10s to enable faster calculations.

Case Twists

Once the estimate is in place, discussion can be evolved to the possible reasons for high truancy and the likely solutions to the same.

It is found that human rights based education in schools (Rights, Respects and Responsibilities of students) results in the following:

• Students more likely to attend school.
• Higher student self-esteem.
• Students taking ownership of their learning and behavior.
• Students begin to behave like citizens, with stronger citizenship behaviors in the following areas: respect for the rights of others, respect for property, and level of participation.
• Students less likely to be excluded.

VIDEO 2 Plan & Structure (Candidate)   **VIDEO 3** Recap & Tips (David Ohrvall)

Blueblood Distribution

Melbourne, Australia

Known for its first-class selection of wines and spirits, Blueblood is facing a lowbrow problem. Some of its distribution centers are not up to snuff. Can you help management raise the bar?

302 FULL ★★★

TRAIN Profile

Type	**R**egion	**A**nalysis	**I**ndustry	**N**umber
4 FULL BUSINESS	MELBOURNE, AUSTRALIA Population: 4M Currency: Australian dollar, AUD	ROADMAP 8 Streamline a Process	Beverages	LEVEL 1

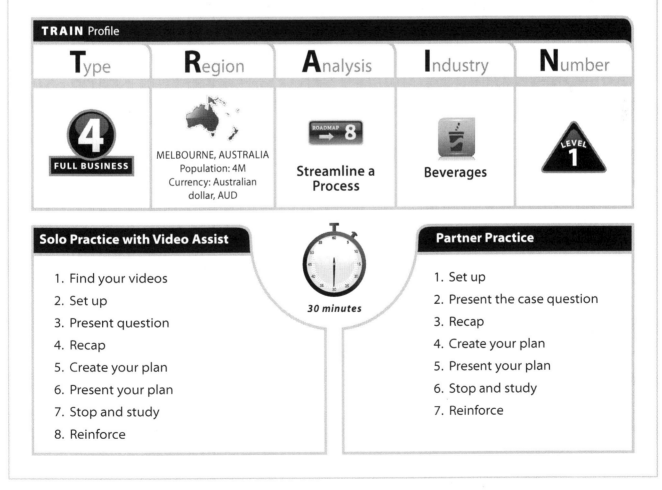

Solo Practice with Video Assist

1. Find your videos
2. Set up
3. Present question
4. Recap
5. Create your plan
6. Present your plan
7. Stop and study
8. Reinforce

30 minutes

Partner Practice

1. Set up
2. Present the case question
3. Recap
4. Create your plan
5. Present your plan
6. Stop and study
7. Reinforce

Blueblood Distribution

Melbourne, Australia

Interview Guide

Case Situation and Question

Blueblood Distribution is a $300M, nationwide distributor of wines and spirits. Their main customers are wine and spirit retailers, major grocery stores and food-marts. Presently they own 22 distribution sites and are trying to determine what factors make some sites more profitable than others.

What metrics would you use to compare distribution sites? Which metrics would be the most insightful?

Case Twist

Management wants you to pick only one metric to use in eliminating 5 of the 22 sites. What metric would you use? Why?

VIDEO 1
Case Question
(Interviewer)

Feedback

Physical Skills

	Weak		Strong
Body Language	①	②	③
Verbal	①	②	③
Listening	①	②	③

Thinking Skills

Hypothesis Generation	①	②	③
Comfort with Ambiguity	①	②	③
Initial Plan & Output	①	②	③
Data Analysis	①	②	③
Basic Business Intuition	①	②	③
Integration	①	②	③
2nd Level Insights	①	②	③
Creativity	①	②	③

Total Score _____ / 33

Intro Facts (Tell the Candidate if Asked)

Ownership

Each location is "owned" by the Regional VP, a company employee with incentive compensation consisting of 75% from regional performance and 25% from overall corporate performance. An additional bonus is available to the 5 top-performing regions.

Sales force

Each distribution site is responsible for generating sales near the site with grocery chains, restaurants and wine and spirit retailers.

Regions

There was little planning around how each region was developed; the Regional VP determined most of the regional locations according to his/her preferences.

Information sharing across regions

Distribution centers are encouraged to share best practices to increase the overall performance of the company.

Key Insights (Do Not Tell the Candidate)

Common Sense Review

This case is not complicated, but it does require the Candidate to think clearly about which metrics will have the most impact.

4 Key Metrics

These four metrics have the biggest impact on performance:

• Relative market share (RMS): indicates market strength, an important factor in pricing power and customer relationships.

• Inventory turns: high turns indicate a focused, well-chosen set of SKUs.

• Route density: gives insight on how costly it is to deliver to customers.

• Limiting the number of SKUs: keeping the number of products down saves warehousing costs.

Mid-case Data (Tell Only at Appropriate Time)

The first part of this case is a discussion of metrics for a distribution facility. Refer to the Data Guide for relevant metrics. After talking about the metrics, hand out some performance data (Handout A). This is all the information that the Candidate needs to do well on the case.

If there is remaining time after the candidate answers the main case question, introduce the Case Twist (see above).

For an additional twist on this case, ask the candidate:

"If you had to fix a 'poor performer' what would you do first?"

Blueblood Distribution

Melbourne, Australia

302 FULL ★★★

Case Flow and Milestones

1 Present Main Question	**2** Answer any Basics	**3** Ask for Clarification	**4** Guide Discussion	**5** Get Recommendation
Candidate takes notes, asks for a minute, forms a plan and presents it.	This case has a large brainstorming component so it would be easy to slide into that discussion. Hold off, though, and wait to fully understand her Plan.	Prompt for clarification with questions like, "Tell me more about this area (you choose). What are you thinking about here?" or "Tell me how the parts of your structure link to each other." Look for clear connections between each part of the plan.	Direct the Candidate by asking about metrics. Referring to Data Guide, facilitate a discussion of metrics in a distribution facility. Next, give candidate Handout A. Ask which metrics appear to be the most significant, based on the data provided.	Gauge whether it is data driven and based on the facts of the case. • Options should reference the data from the case. • The Candidate should look for ways to gather more detailed data and try to confirm that these numbers are correct.

Handout and Data Guide

Handout

Candidate: Do you have any data on the 22 distribution centers' metrics?

Interviewer: "Here's a summary of the metrics, broken into 3 performance categories. Looking at the data on this sheet, which metrics are the most useful? Why?"

Re-routers | Questions to Keep Things on Track

- **What other metrics would you consider?**
  - Competitive intensity, measured in relative market share (RMS), is often forgotten
  - Route efficiency, measured by mileage between deliveries and number of deliveries per day

- **Of the metrics you've mentioned thus far, which one or two capture the most important drivers of the business?**
  - RMS is critical to controlling customer relationships and setting price for a region.
  - Route density and average miles per delivery are good measures of how well the sales team is selling along the routes

- **Which metrics can we gather the most easily?**

Data Guide

First, discuss the metrics. Facilitate a discussion about metrics in a distribution facility. Ask questions about which metrics are most meaningful, and how you gather such metrics. If the candidate gets stuck, offer a few of these:

- Receiving—bringing shipments of wine into the warehouse quickly, safely (without breakage) and consistently
- Picking and Packing—minimizing the time to print an order, pick a product and pack it in a box
- Inventory Turns—ensuring breadth of product while "turning" popular SKUs often
- Admin/ Accounting—streamlining all internal processes and minimizing personnel
- SKU Management—keeping the number of products down
- Sales per Customer—trying to increase the average order size and frequency of order
- Delivery Costs—Minimizing the internal cost per order by building route density
- Route Density—Routing trucks to maximize the number of customers in the shortest distance
- Relative Market Share—Increasing dominance by distribution region to better control pricing. RMS = Blueblood's market share compared to next competitor or leader. For example, if RMS = 2, BB has 2x the share of the next competitor; if RMS = .5, BB has a market share half the size of the leader's.

CRACK THE CASE SYSTEM

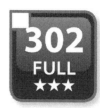

Blueblood Distribution

Melbourne, Australia

302 FULL ★★★

Additional Study Using the FRAME Method

F – Form a Plan

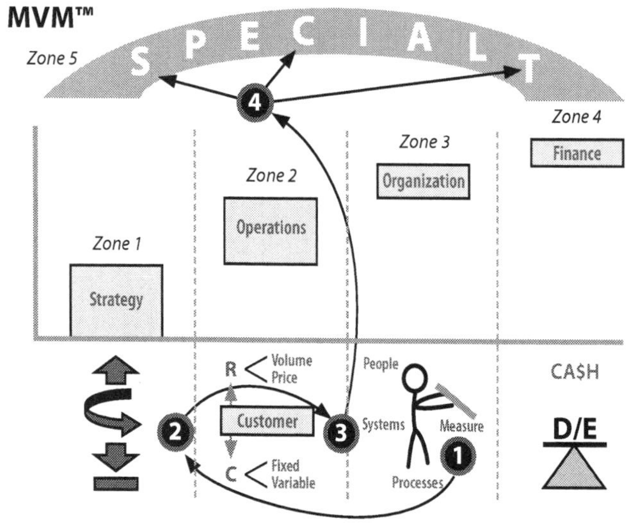

1. Start in Zone 3, Organization/Measure: Although this case is about metrics and comparing distribution sites, to solve it you must move to other parts of the MVM™.

2. Move to Zone 2, Operations/Revenue/Cost: How are the locations performing? What differences do we see in their revenue and costs?

- Volume—how fast do they turn items? Which ones turn more often?
- Price—which products offer a premium?
- Variable Costs—What are the costs of part-time delivery, stocking and administration?
- Fixed Costs—who has the better lease terms on warehousing per square foot?

3. Return to Zone 3, Organization/Processes/People: What internal functions, computer systems or personnel make one site better than another?

4. Finish in Zone 5, External Factors:

- S – Are there any special supplier relationships?
- C – Which site has the most intense competition?
- T – Are there any innovations that separate one site from another?

A - Anchor a Hypothesis

You do not need to explain your hypothesis to the interviewer, but use this mental anchor to help you structure your questions as you move through your plan. Here are some potential hunches:

People: "The quality of the people at the sites is going to be the biggest driver of value. I'll check into their experience, years of work at Blueblood and overall physical strength. I also want to know about the leader of the site."

Processes: "Doing well in distribution is all about executing processes well. I want to know what the time and steps are for all the major processes: picking, packing, loading the trucks and unloading. Office activities are worth looking at as well."

Movement: "Since distribution is about moving items inside the site and eventually to the customer, I'm going to think about all the ways I can measure product movement. In addition to processes inside our site I'll look at the actions at the customer: driving and unloading come to mind immediately."

M—Mine for the Answer

How good were your questions? Aim to ask 2–3 questions in each section you explore. Here are some suggested areas and examples.

Inventory Turns

- **What is the average inventory turn by site?**
  Products (measured by case) typically turn between 7 and 9 times per month
- **What is average for the industry?**
  Industry average for number of turns is 8
- **Which products in the warehouse turn most often and least often?**
  Table wines (retail <$10) move the fastest
  Specialty wines, rare vintages and rare hard liquors move the slowest

Delivery Costs

- **How is product delivered to the customers?**
  Delivery is by a truck driven from the warehouse to the customer site
- **What is the average delivery cost per case of product?**
  Cost per case is about $12
- **What are the key components of delivery?**
  Delivery can be broken down into packing, driving and unloading
- **Which steps in the process have the most variability in terms of cost?**
  Packing varies by skill or experience of packers
  Driving efficiency varies by driver and region

Competitor Intensity

- **How does a distribution site compete?**
  Distributors try to acquire customers through promotions, new products and better delivery schedules
- **Where are Blueblood sites typically strong?**
  Blueblood is known for its wide and deep selection of hard to find products
- **Are there national competitors or regional ones?**
  Few national competitors exist, and in all cases the regional player acts independently
- **How do competitive pressures affect our revenue? Profit?**
  Competitors play tough and consistently try to steal our market share

Blueblood Distribution
Melbourne, Australia

302 FULL ★★★

Post Case Review

Case Insights & Takeaways

A narrow set of metrics turned out to be the indicators of top performance. Two are very important to most businesses: RMS and inventory turns. Route density is a metric particular to distribution.

The chart in this case was fairly simple, but it was key to identifying the most important metrics. When reviewing handouts, look for large fluctuations in the data sets, as this variability often reveals a company's strong and weak spots.

What to Expect with Cases Like These

This case has an unusual topic (metrics) in an industry that may be unfamiliar to you (distribution). When faced with a new topic or industry, start with things that are common knowledge and common sense. For example, here it might be: trucks, warehouses, bottles that can break, heavy crates of liquids. Use these ideas as a starting point.

E - End the Case

Be firm and use data. Here's an option: "From the sample data, four metrics seem to be the most important: inventory turns, limiting the number of SKUs, route density and relative market share (RMS). Our bottom third perform much worse on these. For next steps, I would like to test the full set of metric data to measure the statistical significance. Also, I would rank the sites in detail to determine which ones we should focus on first."

My Takeaways

To build skills and improve, you must apply what you learned to future cases. Take a few moments and review the interviewer feedback and jot down some key insights about your performance in the space below.

Thinking Skills

My top 2 strengths are:

My top 2 soft spots are:

To address these problems I'll begin to:

VIDEO 3
Recap & Tips
(David Ohrvall)

My Performance During the Case

Add up your points. → Total Score: _____ /15

F Form A Plan	**R** Read My Audience	**A** Anchor a Hypothesis	**M** Mine for Answers	**E** End the Case
points	points	points	points	points
③ Structured, clean	③ Good back & forth, caught clues	③ Solid hunch, pursued clue	③ Specific questions, solid analysis	③ Used facts and data, connected the dots
② Somewhat organized and logical	② Awkward, trouble with interviewer style	② Partial direction	② Missed some questions, some math mistakes	② Some data, mostly understood connections
① Messy, overlapping ideas	① Interviewer not interested, couldn't follow	① No hypothesis at all	① Vague questions, weak math, no linkages	① No data, no passion, no connections

Blueblood Distribution

Melbourne, Australia

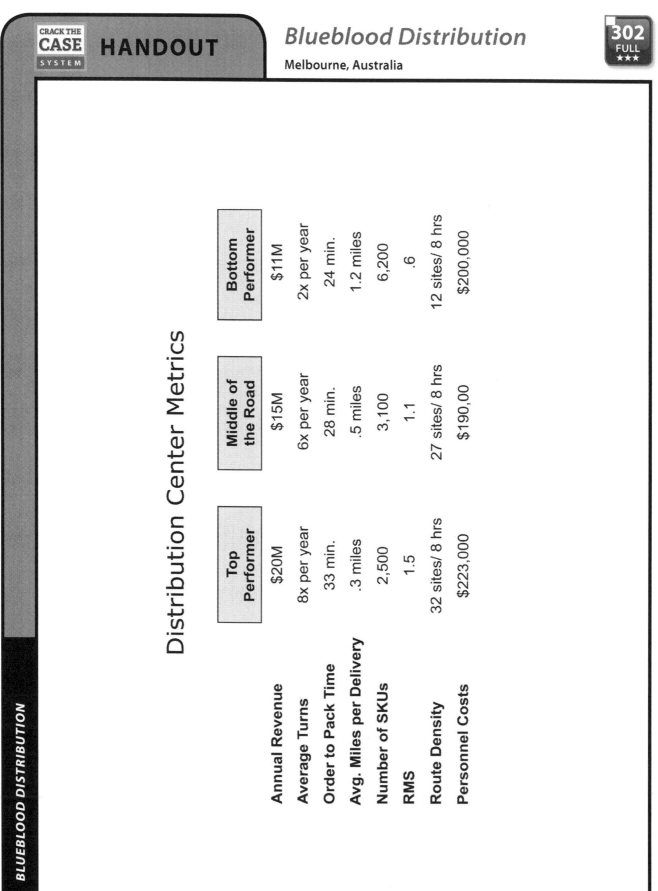

Distribution Center Metrics

	Top Performer	Middle of the Road	Bottom Performer
Annual Revenue	$20M	$15M	$11M
Average Turns	8x per year	6x per year	2x per year
Order to Pack Time	33 min.	28 min.	24 min.
Avg. Miles per Delivery	.3 miles	.5 miles	1.2 miles
Number of SKUs	2,500	3,100	6,200
RMS	1.5	1.1	.6
Route Density	32 sites/ 8 hrs	27 sites/ 8 hrs	12 sites/ 8 hrs
Personnel Costs	$223,000	$190,00	$200,000

CRACK THE CASE SYSTEM

WORKSHEET

Blueblood Distribution

Melbourne, Australia

302 FULL ★★★

BLUEBLOOD DISTRIBUTION

My Initial Plan and Output

Today's date:

2. Be original with your data

4. Leave ample room for a structure and additional notes as the case progresses

1. Zone out your paper

3. Take clean and simple notes

CRACK THE CASE SYSTEM — WORKSHEET

Blueblood Distribution
Melbourne, Australia

302 FULL ★★★

Potential Plan and Output

BLUEBLOOD DISTRIBUTION

How compare distribution sites with metrics?
Which ones are most insightful?

Revenue (price and volume)

Which products bring in the most revenue? Most profit?

What changes have we made to price over time?

What are the volume trends by product?

Costs

Which cost categories are the largest by location? Can they be reduced?

What has been the cost trend line over the last 2 years?

Internal Metrics

Inventory turns

Stocking practices

Management experience

External Metrics

Competitor actions

Supplier pricing

HUNCH: Internal operations will be much more important than the market differences.

Rev – $300M

Costs – ?

Profit – ?

No financial targets

Goal: Which metrics would be the most insightful?

Distributor of wine & spirits

Customers are wine retailers, grocery stores and food marts

22 distribution sites

Voiceover

"To best compare the different distribution sites, I first would like to understand the heart of each site's operations—how they make and spend money. Once we clarify major differences there, I would like to break down the analysis into two parts: internal metrics, like inventory turns, stocking practices and management experience; and external ones, like competitor intensity and supplier pricing. We can dive deep on the ones that are more complex or appear to drive value. To get started, can you tell me more about how these sites generate revenue?"

Additional Study: For more questions to consider, review Section 13: Roadmaps.

VIDEO 2
Plan & Structure
(Candidate)

Dona Air

Barcelona, Spain

Who will Dona invite to dance? How should they evaluate their future partners?

401 START ★★★

BARCELONA CITY FACTS

▸ 2nd largest city in Spain

▸ One of Europe's main Mediterranean ports

▸ Known for the distinctive architecture of Antoni Gaudi

TRAIN Profile

Type	**R**egion	**A**nalysis	**I**ndustry	**N**umber
1 CASE START	BARCELONA, SPAIN Population: 1.5M Currency: Euro, EU	ROADMAP 1 Merge, Acquire, Joint Venture	Airlines	LEVEL 1

Solo Practice with Video Assist

1. Find your videos
2. Set up
3. Present question
4. Recap
5. Create your plan
6. Present your plan
7. Stop and study
8. Reinforce

10 minutes

Partner Practice

1. Set up
2. Present the case question
3. Recap
4. Create your plan
5. Present your plan
6. Stop and study
7. Reinforce

401
START
★★★

Dona Air
Barcelona, Spain

Interview Guide

Case Situation & Question

Dona Airlines is one of the top three established airlines in Spain. Recent growth in the short hop, domestic flight business sparked their interest. Rather than ramp up a new division, management would like to acquire a small successful player. They are reviewing several companies but know that airline regulations will likely only allow them to acquire one.

What factors would be most important in evaluating acquisition targets?

Case Twist

The airline Dona would most like to acquire is balking at the deal. They believe that what sets them apart is their great customer service and Dona is known for its weak to poor customer service. The smaller airline doesn't want their business to shrink after the acquisition.

How would this information affect your decision?

VIDEO 1
Case Question
(Interviewer)

Feedback

Physical Skills

	Weak		Strong
Body Language	①	②	③
Verbal	①	②	③
Listening	①	②	③

Thinking Skills

Hypothesis Generation	①	②	③
Initial Plan & Output	①	②	③
Data Gathering	①	②	③
Basic Business Intuition	①	②	③

Total Score _____ / 21

Case Start Self Study Reminders

Present Question	Recap & Ask for a Minute	Create Your Plan	Present Plan	Stop & Study	Reinforce
Read the question out loud like an interviewer or watch the MBACASE video interviewer.	Briefly recap the situation, the complication, and your task. Speak out loud just like you would in an interview.	Using the paper below, fill in the sections.	Turn your plan toward the interviewer (or mirror or webcam) and present it piece by piece .	Review the roadmaps and the Post Case Review page to see what you missed. Mark up your plan to make it better.	Do the start again with the video interviewer, or find a live partner and get some feedback. Incorporate what you learned the first time.

CRACK THE CASE
SYSTEM

Dona Air
Barcelona, Spain

401 START ★★
★

My Initial Plan and Output

Today's date:

Questions I'm thinking about:

Topics I know to cover:

Profit Tree Approach:

Topic Bucket Approach:

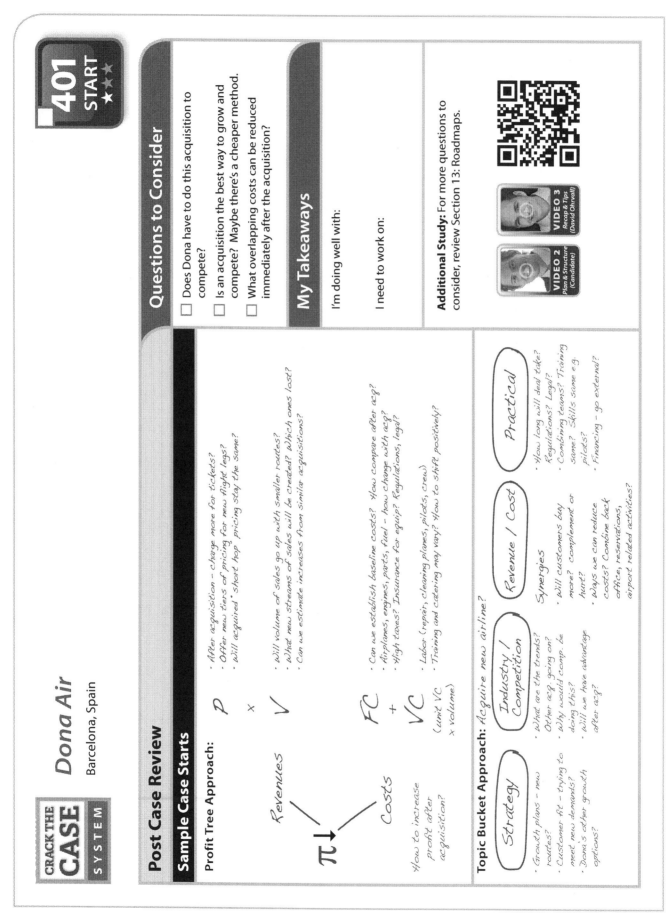

CRACK THE CASE SYSTEM

401 START ★★★

Dona Air
Barcelona, Spain

Post Case Review

Sample Case Starts

Profit Tree Approach:

$$\pi \rightarrow \begin{cases} Revenues \\ Costs \end{cases}$$

$$Revenues = \begin{cases} P \\ \times \\ V \end{cases}$$

P
- After acquisition – charge more for tickets?
- Offer new tiers of pricing for new flight legs?
- Will acquired "short hop" pricing stay the same?

V
- Will volume of sales go up with smaller routes?
- What new streams of sales will be created? Which ones last?
- Can we estimate increases from similar acquisitions?

$$Costs = \begin{cases} FC \\ + \\ VC \end{cases}$$

FC
- Can we establish baseline costs? How compare after acg?
- Airplanes, engines, parts, fuel – how change with acg?
- High taxes? Insurance for equip? Regulations, legal?

VC
- Labor (repair, cleaning planes, pilots, crew)
- Training and catering may vary? How to shift positively?

(unit VC x volume)

How to increase profit after acquisition?

Topic Bucket Approach: Acquire new airline?

Strategy
- Growth plans – new routes?
- Customer fit – trying to meet new demands?
- Dona's other growth options?

Industry / Competition
- What are the trends?
- Other acg going on?
- Why would comp. be doing this?
- Will we have advantage after acg?

Revenue / Cost

Synergies
- Will customers buy more? complement or hurt?
- Ways we can reduce costs? Combine back office, reservations, airport related activities?

Practical
- How long will deal take?
- Regulations? Legal?
- Combining teams? Training same? Skills same e.g. pilots?
- Financing – go external?

Questions to Consider

- [ ] Does Dona have to do this acquisition to compete?
- [ ] Is an acquisition the best way to grow and compete? Maybe there's a cheaper method.
- [ ] What overlapping costs can be reduced immediately after the acquisition?

My Takeaways

I'm doing well with:

I need to work on:

Additional Study: For more questions to consider, review Section 13: Roadmaps.

VIDEO 2 Plan & Structure (Candidate)

VIDEO 3 Recap & Tips (David Ohrvall)

CRACK THE CASE SYSTEM

I ♥ JIT

402 MINI
★★★

Stockholm, Sweden

In the world of fashion, one day it's in and the next day it's out. Can JIT stay cutting edge?

STOCKHOLM CITY FACTS

▶ Stockholm, known as the "Venice of the North," is one of the world's cleanest cities due to strictly limited heavy industry

▶ 30% of the city consists of waterways; another 30% consists of parks and gardens

▶ The service industry accounts for 85% of the jobs in Stockholm

TRAIN Profile

Type	**R**egion	**A**nalysis	**I**ndustry	**N**umber
3 MINI BUSINESS	STOCKHOLM, SWEDEN Population: 829,000 Currency: Swedish Krona, SEK	ROADMAP → **12** Competitor Attack	Advertising	LEVEL **2**

Solo Practice with Video Assist

1. Find your videos
2. Set up
3. Present question
4. Recap
5. Create your plan
6. Present your plan
7. Stop and study
8. Reinforce

20 minutes

Partner Practice

1. Set up
2. Present the case question
3. Recap
4. Create your plan
5. Present your plan
6. Stop and study
7. Reinforce

I ♥ JIT

Stockholm, Sweden

402
MINI
★★★

Interview Guide

Case Situation and Question

I ♥ JIT (Just In Time) is an online shopping site focused on girls ages 18 to 25 years-old. These young women regularly purchase trendy clothes and a variety of accessories.

I ♥ JIT's appeal lies in its ability to buy high-fashion goods directly from the boutiques and fashion houses. I ♥ JIT stirs up demand by offering new goods each day at 4 P.M. A timer shows how fast each product is selling out. This approach creates addiction and daily competition among customers.

I ♥ JIT has a new online competitor with a fresh website and edgier products. I ♥ JIT wants to protect themselves by bulking up their revenue. One idea entails joining forces with a gossip blog heavily trafficked by teens. Another idea is an increase in advertising.

What should they do? What are their options?

Case Twist

Check out the Crack the Case System videos on mbacase.com or scan the Video 3 QR code on the Post Case Review page to hear a twist.

VIDEO 1
Case Question (Interviewer)

Feedback

Physical Skills

	Weak		Strong
Body Language	①	②	③
Verbal	①	②	③
Listening	①	②	③

Thinking Skills

Hypothesis Generation	①	②	③
Comfort with Ambiguity	①	②	③
Initial Plan & Output	①	②	③
Data Gathering	①	②	③
Data Analysis	①	②	③
Basic Business Intuition	①	②	③
Integration	①	②	③
2nd Level Insights	①	②	③
Creativity	①	②	③
Recommendation	①	②	③

Total Score _____ / 39

Intro Facts (Tell the Candidate if Asked)

Management's Perspective: The management team wants to develop several separate options and evaluate which one will bring in the most net profit to I Heart.

Gossip Blogger: Coco Finesse is the name and website of a famous blogger. His snarky comments keep the traffic coming. The blog attracts over 1 million visitors per month.

Customer Time on Website: I Heart boasts about 1.5M visitors per month. The average stay on the site is between 12–15 minutes per visit with 8-10 page views.

Timing: I Heart wants a new option in place within 6 months.

Key Insights (Do Not Tell the Candidate)

Developing the Options: Good candidates will: 1), come up with a title and clear definition for each option 2), think of the attributes that make that specific option special and 3), identify the data that you need to monetize the option. Typically, the data would include revenue and cost drivers and some calculations for profitability.

Small Changes Mean Big Impact: Core customers are critical to I Heart's success. Losing 10% of them with Option 2 would drastically impact profit and not be fully offset by increased advertising revenue. I Heart should be careful with loyal customers and keep their consumer base strong.

Mid-case Data (Tell Only at Appropriate Time)

After Start: After hearing the candidate's initial structure and approach, ask him to lay out the high-level options. Use the Potential Plan and Output page to ask about missing pieces or options that are unclear.

Provide All the Data: If necessary, hint at the topics that the candidate needs to ask about. The candidate will need all the data in order to accurately compare the options. Also, since this is a case heavy on logic and quick math, you want to test both skills.

I Heart JIT Profit: no information

Case Flow and Milestones

1 Present Main Question

Interviewer should read through the case and know the timing for questions, data, charts, and hints. Take on a personality (friendly, firm, or foe). Present the case question. Candidate should then begin to recap and clarify, ask for time to think, form a plan on paper, and present his plan.

2 Assess Structure

Review the Potential Plan and Output page. The answer shown is only one way to approach the problem. Using logical options is an excellent way to determine what to calculate quickly.

3 Look for Specifics

Since timing is tight (6 months), ask and listen for the candidate to be focused on the option that will pay back quickly. Ask questions about any option that does not make sense, or any missing key costs or revenue elements.

4 Guide Discussion

Test the candidate's ability to do detailed math by asking for precise profit comparisons. You will be asking questions and giving data throughout the entire section.

GIVE DATA

5 Get Recommendation

Be exacting and expect a clear recommendation and option from the candidate. Say that you must have an answer and ask for profit numbers and supporting reasons.

I ♥ JIT

Stockholm, Sweden

Interviewer's Data Guide

Step 1 – Ask the candidate for options

- Ask: "How would you describe the separate options they are facing?"
- Let the candidate talk through his approach and options. Give hints if necessary.
  The options below are necessary for analysis. Say, "I like the options you laid out. I Heart came up with similar ones. Let me explain how they defined them."

Option 1	Option 2	Option 3
Tweak & Freshen Up	Ad Plus	Blogger Force
Add features to website to compete	Look into advertising avenues	Join forces with the gossip blogger
Freshen up the image and overall look	Look for other traffic sales opps	Build joint brand
Base traffic/month in M 1.5	Base (same) 1.5	Base (same) 1.5
Increase 15%	Decrease 5%	Increase 70%

Step 2 – Ask for the estimated monthly traffic for each option

- Don't give the numbers unless the candidate is stuck. Calculation = Base traffic/month x Increase or Decrease

New Traffic 1.725	New Traffic 1.425	New Traffic 2.55

Step 3 – Ask about revenue potential

- Say, "What could be the drivers of additional revenue, if any?" Give the data below after your discussion.

Attract same type of customers	Attract same type of customers	Attract many non-buyers
Cust. gross marg. / mo. $5	Cust. gross marg. / mo. $5	Cust. gross marg. / mo. $4
	Monthly ad revenue $750,000	

Step 4 – Measure additional costs

- Say, "What could be the drivers of additional costs, if any?" The candidate will likely have a long list of ideas. Give the data below after your discussion.

Website overhaul, 1 X $500,000	Ad mgmt. per month $30,000	Annual fee to blogger 1.5M
Monthly maintenance $30,000		

Step 5 – Calculate the net margin to I Heart JIT

- Say, "Please calculate the net margin in dollars for each option." Don't give these equations (they are for your own reference):
- Annual revenue in M = traffic per month x Avg. net margin/month x 12 months
- Additional customer costs = 1 time charge + monthly charges x 12 months

Annual cust. gross marg. $113	Annual cust. gross marg. $95	Annual cust. gross marg. $107
Annual costs $860,000	Annual costs $360,000	Annual costs 1.5M
Net Over $111M	Net Over $94M	Net Over $106M

Step 6 – Ask for a final recommendation

- Ask: "What does your analysis say at this point? How does this factor into your final recommendation?" Check for clean options that use data.

CRACK THE CASE SYSTEM

I ♥ JIT

Stockholm, Sweden

402 MINI ★★★

Post Case Review

Case Insights & Takeaways

- **Protect Your Customers:** Not all customers have the same profile. A new customer may not act like a previous customer. When making changes to a company, be sure to understand the core customers and how much money they will bring.
- **Consider Stress on the Organization:** Each option has a different impact on the organization. Options 1 and 2 require little additional change. But Option 3 would have a large impact on almost everything. Always consider how changes may affect your team and their time.

Math Tips

- **Make Clean Options:** Practice structuring your options in columns and your data needs in rows. Look for common variables. Practice laying this out several times so that it will come easily in a new case with options.
- **Data Gathering:** Talk to your interviewer about how the team might gather specific data to prove an option.
- **Look for Estimates:** First make estimates for your numbers. By "ball parking" the numbers quickly, you can determine whether or not an option is going to be successful. You can also consider using ranges.

What to Expect with Cases Like These

- When you have to make a quick decision, try to lay out outcomes or options. Having a few clear "points" on which to lay your recommendation will help you sound more supported and confident.
- Break up the HDDM (Head Down Doing Math) sections by talking to the interviewer and letting him know what you are doing. Learning how to talk through the math will also help you with the phone interviews.
- Stick to your numbers! It is important that you end with crisp data to support what you believe.

My Takeaways

To build skills and improve, you must apply what you learned to future cases. Take a few moments and review the interviewer feedback and jot down some key insights about your performance in the space below.

Thinking Skills

My top 2 strengths are:

My top 2 soft spots are:

To address these problems I'll begin to:

VIDEO 3
*Recap & Tips
(David Ohrvall)*

My Performance During the Case

Add up your points. → Total Score: _____ /15

F Form A Plan	**R** Read My Audience	**A** Anchor a Hypothesis	**M** Mine for Answers	**E** End the Case
points	points	points	points	points
③ Structured, clean	③ Good back & forth, caught clues	③ Solid hunch, pursued clue	③ Specific questions, solid analysis	③ Used facts and data, connected the dots
② Somewhat organized and logical	② Awkward, trouble with interviewer style	② Partial direction	② Missed some questions, some math mistakes	② Some data, mostly understood connections
① Messy, overlapping ideas	① Interviewer not interested, couldn't follow	① No hypothesis at all	① Vague questions, weak math, no linkages	① No data, no passion, no connections

WORKSHEET

CRACK THE CASE SYSTEM

I ♥ JIT

Stockholm, Sweden

I ♥ JIT

My Initial Plan and Output

Today's date:

2. Be original with your data

1. Zone out your paper

3. Take clean and simple notes

4. Leave ample room for a structure and additional notes as the case progresses

CRACK THE CASE SYSTEM

WORKSHEET

I ♥ JIT
Stockholm, Sweden

Potential Plan and Output

I ♥ JIT

How should JIT compete?
New Comp. / better prods / better website

(Revenue)   (Costs / Investment)   (Options)

Price
- Keep low?
- Need to stay competitive
- New competitors – other actions

New website development
- What kind of changes?
- Range of costs? I time only? Upkeep?

1. Do Nothing
2. New website
3. New advertising and promotion
4. Join with blogger

- Combination of these options?

Volume
- Pump up advertising?
- Easier, more attractive website
- More variety?
- Blog partnership – but will they buy? Same people 18–25 years may be too old

- More variety = more inventory

- Blogger referrals = payments, fees?

I Heart JIT – Just In Time

online shopping site

girls 18 to 25 years-old

trendy clothes & accessories

Buy direct high fashion houses

✓ 4 p.m. – new products / timer shows

Addiction / competition (like eBay?)

New competition fresh website / edgier products

Protect & bulking up their revenue

Gossip blog / increase in advertising?

What to do? Options?"

Rev. – no data (bulk it up)

Costs – no data, may

increase with new

website

Additional Study: For more questions to consider, review Section 13: Roadmaps.

VIDEO 2 Plan & Structure (Candidate)

Blaustahl

Frankfurt, Germany

Blaustahl needs to test its mettle with an acquisition. Can you help it find one for a steal?

FRANKFURT CITY FACTS

- ▶ Germany's financial and transportation center; largest financial center in continental Europe
- ▶ Home of the European Central Bank, which sets monetary policy for the Eurozone economy
- ▶ The highest concentration of jobs and of homeowners in Germany

TRAIN Profile

Type	**R**egion	**A**nalysis	**I**ndustry	**N**umber
4 FULL BUSINESS	FRANKFURT, GERMANY Population: 667,000 Currency: Euro, EUR, €	ROADMAP →10 **Valuation**	**Metals & Mining**	LEVEL **3**

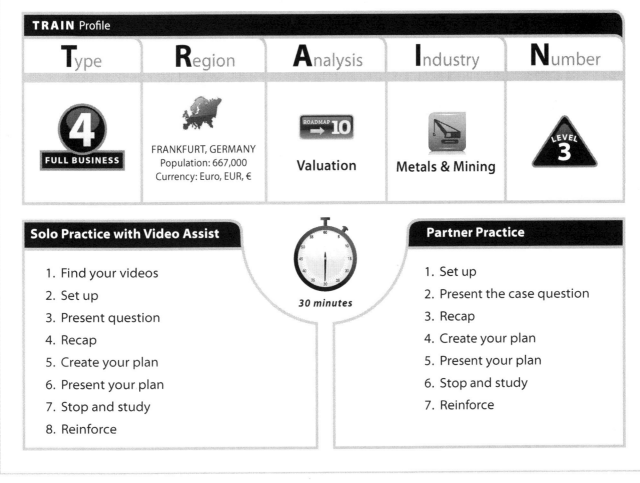

Solo Practice with Video Assist	*30 minutes*	**Partner Practice**
1. Find your videos		1. Set up
2. Set up		2. Present the case question
3. Present question		3. Recap
4. Recap		4. Create your plan
5. Create your plan		5. Present your plan
6. Present your plan		6. Stop and study
7. Stop and study		7. Reinforce
8. Reinforce		

Blaustahl

Frankfurt, Germany

403 FULL
★★★

Interview Guide

Case Situation and Question

Blaustahl is a $2B producer of rebar steel based in Frankfurt, Germany. Its primary customers are German and Baltic construction companies. Over the past five years, Blau has experienced declining profitability. Looking for strategic options, it is considering whether to acquire Tiger Steel, a $1B producer based in Pittsburgh, USA. Tiger looks attractive because it recently developed a technology for producing high-quality steel. Additionally, its customers include aircraft manufacturers and US government agencies.

Blau has asked you to determine whether or not it should acquire Tiger. Walk me through your evaluation.

Case Twist

You discover that three other US-based steel companies are close to implementing their own process technologies for making high-quality steel. Additionally, you discover that several of Tiger's clients do not plan to re-contract because Tiger's prices are much higher than the competition. How will your advice be impacted by each discovery?

VIDEO 1
*Case Question
(Interviewer)*

Feedback

Physical Skills

	Weak		Strong
Body Language	①	②	③
Verbal	①	②	③
Listening	①	②	③

Thinking Skills

Hypothesis Generation	①	②	③
Comfort with Ambiguity	①	②	③
Initial Plan & Output	①	②	③
Data Analysis	①	②	③
Basic Business Intuition	①	②	③
Integration	①	②	③
2nd Level Insights	①	②	③
Creativity	①	②	③

Total Score _____ / 33

Intro Facts (Tell the Candidate if Asked)

Organization: Blau and Tiger are both public companies. Assume US accounting standards.

Financing: Blau is financed 50% with equity and 50% with debt. Tiger is 100% equity.

Customer contracts: Tiger's customers renegotiate contracts every 4 years. Blau's customers renegotiate contracts every year.

Customer loyalty: Blau has retained 80% of its customers the last 5 years; Tiger, 100%.

Customer requirements: Tiger's government clients do not need to source only from US suppliers.

Products: Blau produces low- and medium-grade steel for construction. Tiger makes high-quality steel for aircraft and NASA, even without the new technology.

Competitors: Blau faces two similar-sized European competitors, both of whom also suffer from declining profits.

Market: The market for steel among German and Baltic construction companies is fairly strong, but not enough to keep prices stable. The market among US aircraft manufacturers and government is stable.

Key Insights (Do Not Tell the Candidate)

Quality: Tiger's customers want higher-quality steel but Blau's customers do not need it.

Technology: Blau can use Tiger's new technology in its own processes, but it may take up to three years to implement given the differences in their equipment.

Contracts: Several of Tiger's customers have begun to solicit Tiger's competitors for price proposals.

Mid-case Data (Tell Only at Appropriate Time)

Give handout: After hearing the candidate's initial rationale and questions, ask the candidate to review Handout A.

Expect a precise answer: Ensure candidate uses current price, comps, precedent transactions, and DCF approaches (candidate will need to calculate free cash flow). If necessary, ask for the math. Follow how his logic fits with your data sheet.

Give clue: To calculate DCF, the candidate will need to estimate a growth rate and a discount rate. Ask how he will estimate these rates using existing info. If he calculates WACC, ensure he derives K_b and K_E. K_E comes from the CAPM, so ensure he walks through how to estimate β, r_f, and r_m. (See any finance textbook for a list of definitions.)

Blaustahl

Frankfurt, Germany

Case Flow and Milestones

1 Present Main Question

Interviewer should read through the case and know the timing for questions, data, and hints. Take on a personality (friendly, firm, or foe). Present the case question. Candidate will then likely recap and clarify, ask for time to think, form a plan on paper, and present his plan.

2 Assess Structure

Candidate should discuss why Blau wants to acquire Tiger and how that would affect its profitability. If the candidate jumps right into valuation, push back. Ask, "First, help me understand why Blau wants Tiger," and look for his reasoning. When discussing valuation, he should have a precise answer (see Mid-Case Data).

GIVE HANDOUT A

3 Look for Specifics

Acquisition will involve a revenue synergy, from obtaining new customers and intellectual property for steelmaking; it will also involve a cost synergy, from obtaining redundant operations. These assets together will drive growth in profits and cash flow.

4 Guide Discussion

Give Handout B and follow the steps from Mid-Case Data and Handout & Data Timing. After the candidate performs the valuations, ask for the logic around the growth and discount rates he chooses. If necessary, ask, "What methods should Blau use to find that multiple?" If the candidate asks for comps, provide Handout C.

GIVE HANDOUTS B & C

5 Get Recommendation

A good recommendation should explain why Blau would acquire Tiger, and then support or reject that view using comparables analysis and DCF. The candidate should note that Tiger's DCF multiple is far higher than other multiples, suggesting that Tiger is undervalued from Blau's perspective. He might also suggest that Blau has an over-optimistic view of Tiger's prospects.

Handout and Data Guide

Handout A:

Give when candidate asks for financial information.

Handout B:

Give when candidate specifically asks for cash flow information.

Handout C:

Give when candidate asks for ratios or comparables.

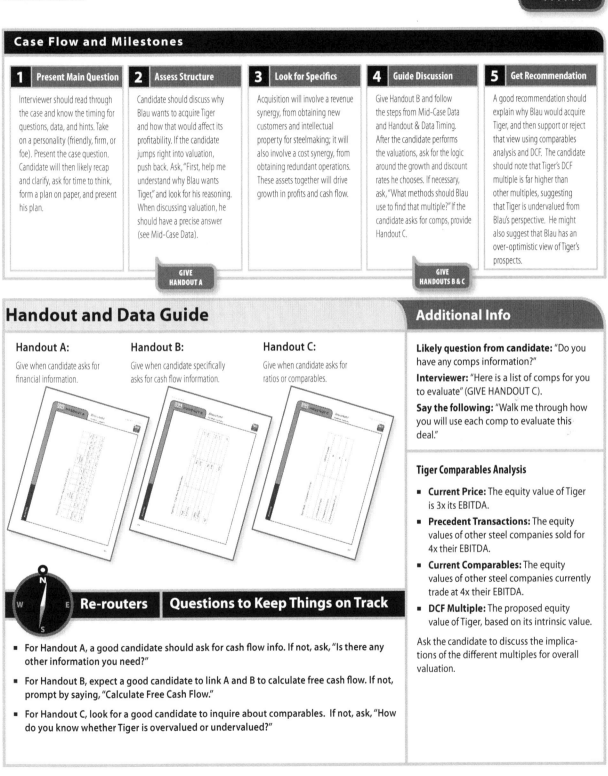

Additional Info

Likely question from candidate: "Do you have any comps information?"

Interviewer: "Here is a list of comps for you to evaluate" (GIVE HANDOUT C).

Say the following: "Walk me through how you will use each comp to evaluate this deal."

Tiger Comparables Analysis

- **Current Price:** The equity value of Tiger is 3x its EBITDA.
- **Precedent Transactions:** The equity values of other steel companies sold for 4x their EBITDA.
- **Current Comparables:** The equity values of other steel companies currently trade at 4x their EBITDA.
- **DCF Multiple:** The proposed equity value of Tiger, based on its intrinsic value.

Ask the candidate to discuss the implications of the different multiples for overall valuation.

Re-routers | Questions to Keep Things on Track

- For Handout A, a good candidate should ask for cash flow info. If not, ask, "Is there any other information you need?"
- For Handout B, expect a good candidate to link A and B to calculate free cash flow. If not, prompt by saying, "Calculate Free Cash Flow."
- For Handout C, look for a good candidate to inquire about comparables. If not, ask, "How do you know whether Tiger is overvalued or undervalued?"

Blaustahl

Frankfurt, Germany

403 FULL ★★★

Post Case Review

Case Insights & Takeaways

Your valuation should show Tiger with multiples for unproven technology (precedent transactions, trading comps) and proven technology (DCF).

The government contracts allow you to show your creativity as you discuss the benefits and costs of having them in the deal.

You should determine if the deal makes sense based on whether it is accretive or dilutive to earnings.

Math Tips

- Know how to calculate Free Cash Flow.
- Calculate your comps quickly so you can address the broader issues in valuation.
- Use "math lite" techniques to calculate terminal value in your head or on paper. In this example, the Perpetuity Growth Method fits the data available.

$$\text{Terminal Value} = \frac{FCF_n \times (1 + g)}{(r - g)}$$

What to Expect with Cases Like These

- Understand which assets in the company drive cash flow and profitability. They will appear indirectly through comps, but you can demonstrate them through a DCF.
- Understand why an acquirer wants to buy those key assets. What can it do with them to increase performance?
- Remember, understanding valuation is important, but *framing* valuation in the context of company strategy will help you structure your thought process and presentation.

My Takeaways

To build skills and improve, you must apply what you learned to future cases. Take a few moments and review the interviewer feedback and jot down some key insights about your performance in the space below.

Thinking Skills

My top 2 strengths are:

My top 2 soft spots are:

To address these problems I'll begin to:

VIDEO 3
Recap & Tips
(David Ohrvall)

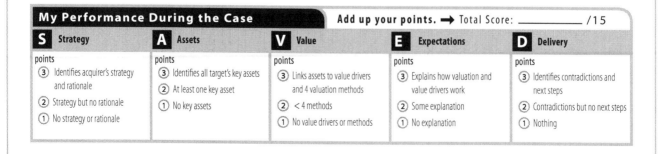

My Performance During the Case

Add up your points. → Total Score: _____ /15

S Strategy	**A** Assets	**V** Value	**E** Expectations	**D** Delivery
points	points	points	points	points
③ Identifies acquirer's strategy and rationale	③ Identifies all target's key assets	③ Links assets to value drivers and 4 valuation methods	③ Explains how valuation and value drivers work	③ Identifies contradictions and next steps
② Strategy but no rationale	② At least one key asset	② < 4 methods	② Some explanation	② Contradictions but no next steps
① No strategy or rationale	① No key assets	① No value drivers or methods	① No explanation	① Nothing

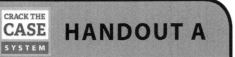

HANDOUT A

Blaustahl
Frankfurt, Germany

403 FULL ★★★

BLAUSTAHL

Blaustahl, Tiger Steel - Partial Financial Snapshot

Company	LTM Financial Statistics						LTM Profitability Margins				
	Sales	Gross Profit	EBITDA	EBIT	EBT	Net Income	Gross Profit	EBITDA	EBIT	EBT	Net Income
Blau	5,000	750	375	225	125	75	15.0%	7.5%	4.5%	2.5%	1.5%
Tiger	1,000	200	100	70	70	42	20.0%	10.0%	7.0%	7.0%	4.2%

Blaustahl

Frankfurt, Germany

BLAUSTAHL

Tiger Steel – Cash Flow Statement Data

	CY	LY
D&A	30.0	27.8
% of Sales	3.0%	3.0%
Cap Ex	30.0	30.0
% of Sales	3.0%	3.2%
WC	40.0	30

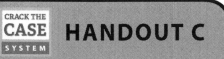

HANDOUT C

Blaustahl
Frankfurt, Germany

Tiger Steel – Comparables Analysis

	EBITDA multiple
Current price of Tiger	3x
Precedent transactions	4x
Current comparables of Tiger	4x

WORKSHEET

CRACK THE CASE SYSTEM

Blaustahl

Frankfurt, Germany

403 FULL ★★★

BLAUSTAHL

My Initial Plan and Output

Today's date:

2. Be original with your data

4. Leave ample room for a structure and additional notes as the case progresses

1. Zone out your paper

3. Take clean and simple notes

WORKSHEET

CRACK THE CASE SYSTEM

Blaustahl
Frankfurt, Germany

403 FULL ★★★

Potential Plan and Output

BLAUSTAHL

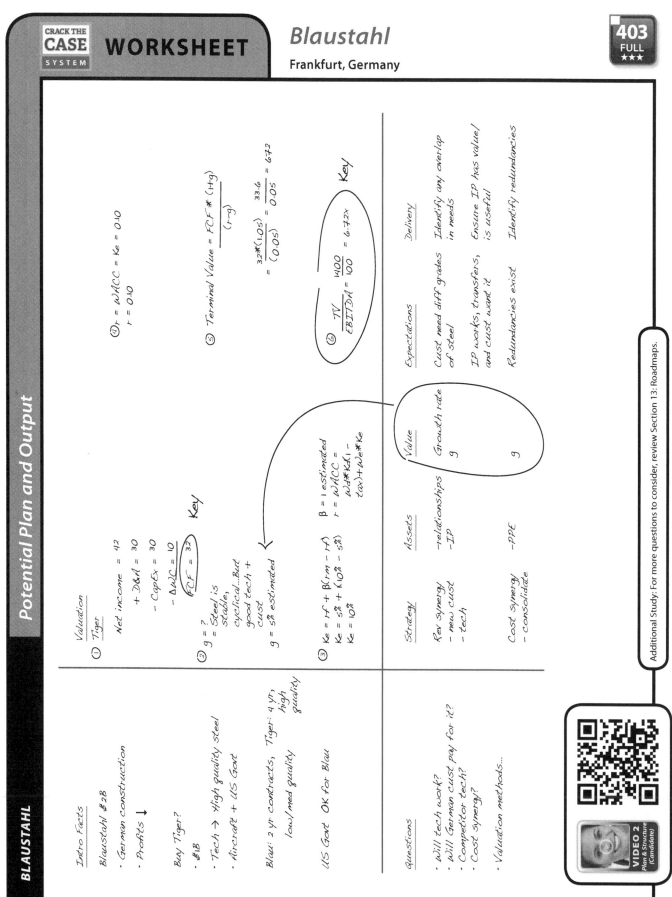

Intro Facts

Blaustahl #2B
- German construction
- Profits ↑

Buy Tiger?
- $1B
- Tech → High quality steel
- Aircraft + US Govt

Blau: 2 yr contracts, Tiger: 4 yr, high quality
low/med quality

US Govt OK for Blau

Valuation

① _Tiger_

Net income = 42
+ D&A = 30
- CapEx = 30
- ΔNWC = 10
FCF = 32   Key

② g = ?
= Steel is stable, cyclical...But good tech + cust
g = 5% estimated

③ ke = rf + β(rm - rf)   β = 1 estimated
ke = 5% + 1(10% - 5%)   r = WACC = wd*kd(1-tax)+we*ke
ke = 10%

④ r = WACC = ke = 0.10
r = 0.10

⑤ Terminal Value = $\frac{FCF*(1+g)}{(r-g)}$

= $\frac{32*(1.05)}{(0.05)}$ = $\frac{33.6}{0.05}$ = 672

⑥ $\frac{TV}{EBITDA}$ = $\frac{400}{100}$ = 6.72x   Key

Questions
- Will tech work?
- Will German cust pay for it?
- Competitor tech?
- Cost synergy?
- Valuation methods...

Strategy	_Assets_	_Value_	_Expectations_	_Delivery_
Rev Synergy - new cust - tech	-relationships -IP	Growth rate g	Cust need diff grades of steel	Identify any overlap in needs
Cost synergy - consolidate	-PPE	g	IP works, transfers, and cust want it	Ensure IP has value/ is useful
			Redundancies exist	Identify redundancies

Additional Study: For more questions to consider, review Section 13: Roadmaps.

VIDEO 2 Plan & Structure (Candidate)

CRACK THE CASE SYSTEM

Noble Line Travel

London, England

"Travel the World like Royalty" has been Noble Line's motto for the last ten years. But will the harsh realities of terrorism, video conferencing, and corporate budget cuts finally catch up with their grandiose ways?

404 FULL ★★★

LONDON CITY FACTS

▸ London Heathrow is the world's busiest airport

▸ The Tower of London, built by William the Conqueror in 1078, is the oldest building used by the British Government

▸ Over 1B journeys a year are made on the underground railway system, which is known as the Tube

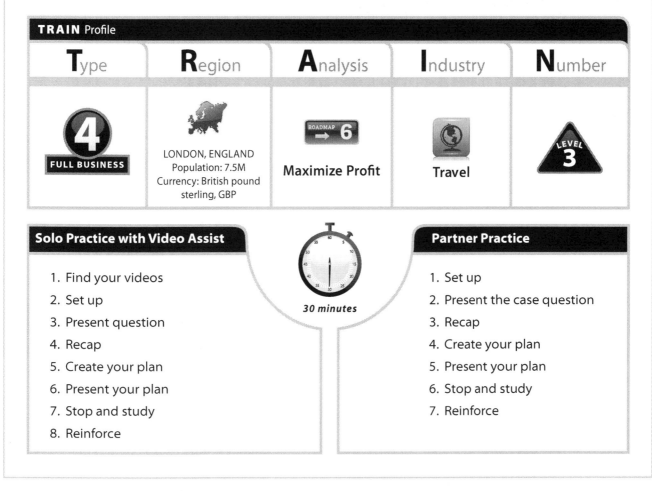

TRAIN Profile

Type	**R**egion	**A**nalysis	**I**ndustry	**N**umber
4 FULL BUSINESS	LONDON, ENGLAND Population: 7.5M Currency: British pound sterling, GBP	ROADMAP → **6** Maximize Profit	Travel	LEVEL **3**

Solo Practice with Video Assist

1. Find your videos
2. Set up
3. Present question
4. Recap
5. Create your plan
6. Present your plan
7. Stop and study
8. Reinforce

30 minutes

Partner Practice

1. Set up
2. Present the case question
3. Recap
4. Create your plan
5. Present your plan
6. Stop and study
7. Reinforce

Noble Line Travel

London, England

404 FULL ★★☆

Interview Guide

Case Situation and Question

Noble Line Travel (NLT) is one of the largest travel agencies in Europe. They recently purchased a well-known US travel agency that focuses on business travel; they do not book any leisure travel. They call it NLT-US. NLT-US's customer base comprises medium to large companies, whom they serve with both on-site agents and a call center. NLT-US is facing declining profits due to the general reduction in business travel. There is also a rumor that airlines may reduce or eliminate the commission they pay travel agencies.

How can NLT increase it's profits?

Case Twist

- If the investors came back and said they needed $750M rather than $500M, would you change your answer? What would you do differently?
- Imagine that commissions don't exist. Instead, for each ticket sold NLT-US gets a flat management fee (bottom row of data, Handout B). How would your answer change?

VIDEO 1
Case Question
(Interviewer)

Feedback

Physical Skills

	Weak		Strong
Body Language	①	②	③
Verbal	①	②	③
Listening	①	②	③

Thinking Skills

Hypothesis Generation	①	②	③
Comfort with Ambiguity	①	②	③
Initial Plan & Output	①	②	③
Data Analysis	①	②	③
Basic Business Intuition	①	②	③
Integration	①	②	③
2nd Level Insights	①	②	③
Creativity	①	②	③

Total Score _____ / 33

Intro Facts (Tell the Candidate if Asked)

Major assumption: Airlines still pay commissions regardless of today's current practices. Otherwise all other current trends in travel are applicable.

Commission rate: Stress that these rates are set by country of origin for all flights. They vary by country. The US rate is 10%.

Leisure travel business: Management does not want to pursue this option.

Service line: Basic airplane reservations are about 90% of NLT-US's business.

Locations: Over 500 agents in "travel departments" of customers; 3 call centers (East, Midwest, West).

Financial targets: Management needs to know whether NLT-US can survive profitably in this industry.

Suppliers: Airlines supply the travel routes and pay a commission on each ticket sold.

Government/ Legislation: No barriers or legislation at this time.

Key Insights (Do Not Tell the Candidate)

General Tips: A simple revenue and cost structure will suffice. Don't get caught up over-analyzing the cost data (Handout C) as it has little impact on the bottom line.

Revenue calculation: Revenue = Ticket Volume x Price x Commission Rate (the portion of the ticket price NLT-US receives). Lines 4 & 5 on Handout B should only be used if you ask the Case Twist.

Revenue drivers: Commission and ticket price have a big impact on overall revenue. Commission varies by country. Many European countries have commissions over 10%. Long distance tickets are usually more per unit when compared to domestic.

Competitors: Some are out-performing NLT-US due to more international travel.

Costs: Few variables you can push on to make a difference. Ticket price increase is the most critical action to take.

Profit: Competitors are making more profit. Refocusing on long haul and international flights is the solution if NLT-US wants to increase profit.

Mid-case Data (Tell Only at Appropriate Time)

Before you begin discussing costs (details in Handout C), ask the Candidate about what type of costs a travel company might have. Here are some examples:

People: The highest portion of costs. Most of the work is administrative.

Systems: Most travel companies use reservation systems that require maintenance fees and an initial purchase fee.

Office rental: Space is required for the hubs. Locations at a client site usually have no fee.

Sales and service: Sales people meet with corporate clients. Service would be handled by the reservation people.

Back-office: Typical support functions like HR, IT, and admin personnel.

Noble Line Travel
London, England

Case Flow and Milestones

1 Give Handout	**2** Answer Any Basics	**3** Ask for Clarification	**4** Guide Discussion	**5** Get a Recommendation
Say that NLT-US is a recently acquired, business (not leisure) travel company and give Handout A. Mention that NLT in all handouts refers to the NLT-US entity.	Questions may come up after the candidate reviews Handout A. Review the Intro Facts to know what to say.	Be sure to make him explain anything you do not fully understand. Look for solid logic on how this plan will drive data, root causes and eventually answers to your questions.	There are several handouts, and the case flows better if they are given in order. See the Mid-Case Data section.	Since it is clear that some companies are making significant profit, and the drivers of that profit are the higher commission rate and average ticket price, NLT-US should consider refocusing its marketing.

Handout and Data Guide

Handout A:

Give this handout at the beginning of the case.

Candidate: What about the other two divisions, or, when will commissions be cut?

Interviewer: Ignore those divisions for now. Commissions will not be cut for now.

Insight: This is a profit maximization case, so stay focused on revenue and costs.

Handout B:

Candidate: Do you have any sales information?

Interviewer: Here's sales information by competitor.

You Must Say: Calculate revenue for me. Please only use the top 3 lines. What's driving the revenue for Excursions? How about the others?

Insight: No single driver, but the key elements are price and volume.

Handout C: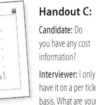

Candidate: Do you have any cost information?

Interviewer: I only have it on a per ticket basis. What are your thoughts here?

You Must Ask: Which costs seem to have the most impact? Who is leading in terms of cost control or economies of scale?

Insight: Spread between lowest cost per ticket and highest is $4. A $40 ticket price increase at 10% achieves the same profit increase for less effort.

Handout D:

Candidate: Do we know anything about the market focus of each company?

Interviewer: Here's some qualitative info a consultant put together quickly. What can you infer about each player?

Insight: Regional players make less money. Companies that book international flights are getting higher commission rates. Flights originating from certain countries must pay more than the US rate of 10%.

Re-routers | Questions to Keep Things on Track

- **How do you think a travel agency makes money?**
  - Small commissions for each transaction
  - Additional commissions for services like booking hotels, cars, business meetings, conventions and side trips

- **What do you think would be in the indirect labor category?**
  - Any labor that is not a ticket agent (e.g. corporate support functions like marketing and IT and agent supervisors).

- **What can you infer about the total costs per ticket when you look at all of the competitors?**
  - Either cost cutting is over and most of the firms are lean, or all of the firms have high costs and additional cost savings are available.

- **If you and your team could focus on improving only one area—revenue or cost reduction—what would you do and why?**
  - Choose revenue, because it is easier and has more upside. Even with major, difficult cost reductions, savings would most likely be small.

Noble Line Travel

London, England

404 FULL ★★★

Additional Study Using the FRAME Method

F – Form a Plan

MVM™

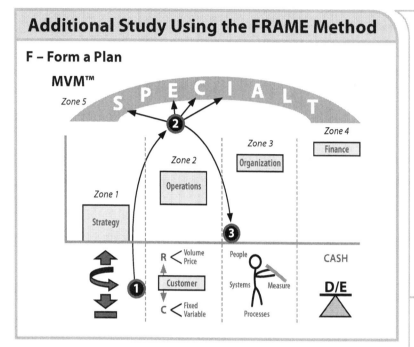

1. **Start in Zone 2, Operations:** Break profit into revenue and costs. Determine which one will be the biggest driver of increased profit (the main question of the case).

2. **Move to Zone 5, External Factors:** TConsider how NLT can increase profit:
   - Competitors – What is their overall margin? Are they succeeding? How?
   - Suppliers – What are the airlines' plans for the near future and the long-term?
   - Industry – What other barriers exist in this industry? What about in foreign countries?
   - Economy – What additional barriers may exist due to slow economic times?

3. **Finish in Zone 3 with People:** Can NLT provide the kind of leadership and manpower necessary to carry out new initiatives?

A – Anchor a Hypothesis

A hypothesis structure can be helpful, even in a case where you think you need to see the data first. By anticipating one or two issues a company may have, you give yourself a focus for your questions; you have "turned your mind on" and readied it for the data. The data may give you a different answer than expected, but that is the beauty of a hypothesis: the data will prove it or disprove it.

Scale is the Issue

"Since NLT is fifth in terms of revenue, they are probably missing out on some scale advantages that larger organizations have."

Costs

"Costs may be out of control, which could be hampering bottom line profit."

Revenue by Segment

"These companies probably differentiate themselves by going after different segments. I want to make sure we are going after the most profitable corporate clients."

E – End the Case

"'Noble Line Travel can increase its profit by focusing on revenue rather than cost reduction, since costs are already in line with competitors'. To increase revenue, international bookings will drive increases in our commission rate and our average ticket price. A 20% increase in revenue will result in $15M being added to the bottom line. I recommend that we quickly look into what clients we need to pursue to increase our number of international bookings."

M—Mine for the Answer

What kind of questions did you ask? Usually it takes 2–3 questions per topic to uncover what is really happening. See how many you asked during the case.

Revenue & Costs	Specific Markets	Entering New Space
■ **What is the revenue of each company? Who is making more money?** *Calculate revenue by taking transactions x average ticket price x commission rate.* ■ **Which variable is the biggest driver?** *No one variable is dominant.* ■ **Who has higher costs per ticket?** *Excursions (highest commission rate) and Destinations (highest volume) are leading.* ■ **Who has benefited from scale? Should we focus on cost reductions?** *Cost reduction provides little profit leverage compared to revenue.*	■ **How are some companies earning more revenue than others? What are the various niches?** *Handout D shows that companies who focus on international travel tend to do better.* ■ **Which niche seems to be offering the most revenue? Are there correlating increases in cost with these markets?** *Regional transportation keeps the average ticket price low and the commission rate at 10% (US rate).*	■ **What are the barriers to entering a new space?** *Doing more international bookings will require us to have more of a presence in several foreign locations.* ■ **Is NLT suited to play in that space? What challenges will we face?** *Many of these regions may be tough to enter, and increasing our brand awareness may be difficult.* ■ **What would it take to get our organization ready?** *Internally, we need people with international experience to market us.*

Noble Line Travel

London, England

404
FULL
★★★

Post Case Review

Case Insights & Takeaways

- NLT-US is focused mainly on short-haul, US based flights. They rarely sell domestic flights.
- Given that longer flights command larger dollars and non-US flights may be at a higher commission rate, NLT-US may be missing out on a growth opportunity. They should consider booking more international flights.
- NLT-US seems to have gotten their costs in line with the other companies. A 10% reduction would only result in $4.1 per ticket.
- NLT-US should align resources behind revenue changes, as a small price change results in a greater impact than cost reductions.

Math & Logic Tips

- With multiple slides and numbers, your goal should be to standardize the *scale and comparison metrics* as quickly as possible.
- Handout C introduced the cost per ticket metric which should have been a clue to switch to that approach for all remaining math. When you compare revenue and cost on a per ticket basis, the math is much easier.
- Always do a quick check on which drivers will make the most impact. In this situation, revenue changes seem like an easier approach and provide more upside than making cost reductions.

How It Ties Together

- With multiple slides, remember that the interviewer is looking for you to *integrate* the findings. In this case you needed Handouts B and C to calculate profitability. Handout A provided direction and Handout D should have confirmed your recommendations.
- After you understand how the slides connect then consider digging deeper for additional insights. If there are additional pieces of information that you are not using, ask about them after you have developed your base answer.

My Takeaways

To build skills and improve, you must apply what you learned to future cases. Take a few moments and review the interviewer feedback and jot down some key insights about your performance in the space below.

Thinking Skills

My top 2 strengths are:

My top 2 soft spots are:

To address these problems I'll begin to:

VIDEO 3
Recap & Tips
(David Ohrvall)

My Performance During the Case

Add up your points. ➡ Total Score: _____ /15

F Form A Plan	**R** Read My Audience	**A** Anchor a Hypothesis	**M** Mine for Answers	**E** End the Case
points	points	points	points	points
③ Structured, clean	③ Good back & forth, caught clues	③ Solid hunch, pursued clue	③ Specific questions, solid analysis	③ Used facts and data, connected the dots
② Somewhat organized and logical	② Awkward, trouble with interviewer style	② Partial direction	② Missed some questions, some math mistakes	② Some data, mostly understood connections
① Messy, overlapping ideas	① Interviewer not interested, couldn't follow	① No hypothesis at all	① Vague questions, weak math, no linkages	① No data, no passion, no connections

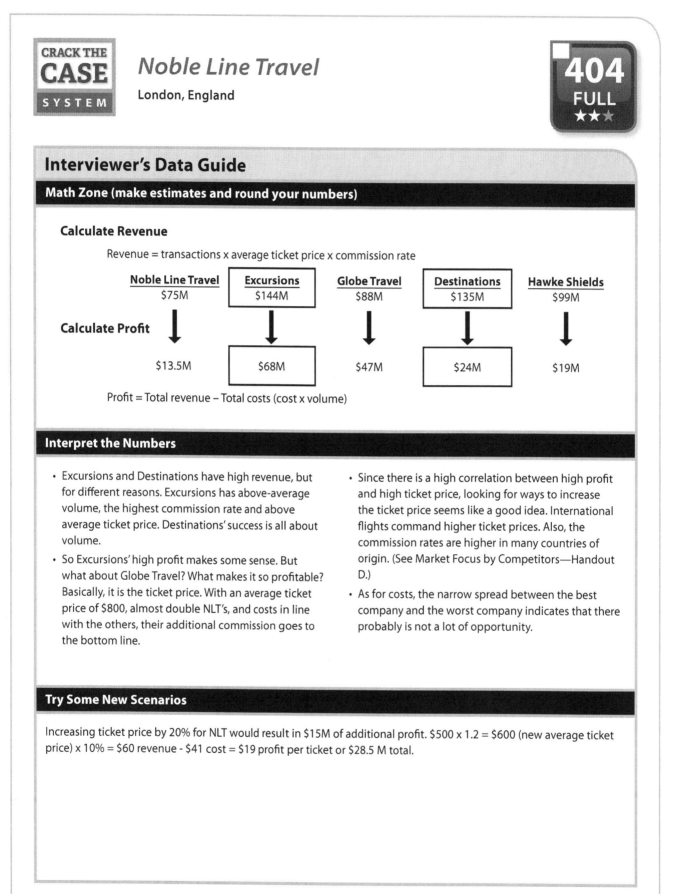

CRACK THE CASE SYSTEM

Noble Line Travel
London, England

404 FULL ★★☆

Interviewer's Data Guide

Math Zone (make estimates and round your numbers)

Calculate Revenue

Revenue = transactions x average ticket price x commission rate

Noble Line Travel	Excursions	Globe Travel	Destinations	Hawke Shields
$75M	$144M	$88M	$135M	$99M

Calculate Profit

$13.5M	$68M	$47M	$24M	$19M

Profit = Total revenue – Total costs (cost x volume)

Interpret the Numbers

- Excursions and Destinations have high revenue, but for different reasons. Excursions has above-average volume, the highest commission rate and above average ticket price. Destinations' success is all about volume.

- So Excursions' high profit makes some sense. But what about Globe Travel? What makes it so profitable? Basically, it is the ticket price. With an average ticket price of $800, almost double NLT's, and costs in line with the others, their additional commission goes to the bottom line.

- Since there is a high correlation between high profit and high ticket price, looking for ways to increase the ticket price seems like a good idea. International flights command higher ticket prices. Also, the commission rates are higher in many countries of origin. (See Market Focus by Competitors—Handout D.)

- As for costs, the narrow spread between the best company and the worst company indicates that there probably is not a lot of opportunity.

Try Some New Scenarios

Increasing ticket price by 20% for NLT would result in $15M of additional profit. $500 x 1.2 = $600 (new average ticket price) x 10% = $60 revenue - $41 cost = $19 profit per ticket or $28.5 M total.

HANDOUT A

Noble Line Travel
London, England

NOBLE LINE TRAVEL

Overview

- Noble Line Travel is a travel agency with three divisions: corporate travel and two others

- Corporate travel agencies have two types of sites: offices at their customers (e.g. IBM travel department) and reservation sites throughout the world

- Noble Line is ranked fifth in terms of revenues but they do not know how their profits compare to their competitors

- Several employees have discussed starting a union, but only in certain regions

- Customers like Noble Line's quality and service but perceive them to be expensive

- Airlines are considering eliminating the commission structure on ticket sales, a trend that makes Noble Line uncertain about its future

How can Noble Line Travel increase profitability in this changing industry?

HANDOUT B

Noble Line Travel
London, England

404 FULL ★★★

Sales by Competitor

	Noble Line Travel	Excursions	Globe Travel	Destinations	Hawke Shields
Transactions Per Year	1.5 MM	2MM	1MM	3MM	2MM
Average Ticket Price	$500	$600	$800	$450	$550
Commissions Per Ticket	10%	12%	11%	10%	9%
Override / Fee Per Ticket	1MM/$5	1.9MM/$7	900K/$5	3.5MM/$6	1.8MM/$5
Management Fee	$55	$43	$45	$48	$50

Noble Line Travel
London, England

Costs per Ticket

	Noble Line Travel	Excursions	Globe Travel	Destinations	Hawke Shields
Non-Labor	$41	$38	$41	$37	$40
	Indirect Labor	Indirect Labor	Indirect Labor	Indirect Labor	Indirect Labor
	Ticket Agents	Ticket Agents	Ticket Agents	Ticket Agents	Ticket Agents

Market Focus and Image by Competitors

	Noble Line Travel	Excursions	Globe Travel	Destinations	Hawke Shields
Regional, short flights	Yes	No	No	Yes	Yes
National Domestic	Yes	Yes	Yes	Yes	Yes
International	Rarely	Yes	Yes	Rarely	Rarely
Public Perception	High Priced	Sophisticated, experienced	International expert	Quick service	Mid-priced
Industry Inside Perspective	Good with service, technically behind	Premium player with great client list	Leader in global alliances	Gets the job done, no frills	Average on all dimensions

CRACK THE CASE SYSTEM

WORKSHEET

Noble Line Travel
London, England

404 FULL ★★☆

NOBLE LINE TRAVEL

My Initial Plan and Output

Today's date:

2. Be original with your data

1. Zone out your paper

3. Take clean and simple notes

4. Leave ample room for a structure and additional notes as the case progresses

WORKSHEET

Noble Line Travel
London, England

Potential Plan and Output

How can NLT increase profit?

Price | Volume | Fixed Costs | Variable Costs

Price
Can we increase price / commission / how do we charge?

Are there customer segments that pay more?

Where have we not taken price increases recently?

Volume
Which segments drive our volume? Have they shrunk?

Which segments are growing the fastest?

Are there segments we need to enter? Do they need products?

Fixed Costs
What are the basic fixed costs? Computers, office space, fees for travel systems, office machines

HUNCH: prices cannot be changed due to competition. Fixed and variable costs are out of control.

Variable Costs
Personnel, paper, tickets, brochures, marketing materials

NOBLE LINE TRAVEL

Rev. – no data, 5th overall

Costs – ?

Profit Margin – unknown, don't know competitor profit

Goal: how increase profit?

NLT–US, just bought, 3 divisions

Unionizing the workers?

Quality and service high

Customers think they are expensive

Commission structure may disappear

Voiceover

"Since Noble Line Travel wants to increase profit, I want to review both revenue and costs to determine which one will give us the most bottom-line impact. Looking first at volume and price, I'd like to explore what price points we offer today and whether they are competitive. As for volume, we should understand which customer and product segments are the most important now and going forward. On the cost side, we'll need to see what can be done feasibly to reduce our fixed costs in perhaps leased spaced or travel computer systems. Variable costs will likely be linked to what we pay for personnel and marketing. I would like to begin with any revenue data you have, unless you would prefer that we discuss another area first."

Additional Study: For more questions to consider, review Section 13: Roadmaps.

VIDEO 2 Plan & Structure (Candidate)

Ricci Carta

Rome, Italy

Will cheap paper threaten the livelihood of 5th generation
Italian artistry? How can you craft a strategy?

405
START
★ ★ ★

ROME CITY FACTS

▸ Economy is
dominated by
services and high
tech with little
heavy industry

▸ Rome's "talking
statues" serve as
soapboxes, where
people post their
political views with
placards or graffiti
directly on the
statues

▸ Famous for its seven
hills east of the river
Tiber

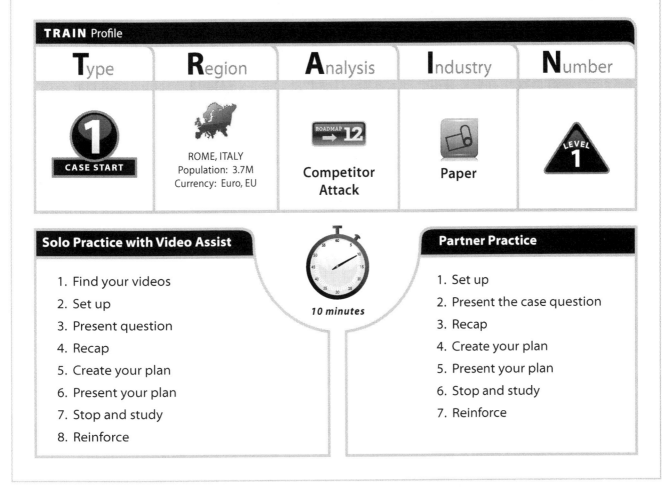

TRAIN Profile

Type	**R**egion	**A**nalysis	**I**ndustry	**N**umber
1 CASE START	ROME, ITALY Population: 3.7M Currency: Euro, EU	ROADMAP ➔ **12** Competitor Attack	Paper	LEVEL 1

Solo Practice with Video Assist

1. Find your videos
2. Set up
3. Present question
4. Recap
5. Create your plan
6. Present your plan
7. Stop and study
8. Reinforce

10 minutes

Partner Practice

1. Set up
2. Present the case question
3. Recap
4. Create your plan
5. Present your plan
6. Stop and study
7. Reinforce

405 START ★★★
★★
★

Ricci Carta
Rome, Italy

Interview Guide

Case Situation & Question

Ricci Carta is a 5th generation, custom artisan paper manufacturing facility. They supply all of Italy as well as parts of Europe with sophisticated grades of writing and artisan papers. Through custom dying, acid application and other proprietary techniques, they have been established as the market leader for over 130 years. Recent Taiwanese and Chinese entrants are now threatening their business.

How would you help them?

Case Twist

In addition to competitor quality being about 90% as good as the typical Ricci product, competitor prices are now 20% less.

How would this data affect your approach?

Feedback

Physical Skills

	Weak		Strong
Body Language	①	②	③
Verbal	①	②	③
Listening	①	②	③

Thinking Skills

Hypothesis Generation	①	②	③
Initial Plan & Output	①	②	③
Data Gathering	①	②	③
Basic Business Intuition	①	②	③

Total Score _____ / 21

VIDEO 1
Case Question
(Interviewer)

Case Start Self Study Reminders

Present Question	Recap & Ask for a Minute	Create Your Plan	Present Plan	Stop & Study	Reinforce
Read the question out loud like an interviewer or watch the MBACASE video interviewer.	Briefly recap the situation, the complication, and your task. Speak out loud just like you would in an interview.	Using the paper below, fill in the sections.	Turn your plan toward the interviewer (or mirror or webcam) and present it piece by piece.	Review the roadmaps and the Post Case Review page to see what you missed. Mark up your plan to make it better.	Do the start again with the video interviewer, or find a live partner and get some feedback. Incorporate what you learned the first time.

CRACK THE CASE
CASE
SYSTEM

Ricci Carta
Rome, Italy

My Initial Plan and Output

Today's date:

Questions I'm thinking about:

Topics I know to cover:

Profit Tree Approach:

Topic Bucket Approach:

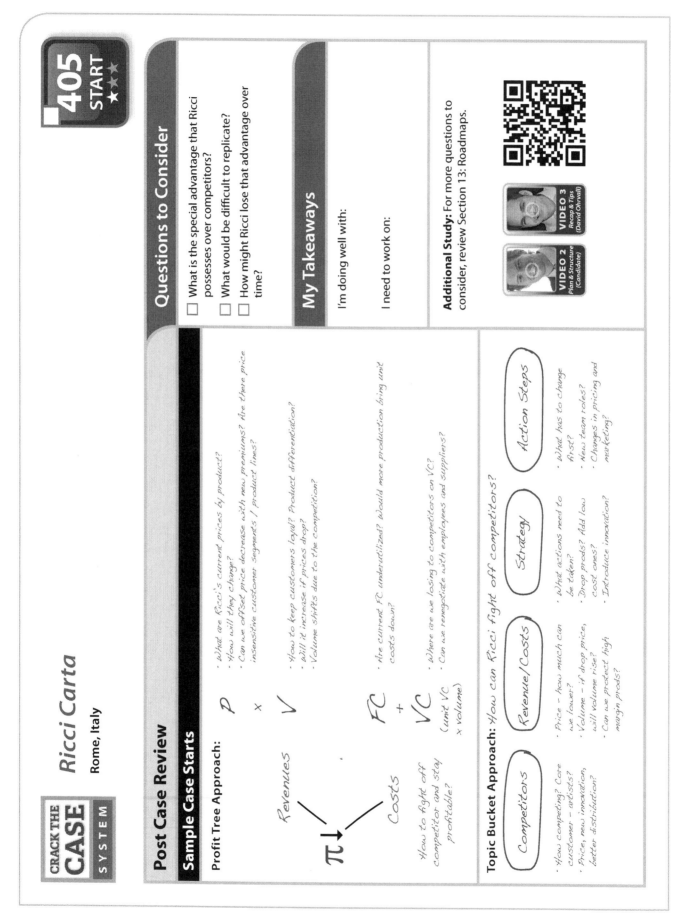

CRACK THE CASE SYSTEM

EU Oil Consumption

Brussels, Belgium

How green is the EU when it comes to oil consumption?

406
SIZING
★★★

BRUSSELS CITY FACTS

▸ De facto capital city of the European Union

▸ French-speaking

▸ "Capital of the comic strip" with city walls covered in comic motif

▸ Known for its chocolate, waffles, beer and frites

TRAIN Profile

Type	**R**egion	**A**nalysis	**I**ndustry	**N**umber
2 MARKET SIZING	BRUSSELS, BELGIUM Population: 1.8M Currency: Euro, EUR, €	Observe, Range	Oil & Gas	**2**

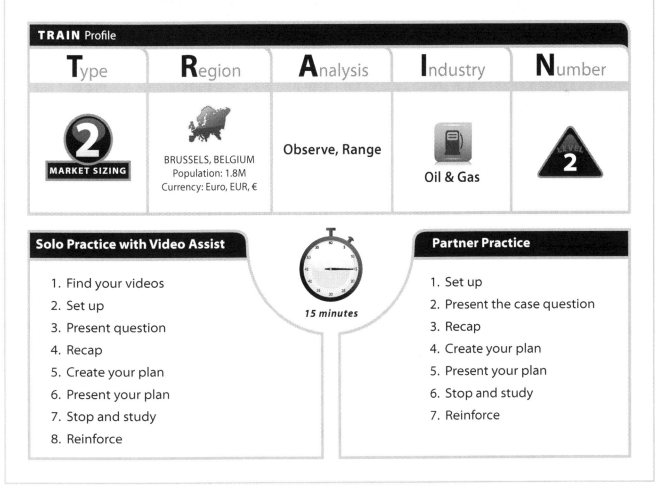

Solo Practice with Video Assist

1. Find your videos
2. Set up
3. Present question
4. Recap
5. Create your plan
6. Present your plan
7. Stop and study
8. Reinforce

15 minutes

Partner Practice

1. Set up
2. Present the case question
3. Recap
4. Create your plan
5. Present your plan
6. Stop and study
7. Reinforce

EU Oil Consumption

Brussels, Belgium

406
SIZING
★ ★ ★

Interview Guide

Initial Question

The EU is running a study on consumption habits and wants to know how much oil is consumed daily by the European Union. Several multinational companies may use this data for expansion plans, so they want to make sure it is accurate. They need an answer quickly as there's a Brussels conference in two days.

Case Twist

Check out the Crack the Case System videos on mbacase.com or scan the Video 3 QR code on the Post Case Review page to hear an additional challenge.

VIDEO 1
Case Question
(Interviewer)

Feedback

Physical Skills	Weak		Strong
Body Language	①	②	③
Verbal	①	②	③
Listening	①	②	③

Thinking Skills

Initial Plan & Output	①	②	③
Data Gathering	①	②	③
Data Analysis	①	②	③

Total Score _____ / 18

Intro Facts (Tell the Candidate if Asked)	**Key Insights** (Do Not Tell the Candidate)	**Mid-case Data** (Tell Only at Appropriate Time)
Any specific country data? Japan consumes 5.5 million barrels (bbls) per day and Spain uses 1.5 million bbls/day. **Countries in the EU (according to your data, it may have changed):** Austria, Belgium, Bulgaria, Cyprus, Czech Republic, Denmark, Estonia, Finland, France, Germany, Greece, Hungary, Ireland, Italy, Latvia, Lithuania, Luxembourg, Malta, Netherlands, Poland, Portugal, Romania, Slovakia, Slovenia, Spain, Sweden, United Kingdom).	**Extrapolation:** This case requires the candidate to think through how data about Japan and Spain could be useful in the consumption analysis. **Growth Potential:** Strong candidates will return to the scenario of the meeting and want to think through which specific countries would be attractive for expansion. You won't have data for these questions but look for this kind of thinking.	**Give idea:** If the candidate is stuck consider giving tips about comparing consumption and size across countries.

Case Flow and Milestones

1 Prep and Review

Read all the notes in the Interview Guide. Understand when to ask certain questions and when to give data and clues.

2 Present Main Question

Take on a personality (friendly, firm, or foe). Ask one or two background questions. Present the question. Candidate will take notes and ask for time to think or begin talking. Discourage silence as market sizing cases are meant to be interactive.

3 Answer & Ask

This is an ambiguous problem. Try to help the candidate by offering ideas if he is stuck. Continue to ask why he is thinking a certain way.

4 Guide Discussion

Give any missing data if needed, as well as the Mid-Case Data tips. Review the answer on page 4 of the case pack and offer suggestions if the candidate needs help.

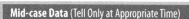

GIVE CLUE

5 Get Recommendation

Be firm and expect a final number. To see if the candidate is thinking about broader business issues, ask what he would do with this information.

406 SIZING ★★★

EU Oil Consumption
Brussels, Belgium

My Initial Plan and Output — Use the space below to write your thoughts.

State your assumptions

Pick your main metrics and approach

Estimate quickly and with round numbers

Assess your approach and answer

Keep exceptions and next steps in mind.

My Numbers

What are some simple estimates for getting started?

How might you refine these numbers?

EU Oil Consumption

Brussels, Belgium

Post Case Review	My Score	
Potential Solution & Output	Weak	Strong

State your assumptions
① ② ③

- Approximately 20 countries in the European Union.
- With the given usage of Japan and Spain, assuming the average usage of a EU country is less than Spain.

Pick your main metrics and approach
① ② ③

- Number of countries that are similar in size.
- Economic sophistication and demand for similar rates of oil.

Estimate quickly and with round numbers
① ② ③

- 3 EU countries with greater economic and military sophistication than Spain.
- 3 x ≈3 million = 9 million.
- 3 EU countries on par with Spain = 3 x 1.5 = 4.5 million.
- 14 small, poor EU countries averaging 25% Spain.
- 25% of 1.5 million = 375,000.

Assess your approach and answer
① ② ③

- European Union consumes 14 million barrels of oil per day.
- Alternative approach: extrapolate from worldwide population ratios or overall production.

Keep exceptions and next steps in mind
① ② ③

- Critical steps: determining exactly how many countries are in the EU and verifying Spain's economic strength comparatively.

Total:

BASIC RESOURCES AND PROCESSING
RESOURCES
　Coal
PROCESSING
　Iron and steel
　Nonferrous metals
　Petroleum

Different Approaches to Consider

- Draw a visual, like a map, to help think about population, density and sophistication of each country.
- Try a quick solution, like assuming every country consumes the same amount. Then refine the solution with variations that are logical.
- Consider what kinds of businesses would care about oil consumption for the EU and by country.

Tips and Takeaways

- Calculate your "close to" estimates by thinking High Quality products shrank by half, and Low Quality products almost doubled.
- Avoid lots of zeroes by picking a scale, like M for millions.
- Use 40% of 10M, 4M, as an anchor to quickly help you calculate the other revenue ($2.5M, 3.5M, etc.).

VIDEO 2
Plan & Structure
(Candidate)

VIDEO 3
Recap & Tips
(David Ohrvall)

RussoGaz

St. Petersburg, Russia

An investor group says RussoGaz will be the hot commodity in the energy sector. Do they have a plan to make it rise, or will it go down in flames?

407
FULL
★★★

ST. PETERSBURG CITY FACTS

▶ The capital of the Russian Empire from 1703 to 1918

▶ The city contains more than 200 museums

▶ As a port city, it has a strong commercial presence, particularly around oil and gas trading and finance

▶ The distillery owned by Russian Standard Vodka produces approximately 22,500 bottles of vodka per hour

TRAIN Profile

Type	**R**egion	**A**nalysis	**I**ndustry	**N**umber
4 FULL BUSINESS	ST. PETERSBURG, RUSSIA Population: 4.6M Currency: Russian Rubles, RUB, руб. / Р. / р.	ROADMAP → **10** Valuation	Oil & Gas	LEVEL **3**

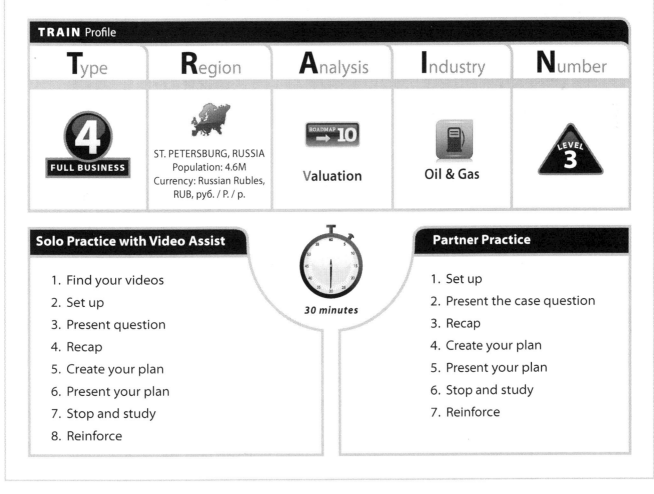

Solo Practice with Video Assist	*30 minutes*	**Partner Practice**
1. Find your videos		1. Set up
2. Set up		2. Present the case question
3. Present question		3. Recap
4. Recap		4. Create your plan
5. Create your plan		5. Present your plan
6. Present your plan		6. Stop and study
7. Stop and study		7. Reinforce
8. Reinforce		

RussoGaz

St. Petersburg, Russia

407
FULL
★★★

Interview Guide

Case Situation and Question

Ex-Russian officials want to buy out RussoGaz, a $500M state-run gas exploration company on the verge of privatization. It has 40 operating gas wells and 20 dormant wells. This group has lined up $400M in debt financing to buy RussoGaz, and would like your firm to put up the remaining $100M as private equity.

The officials claim that they can increase the value of the business by 50% over 5 years, by activating 20% of their dormant gas wells each year. After 5 years, they will sell the company.

Before you fly to St. Petersburg to meet the buyout group, the senior partner wants you to examine the group's financial projections and lay out key areas for due diligence.

VIDEO 1
Case Question
(Interviewer)

Feedback

Physical Skills

	Weak		Strong
Body Language	①	②	③
Verbal	①	②	③
Listening	①	②	③

Thinking Skills

Hypothesis Generation	①	②	③
Comfort with Ambiguity	①	②	③
Initial Plan & Output	①	②	③
Data Analysis	①	②	③
Basic Business Intuition	①	②	③
Integration	①	②	③
2nd Level Insights	①	②	③
Creativity	①	②	③

Total Score _____ / 33

Intro Facts (Tell the Candidate if Asked)	**Key Insights** (Do Not Tell the Candidate)	**Mid-case Data** (Tell Only at Appropriate Time)
Management: The buyout group comes from the Soviet/Russian Energy Ministry. They plan to hire an experienced manager to run operations at RussoGaz.	**Management:** The buyout group assumes that RussoGaz will be worth 50% more if it has 50% more active wells.	**Give Handout A:** A good candidate will calculate Free Cash Flow unprompted and forecast it for 5 years. Track his work against your answer sheet. When he finishes the forecast, GIVE HANDOUT B.
Product: The natural gas is similar in quality to that of other providers. Reports suggest there is plenty of natural gas in the active wells but levels at the dormant wells are unknown.	**Product:** Half the dormant wells have depleted natural gas reserves.	**Give Handout B and Prompt the Candidate:** Ask, "Can you tell me what's going on in this model?" Look for candidate to connect FCF from his work to that in Handout B. Ask, "Can you connect your projections to this analysis?" He should describe the debt repayment process.
Competitors: Other state-run and private gas companies exist, but overall market size is growing, so competition has not been intense.		**Ask About Valuation:** Prompt the candidate to discuss valuation measure. Ask, "What does IRR tell you about this investment?" and "What does Cash Return tell you?" Check that his answers are more than just definitions of terms.
Financing: The syndicate is led by a major bank. Funding will be used to purchase all the assets from the Russian government, activate dormant wells, operate active wells, and manage overall operations.		
Operations: The activation rate of gas wells depends on having new equipment and government approval.		

RussoGaz
St. Petersburg, Russia

407
FULL
★★★

Case Flow and Milestones

1 Present Main Question	**2** Assess Structure	**3** Look for Specifics	**4** Guide Discussion	**5** Get Recommendation
Interviewer should read through the case and know the timing for questions, data, and hints. Take on a personality (friendly, firm, or foe). Present the case question. Candidate will then likely recap and clarify, ask for time to think, form a plan on paper, and present his plan.	Candidate should address how the buyout group will increase company value. If he jumps right into valuation, push back by asking, "Explain how the buyout group will increase company value" and look for his reasoning. When discussing FCF, he should have a precise answer (See Mid-Case Data).	FCF growth depends on each part of Handout A except for interest and taxes. The candidate should discuss how Revenue is a function of the amount of gas pumped per active well x price. The amount pumped is a function of the number of active wells and their yield. Depreciation is an accounting function. CapEx is how much is spent on the business to activate wells.	Follow the Mid-Case data tips. When examining Handout B, candidate should explain what IRR and Cash Return are and why they are used in financial analysis.	Strong candidates will explain whether the group's projections make sense based on forecasts of full use of all wells and also based on certain wells not yielding natural gas (and cash flow). A good answer will highlight these risks. Also, good answers will highlight how the activation rate, price of gas, and net margin could change and affect FCF. Finally, the projected 50% increase in terminal value is not justified by the buyout group and needs further analysis.

GIVE HANDOUT A

Handout and Data Guide

Handout A:

Give Handout A after reading the case question. Ask, "Do you have any questions about the company before you begin your analysis?"

Handout B:

Give Handout B when candidate completes Free Cash Flow projections.

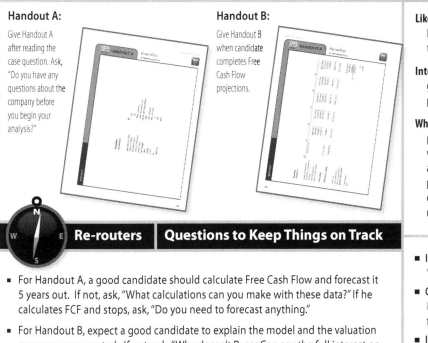

Additional Info

Likely question from Candidate: "Do you have any more financial or company info than what you presented?"

Interviewer: "This is everything the buyout group has provided to you. Do you have particular concerns that you want to raise?"

What to look for: A good candidate would point out that the 50% increase in terminal value is too high or is based on weak assumptions. Look for the candidate to propose different valuation methods (e.g., comps) and to propose examining the gas reserves more closely.

■ **Interest:** Interest on debt is tax deductible, hence "interest tax savings" entry on Handout B.

■ **Cash Return:** A ratio of terminal equity value to initial equity investment, without accounting for the time value of money.

■ **IRR (Internal Rate of Return):** The discount rate that makes the net present value of current and future cash flows from a project equal to zero.

Re-routers | Questions to Keep Things on Track

- For Handout A, a good candidate should calculate Free Cash Flow and forecast it 5 years out. If not, ask, "What calculations can you make with these data?" If he calculates FCF and stops, ask, "Do you need to forecast anything."

- For Handout B, expect a good candidate to explain the model and the valuation measure unprompted. If not, ask, "Why doesn't RussoGaz pay the full interest on debt?" If necessary, also ask, "Tell me what is going on in Year 5."

RussoGaz

St. Petersburg, Russia

407 FULL ★★★

Post Case Review

Case Insights & Takeaways

- This is a leveraged buyout question, so valuation must address debt repayment and terminal value. That means you will comment on debt service, interest, and tax savings on interest.
- Understand simple valuation measures for investing in projects, such as cash return and IRR.

Math Tips

- Know how to calculate Free Cash Flow.
- Organize your paper so that you can manually write financial projections.
- Use percentages for easier forecasting. In this case, FCF is assumed as 30% of revenue, so once you calculate revenue, you can calculate FCF without interim steps.

What to Expect with Cases Like These

- Understand which assets in the company drive cash flow. Ensure that you account for the risk of the asset NOT contributing to cash flow. This will ultimately affect your recommendation.

My Takeaways

To build skills and improve, you must apply what you learned to future cases. Take a few moments and review the interviewer feedback and jot down some key insights about your performance in the space below.

Thinking Skills

My top 2 strengths are:

My top 2 soft spots are:

To address these problems I'll begin to:

VIDEO 3
*Recap & Tips
(David Ohrvall)*

My Performance During the Case

Add up your points. → Total Score: _____ /15

S Strategy	**A** Assets	**V** Value	**E** Expectations	**D** Delivery
points	points	points	points	points
③ Identifies group's strategy and rationale	③ Identifies all target's key assets	③ Links assets to value drivers and 2 valuation methods	③ Explains how valuation and value drivers work	③ Identifies contradictions and next steps
② Identifies strategy but no rationale	② Identifies at least one key asset	② Links assets to value drivers and < 2 methods	② Explains how some valuation and value drivers work	② Identifies contradictions but no next steps
① Fails to identify strategy or rationale	① Fails to identify any key assets	① Fails to link assets to value drivers or methods	① Fails to explain how any valuation and value drivers work	① No contradictions or next steps

HANDOUT A

RussoGaz
St. Petersburg, Russia

RussoGaz
Handout A

	t1	
Operational Wells	40	
Dormant Wells	20	
Activation Rate	20%	annually
Annual Yield/Well	1,000	thousand cc ft
Price of gas	$4.00	per thousand cc
Net margin	40%	
D&A	20%	of sales
CapEx	30%	of sales
Δ WC	0	
k_D	8%	
Tax Rate	40%	

HANDOUT B

RussoGaz
St. Petersburg, Russia

RussoGaz
Handout B

	t0	t1	t2	t3	t4	t5	
Equity Participation	($100,000.0)						
Total Debt, beg balance		$400,000.0	$371,200.0	$336,217.6	$294,756.0	$246,504.3	
FCF beg		$48,000.0	$52,800.0	$57,600.0	$62,400.0	$67,200.0	
Interest Expense		$32,000.0	$29,696.0	$26,897.4	$23,580.5	$19,720.3	
Interest Tax Savings		$12,800.0	$11,878.4	$10,759.0	$9,432.2	$7,888.1	
FCF ending	($100,000.0)	$28,800.0	$34,982.4	$41,461.6	$48,251.7	$55,367.8	
Total Debt, ending		$400,000.0	$371,200.0	$336,217.6	$294,756.0	$246,504.3	$191,136.5
Sale Price							$750,000.0
Less: Total Debt							400,000.0
Plus: Cumulative FCF							208,863.5
Equity Value at Exit						$	558,863.5
Cash Return							5.6
IRR							27.0%

WORKSHEET

RussoGaz
St. Petersburg, Russia

CRACK THE CASE SYSTEM

RUSSOGAZ

My Initial Plan and Output

Today's date:

2. Be original with your data

4. Leave ample room for a structure and additional notes as the case progresses

1. Zone out your paper

3. Take clean and simple notes

CRACK THE CASE SYSTEM — WORKSHEET

RussoGaz
St. Petersburg, Russia

407 FULL ★★★

RUSSOGAZ

Potential Plan and Output

Data

RussoGaz $500M
- 400 debt
- 100 equity

Sales price in T5 = $750M
40 wells now
20 wells dormant
60 total in T5

Mgt team former Soviet/ Russian officials

Questions

Faster activation rate?
Wells have good reserves?
Competent management?
↑Yield/well?
Buyer in T5?

	T1	T2	T3	T4	T5
Dormant wells	20	16	12	8	4
Active rate (20%)					
Active wells	40	44	48	52	56
Gas Yield (1,000)					
Total Gas	40,000	44,000	48,000	52,000	56,000
Gas Price ($4)					
Total Rev	160,000	176,000	192,000	208,000	224,000
Net Margin (40%)					
Net Income	64,000	70,400	76,800		
+D&A (20%)	32,000	35,200	38,400		
−CapEx (30%)	48,000	52,800	57,600		
−ΔWC (0%)	0	0	0		
FCF	48,000	52,800	57,600	62,400	67,200

Strategy	Assets	Value	Expectations	Delivery
• Activate wells	• Gov't contracts • Equipment • Wells	• Activation rate • Activation rate • Gas yield	• Clearance for wells • Equip does the job • Enough reserves	• Anticipate holdups/corrupt officials • Assess equipment • Investigate dormant wells

Additional Study: For more questions to consider, review Section 13: Roadmaps.

VIDEO 2
Plan & Structure
(Candidate)

Foundation Bank

Istanbul, Turkey

Foundation Bank was built on plastic. Will they succeed again in a new territory?

ISTANBUL CITY FACTS

▸ Known as The City on the Seven Hills (Like Rome, built on 7 hills)

▸ Fourth largest billionaire city, home to approximately 35 billionaires

▸ The only metropolis in the world situtated on two continents: Europe and Asia

TRAIN Profile

Type	**R**egion	**A**nalysis	**I**ndustry	**N**umber
1 CASE START	ISTANBUL, TURKEY Population: 12.8M Currency: Turkish Lira, TL	ROADMAP → **4** Enter a New Geography or Market	Banking	LEVEL **1**

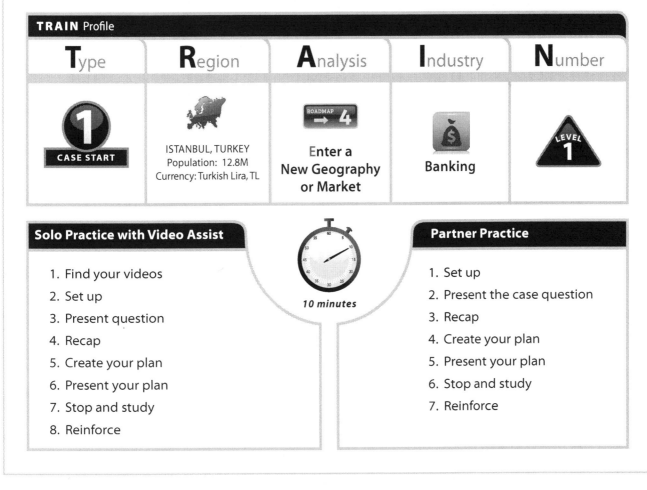

Solo Practice with Video Assist

1. Find your videos
2. Set up
3. Present question
4. Recap
5. Create your plan
6. Present your plan
7. Stop and study
8. Reinforce

10 minutes

Partner Practice

1. Set up
2. Present the case question
3. Recap
4. Create your plan
5. Present your plan
6. Stop and study
7. Reinforce

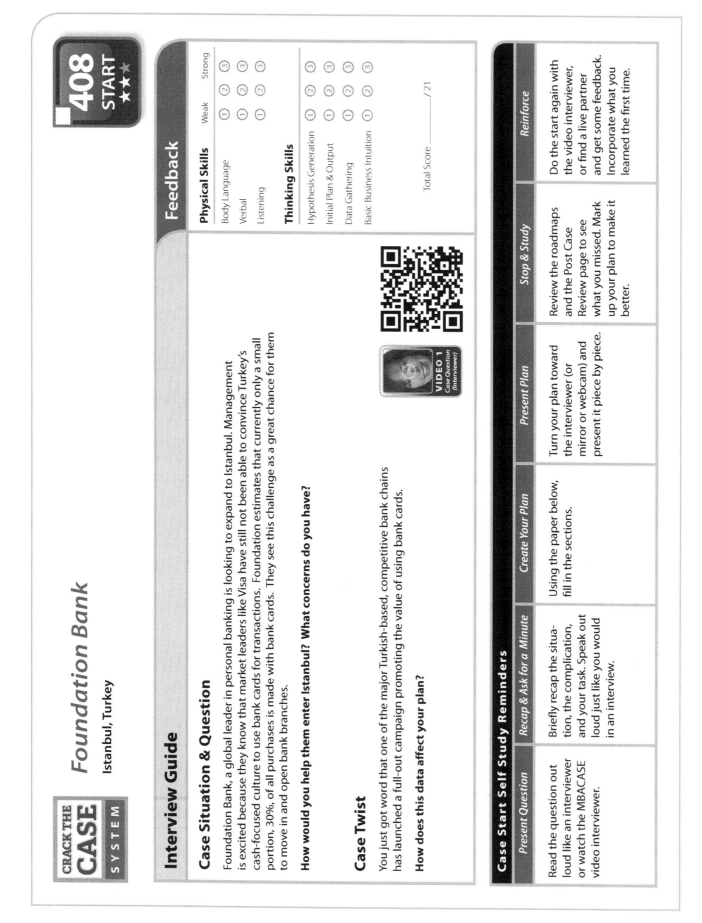

408 START ★★

CRACK THE CASE SYSTEM

Foundation Bank
Istanbul, Turkey

Interview Guide

Case Situation & Question

Foundation Bank, a global leader in personal banking is looking to expand to Istanbul. Management is excited because they know that market leaders like Visa have still not been able to convince Turkey's cash-focused culture to use bank cards for transactions. Foundation estimates that currently only a small portion, 30%, of all purchases is made with bank cards. They see this challenge as a great chance for them to move in and open bank branches.

How would you help them enter Istanbul? What concerns do you have?

Case Twist

You just got word that one of the major Turkish-based, competitive bank chains has launched a full-out campaign promoting the value of using bank cards.

How does this data affect your plan?

VIDEO 1
Case Question (Interviewer)

Feedback

Physical Skills	Weak		Strong
Body Language	①	②	③
Verbal	①	②	③
Listening	①	②	③

Thinking Skills			
Hypothesis Generation	①	②	③
Initial Plan & Output	①	②	③
Data Gathering	①	②	③
Basic Business Intuition	①	②	③

Total Score _____ / 21

Case Start Self Study Reminders

Present Question	Recap & Ask for a Minute	Create Your Plan	Present Plan	Stop & Study	Reinforce
Read the question out loud like an interviewer or watch the MBACASE video interviewer.	Briefly recap the situation, the complication, and your task. Speak out loud just like you would in an interview.	Using the paper below, fill in the sections.	Turn your plan toward the interviewer (or mirror or webcam) and present it piece by piece.	Review the roadmaps and the Post Case Review page to see what you missed. Mark up your plan to make it better.	Do the start again with the video interviewer, or find a live partner and get some feedback. Incorporate what you learned the first time.

CRACK THE CASE
SYSTEM

Foundation Bank
Istanbul, Turkey

408
START
★★

My Initial Plan and Output

Today's date:

Questions I'm thinking about:

Topics I know to cover:

Profit Tree Approach:

Topic Bucket Approach:

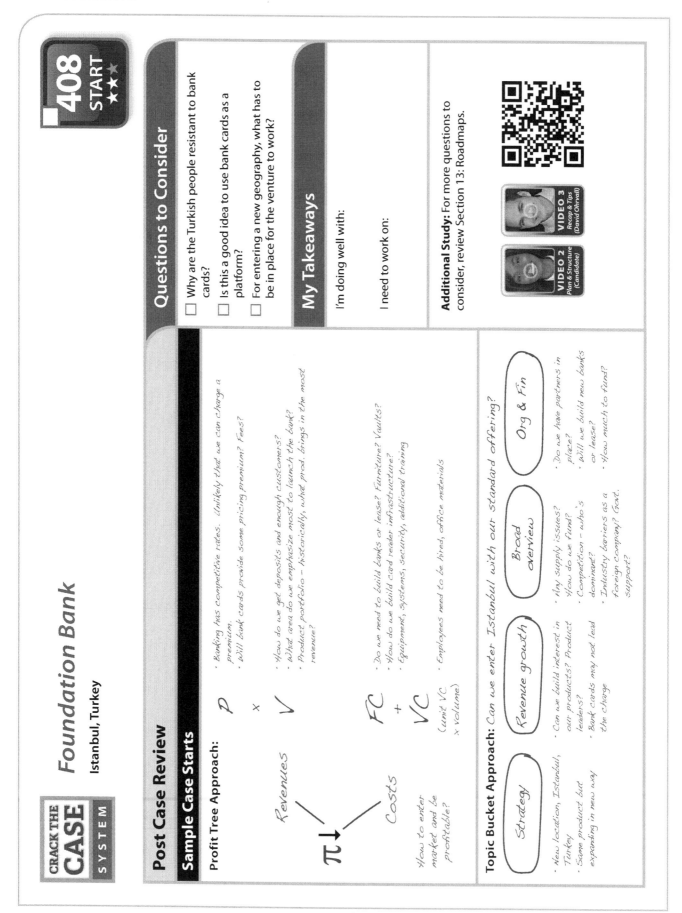

CRACK THE CASE SYSTEM

408 START ★★★

Foundation Bank
Istanbul, Turkey

Questions to Consider

- ☐ Why are the Turkish people resistant to bank cards?
- ☐ Is this a good idea to use bank cards as a platform?
- ☐ For entering a new geography, what has to be in place for the venture to work?

My Takeaways

I'm doing well with:

I need to work on:

Additional Study: For more questions to consider, review Section 13: Roadmaps.

VIDEO 2 Plan & Structure (Candidate)

VIDEO 3 Recap & Tips (David Ohrvall)

Post Case Review

Sample Case Starts

Profit Tree Approach:

$$\pi \rightarrow$$

Revenues

P
×
V

Costs

FC
+
VC
(unit VC × volume)

How to enter market and be profitable?

- Banking has competitive rates. Unlikely that we can charge a premium.
- Will bank cards provide some pricing premium? Fees?

- How do we get deposits and enough customers?
- What area do we emphasize most to launch the bank?
- Product portfolio – historically, what prod. brings in the most revenue?

- Do we need to build banks or lease? Furniture? Vaults?
- How do we build card reader infrastructure?
- Equipment, systems, security, additional training

- Employees need to be hired, office materials

Topic Bucket Approach: Can we enter Istanbul with our standard offering?

Strategy
- New location, Istanbul, Turkey
- Same product but expanding in new way

Revenue growth
- Can we build interest in our products? Product leaders?
- Bank cards may not lead the charge

Broad overview
- Any supply issues?
- How do we fund?
- Competition – who's dominant?
- Industry barriers as a foreign company? Govt. support?

Org & Fin
- Do we have partners in place?
- Will we build new banks or lease?
- How much to fund?

Bhawani Print

Hyderabad, India

Bhawani is looking for growth? Can they press through and meet demand?

501 START ★★★

HYDERABAD CITY FACTS

▸ Nickname: City of Pearls

▸ Home to Indian headquarters of Microsoft and Google

▸ Famous for its booming film industry, the city is home to the world's largest film studio: Ramoji Film City

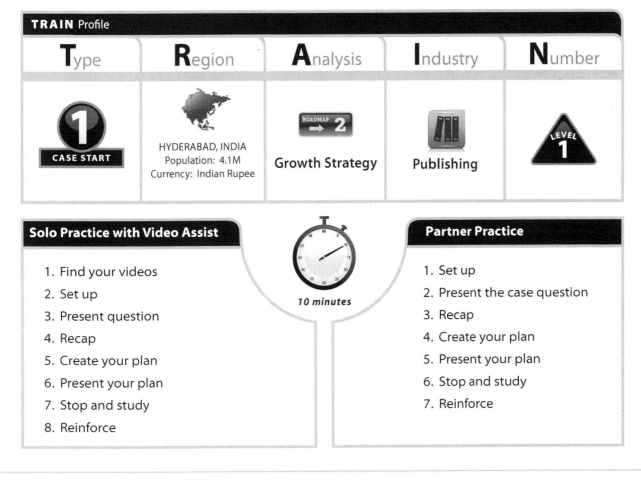

TRAIN Profile

Type	**R**egion	**A**nalysis	**I**ndustry	**N**umber
1 CASE START	HYDERABAD, INDIA Population: 4.1M Currency: Indian Rupee	ROADMAP → **2** **Growth Strategy**	**Publishing**	LEVEL **1**

Solo Practice with Video Assist

1. Find your videos
2. Set up
3. Present question
4. Recap
5. Create your plan
6. Present your plan
7. Stop and study
8. Reinforce

10 minutes

Partner Practice

1. Set up
2. Present the case question
3. Recap
4. Create your plan
5. Present your plan
6. Stop and study
7. Reinforce

CRACK THE CASE SYSTEM

501 START ★★★

Bhawani Printing
Hyderabad, India

Interview Guide

Case Situation & Question

Bhawani Print is known for its high quality printing. They specialize in very affordable offset printing, which is the most common technique for producing high quality, black and white and color books you would find in a typical bookstore like Barnes & Noble. Several large US based publishers have approached them to do their book printing.

How would you help Bhawani anticipate growth?

Case Twist

Flash forward 6 months and Bhawani's growth plans are right on track. Unfortunately, they just got slapped with a cease and desist lawsuit on several titles. Authors are claiming that Bhawani is producing titles without the correct international rights.

How might this situation affect their growth plans? List out some financial implications.

VIDEO 1
Case Question
(Interviewer)

Feedback

Physical Skills

	Weak		Strong
Body Language	①	②	③
Verbal	①	②	③
Listening	①	②	③

Thinking Skills

Hypothesis Generation	①	②	③
Initial Plan & Output	①	②	③
Data Gathering	①	②	③
Basic Business Intuition	①	②	③

Total Score _____ / 21

Case Start Self Study Reminders

Present Question	Recap & Ask for a Minute	Create Your Plan	Present Plan	Stop & Study	Reinforce
Read the question out loud like an interviewer or watch the MBACASE video interviewer.	Briefly recap the situation, the complication, and your task. Speak out loud just like you would in an interview.	Using the paper below, fill in the sections.	Turn your plan toward the interviewer (or mirror or webcam) and present it piece by piece .	Review the roadmaps and the Post Case Review page to see what you missed. Mark up your plan to make it better.	Do the start again with the video interviewer, or find a live partner and get some feedback. Incorporate what you learned the first time.

CRACK THE CASE SYSTEM

Bhawani Printing
Hyderabad, India

501 START ★★★

My Initial Plan and Output

Today's date:

Questions I'm thinking about:

Topics I know to cover:

Profit Tree Approach:

Topic Bucket Approach:

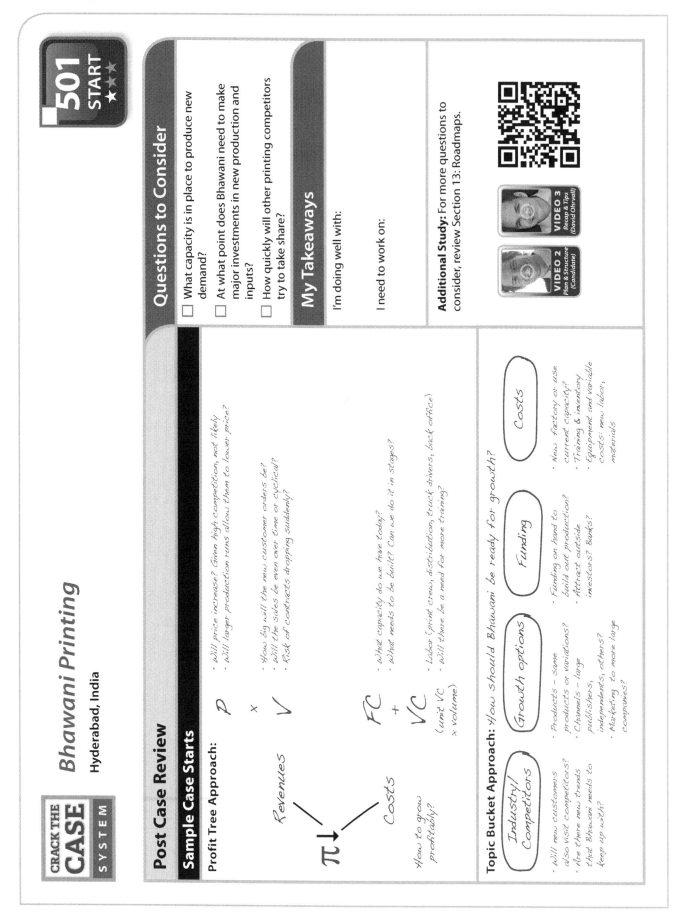

CRACK THE CASE SYSTEM

501 START ★★★
★☆☆

Bhawani Printing
Hyderabad, India

Post Case Review

Sample Case Starts

Profit Tree Approach:

$$\pi \rightarrow \begin{array}{l} Revenues \\ Costs \end{array}$$

Revenues: $P \times V$

- Will price increase? Given high competition, not likely
- Will larger production runs allow them to lower price?

- How big will the new customer orders be?
- Will the sales be even over time or cyclical?
- Risk of contracts dropping suddenly?

Costs: $FC + VC$ (unit VC × volume)

FC:
- What capacity do we have today?
- What needs to be built? Can we do it in stages?

VC:
- Labor (print crew, distribution, truck drivers, back office)
- Will there be a need for more training?

How to grow profitably?

Topic Bucket Approach: How should Bhawani be ready for growth?

Industry/ Competitors
- Will new customers also visit competitors?
- Are there new trends that Bhawani needs to keep up with?

Growth options
- Products – same products or variations?
- Channels – large publishers, independents, others?
- Marketing to more large companies?

Funding
- Funding on hand to build out production?
- Attract outside investors? Banks?

Costs
- New factory or use current capacity?
- Training & inventory
- Equipment and variable costs: new labor, materials

Questions to Consider

- [ ] What capacity is in place to produce new demand?
- [ ] At what point does Bhawani need to make major investments in new production and inputs?
- [ ] How quickly will other printing competitors try to take share?

My Takeaways

I'm doing well with:

I need to work on:

Additional Study: For more questions to consider, review Section 13: Roadmaps.

VIDEO 3
Recap & Tips
(David Ohrvall)

VIDEO 2
Plan & Structure
(Candidate)

Rickshaw Rules of the Road

Punjab Province, Pakistan

How many Rickshaws are there in Pakistan?

502
SIZING
★★★

PUNJAB PROVINCE FACTS

▶ Contains nearly 60% of all Pakistan's population, 92.5M

▶ The most industrialized region of Pakistan, producing textiles, sporting goods, machinery, electrical appliances, and surgical tools

▶ 50 colleges and universities

▶ Nickname: "The Land of the Five Rivers"

TRAIN Profile

Type	**R**egion	**A**nalysis	**I**ndustry	**N**umber
2 MARKET SIZING	PUNJAB, PAKISTAN Population: 92.5M Currency: Pakistani Rupee, PKR	Funnel	Electronics	LEVEL 1

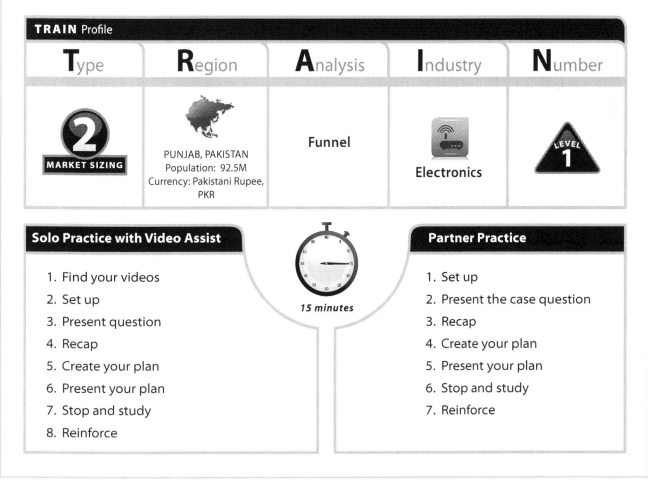

Solo Practice with Video Assist

1. Find your videos
2. Set up
3. Present question
4. Recap
5. Create your plan
6. Present your plan
7. Stop and study
8. Reinforce

15 minutes

Partner Practice

1. Set up
2. Present the case question
3. Recap
4. Create your plan
5. Present your plan
6. Stop and study
7. Reinforce

Rickshaw Rules of the Road

Punjab Province, Pakistan

502 SIZING
★★★

Interview Guide

Initial Question

The provincial government of Punjab, Pakistan has mandated that all autorickshaw drivers must wear bluetooth headsets. A headset manufacturer is deciding whether to invest in a new factory in South Asia and would like to estimate how many autorickshaw drivers there are in Pakistan.

VIDEO 1
Case Question (Interviewer)

Feedback

Physical Skills   Weak   Strong

Body Language	①	②	③
Verbal	①	②	③
Listening	①	②	③

Thinking Skills

Initial Plan & Output	①	②	③
Data Gathering	①	②	③
Data Analysis	①	②	③

Total Score _____ / 18

Intro Facts (Tell the Candidate if Asked)	**Key Insights** (Do Not Tell the Candidate)	**Mid-case Data** (Tell Only at Appropriate Time)
There are 187M people in Pakistan. The urban population is around 30% of Pakistan population. The labor force is 50M people. Rickshaws represent around 20% of commuters. Rickshaws average around 2 people per vehicle.	Rickshaws serve Urban areas exclusively.	If the candidate is stuck suggest focusing on working population and using the "funnel" method.

Case Flow and Milestones

1 Prep and Review

Read all the notes in the Interviewer Guide. Understand when to ask certain questions and when to give data and clues.

2 Present Main Question

Take on a personality (friendly, firm or foe). Ask one or two background questions. Present the question. Candidate will take notes and ask for time to think or begin talking. Discourage silence as market sizing cases are meant to be interactive.

3 Answer & Ask

This is an ambiguous problem. Try to help the candidate by offering ideas if he is stuck. Continue to ask why he is thinking a certain way

4 Guide Discussion

Give any missing data if necessary and the Mid-case Data tips. Review the answer on page 4 of the case pack and offer suggestions if the candidate needs help.

GIVE CLUE

5 Get Recommendation

Be firm and expect a final number. To see if the candidate is thinking about broader business issues ask what he would do with this information.

CRACK THE CASE
SYSTEM

502 SIGZING
★★★

Rickshaw Rules of the Road
Punjab Province, Pakistan

My Initial Plan and Output — Use the space below to write your thoughts.

State your assumptions

Pick your main metrics and approach

Estimate quickly and with round numbers

Assess your approach and answer

Keep exceptions and next steps in mind.

My Numbers

What are some simple estimates for getting started?

How might you refine these numbers?

Rickshaw Rules of the Road

Punjab Province, Pakistan

502
SIZING
★★★

Post Case Review	My Score		
Potential Solution & Output	**Weak**		**Strong**
State your assumptions	①	②	③
• Only the Urban working population uses autorickshaws.			
• "Rush hour" will bring out nearly all autorickshaws and people.			
Pick your main metrics and approach	①	②	③
• Top-down, population-based approach.			
Estimate quickly and with round numbers	①	②	③
• Working urban population is around 17M.			
• Those riding a rickshaw is around 4M.			
• Assuming 4 rides during rush hour, there are 1M rickshaws required.			
• Assuming 2 people per rickshaw, 500K rickshaws required.			
Assess your approach and answer	①	②	③
• 500K rickshaws means that there is 1 autorickshaw for every 300 people in the country. Compared to New York City, this seems reasonable.			
Keep exceptions and next steps in mind	①	②	③
• Enforcement is unlikely to be 100% across the country. There may be ways around enforcement depending on the "willingness" of local authorities (Pakistan ranks 143 out of 178 countries in the Corruption Perceptions Index published by Transparency International).			
Total:			

Different Approaches to Consider

- Assess the size of Pakistan overall. Roughly compares to the size of Texas. Assume same proportion of large and small cities. Determine total length of all roads, prevalence of rickshaws, and length of rickshaws.

Tips and Takeaways

- Describe each step of the funnel to the interviewer.
- Remain flexible if interviewer disagrees with assumptions.
- Avoid lots of zeroes by picking M for millions.

VIDEO 2
Plan & Structure
(Candidate)

VIDEO 3
Recap & Tips
(David Ohrvall)

Man in the Mirror

Manila, Philippines

How many men's facial products could be sold in the Philippines?

503
SIZING
★★★

MANILA CITY FACTS

▶ Capital of the Philippines

▶ One of 16 cities that comprise Metro Manila

▶ Has highest population density in the world

▶ Suffers from major environmental issues

▶ Tourism is vital to its economy, with over 1 million visitors per year

TRAIN Profile

Type	**R**egion	**A**nalysis	**I**ndustry	**N**umber
2 CASE START	MANILA, PHILIPPINES Population: 1.7M Currency: Philippine Peso, PHP	Funnel	Consumer Products	LEVEL 2

Solo Practice with Video Assist

1. Find your videos
2. Set up
3. Present question
4. Recap
5. Create your plan
6. Present your plan
7. Stop and study
8. Reinforce

15 minutes

Partner Practice

1. Set up
2. Present the case question
3. Recap
4. Create your plan
5. Present your plan
6. Stop and study
7. Reinforce

Man in the Mirror

Manila, Philippines

503
SIZING
★★★

Interview Guide

Initial Question

M'Oreal, an Asian cosmetics manufacturer, is looking for the next $100M blockbuster product. Its VP of Strategy has heard that men in the Philippines are using facial creams at a growing rate. How big could the market get? Facial cream costs an average of $30 and lasts about 3 months. Assume 1 of 5 grown men would eventually buy this product.

VIDEO 1
Case Question
(Interviewer)

Feedback

Physical Skills	Weak		Strong
Body Language	①	②	③
Verbal	①	②	③
Listening	①	②	③

Thinking Skills

Initial Plan & Output	①	②	③
Data Gathering	①	②	③
Data Analysis	①	②	③

Total Score _____ / 18

Intro Facts (Tell the Candidate if Asked)	**Key Insights** (Do Not Tell the Candidate)	**Mid-case Data** (Tell Only at Appropriate Time)
The population of the Philippines is around 100M. Population is distributed evenly.	1 of 5 men would buy this product. Men will buy the product around 4 times per year.	If the candidate is stuck, suggest focusing on working population and using the "funnel" method.

Case Flow and Milestones

1 Prep and Review	**2** Present Main Question	**3** Answer & Ask	**4** Guide Discussion	**5** Get Recommendation
Read all the notes in the Interviewer Guide. Understand when to ask certain questions and when to give data and clues.	Take on a personality (friendly, firm or foe). Ask one or two background questions. Present the question. Candidate will take notes and ask for time to think or begin talking. Discourage silence as market sizing cases are meant to be interactive.	This is an ambiguous problem. Try to help the candidate by offering ideas if he is stuck. Continue to ask why he is thinking a certain way.	Give any missing data if necessary and the Mid-case Data tips. Review the answer on page 4 of the case pack and offer suggestions if the candidate needs help.	Be firm and expect a final number. To see if the candidate is thinking about broader business issues ask what he would do with this information.

GIVE CLUE

CRACK THE CASE
SYSTEM

503 SIZING ★★★

Man in the Mirror
Manila, Philippines

My Initial Plan and Output
Use the space below to write your thoughts.

State your assumptions

Pick your main metrics and approach

Estimate quickly and with round numbers

Assess your approach and answer

Keep exceptions and next steps in mind.

My Numbers

What are some simple estimates for getting started?

How might you refine these numbers?

Man in the Mirror

Manila, Philippines

503
SIZING
★★★

Post Case Review	My Score		
Potential Solution & Output	**Weak**		**Strong**
State your assumptions	①	②	③
• All men will use this product.			
• Population distribution is even across age.			
Pick your main metrics and approach	①	②	③
• Top-down, population-based funnel.			
Estimate quickly and with round numbers	①	②	③
• Overall population is around 100M, male population is 50M.			
• Assuming average of 70, then around 11/14 of population is eligible or ¾.			
• 1 of 5 men would buy this product = 7.5M.			
• Product purchased 4 times per year = 30M products.			
• With price of $30 then market size is $900M/year.			
Assess your approach and answer	①	②	③
• If every woman in the Philippines spent $50 per year on makeup, this would be a ~$2.5B market. Comparatively speaking $900M for men does not seem unreasonable. It may be possible to benchmark this segment against other new segments and categories.			
Keep exceptions and next steps in mind	①	②	③
• May want to exclude married men from the calculation, who may be less inclined to purchase facial products.			
• Decide whether you can expand the market size to adjacent geographies where lighter skin is also highly prized (such as Pakistan, India, and other SE Asian countries).			
Total:			

Different Approaches to Consider

• Take population and break into market areas for grocery stores. Assume each market area has x completive outlets. Use average time on the shelf to determine the market size from a bottom-up approach.

Tips and Takeaways

• Turn "strange" fractions into easy ones (e.g., 11/14 to ¾).

• Don't forget to factor in product life to assess frequency of purchase.

VIDEO 2
Plan & Structure
(Candidate)

VIDEO 3
Recap & Tips
(David Ohrvall)

Siam Tea Company

Bangkok, Thailand

Siam Tea is brewing up an IPO. Should CTC Partners pour in some capital or let the company steep a little longer?

TRAIN Profile

Type	**R**egion	**A**nalysis	**I**ndustry	**N**umber
3 MINI BUSINESS	BANGKOK, THAILAND Population: 7M Currency: Thai Baht, THB	ROADMAP → 10 **V**aluation	Beverage	LEVEL 5

Solo Practice with Video Assist

1. Find your videos
2. Set up
3. Present question
4. Recap
5. Create your plan
6. Present your plan
7. Stop and study
8. Reinforce

20 minutes

Partner Practice

1. Set up
2. Present the case question
3. Recap
4. Create your plan
5. Present your plan
6. Stop and study
7. Reinforce

Siam Tea Company

Bangkok, Thailand

504
MINI
★★★

Interview Guide

Case Situation and Question

The Siam Tea Company, based out of Bangkok, Thailand, is a producer of premium bottled organic teas. It enjoys a reputable brand, both for its products and its company culture, throughout Asia and among urban Asian Americans on the west coast.

Sales of its teas grew 30% last year, and are expected to grow another 25% this year to $200M. Nearly 90% of its revenues come from sales to supermarkets, cafes, grocery stores and other outlets. It earns a 10% profit margin.

Siam Tea is conducting an IPO to maintain its growth rate.

An investment fund, CTC Partners, is considering investing in the Siam Tea IPO. Do you think they should invest or not?

Feedback

Physical Skills
	Weak		Strong
Body Language	①	②	③
Verbal	①	②	③
Listening	①	②	③

Thinking Skills
Hypothesis Generation	①	②	③
Comfort with Ambiguity	①	②	③
Initial Plan & Output	①	②	③
Data Gathering	①	②	③
Data Analysis	①	②	③
Basic Business Intuition	①	②	③
Integration	①	②	③
2nd Level Insights	①	②	③
Creativity	①	②	③
Recommendation	①	②	③

Total Score _____ / 39

Intro Facts (Tell the Candidate if Asked)

Customers: Not well known outside Asia.

Sales: 75% of sales come from Asia and 25% from the U.S.

Product: One flavor, Orange Blossom, with or without condensed milk. Both versions sell well.

Manufacturing: Siam grows, produces, brews, and bottles its teas locally. They ship across Asia and to the U.S.

Competitors: Several major competitors producing different teas.

Comparables: Other beverage companies are trading between 15x and 25x P/E.

Key Insights (Do Not Tell the Candidate)

Geography: Recent studies of American beverage consumption show negative feelings for drinks enriched with condensed milk.

Product: The teas that are shipped to the U.S. have Thai and Chinese labeling on the bottles.

Growth: Scale economies will contribute to profit margin when sales cross $300M.

Mid-case Data (Tell Only at Appropriate Time)

Handout: There is no handout for this case.

Questions to ensure candidate is on track:

1) "Under what multiples or growth rates should we not invest?"

2) "What do you think are appropriate multiples for Siam?"

3) "If sales grow but profit margin does not, how will that impact your valuation?"

Case Flow and Milestones

1 Present Main Question

Interviewer should read through the case and know the timing for questions, data, and hints. Take on a personality (friendly, firm, or foe). Present the case question. Candidate will then likely recap and clarify, ask for time to think, form a plan on paper, and present his plan.

2 Assess Structure

Candidate should discuss reasons to IPO and how it affects growth plans. If he jumps to valuation, push back: "Why does Siam want to IPO?" If necessary, ask what "growth" means. Candidate should discuss P/E multiple, PEG ratios, and implied revenue multiples. Follow how his logic fits your worksheet.

3 Look for Specifics

Growth will involve entering specific markets and increasing tea production. Look for a grasp of what assets will drive this growth and how the candidate will translate that into a valuation.

4 Guide Discussion

Follow the Mid-case Data steps. After the candidate performs the valuations, ask him to pick the best multiple and discuss why he chose it. Ask if the growth rate and margins are sustainable.

5 Get Recommendation

A good recommendation will approve investing in the IPO because expected growth and scale economies will increase value as shown by P/E and P/S. Candidate should discuss scenarios with different growth rates, P/E multiples, and margins. See worksheet for details.

Siam Tea Company

Bangkok, Thailand

504
MINI
★★★

Post Case Review

Case Insights & Takeaways

- Valuation should show Siam with equity values under different P/E multiples and growth rates. Candidate should also show P/S multiples and explain their use for this case.
- The organizational structure, production process, and brand of Siam Tea allow the candidate to show creativity when discussing whether the IPO is fairly priced. There is no correct answer.

Math Tips

- Know how to calculate value using simple measures such as P/E, P/S, and PEG ratio: (Price/Earnings) / (Annual Earnings Growth Rate).
- Lay out your math either on paper or in your head so that you can move through data quickly. For example, $200M in revenue x 10% profit margin x P/E of 25 = $500M equity value. It also means a P/S of 2.5 ($500 / $200). You can create a table for these calculations.

What to Expect with Cases Like These

- Develop and walk through your assumptions behind growth rates and margins and discuss valuation under different conditions.
- Know how to calculate values in your head. Use numbers that facilitate easy math. Practice creating tables that yield values so you can perform the math more quickly over time.
- Know how to integrate the different measures into your analysis. For example, for a growth rate of 20%, Siam's P/E must be under 20 to ensure its equity is undervalued. At $200M in revenue, that means investing in Siam's IPO if equity value is priced under $400M.
- Once you have developed your main valuation scenario, you can then discuss the assumptions behind growth and margin.

My Takeaways

To build skills and improve, you must apply what you learned to future cases. Take a few moments and review the interviewer feedback and jot down some key insights about your performance in the space below.

Thinking Skills

My top 2 strengths are:

My top 2 soft spots are:

To address these problems I'll begin to:

VIDEO 3
Recap & Tips
(David Ohrvall)

My Performance During the Case

Add up your points. → Total Score: _____ /15

S Strategy	**A** Assets	**V** Value	**E** Expectations	**D** Delivery
points	points	points	points	points
③ Identifies company strategy and reasoning	③ Identifies all key assets	③ Links assets to all value drivers	③ Explains how all value drivers work	③ Identifies contradictions and next steps
② Identifies strategy but no reasoning	② Identifies at least one key asset	② Links assets to some value drivers	② Explains how some value drivers work	② Identifies contradictions but no next steps
① Fails to identify strategy or reasoning	① Fails to identify any key assets	① Fails to link assets to any value drivers	① Fails to explain how any value drivers work	① No contradictions or next steps

WORKSHEET

Siam Tea Company
Bangkok, Thailand

504 MINI ★★★

CRACK THE CASE SYSTEM

SIAM TEA COMPANY

My Initial Plan and Output

Today's date:

2. Be original with your data

4. Leave ample room for a structure and additional notes as the case progresses

1. Zone out your paper

3. Take clean and simple notes

CRACK THE CASE SYSTEM — WORKSHEET

Siam Tea Company
Bangkok, Thailand

504 MINI ★★★

Potential Plan and Output

SIAM TEA COMPANY

Data
Organic tea
Across Asia and
West Coast US
Sales = $200M
90% of rev from
supermarkets, etc.
75% of sales Asia,
25% US

Net margin = 10%
g = 25% CY, 30% LY

locally produced, bottled
1 flavor, 2 types
Competitors trade at
15x - 25x P/E

IPO will fund growth

Questions
Is growth rate sustainable?
Will margins improve?
Valuation methods...

Valuation:
Should CTC invest in Siam IPO?

Sales × Net Margin = Earnings
Earnings × P/E = Equity Value

$PEG\ ratio = \dfrac{(P/E)}{g}$
PEG > 1: overvalued
PEG = 1: fairly valued
PEG < 1: undervalued

$200M	P/E		
	15	20	25
10%	300	400	500
15%	450	600	750
20%	600	800	1,000

margins

Price to Sales ratio: $\dfrac{P}{S}$

At a P/E of 15x and 10%
margin, P/S = 1.5x

	P/E		
	15	20	25
20%	.75	1	1.25
25%	0.60	0.80	1.00
30%	0.50	0.67	0.83

Strategy

retailers
- US and non-US

Diversify retailer type

production
- land
- facilities

Assets
- reputation/ brand
- reputation/ brand
- PPE

Value
Growth rate
g

Expectations
New regions accept brand over competitors

New retailers will carry brand. Cust will buy it

Scale economies

Delivery
Evaluate demand for brand

See who will carry it"

Identify possible limitations to scale

Additional Study: For more questions to consider, review Section 13: Roadmaps.

VIDEO 2
Plan & Structure (Candidate)

Virtual Vietnam

Ho Chi Minh City (formerly Saigon), Vietnam

How many computers could Vietnamese public schools purchase per year?

505
SIZING
★★★

HO CHI MINH CITY FACTS

▸ Most important economic center in Vietnam, with booming industries like seafood, mining, agriculture, construction, tourism, finance, industry, and trading

▸ Motorbikes are the preferred form of transportation in the city

▸ Known for its numerous theater companies

TRAIN Profile

Type	**R**egion	**A**nalysis	**I**ndustry	**N**umber
2 MARKET SIZING	HO CHI MINH CITY VIETNAM Population: 716,000 Currency: đồng, VND	Funnel	Computers	LEVEL 2

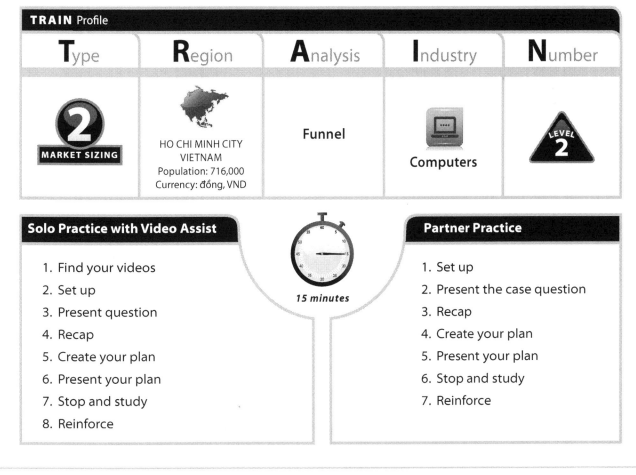

Solo Practice with Video Assist	**Partner Practice**
1. Find your videos	1. Set up
2. Set up	2. Present the case question
3. Present question	3. Recap
4. Recap	4. Create your plan
5. Create your plan	5. Present your plan
6. Present your plan	6. Stop and study
7. Stop and study	7. Reinforce
8. Reinforce	

15 minutes

Virtual Vietnam

Ho Chi Minh City, Vietnam

505
SIZING
★★☆

Interview Guide

Initial Question

The National Assembly of Vietnam announced a plan to enhance digital literacy. Like mathematics or literature, a computer education will now be mandatory in Vietnam. A Chinese PC manufacturer sees this as an opportunity to expand its stable of governmental customers. What is the maximum number of computers in this segment? Assume the computer price is around $200.

VIDEO 1
Case Question
(Interviewer)

Feedback

Physical Skills	Weak		Strong
Body Language	①	②	③
Verbal	①	②	③
Listening	①	②	③

Thinking Skills			
Initial Plan & Output	①	②	③
Data Gathering	①	②	③
Data Analysis	①	②	③

Total Score _____ / 18

Intro Facts (Tell the Candidate if Asked)	**Key Insights** (Do Not Tell the Candidate)	**Mid-case Data** (Tell Only at Appropriate Time)
The GDP of Vietnam is around $100B. The percent of GDP spent on education is 5%. Non-personnel costs are around 25% of education expenditures.	Computers could be only a portion of the overall technology budget.	Technology can be no more than 10% of non-education costs.

Case Flow and Milestones

1 Prep and Review

Read all the notes in the Interviewer Guide. Understand when to ask certain questions and when to give data and clues.

2 Present Main Question

Take on a personality (friendly, firm or foe). Ask one or two background questions. Present the question. Candidate will take notes and ask for time to think or begin talking. Discourage silence as market sizing cases are meant to be interactive.

3 Answer & Ask

This is an ambiguous problem. Try to help the candidate by offering ideas if he is stuck. Continue to ask why he is thinking a certain way.

4 Guide Discussion

Give any missing data if necessary and the Mid-case Data tips. Review the answer on page 4 of the case pack and offer suggestions if the candidate needs help.

GIVE CLUE

5 Get Recommendation

Be firm and expect a final number. To see if the candidate is thinking about broader business issues ask what he would do with this information.

CRACK THE CASE SYSTEM

505 SIZING ★★★

Virtual Vietnam
Ho Chi Minh City, Vietnam

My Initial Plan and Output   Use the space below to write your thoughts.

State your assumptions

Pick your main metrics and approach

Estimate quickly and with round numbers

Assess your approach and answer

Keep exceptions and next steps in mind.

My Numbers

What are some simple estimates for getting started?

How might you refine these numbers?

Virtual Vietnam

Ho Chi Minh City, Vietnam

505
SIZING
★★☆

Post Case Review	My Score		
Potential Solution & Output	**Weak**		**Strong**
State your assumptions	①	②	③
• The % of GDP spent on education represents a maximum school budget.			
Pick your main metrics and approach	①	②	③
• Top-down GDP based funnel.			
Estimate quickly and with round numbers	①	②	③
• Education spending is $100B * 5% = $5B			
• Nonpersonnel = $5B * 25% = $1B			
• Technology = 10%*$1B = $100M			
• Maximum computers = $100M / $200 = 500,000			
Assess your approach and answer	①	②	③
• The population of Vietnam is around 100M. This means that the school age population is probably around 15% or 15M. 1 computer shared by 30 school children seems reasonable with multiple sessions per day and some days off.			
Keep exceptions and next steps in mind	①	②	③
• The entire technology budget will likely include some software or maintenance costs, which would drive the number downward. Alternatively, the % of budget devoted to technology may rise as a result of shifting priorities.			
Total:			

Different Approaches to Consider

• Assess based on population. Make assumptions for average school day length, computer sharing, and frequency of use.

Tips and Takeaways

• If you are not using a population-based approach, use population as a sanity check.

VIDEO 2
*Plan & Structure
(Candidate)*

VIDEO 3
*Recap & Tips
(David Ohrvall)*

E&M Brothers Beer

Beijing, China

With growth in parent market (US) stagnating, company is looking at emerging markets to deliver the numbers.

506
MINI
★★★

BEIJING, CHINA CITY FACTS

▸ Capital of China, also known as Peking

▸ One of China's most developed cities, with its industry accounting for 73.2% of GDP

▸ Recognized as China's entrepreneurial center; the city is home to numerous venture capital firms

TRAIN Profile

Type	**R**egion	**A**nalysis	**I**ndustry	**N**umber
3 MINI BUSINESS	BEIJING, CHINA Population: 22M Currency: Chinese Yuan, CNY	ROADMAP → 1 Merge, Acquire, Joint-venture	Beverages	LEVEL 3

Solo Practice with Video Assist

1. Find your videos
2. Set up
3. Present question
4. Recap
5. Create your plan
6. Present your plan
7. Stop and study
8. Reinforce

20 minutes

Partner Practice

1. Set up
2. Present the case question
3. Recap
4. Create your plan
5. Present your plan
6. Stop and study
7. Reinforce

E&M Brothers Beer

Beijing, China

506 MINI ★★☆

Interview Guide

Initial Question

E&M Brothers Beer is a global beer conglomerate with a strong presence in the US and other developed markets. They are building market share in various developing markets across the globe. Their sales in the US are flat and management is under pressure from the Board of Directors to deliver a solid growth plan. To deliver the numbers, E&M Brothers Beer management is looking at emerging markets, specifically China.

How would you help them build their growth strategy?

VIDEO 1
Case Question
(Interviewer)

Feedback

Physical Skills   Weak   Strong

Body Language	①	②	③
Verbal	①	②	③
Listening	①	②	③

Thinking Skills

Initial Plan & Output	①	②	③
Data Gathering	①	②	③
Data Analysis	①	②	③
Basic Business Intuition	①	②	③
Integration	①	②	③
2nd Level Insights	①	②	③

Total Score _____ / 27

Intro Facts (Tell the Candidate if Asked)

Competitors: There are 4 big beer companies operating in China accounting for 57% of total volume sold. 43% of beer volume is sold by a number of small regional players.

Market / Landscape: China is the world's largest beer market in terms of total volume of consumption. The 4 regions of China have different levels of socio-economic development. All the key cities (e.g. Shanghai, Beijing) are in the Eastern Region.

Company Targets: E&M likes to see new acquisitions double their market share by 2 yrs. as a result of strong marketing support.

Price / Volume: Give the candidate Handout A.

Key Insights (Do Not Tell the Candidate)

Per Capita Consumption: Overall, China has per capita consumption of 21 bottles per person per year, low compared to other markets (Brazil: 45; UK: 100). China's, Eastern Region is the clear consumption leader with per capita of 48.

Acquisition Targets:

- Xingfu is the clear market share leader in the Eastern region. (Best choice.)
- Singsing in Central and Flakes in the North East have profitable business models and are ripe for acquisition to give E&M access in those regions.
- Acquiring other small players will not add profitability.

Mid-case Data (Tell Only at Appropriate Time)

Consumption Occasions: Give Handout B after discussion of acquisition targets. Ask the candidate for an interpretation. Insight: Need to drive consumption in the Eastern region by targeting new occasions (lunches, early afternoons).

Expect a precise answer: Next, ask the candidate to calculate incremental volume share gained by increasing new consumption occasion in Eastern Region. Reasonable assumptions are fine.

Give clue: Ask "What are the various ways to quantify the growth opportunity? Can E&M reach its goal of 2x market share for newly acquired companies?"

Case Flow and Milestones

1 Prep and Review
Read all the notes in the Interviewer Guide. Understand when to ask certain questions and when to give data and clues.

2 Present Main Question
Take on a personality (friendly, firm or foe). Ask one or two background questions. Present the question. Candidate will take notes, ask for a minute, form a plan and present it.

3 Answer & Ask
This is an acquisition and incremental consumption strategy case. Answer initial questions using the Intro Facts. As the candidate explains his plan, ask him how he connects the parts and push for more info.

4 Guide Discussion
Give the handout and follow the Mid-case Data tips. After the candidate interprets the data, give the clue. This clue should trigger a discussion of whether E&M can reach its targets in Eastern China.

GIVE CLUE

5 Get Recommendation
The best recommendation is to acquire stake in Xingfu. It's strong presence in the Eastern Region can be leveraged by E&M to drive more consumption occasions like lunches and early afternoons.

E&M Brothers Beer

Beijing, China

Interviewer's Data Guide

Step 1 – Determine where E&M is most likely to grow and how. Look at Handout A.

- Driving up consumption would point E&M to the east.
- Eastern consumers are heavier beer drinkers and are likely open to new ideas of how to consume more.

Step 2 – Calculate reasonable growth in consumption. Look at Handout B.

- Use Germany's consumption for occasions as a benchmark.
- If Eastern China continues to develop more Western consumption habits, lunch and early afternoon shares could double.
- Double the consumption in these two areas to approximately 12%, which is still below the Germany number.
- This increase in occasion consumption would imply a net increase of 13% in total beer category sales in Eastern China.

Occasion	Eastern China	New Goal	Net Change	Germany
Lunches	5%	12%	7%	14%
Early Afternoon	6%	12%	6%	21%
			13%	(assume 12%)

Step 3 – Determine what share of this increasing market (or "pie") E&M will capture.

- Of this E&M will grab double fair share (2x35%=70%) since they are leading the category development initiative.
- Thus E&M will increase its volumes in eastern china by 8.4% of total beer sales (all brands) in eastern china.

Eastern China	Current Share	Net Increase	Increased Consumption	New Share
Xingfu	35%	8.4% = 70% x 12%	43.4	39%
Rest	65%	3.6%	68.6	61%
Total	100%	12%	112	100%

E&M Brothers Beer

Beijing, China

506
MINI
★★★

Post Case Review	My Takeaways

Case Insights & Takeaways

- E&M Brothers Beer should acquire China's Eastern Region brand leader, Xingfu, to secure a large share of the market in China's top beer-consuming region.
- E&M could also consider acquiring a stake in a few smaller companies with strong presence in the mid-tier segment (Singsing in central and Flakes in North East). This strategy will give E&M a distribution network throughout China.
- E&M Brothers Beer should leverage the current premium brand in high per capita beer consumption regions of China (Eastern) to trade up consumers and drive more consumption occasions like lunches and early afternoons.

Math Tips

- Scan and focus on per capita consumption in different countries and across regions of China.
- A quick review shows that the category is significantly more developed in Eastern China.
- Scan the volume and value shares. Story emerges around the strengths of different companies in different regions of China playing across different pricing segments. This indicates potential acquisition targets.
- To calculate incremental volume share from new consumption occasions, benchmark to a high per-capita market occasions and extrapolate the most probable occasion currently not tapped in China to similar ratios as the benchmark market.

What to Expect with Cases Like These

- For cases based out of emerging markets, it's common to find that the development indices in some regions / cities is significantly higher (equal to some of the best markets globally) than the rest of the country. This will impact growth strategy for those specific cities.
- Present all of your areas and show that you have considered other options. Don't jump to the perceived answer too quickly.

To build skills and improve, you must apply what you learned to future cases. Take a few moments and review the interviewer feedback and jot down some key insights about your performance in the space below.

Thinking Skills

My top 2 strengths are:

My top 2 soft spots are:

To address these problems I'll begin to:

VIDEO 3
Recap & Tips
(David Ohrvall)

My Performance During the Case

Add up your points. → Total Score: _____ /15

F Form A Plan	**R** Read My Audience	**A** Anchor a Hypothesis	**M** Mine for Answers	**E** End the Case
points	points	points	points	points
③ Structured, clean	③ Good back & forth, caught clues	③ Solid hunch, pursued clue	③ Specific questions, solid analysis	③ Used facts and data, connected the dots
② Somewhat organized and logical	② Awkward, trouble with interviewer style	② Partial direction	② Missed some questions, some math mistakes	② Some data, mostly understood connections
① Messy, overlapping ideas	① Interviewer not interested, couldn't follow	① No hypothesis at all	① Vague questions, weak math, no linkages	① No data, no passion, no connections

HANDOUT A

E&M Brothers Beer
Beijing, China

506 MINI

E&M Beer Bros	Rev (%)	Vol (%)
Argentina	10%	6%
Brazil	34%	47%
China	7%	28%
Russia	14%	9%
UK	18%	5%
United States	17%	6%
	100%	100%

Total China	Vol Share	Val share	Price (Yuan) – Can (355ml)
Xingfu	15%	25%	5
Singsing	13%	22%	3.6
Flakes	18%	20%	3
Yingyang	11%	6%	1.8
Others	43%	27%	1.9
100%	100%		

	China	China Regions			
		Eastern	Western	Central	NorthEast
Bottles of Beer Consumption (per capita)	21	48	9	12	9
Vol Share					
Xingfu	15%	35%	7%	8%	2%
Singsing	13%	15%	3%	27%	2%
Flakes	18%	19%	19%	8%	28%
Yingyang	11%	13%	4%	5%	27%
Others	43%	18%	67%	52%	41%
	100%	100%	100%	100%	100%

HANDOUT B

E&M Brothers Beer
Beijing, China

506 MINI ★★☆

Occasion	Eastern China	Germany
Lunches	5%	14%
Early Afternoon	6%	21%
Nightcaps	23%	22%
Picnics	8%	17%
Evening Entertainment	58%	26%
	100%	100%

What beer experts have to say about beer consumption occasions:

Lunches
Earliest occasion to sensibly drink beer. By this time we have not eaten much and it's best to enjoy a light beer ('session' bitter or lager).

Early Afternoon
An early afternoon beer with a snack is a welcome refreshment in the summer (when it will help you to cool down) or winter (to warm you up).

Nightcaps
To relax and send you nodding off.

Picnics
Fruity, crisp chilled beer to compliment picnic food.

Evening Entertainment
Beer cocktails to get a party going; luxuriant, darker beers.

WORKSHEET

E&M Brothers Beer
Beijing, China

CRACK THE CASE SYSTEM

E&M BROTHERS BEER

My Initial Plan and Output

Today's date:

2. Be original with your data

4. Leave ample room for a structure and additional notes as the case progresses

1. Zone out your paper

3. Take clean and simple notes

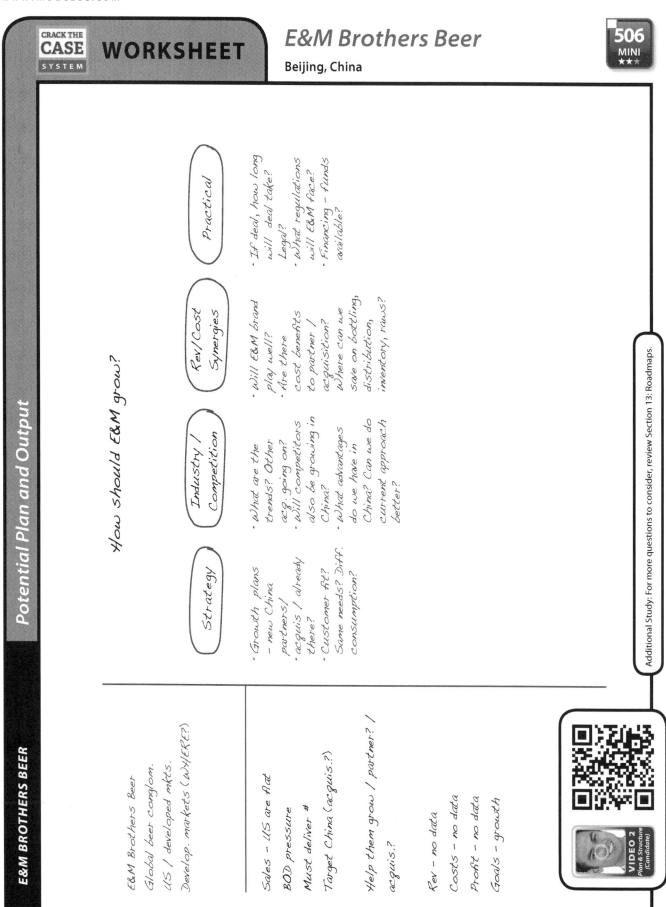

WORKSHEET

E&M Brothers Beer

Beijing, China

506 MINI ★★☆

Potential Plan and Output

E&M BROTHERS BEER

How should E&M grow?

Strategy
- Growth plans – new China partners / acquis / already there?
- Customer fit? Same needs? Diff. consumption?

Industry / Competition
- What are the trends? Other acg. going on?
- Will competitors also be growing in China?
- What advantages do we have in China? Can we do current approach better?

Rev/Cost Synergies
- Will E&M brand play well?
- Are there cost benefits to partner / acquisition?
- Where can we save on bottling, distribution, inventory, raws?

Practical
- If deal, how long will deal take?
- Legal?
- What regulations will E&M face?
- Financing – funds available?

E&M Brothers Beer
Global beer conglom.
US / developed mkts.
Develop. markets (WHERE?)

Sales – US are flat
BOD pressure
Must deliver #
Target China (acquis.?)

Help them grow / partner? / acquis.?

Rev – no data
Costs – no data
Profit – no data
Goals – growth

Additional Study: For more questions to consider, review Section 13: Roadmaps.

VIDEO 2
Plan & Structure
(Candidate)

Kryptonite Toys & Parts

Taipei, Taiwan

Kryptonite thought they were on top of the world, but customers think their service is plummeting. Can you save the day before Kryptonite loses its power over competitors?

507
FULL
★★★

TAIPEI CITY FACTS

▸ Taipei is regarded as the cultural, economic, and political center of Taiwan

▸ Nickname: The City of Azaleas

▸ The city of Taipei is home to 20 university campuses

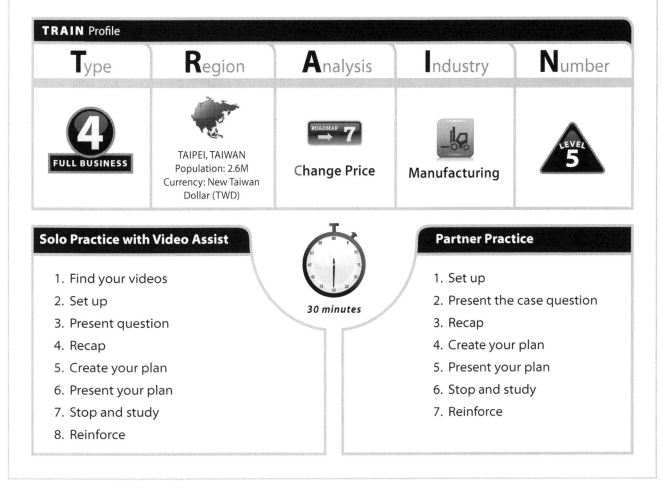

TRAIN Profile

Type	**R**egion	**A**nalysis	**I**ndustry	**N**umber
4 FULL BUSINESS	TAIPEI, TAIWAN Population: 2.6M Currency: New Taiwan Dollar (TWD)	ROADMAP **7** Change Price	Manufacturing	LEVEL **5**

Solo Practice with Video Assist

1. Find your videos
2. Set up
3. Present question
4. Recap
5. Create your plan
6. Present your plan
7. Stop and study
8. Reinforce

30 minutes

Partner Practice

1. Set up
2. Present the case question
3. Recap
4. Create your plan
5. Present your plan
6. Stop and study
7. Reinforce

Kryptonite Toys & Parts

Taipei, Taiwan

507 FULL ★★★

Interview Guide

Case Situation and Question

Kryptonite Toys & Parts (KTP), a $250M manufacturer of handheld game components, has recently received complaints from several long-time customers. The customers are having trouble securing consistent global prices with Kryptonite. When one KTP location promises a favorable price, other KTP manufacturing locations will not support that price. From the customers' perspective, KTP is acting more like a consortium of different companies than a unified global entity. KTP's management has reviewed the problem, but does not have a clear solution. Several executives believe the problem stems from the company's internal transfer pricing policies.

How would you dissect this problem? What solutions can you offer management?

Case Twist

If management does want to create a global pricing approval process, what other options are there for solving this problem?

How would you implement a new global pricing policy if you only had two months to do it?

VIDEO 1
Case Question
(Interviewer)

Feedback

Physical Skills   Weak   Strong

	Weak		Strong
Body Language	①	②	③
Verbal	①	②	③
Listening	①	②	③

Thinking Skills

Hypothesis Generation	①	②	③
Comfort with Ambiguity	①	②	③
Initial Plan & Output	①	②	③
Data Analysis	①	②	③
Basic Business Intuition	①	②	③
Integration	①	②	③
2nd Level Insights	①	②	③
Creativity	①	②	③

Total Score _____ / 33

Intro Facts (Tell the Candidate if Asked)

Locations: Kryptonite has divided the world into four major regions: North America (NAM), Latin America (LAM), Europe (EU), and Asia Pacific (AP).

Manufacturing: Most electronic parts are made in LAM and AP because of low labor costs and cheap raw materials. They are then sold to manufacturers who use the parts to make finished handheld products.

Shipping: Some parts are shipped to various customer facilities in NAM and EU and then put into finished handheld products.

Distribution: Some KTP parts are sold to distributors or outsourced assemblers.

Deal Sheets: Sales people in every region fill out "deal sheets" for potential sales with customers. These sheets capture overall margin for the deals and determine whether or not they should be approved. Historic policy requires every deal to generate "net 15%" (net margin) by region.

Key Insights (Do Not Tell the Candidate)

General Tips: This case has several interesting elements: basic accounting, historic policy review, and policy enforcement. Most candidates will piece together the transfer pricing transaction flow, but will struggle with the dollar impact (the "so what?").

Net 15 policy is hurting the company: By requiring that every region involved in a deal must achieve a net 15% profit on the transaction, many deals are being eliminated that could benefit the company overall.

Decentralized decision making: Present decision making is decentralized, which is one of the root causes of the poor management. Centralized decision making would promote deals that benefit the whole company.

Regional profitability—If changes are made to the net 15% policy, some regions will look less profitable than they do today. A new internal accounting system would minimize this effect.

Mid-case Data (Tell Only at Appropriate Time)

Give the following information if asked about how big the problem is:

Number of deals lost to pricing disputes: 322 deals in the first year; the second year is expected to be higher.

Average revenue per deal: $54,000

Estimated net profit per deal: 22%

Recent comments from the Regional Leaders (RL):

"If the European sales guys weren't so expensive and greedy, we wouldn't have so many pricing disputes." Asia Pacific

"Asia is always complaining about price. They just don't know how hard and expensive it is to scare up business here." Europe

"What pricing problem?" North America

"The heart of the issue is communication. We need more." Latin America

See the Mine for the Answer Section later in this case for additional questions and answers. Please review these before giving the case.

www.mbacase.com

404

CRACK THE CASE SYSTEM

Kryptonite Toys & Parts

Taipei, Taiwan

507 FULL ★★☆

Case Flow and Milestones

1 Present Main Question	**2** Answer Any Basics	**3** Ask for Clarification	**4** Guide Discussion	**5** Get Recommendation
Candidate takes notes, asks for a minute, forms a plan and presents it.	Transfer pricing can be confusing, so make sure you have reviewed the handouts. It is important for the Candidate to understand the net 15% rule.	Be sure to make him explain anything you do not fully understand. Look for clear connections between each part of the plan and an understanding of how each part contributes to the whole. Look for solid logic on how this plan will get some answers.	Expect questions about deals and historical pricing transactions. Your goal should be to hand out the two transfer pricing handouts (A and B) and then ask any questions about the volume of deals. Look at the additional info section below.	Ask the Candidate to create a solution to the problems. Options include: • Create a new global pricing review process to ensure that deals exceeding net 15% globally are accepted. • Develop a global accounting system so that regions share the value of deals equally.

Handout and Data Guide

Handout A:

Candidate: Do you have any data on failed price quotations?

Interviewer: Here's an example of a deal that did not go through in one of KTP's manufacturing locations. Why do you think the deal was rejected?

Insight: Each region must achieve 15% net margin on every deal. This deal fell short at 12%.

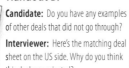

Handout B:

Candidate: Do you have any examples of other deals that did not go through?

Interviewer: Here's the matching deal sheet on the US side. Why do you think this deal was rejected?

Insight: Even though the Indiana plant's margin was well over 15%, they were denied. It looks like the US tried to get the customer to pay more, but the customer refused.

Re-routers | Questions to Keep Things on Track

- **What profit goals does each region have to meet?**
  - ‣ Net 15% on every deal, no exceptions
- **Why would a company have such a rule?**
  - ‣ To ensure that regions do not take low-margin deals and then hope to make up losses with high-margin deals later.
  - ‣ To provide a simple control that any employee can understand
- **What additional data would you like to see?**

- **How can you make your answer more quantitative?**

- **What are some simple ways that KTP can encourage the management team to adopt a more global focus?**
  - ‣ Develop more global infrastructure and information sharing, e.g. international sales teams or global pricing approval.
  - ‣ Revise incentive programs to reward global profitability and reduce the "penalty" incurred by deals with lower local margins.

Additional Info

Below is a recommended approach to solving the analytics. Give hints if necessary:

Review the slides: It is clear that Japan rejected the deal due to margin shortfall. Even though the US plant was well over 15% and could make up Japan's 3% shortfall (15%–12%), the deal was cancelled.

Calculate global value to KTP: Killing deals that could profit the global entity does not make sense. To determine what the margin would be on the global deal, create the following table:

Units:	10,000
Global Revenue:	$4.10
Direct Costs:	$1.12
Gross Profit:	$2.98
Gross Profit Margin:	73%
Selling and Service:	$1.30
Admin:	$0.61
Net Profit:	$1.07
Net Margin:	26%

From a global perspective, the deal offers a net margin of 26%! Certainly, this is a good deal to pursue!

Total value of this problem to KTP: $54k (average deal revenue) x 22% (average net margin) x 322 (year 1 deals killed) = $3.8M.

$ 3.8M / ($ 250 x net 15%) = 10% of total net profit. This is a big issue.

Kryptonite Toys & Parts

Taipei, Taiwan

507
FULL
★★★

Additional Study Using the FRAME Method

F – Form a Plan

MVM™

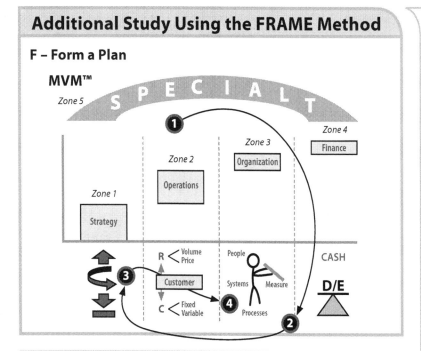

1. **Start in Zone 5, External Factors:** This case starts off with customers complaining about their supplier (KTP). KTP has failed to keep up with an industry shift toward global pricing. Why is the company lagging behind?

2. **Move to Zone 3, Organization/ Processes:** What is happening with the pricing approval process today? How is it integrated with the sales approval process? Is there any data on why the deals are rejected, and, how many are rejected?

3. **Move to Zone 2, Revenue/ Price:** How do the regions set pricing policy? Is this an internal problem, or is it being driven by some external market factors?

4. **Finish in Zone 3, Organization/ Systems:** How can the deal approval process be changed? What changes in regional and global accounting need to happen? What are the rollout implications?

M—Mine for the Answer

The key to this case was discovering how pricing quotes were rejected and approved. Other critical areas to drill into are global unity and regional differences. With any potential change, it is also good to get a perspective on what that change will do to the organization.

Deal Rejections	Global View	Performance
■ **How many deals are rejected per year because one region won't support them?** *233 price quotes were cancelled last year due to "regional disagreement."*	■ **How do the different regions work together?** *Cooperation is based on transactions; the manufacturing region transfers parts to the assembling region.*	■ **What global policies or systems has KTP rolled out in the past?** *SAP (global computer information system) was rolled out 2 years ago. There have been no other global rollouts.*
■ **What are the reasons for not supporting the price?** *One region is either not achieving enough margin on the deal, or has limited capacity. Thus, priority is given to high margin deals.*	■ **Where do the regions typically have disagreement with one another?** *Disagreement is almost always based on profitability and who will make more by region.*	■ **What were the reasons for their success or failure?** *SAP succeeded somewhat, but there were many disputes over universal standards.*
■ **Do we have regional policy on profit margin and deal approval?** *Each region must make net 15% on every transaction. Sales people can approve/ reject deals.*	■ **How does KTP resolve regional differences when they arise?** *KTP lets the regions resolve their own disputes.*	■ **What is leadership's attitude (by region) toward change?** *Each region wants to roll out their own policies; they seldom want to explore policies developed in other regions.*
■ **Do we have a global policy?** *No global policy. Each region has veto power.*		

A - Anchor a Hypothesis

So where could you build some initial hunches? Did you suspect that the company is disorganized? Is KTP outdated in terms of their policies? Those thoughts would have been a good beginning.

Here are some examples:

Internal Policy, Not Employees

"I bet that some deals are being rejected due to company policy or something out of the control of the employees."

Communication

"My hunch is that the procedures are probably appropriate, but communication is breaking down for some reason."

Incentives

"People are wallet-driven, looking to fill their own pocket as much as possible. The leaders in the company are doing things that suit their own best interests."

Kryptonite Toys & Parts

Taipei, Taiwan

507
FULL
★★★

Post Case Review

Case Insights & Takeaways

- Deals that would be profitable to the global company are rejected if they don't meet the net 15% rule at every single region.
- One sample (shown on the handouts) indicates that Kryptonite rejected a 26% margin opportunity (using a global perspective).
- Lost profits from this policy add up to about $3.8M or 10% of net profit.

Options for solving the problem include:

- Create a new global pricing review process. This process would ensure that the deals that benefit KTP and exceed net 15% globally are accepted.
- Develop a new, global accounting system to support the new policy. Through an internal set of accounting "books," regions share the value of deals equally. This approach encourages participation in global deals.

Math & Logic Tips

- When reviewing several handouts, be prepared to do a new calculation on a separate piece of paper.
- Create sample tables or charts whenever possible to show your interviewer as you are integrating your findings (see the table under Additional Info).

What to Expect with Cases Like These

- Even though transfer pricing may be a new concept to you, the math is simple. Many cases with unusual concepts will have straightforward math.
- Feel free to interact with your interviewer over new concepts and ask questions when something is unclear.
- When making new calculations, show your work and explain what you are doing.
- To solve a case like this you may have to try several options. Don't be shy about working through your thoughts out loud.

My Takeaways

To build skills and improve, you must apply what you learned to future cases. Take a few moments and review the interviewer feedback and jot down some key insights about your performance in the space below.

Thinking Skills

My top 2 strengths are:

My top 2 soft spots are:

To address these problems I'll begin to:

VIDEO 3
Recap & Tips
(David Ohrvall)

My Performance During the Case

Add up your points. ➡ Total Score: _____ / 15

F Form A Plan	**R** Read My Audience	**A** Anchor a Hypothesis	**M** Mine for Answers	**E** End the Case
points	points	points	points	points
③ Structured, clean	③ Good back & forth, caught clues	③ Solid hunch, pursued clue	③ Specific questions, solid analysis	③ Used facts and data, connected the dots
② Somewhat organized and logical	② Awkward, trouble with interviewer style	② Partial direction	② Missed some questions, some math mistakes	② Some data, mostly understood connections
① Messy, overlapping ideas	① Interviewer not interested, couldn't follow	① No hypothesis at all	① Vague questions, weak math, no linkages	① No data, no passion, no connections

Kryptonite Toys & Parts
Taipei, Taiwan

Kyoto Japan Plant
Deal Sheet (proposed quotation)

REJECTED

Customer: Hand Glove Toys

Part #: 590234PLU4492

KJP Sales Rep: Shinju Mori

Customer Contact: Roy Headstrong (KTP Indiana)

Per unit costs

		amount requested by Indiana USA plant
Units	10,000	
Revenue – Transfer Price	$ 1.75	← amount requested by Indiana USA plant
Direct Costs	$ 1.12	
Gross Profit	$ 0.63	
Gross Profit Margin	36%	
Selling and Service	$ 0.25	
Admin	$ 0.17	
Net Profit	$ 0.21	
Net Margin	12.0%	

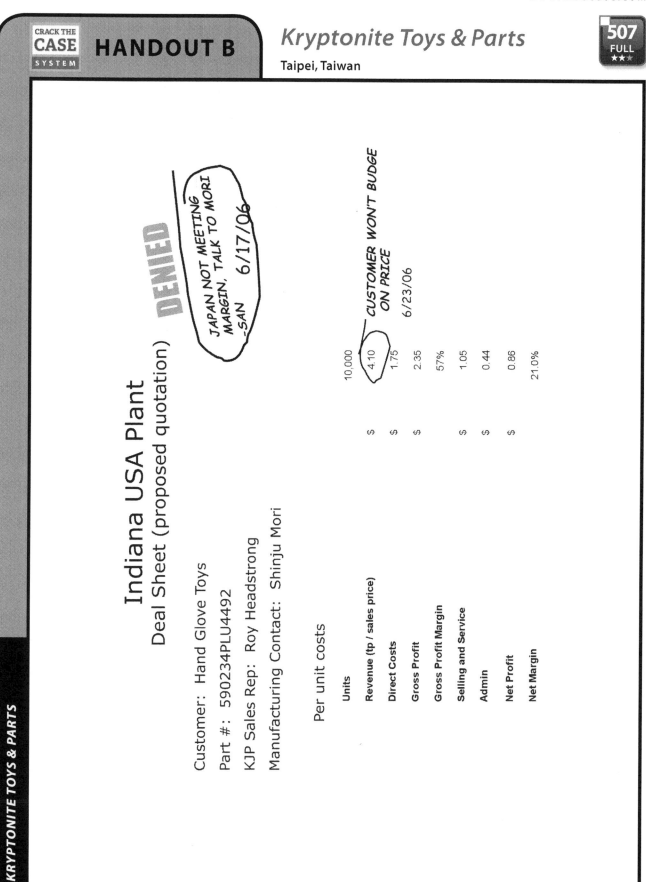

Indiana USA Plant
Deal Sheet (proposed quotation)

DENIED

JAPAN NOT MEETING MARGIN, TALK TO MORI —SAN 6/17/06

Customer: Hand Glove Toys

Part #: 590234PLU4492

KJP Sales Rep: Roy Headstrong

Manufacturing Contact: Shinju Mori

Per unit costs

Units			10,000
Revenue (tp / sales price)	$	4.10	*CUSTOMER WON'T BUDGE ON PRICE 6/23/06*
Direct Costs	$	1.75	
Gross Profit	$	2.35	
Gross Profit Margin		57%	
Selling and Service	$	1.05	
Admin	$	0.44	
Net Profit	$	0.86	
Net Margin		21.0%	

WORKSHEET

CRACK THE CASE SYSTEM

Kryptonite Toys & Parts
Taipei, Taiwan

507 FULL ★★☆

KRYPTONITE TOYS & PARTS

My Initial Plan and Output

Today's date:

2. Be original with your data

4. Leave ample room for a structure and additional notes as the case progresses

1. Zone out your paper

3. Take clean and simple notes

CRACK THE CASE SYSTEM — WORKSHEET

Kryptonite Toys & Parts
Taipei, Taiwan

Potential Plan and Output

KRYPTONITE TOYS & PARTS

How fix transfer pricing?

Pricing Policy	Industry / Competitors	Measurement	Options Forward
What's the pricing method today?	Have they not adopted industry trends?	How do they work in each region?	How can we change it going forward?
How are they approved by region?	What are competitors doing?	What is the global goal?	How quickly can we make the change?
Baseline data. Do we have examples of bad decisions?	Who has power to impact price? Suppliers? Distributors?	What do the customers want? How do we measure success with them?	What will be the impact on the products and the organization?

HUNCH: out of date policies that need to be revamped.

- Rev. – $250M
- Costs – no data
- Profit margin – no %, no $
- What's the goal financially?

- Handheld game components
- Customer complaints
- Global prices ??
- Regions – not same price
- Transfer pricing problems

Voiceover

"To better understand the pricing issue, I would like to know how prices are defined and approved by region. I'll be looking for data that shows where the lack of coordination is a problem. Second, I want to know whether there are any industry pricing trends that KTP has not adopted. Or perhaps they are following an industry standard that does not work for their customers. Third, I'd like to understand how they measure success and failure today. You mentioned the regions. What specifically are the customers complaining about their interaction with the regions. Finally, I'd like to put together some options and discuss how those changes will affect the organization. I'd like to start with the internal deal approval process, unless you'd prefer me to start elsewhere."

Additional Study: For more questions to consider, review Section 13: Roadmaps.

VIDEO 2 — Plan & Structure (Candidate)

Albion Inc.

Hong Kong, People's Republic of China

Albion thrived in the financial crisis, but regulators think it is due for a crash. Can you help Albion show that its business model is rock solid?

508 START ★★★

HONG KONG CITY FACTS

▶ British colony (1842–1997) transferred to the People's Republic of China in 1997

▶ Major world financial center: raised 22% of worldwide IPO capital in 2009, making it largest center of IPOs

▶ Buildings often lack any floor number that has 4 in it, due to its similarity to the word for "die" in Cantonese

▶ The city has approximately 7,650 skyscrapers, putting it at the top of world rankings

TRAIN Profile

Type	**R**egion	**A**nalysis	**I**ndustry	**N**umber
1 CASE START	HONG KONG, PRC Population: 7M Currency: HKD	ROADMAP 11 Risk Management	Securities	LEVEL 1

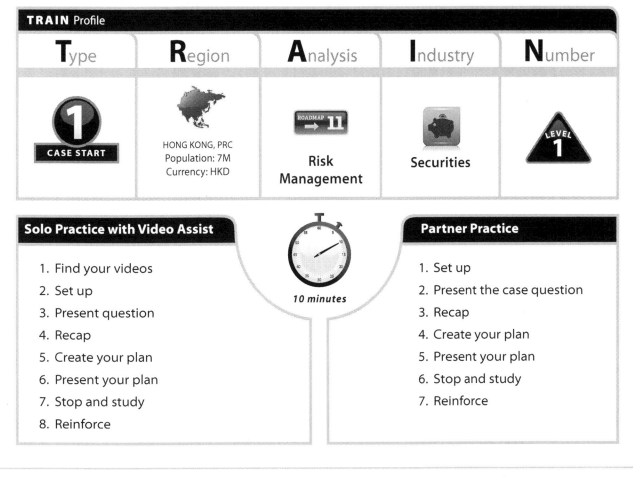

Solo Practice with Video Assist

1. Find your videos
2. Set up
3. Present question
4. Recap
5. Create your plan
6. Present your plan
7. Stop and study
8. Reinforce

10 minutes

Partner Practice

1. Set up
2. Present the case question
3. Recap
4. Create your plan
5. Present your plan
6. Stop and study
7. Reinforce

CRACK THE CASE SYSTEM

Albion Inc.
Hong Kong, PRC

Interview Guide

Case Situation and Question

Albion Inc. is a successful brokerage firm catering to institutional and high-net-worth clients. Its client base consists primarily of wealthy Chinese and Taiwanese nationals, as well as British expatriates.

Business has never been better, but with regulators scrutinizing the risk profiles of financial institutions, management wants to take proactive steps to show high quality risk management in its lines of business.

Help them figure out how to solidify their reputation.

Case Twist

After an extensive analysis, you discover that 40% of Albion's clients are mid-sized businesses located in Spain. Discuss the risks associated with this finding and how to manage them.

Feedback

Physical Skills

	Weak		Strong
Body Language	①	②	③
Verbal	①	②	③
Listening	①	②	③

Thinking Skills

	Weak		Strong
Hypothesis Generation	①	②	③
Comfort with Ambiguity	①	②	③
Initial Plan & Output	①	②	③
Data Analysis	①	②	③
Basic Business Intuition	①	②	③
Integration	①	②	③
2nd Level Insights	①	②	③
Creativity	①	②	③

Total Score _____ / 33

VIDEO 1
Case Question (Interviewer)

Case Start Self Study Reminders

Present Question	Recap & Ask for a Minute	Create Your Plan	Present Plan	Stop & Study	Reinforce
Read the question out loud like an interviewer or watch the MBACASE video interviewer.	Briefly recap the situation, the complication, and your task. Speak out loud just like you would in an interview.	Using the paper below, fill in the sections.	Turn your plan toward the interviewer (or mirror or webcam) and present it piece by piece.	Review the roadmaps and the Post Case Review page to see what you missed. Mark up your plan to make it better.	Do the start again with the video interviewer, or find a live partner and get some feedback. Incorporate what you learned the first time.

508 START ★★★

Albion Inc.

Hong Kong, PRC

My Initial Plan and Output

Today's date:

Questions I'm thinking about:

Topics I know to cover:

Profit Tree Approach:

Topic Bucket Approach:

WORKSHEET

CRACK THE CASE SYSTEM

Albion Inc.
Hong Kong, PRC

508 START ★★★

ALBION INC.

Post Case Review

Questions I'm Thinking About

What do they do?
- Invest
- Lend
- Borrow

Investment/Lending/Borrowing have what types of risks?

How to address that?

Strategy	Assets
↑% investments with risk-adjusted profit	Positions in market
↑% of clients with good credit	Receivables
↑equity base for solvency	

Topics I Know To Cover

Risk Management for:
- Investing
- Customers
- Overall Organization

How to measure risk:
- Good MIS capability
- Good data
- Available risk tools

TOPIC BUCKET APPROACH

Value	Expectations	Delivery
Market risk	Measure risk of investments	Diversify investments
Interest rate risk		
Liquidity risk		
Country Risk		
FX Risk		
Credit Risk	Assess customer risk profiles	Diversify Customer base
		Cull Risky clients
Leverage	Reduce leverage	Hold more capital

Additional Study: For more questions to consider, review Section 13: Roadmaps.

VIDEO 3 Recap & Tips (David Ohrvall)

VIDEO 2 Plan & Structure (Candidate)

Kawaguchi Labs

Sapporo, Japan

Should Kawaguchi bow out of this partnership?

509
START
★★★

Sapporo CITY FACTS

▸ Sixth-largest city in Japan by population

▸ Sapporo is a famous destination for winter sports and activities

▸ Famous for the Sapporo Brewery and white chocolate biscuits called "White Lovers"

TRAIN Profile

Type	**R**egion	**A**nalysis	**I**ndustry	**N**umber
1 CASE START	SAPPORO, JAPAN Population: 1.9M Currency: Japanese Yen	ROADMAP → **13** **Market Shift**	**Pharmaceutical**	LEVEL **1**

Solo Practice with Video Assist

1. Find your videos
2. Set up
3. Present question
4. Recap
5. Create your plan
6. Present your plan
7. Stop and study
8. Reinforce

10 minutes

Partner Practice

1. Set up
2. Present the case question
3. Recap
4. Create your plan
5. Present your plan
6. Stop and study
7. Reinforce

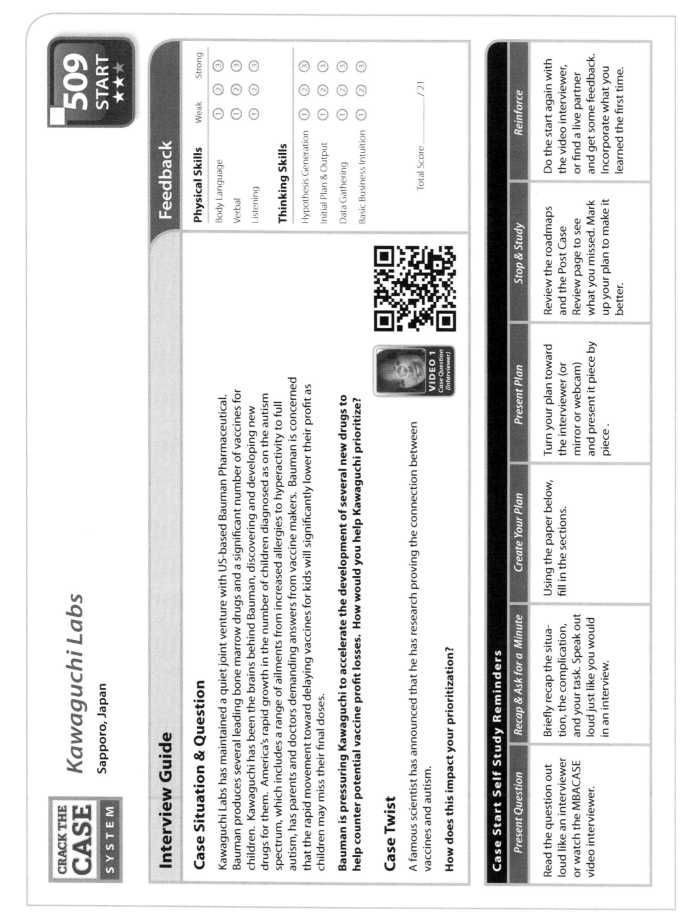

CRACK THE CASE SYSTEM

509
START ★★★

Kawaguchi Labs
Sapporo, Japan

Interview Guide

Case Situation & Question

Kawaguchi Labs has maintained a quiet joint venture with US-based Bauman Pharmaceutical. Bauman produces several leading bone marrow drugs and a significant number of vaccines for children. Kawaguchi has been the brains behind Bauman, discovering and developing new drugs for them. America's rapid growth in the number of children diagnosed as on the autism spectrum, which includes a range of ailments from increased allergies to hyperactivity to full autism, has parents and doctors demanding answers from vaccine makers. Bauman is concerned that the rapid movement toward delaying vaccines for kids will significantly lower their profit as children may miss their final doses.

Bauman is pressuring Kawaguchi to accelerate the development of several new drugs to help counter potential vaccine profit losses. How would you help Kawaguchi prioritize?

Case Twist

A famous scientist has announced that he has research proving the connection between vaccines and autism.

How does this impact your prioritization?

VIDEO 1
Case Question
(Interviewer)

Feedback

Physical Skills

	Weak		Strong
Body Language	①	②	③
Verbal	①	②	③
Listening	①	②	③

Thinking Skills

Hypothesis Generation	①	②	③
Initial Plan & Output	①	②	③
Data Gathering	①	②	③
Basic Business Intuition	①	②	③

Total Score _____ / 21

Case Start Self Study Reminders

Present Question	Recap & Ask for a Minute	Create Your Plan	Present Plan	Stop & Study	Reinforce
Read the question out loud like an interviewer or watch the MBACASE video interviewer.	Briefly recap the situation, the complication, and your task. Speak out loud just like you would in an interview.	Using the paper below, fill in the sections.	Turn your plan toward the interviewer (or mirror or webcam) and present it piece by piece.	Review the roadmaps and the Post Case Review page to see what you missed. Mark up your plan to make it better.	Do the start again with the video interviewer, or find a live partner and get some feedback. Incorporate what you learned the first time.

CRACK THE CASE SYSTEM

Kawaguchi Labs

Sapporo, Japan

My Initial Plan and Output

Today's date:

Questions I'm thinking about:

Topics I know to cover:

Profit Tree Approach:

Topic Bucket Approach:

CRACK THE CASE
SYSTEM

509 START ★★
★★★

Kawaguchi Labs
Sapporo, Japan

Post Case Review

Sample Case Starts

Profit Tree Approach:

$$\pi \rightarrow \begin{array}{l} \text{Revenues} \\ \text{Costs} \end{array}$$

Revenues:
$$P \times V$$

- *P*: What is happening to current prices? What's the prediction over time?
- How might new products be priced?
- *V*: How fast will volume drop for current products?
- What is the estimated volume for new products?

Costs:
$$FC + VC$$
(unit VC × volume)

- *FC*: What kind of fixed cost investment will Kawaguchi need to make?
- *VC*: Will new production require more man hours or input costs?
- What are the estimates in the short and mid-term?

How to shift the company to make up losses?

Topic Bucket Approach: How to deal with shift in consumption?

(External Forces)
- How fast is the shift taking place?
- What is the specific impact – inputs and outputs?

(Revenue / Costs)
- How steep is the revenue drop off?
- Will this continue?
- Can it be brought back?

(Organization)
- How do we realign our people, systems and technology?

(Strategy)
- Are there actions we can take to win back lost profit?
- Acq./merger target that has wider product portfolio?
- Reposition drugs to serve additional markets?

Questions to Consider

☐ When a product shifts, is there another part of the business that can grow?

☐ What are your biggest concerns about the drug pipeline?

☐ Do you think parents will shift their thinking back to previous norms with regard to vaccines?

My Takeaways

I'm doing well with:

I need to work on:

Additional Study: For more questions to consider, review Section 13: Roadmaps.

VIDEO 2
Plan & Structure
(Candidate)

VIDEO 3
Recap & Tips
(David Ohrvall)

Clark & Gable Shoes

Seoul, South Korea

Clark & Gable Shoes is stepping out in a new direction. They want to offer hip, fresh styles to the business casual crowd. Will their Italian design firm help them walk on air or wade into red ink?

510 FULL ★★★

SEOUL CITY FACTS

▸ Was almost completely destroyed during the Korean War

▸ The old city center holds a pavilion with a large bell which once controlled the four major gates to the city; it is now rung 33 times at midnight on New Year's Eve

▸ Location of the world headquarters of taekwondo (the national sport)

TRAIN Profile

Type	**R**egion	**A**nalysis	**I**ndustry	**N**umber
4 FULL BUSINESS	SEOUL, SOUTH KOREA Population: 10M Currency: South Korean won (KRW)	ROADMAP → **3** New Business or Product	Apparel	LEVEL **3**

Solo Practice with Video Assist

1. Find your videos
2. Set up
3. Present question
4. Recap
5. Create your plan
6. Present your plan
7. Stop and study
8. Reinforce

30 minutes

Partner Practice

1. Set up
2. Present the case question
3. Recap
4. Create your plan
5. Present your plan
6. Stop and study
7. Reinforce

Clark & Gable Shoes

Seoul, South Korea

510 FULL ★★★

Interview Guide

Case Situation and Question

Clark & Gable Shoes, a $300M shoe manufacturer and retailer, has a 70-year tradition of making fine men's dress shoes. In the last two years sales have been gradually slipping, mainly due to the business casual trend and C&G's lack of less formal shoes. To fill the gap in its product line and put some energy into the brand, C&G enlisted Luigi, a well known, avant-garde Italian design firm. After six months of sales, management wants to review the results of the ten shoes in their Everyday Style line and eliminate four "dogs" to make way for Luigi's second wave of shoes.

Management wants you to recommend which six styles of shoes to keep and to discuss the implications of eliminating four.

Case Twist

If you had to cut two more shoe styles, which shoe styles would you take out?

VIDEO 1
Case Question
(Interviewer)

Feedback

Physical Skills	Weak		Strong
Body Language	①	②	③
Verbal	①	②	③
Listening	①	②	③

Thinking Skills

Hypothesis Generation	①	②	③
Comfort with Ambiguity	①	②	③
Initial Plan & Output	①	②	③
Data Analysis	①	②	③
Basic Business Intuition	①	②	③
Integration	①	②	③
2nd Level Insights	①	②	③
Creativity	①	②	③

Total Score _____ / 33

Intro Facts (Tell the Candidate if Asked)

Revenue targets: None. Management is more interested in knowing how the launch of these ten shoes compares to previous successful launches. The second wave of Luigi-designed shoes is certain.

Distribution channels: All shoes are sold through C&G's stores, catalogs or online store. For this case, the focus will be on the new line and how it is performing, not on improving the distribution channels. Not using third party retailers means that more profit will hit C&G's bottom line.

Cost structure: Not a focus of this case. The main discussion around costs will center on why some shoes cost more to make than others, resulting in lower gross margins.

Competitors: Most have casual lines. C&G is a laggard.

Suppliers, government and legislation: No issues.

Key Insights (Do Not Tell the Candidate)

General tips: This case is very straightforward: look at the data and eliminate four out of ten products. It requires a quick ability to integrate data from many sources. Star candidates build a logical solution quickly. Since most people will not have trouble coming up with a recommendation, push hard to understand the flaws in the logic. At the end ask, "If you had to eliminate two more, which ones would you pick?"

Product elimination: Eliminating the following four shoes is the best solution for Clark & Gable: Everyday Camel, the Sierra, the Randy and Neuman.

Gross margin: The four eliminated shoes do represent 1/3 of gross margin from 6 months, which is less than the 4/10 they would provide if all 10 shoes were equal.

Unit sales: All previous successful new product launches have had one critical element in common; baseline sales of 2952 units over the first 6 months. The four shoes above do not meet this threshold.

Product appeal: These 4 shoes have not shown much appeal with our most loyal customers.

Product line gaps: After removing the products, there will be a gap in the offering, namely the beach category.

Mid-case Data (Tell Only at Appropriate Time)

"What is the most efficient way to determine which products are going to succeed long-term?"

■ Give the candidate Handout A. Ask, "Which products have contributed the most in terms of gross margin dollars?"

"What role would historical data play?"

■ Give the candidate Handout C, historical product launches. Ask, "What can you infer about previous launches and their ability to succeed?"

"How would you gather data around preferences for certain product types over others?"

■ Give the candidate Handout B, purchases of highly loyal customers. Ask, "How does this data align or disagree with other information you may have?"

"What other considerations do you need to account for when reducing a product line?"

■ Give the candidate Handout D, qualitative description of the product lines. Ask, "Where is our product line weak and strong today?"

Clark & Gable Shoes

Seoul, South Korea

Case Flow and Milestones

1 Present Main Question	**2** Answer Any Basics	**3** Ask for Clarification	**4** Guide Discussion	**5** Get Recommendation
Candidate takes notes, asks for a minute, forms a plan and presents it.	These may come up after you read the question or later.	"Tell me more about this area (you choose). What are you thinking about here?" or "Tell me how the parts of your structure link to each other." No data. Ask questions about his approach.	To solve the case he will need data on units, revenue and gross margin. Your main goal with giving this case is to eventually get all 4 slides in front of the candidate. Review the Mid-Case Data on page 2 to prompt him.	The candidate needs to integrate his insights into a selection process. Staying data-driven is the best course of action, so the candidate should calculate the bottom-line implication of his choice. A good conclusion will make sense mathematically and logically.

Handout and Data Guide

Additional Info

Handout A:

Candidate: Do you have any sales data?

Interviewer: Here's what we know about the six month launch in terms of unit volume. Revenue and gross margin per shoe are also shown.

Ask: Which products are contributing the most in gross margin dollars?

Insight: Revenue per shoe varies quite a bit, but a majority of the shoes contribute $100 in gross margin per sale.

Handout B:

Candidate: Do customers like the products?

Interviewer: We polled our most loyal customers with pictures and prices of each new shoe. Here's what they said.

You Must Ask: Which shoes seem to be most disliked? Which ones are the favorites?

Insight: Three shoes rated poorly: Neuman, the Randy, and Everyday Camel. People either loved or hated Berks.

Handout C:

Candidate: Do we have any historical benchmarks for product launches?

Interviewer: C&G has tracked their last 25 launches.

You Might Ask: What can you infer from the data about the minimum required for success?

Insight: Previous launches that succeeded all had sales of at least 2,952 units in their first six months.

Handout D:

Candidate: Do you have any descriptions of the shoes and how they differ?

Interviewer: Here is a qualitative style map. This depicts the niche each shoe fills.

You Must Ask: What would be the implications of removing the shoes you are considering eliminating?

Insight: Gaps will occur as a result of removing some shoes. Wave 2 from Luigi will need to fill these gaps.

Prompt the Candidate by asking the following questions:

(See Post Case Review page for answers)

Company Philosophy: How long does Clark & Gable test their new products?

Units and Gross Margin: Are there any similarities across gross margin by product?

Historical Success: Is there an historical unit sales threshold?

Customer Feedback: What shoes do the customers like best?

Style: How do your cuts impact C&G's portfolio of styles?

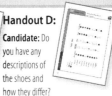

Re-routers | Questions to Keep Things on Track

- **What do you think is a good basis for making this decision?**
  - ‣ Historical launches and their units sold
  - ‣ Gross margin contribution
  - ‣ Customer feedback or interest

- **What value is there in looking at gross margin?**
  - ‣ Gross margin is defined as revenue minus direct labor and materials. Gross margins tell

you how much of a product's revenue is eaten up by the cost to produce it.

  - ‣ In the case of C&G, most of the gross margin percentages were the same, so there was not a lot to explore. Making labor more efficient and/or reducing material costs would result in higher gross margins.

- How can you make your answer more quantitative?

Clark & Gable Shoes
Seoul, South Korea

Additional Study Using the FRAME Method

F – Form a Plan

MVM™

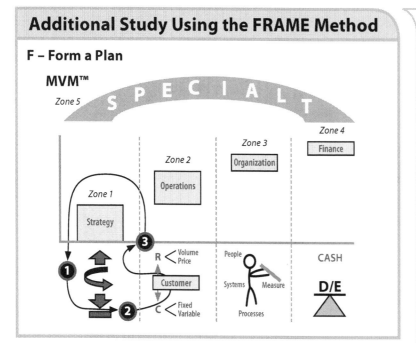

M—Mine for the Answer

Now you can mine for data. Use your plan as a guide along with your initial hypothesis. Try to ask 2–3 questions in each section you explore.

Revenue & Costs	Customer Reaction	Shoe Portfolio
■ **How much revenue do we typically make per shoe?** *Revenue per shoe for the new line averages around $150, plus or minus $30 for exceptions.*	■ **Will customers respond negatively when the shoes are cut from the line?** *Using unit sales of 2,952 as a threshold, the four lowest performers are Everyday Camel, the Randy, the Sierra and Neuman. By selecting the ones that have the lowest unit sales, the smallest number of customers will be disturbed.*	■ **What various lifestyle needs is our line trying to address?** *The most well-represented categories are office casual, club (evening), and hip (fashion-forward). This suggests a young and affluent customer.*
■ **What are the costs and resulting gross margin per shoe?** *Gross Margin % is hard to estimate from the chart but $ are easy to see: five shoes earn ~$100, 3 shoes earn ~ $75, 1 earns $125 and another $150.*	■ **What kind of shoes do our most loyal customers like?** *Loyal customers were not fond of three of the four. The Sierra elicited an average response.*	■ **What gaps will result from these eliminations? Will the gaps hurt our long-term sales?** *If you eliminate four shoe lines, gaps will result in the beach and club categories. Shoes, considered to be more hip, will disappear. This gap could be a problem as C&G tries to reach new customers. The businesses want freedom to make independent decisions more quickly without having to obtain senior management's approval.*
■ **In past launches, what is the typical number of units sold in the first six months?** *Past successful shoes had at least 2,952 units sold in the first six months. This is a good benchmark.*		

---

1. **Start in Zone 1, Strategy – Change Direction.** This is a mental placeholder until you answer the question of narrowing the new shoe line. You should return here if possible.

2. **Move to Zone 2, Operations.** How are the shoe lines performing? Compare them in terms of unit sales, revenue and margin.

3. **Stay in Operations.** After you eliminate some styles, consider these issues:

   ■ Customer Response – How will our most loyal customers respond to these cuts? Should we care more about this group, or about to new customers?

   ■ Historical Performance – How have successful shoes performed in the past?

   ■ Product Offering – What gaps will exist in our product line?

4. **Finish back in Zone 1.** Can you estimate the new line's growth and profit potential? Is that enough for management?

A - Anchor a Hypothesis

The key to using a hypothesis well is to anchor your initial thought and then look for data that will help you prove or disprove your hunch.

Look for the Most Profitable Shoes

"Since I have to eliminate shoes based on only six months of data, I need to find the ones that produce the greatest profit or gross margin dollars."

Consider the Portfolio and Seasonal Mix

"Since C&G launched ten shoes, it is likely that each shoe is playing a role in the overall portfolio. I need to look for any seasonal impact in the data and see if "dogs" are performing poorly because of their purpose (e.g., winter boots vs. beach sandals)."

E - End the Case

"I recommend C&G eliminate the following four shoes: Everyday Camel, the Sierra, the Randy and Neuman. I'm basing my decision on historical measures of success for new products. These shoes represent one-third of our total gross margin from the first six months, but because they do not meet our six month benchmark of 2,952 units, I don't think they have long term potential. Most of them turned off our loyal customers as well."

510 FULL ★★★
CRACK THE CASE SYSTEM

Clark & Gable Shoes
Seoul, South Korea

Post Case Review

Case Insights & Takeaways

What did you learn?

Company Philosophy: Clark & Gable has tough standards, shown by its willingness to "cut bait" or eliminate new product lines after only 6 months of data.

Units and Gross Margin: Unit sales and gross margin percentages vary widely, but revenue is roughly in the same range for the ten products. About 7 of the 10 shoes provide gross margin dollars of over $100 each (Handout A).

Historical Success: All shoe lines that succeeded in the last 25 launches exceeded unit sales of 2,952 in their first six months (Handout C).

Customer Feedback: Loyal customers dislike these 4 shoes: Neuman, the Randy, Berks and Everyday Camel.

Style: Most of the products are focused on the office casual, club and hip factor styles. Removing certain products may leave holes in the portfolio.

How does it tie together?

Use a logical rule to make your selection. In this case, sticking to the unit sale requirements is a good method. Four shoes do not make the historical cut-off of 2,952 for the first 6 months. Knowlton is close enough and carries a large GM dollar contribution, so you would probably want to keep it.

Check the downside. From a total, six-month gross margin dollar comparison, these four are good choices. Neuman rivals several others that were not selected, but loyal customers do not like it.

Consider the gaps. Beach will not be covered with these choices. Next steps should include reviewing the portfolio coverage.

My Takeaways

To build skills and improve, you must apply what you learned to future cases. Take a few moments and review the interviewer feedback and jot down some key insights about your performance in the space below.

Thinking Skills

My top 2 strengths are:

My top 2 soft spots are:

To address these problems I'll begin to:

VIDEO 3
Recap & Tips
(David Ohrvall)

My Performance During the Case

Add up your points. → Total Score: _____ / 15

F Form A Plan	**R** Read My Audience	**A** Anchor a Hypothesis	**M** Mine for Answers	**E** End the Case
points	points	points	points	points
③ Structured, clean	③ Good back & forth, caught clues	③ Solid hunch, pursued clue	③ Specific questions, solid analysis	③ Used facts and data, connected the dots
② Somewhat organized and logical	② Awkward, trouble with interviewer style	② Partial direction	② Missed some questions, some math mistakes	② Some data, mostly understood connections
① Messy, overlapping ideas	① Interviewer not interested, couldn't follow	① No hypothesis at all	① Vague questions, weak math, no linkages	① No data, no passion, no connections

Clark & Gable Shoes

Seoul, South Korea

Interviewer's Data Guide

Make estimates and round your numbers

Review the Slides

- Look for a simple method or "cutoff" to eliminate some of the shoes.
- One approach is to use the historical successful launches as a benchmark.
- Since every successful product in the past had at least 2,952 units sold in the first six months, that number may be a good start.

Apply Your Rule

- Shoes that do not have unit sales of at least 2,952 are:
  - ▸ Everyday Camel, Sierra, Randy, Neuman

Check Implications

- **Customers:** Will they be upset if you cut these four? Not likely, given the loyal customer survey. Only the Sierra was borderline in terms of customers being unsure vs. interested in buying it.
- **Shoe Line:** Removing these four will create gaps in the "hip" and "beach" categories. This is a softer point and could lead to a discussion about what Wave 2 should try to fill.
- **Bottom Line:** From a gross margin point of view, what's the impact? The table at the right (make this quickly during the interview) gives us a view.

Shoe	~GM$	UNITS	Rounded Totals (K)
CAMEL	100	1200	120
PIERC	150	3300	500
SULT	75	3500	260
BREAK	75	2900	220
KNOW	100	2950	300
SIERRA	125	1500	200
DULS	100	3200	320
BERKS	100	3150	315
RAND	75	1420	110
NEUM	100	2450	250

Cutting these four will eliminate two that were contributing decent, six-month total gross margin (SIE, N) and two that were, at the bottom (EC, R).

HANDOUT A

Clark & Gable Shoes
Seoul, South Korea

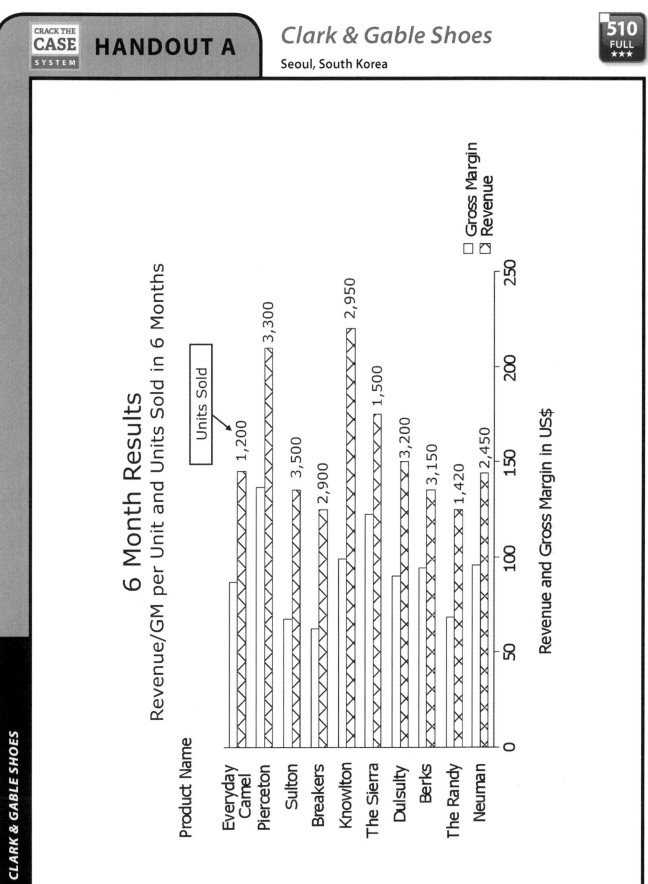

6 Month Results

Revenue/GM per Unit and Units Sold in 6 Months

Product Name

Units Sold

Product	Units Sold
Everyday Camel	1,200
Pierceton	3,300
Sulton	3,500
Breakers	2,900
Knowlton	2,950
The Sierra	1,500
Dulsulty	3,200
Berks	3,150
The Randy	1,420
Neuman	2,450

Revenue and Gross Margin in US$

☐ Gross Margin
☒ Revenue

HANDOUT B

Clark & Gable Shoes

Seoul, South Korea

510 FULL ★★★

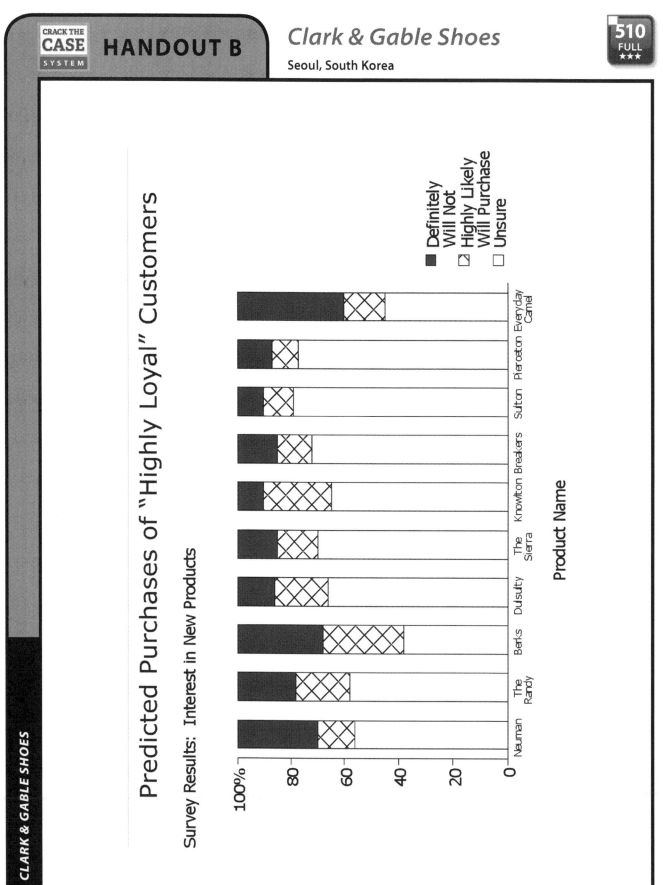

Predicted Purchases of "Highly Loyal" Customers

Survey Results: Interest in New Products

Legend:
- ■ Definitely Will Not
- ▨ Highly Likely Will Purchase
- □ Unsure

Product Names (x-axis): Neuman, The Randy, Berks, Dusuty, The Sierra, Knowlton Breakers, Sutton, Pierceton, Everyday Camel

Y-axis: 0, 20, 40, 60, 80, 100%

Product Name

HANDOUT C

Clark & Gable Shoes
Seoul, South Korea

510 FULL ★★★

Historical Profile of Last 25 Launches
Shaded bars indicate shoe lines that succeeded

Unit Sales Over 6 Months

Product Number	Unit Sales
25	3,243
59	3,493
91	2,952
21	3,363
57	2,725
1	2,441
24	3,609
16	3,574
83	4,133
43	2,771
7	3,346
79	2,647
9	3,268
72	2,212
63	2,636
22	2,328
68	3,913
26	4,415
38	3,911
70	3,980

HANDOUT D

Clark & Gable Shoes
Seoul, South Korea

510
FULL
★★★

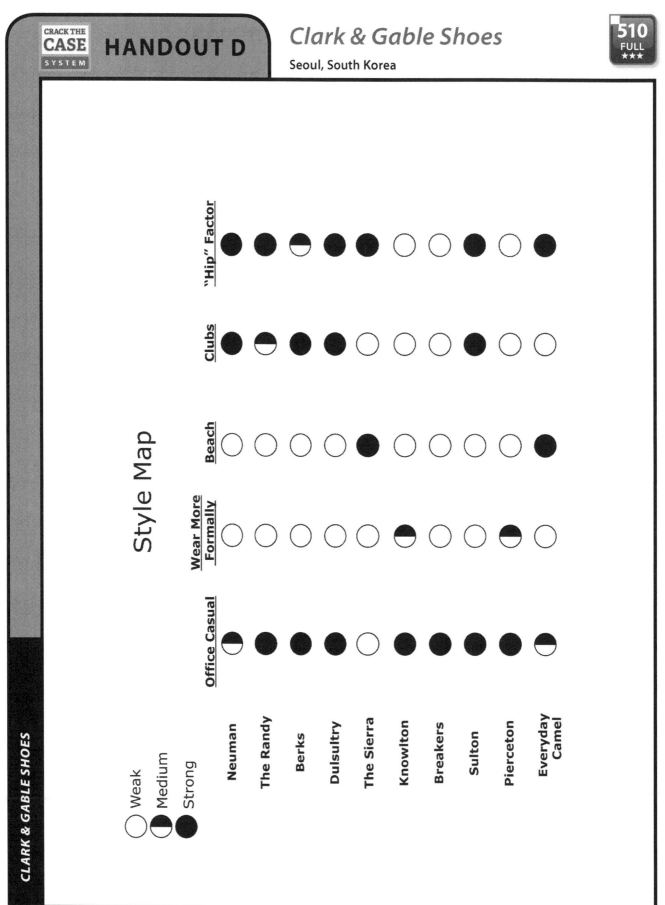

Style Map

Weak ○
Medium ◑
Strong ●

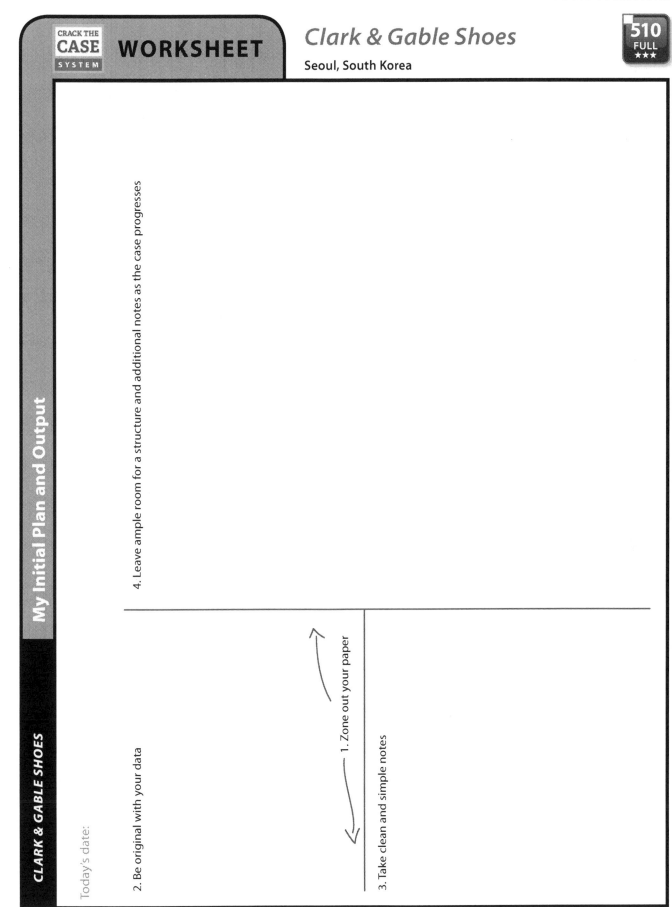

CRACK THE CASE SYSTEM

WORKSHEET

Clark & Gable Shoes

Seoul, South Korea

510 FULL ★★★

CLARK & GABLE SHOES

My Initial Plan and Output

Today's date:

2. Be original with your data

1. Zone out your paper

3. Take clean and simple notes

4. Leave ample room for a structure and additional notes as the case progresses

CRACK THE CASE SYSTEM — WORKSHEET

Clark & Gable Shoes
Seoul, South Korea

510 FULL ★★★

CLARK & GABLE SHOES

Potential Plan and Output

Which 6 styles to keep?
Implications of removing 4?

Metrics > Revenue

What's the total revenue per product?

How steady has each shoe's revenue been over time?

Cost to Produce / profit

Does any shoe line require additional costs, expensive processes or unusual labor?

Units Sold

Which shoe has the largest demand?

Have unit sales been steady or uneven?

Are there any clear "dogs" that are underperforming?

Customer Reaction

Are there any clear favorites?

Do customers dislike any specific shoe?

HUNCH: Focus on units sold. Pricing can vary but units moved will be most important.

Rev – $300M

Costs – ?

Profit – ?

No financial targets

Goal: Review 10 shoes, remove 4 styles

· Clark & Gable Shoes

· 70 year tradition, fine men's shoes

· Sales slipping > casual trend

· Lack less formal shoes

· Luigi – Italian design

· 6 month sales review

· Preparing for 2nd wave

Voiceover

"In order to evaluate the new line's performance to date, I'm going to focus on the basics: revenue, cost to produce, units sold and customer reaction. After I understand the fact base better, I'd like to talk about the strategic implications of my reductions. To begin, may I review any sales results you have for the first six months?"

Additional Study: For more questions to consider, review Section 13: Roadmaps.

VIDEO 2 Plan & Structure (Candidate)

Fitness Xtreme

Naperville, Illinois, US

Fitness Xtreme, land of the lean and limber, needs to go on a diet. Membership fees are down and management is eyeing its costs. Should the trainers get the axe?

601 FULL ★★★

NAPERVILLE CITY FACTS

- ▸ Rated as a Top 10 Best Places to Live in America 3 times by Money Magazine
- ▸ Home to multiple high-tech companies like the BP North American Chemical Headquarters, Nalco Holding Company, Tellabes, and Alcatel-Lucent
- ▸ A thriving downtown anchored by a Riverwalk with fountains and bridges, and one of the world's only 6-octave carillons

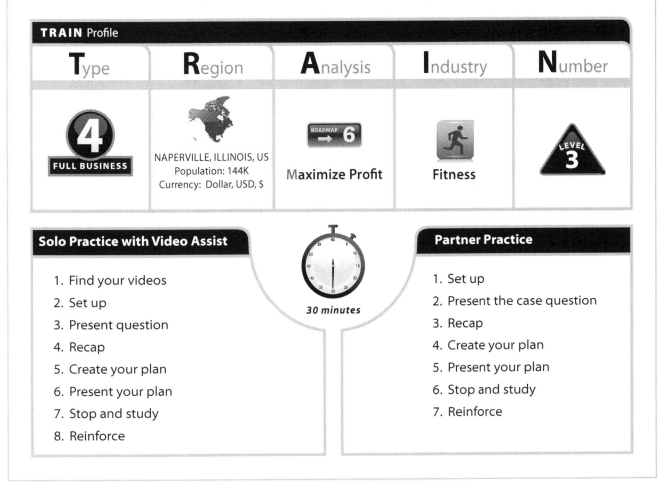

TRAIN Profile

Type	**R**egion	**A**nalysis	**I**ndustry	**N**umber
4 FULL BUSINESS	NAPERVILLE, ILLINOIS, US Population: 144K Currency: Dollar, USD, $	ROADMAP → **6** Maximize Profit	Fitness	LEVEL **3**

Solo Practice with Video Assist

1. Find your videos
2. Set up
3. Present question
4. Recap
5. Create your plan
6. Present your plan
7. Stop and study
8. Reinforce

30 minutes

Partner Practice

1. Set up
2. Present the case question
3. Recap
4. Create your plan
5. Present your plan
6. Stop and study
7. Reinforce

Fitness Xtreme

Naperville, Illinois, US

601 FULL ★★★

Interview Guide

Case Situation and Question

Fitness Xtreme, a mega-gym located in the Midwest, offers its members 45,000 square feet of indoor fitness: state of the art equipment, multiple gymnasiums, dance studios, racquet ball courts, a climbing wall, swimming pools, on-site child care, and a healthy fare café. They even have a day spa on site! In the wake of a recent economic slowdown and waning memberships, it has been difficult to keep such a monstrosity functioning profitably. As a result, management is looking to cut costs. They are eyeing the personal training staff. Half the management team thinks they offer little benefit to members, while the other half believes that they are critical to Fitness Xtreme's value proposition.

What should FX do?

Case Twist

How would you change your answer if trainers were 100% busy with new member sessions and private sessions?

What is the most effective way to get data supporting the true value of the trainers?

VIDEO 1
Case Question
(Interviewer)

Feedback

Physical Skills

	Weak		Strong
Body Language	①	②	③
Verbal	①	②	③
Listening	①	②	③

Thinking Skills

Hypothesis Generation	①	②	③
Comfort with Ambiguity	①	②	③
Initial Plan & Output	①	②	③
Data Analysis	①	②	③
Basic Business Intuition	①	②	③
Integration	①	②	③
2nd Level Insights	①	②	③
Creativity	①	②	③

Total Score _____ / 33

Intro Facts (Tell the Candidate if Asked)

Cost containment: Management is leery of making too many cutbacks for fear of losing members.

Economic outlook: The economy seems to be improving. Many experts predict a recovery in the next six to twelve months. Gym memberships typically rise and fall in line with the economy.

Member opinions: There is no data on what members think of the trainers.

Competitors: FX is the only mega-gym of its kind within 20 miles.

Key Insights (Do Not Tell the Candidate)

General Tips: This is a fun case because it involves something everyone understands (fitness) and something many often wonder about (do fitness trainers add any value?).

Look to see if your candidate could ballpark the numbers quickly (e.g. costs are ~$7M, revenue is about ~$10M) before diving deep. It is a valuable skill, and critical for finishing cases on time.

Trainers are a break-even proposition. Trainers are barely paying for themselves. Without changing their salary structure, we know that their value lies in attracting/retaining members, not generating revenue.

Few members use personal training. Trainers perform 900 (18 trainers x 2.5 sessions x 20 working days) sessions per month. Since the average trainee meets 2X per week, 450 different people are being trained. That's less than 5% of the 14,000 membership base.

To be valuable, trainers must be offering other intrinsic value. Trainers could be adding value by attracting new customers or by giving tips throughout the day that the members appreciate. You do not have any data to show whether or not they are providing a service that draws or keeps members, but it would make a good discussion toward the end of the interview.

Mid-case Data (Tell Only at Appropriate Time)

In this case you will read the Interviewer Data Guide. To draw the Candidate out, ask a few of these questions:

"What kind of data would you need to best understand the potential trainer cuts?"

"What specifically would you be looking for with revenue data?"

"What cost information would be most relevant to you?"

"What other data would you need to support your analysis?"

Is management focused on the right area? Refer to the bar charts in the Handout and Data Guide.

Lease Payments is the largest cost category. Assume it's a fixed cost.

Employee Salaries is the next largest area, so management is right to focus there.

Trainer Salaries is the largest item within Salary Costs, and there is no guarantee that they are helping to retain or attract members. We could also look at Sales Staff, but since memberships are down we don't want to reduce in that category.

Note that membership dues comprise 80% of revenue. Training fees contribute only 7%.

Fitness Xtreme

Naperville, Illinois, US

Case Flow and Milestones

1 Present Main Question	**2** Answer Any Basics	**3** Ask for Clarification	**4** Guide Discussion	**5** Get Recommendation
Candidate takes notes, asks for a minute, forms a plan and presents it.	This case has no handouts, so be prepared to give quite a bit of information.	Be sure to make him explain anything you do not fully understand. You might ask: "Tell me more about this area (you choose). What are you thinking about here?" Or, "Tell me how the parts of your structure link to each other."	To understand the significance of any cost reduction, it is important to understand the full revenue & cost structure of the company. Ask the Candidate what kind of data he wants, and then read the data to him from the Interviewer's Data Guide.	See Additional Info below for the major insights. Consider asking these questions if you have more time: • "Do you think Fitness Xtreme needs to offer this many amenities to be successful?" • "What is your 80/20 hunch about the fastest way to boost membership?"

Handout and Data Guide

A few 100% bar charts can help keep the data organized.

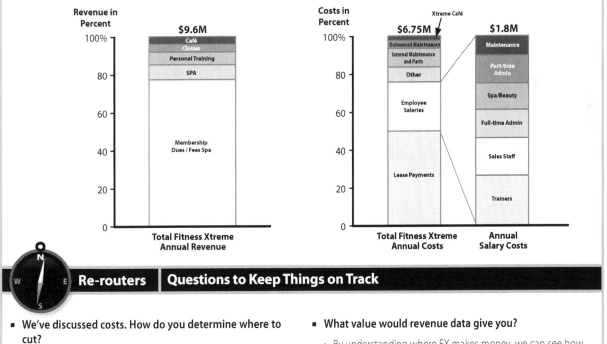

Re-routers — Questions to Keep Things on Track

- **We've discussed costs. How do you determine where to cut?**
  - Look at the largest buckets and the ones that are the most controllable.
  - In this case, lease payments are large but hard to change. Salaries are easier to change, but cutting them can be complicated.

- **What value would revenue data give you?**
  - By understanding where FX makes money, we can see how cost cuts would have an impact.
  - In this case, membership fees comprise 80% of revenue; training comprises less than 10%.
- **What additional data would you like to see?**
- **How can you make your answer more quantitative?**

435

Fitness Xtreme

Naperville, Illinois, US

601
FULL
★★★

Additional Study Using the FRAME Method

F – Form a Plan

MVM™

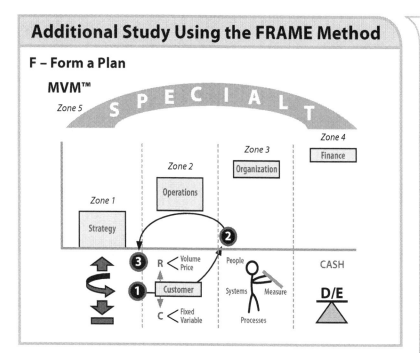

1. **Start in Zone 2, Operations, Costs.** First, understand the size of the cost bar and how it relates in proportionally to the revenue line. In general, personnel costs will be variable, but FX may believe it needs a "fixed" or minimum set of trainers to do well.

2. **Move to Zone 3, Organization, People.** Understand the structure of the training staff; then discuss how FX might restructure the staff and their schedules. Relate these new ideas back to the costs.

3. **Move to Zone 2, Operations, Revenue.** How would changes to the cost bar impact total revenue? Would there be a dip in revenues because the overall "quality of the gym" has declined? Would current members miss having the staff available for personal training and join another gym? Would potential members decide against joining FX if personal training is unavailable?

M—Mine for the Answer

What kind of questions did you ask? Even though the categories are simple, there are all kinds of questions that you can ask. Consider the following:

Costs	Revenue	Hybrid Solution
■ **What does the total cost bar look like?** *Total annual costs are $6.75M.*	■ **What is membership revenue?** *Total annual revenue is $9.5M.*	■ **What portion of the trainer's time is unused?** *Trainers on average have only two appointments per day (20 days out of the month).*
■ **What portion of costs do the trainers' salaries represent?** *Trainer salaries are 9% of total costs.*	■ **What portion of it is tied to using a personal trainer?** *Personal trainer fees amount to 9% of the total revenue.*	■ **If we reduce the number of trainers could we still meet demand?** *It would be easy to meet demand with a reduced number of trainers.*
■ **How much of the cost is for full-time salaries and how much is for part-time salaries?** *All the trainer salaries are full-time at this point.*	■ **What do we know about members and their use of trainers?** *Some members are heavy users while others never use trainers. All members get one free session with a trainer when they join.*	■ **What risk is there to having fewer, higher quality trainers?** *Little risk since there are so many trainers who are unutilized.*
■ **At what point will trainers leave due to salary cuts?** *Most of the trainers are looking to make at least $30K per year.*	■ **How many members would leave the gym if trainers were no longer available?** *We don't have data on how many may potentially leave the gym.*	

A - Anchor a Hypothesis

What were your thoughts here? If you are new to forming a hunch, try one of these simple options below. Pay close attention to the data, though, as your hunch may be wrong.

Keep the Trainers

"Trainers can't cost that much and it is likely that they earn their keep through special member charges."

Cut the Trainers

"In my own experience, I never see the trainers adding all that much value. It is unlikely that they are used often, and it does seem that there might be some savings potential."

Optimize the Trainers

"Keeping or cutting is too black and white. I think there are some inefficiencies that we can remove. Also, I think there are benefits to having the trainers on-site as they often help train new members and lend an air of professionalism to the gym."

E - End the Case

"Our investment in trainers today represents about 10% of our overall costs, but provides little more than break-even revenue. The real question is whether they are providing some intrinsic value that, when removed, would hurt our revenue. For instance, if all 450 members being trained in one-on-one sessions left, we'd lose about 3% of our annual revenue. Since trainers are only utilized two-thirds of the time, we could reduce the staff by a third, saving a quarter million in annual revenue. Another idea would be to boost revenue and loyalty by giving away their time or discounting the hourly rate. I recommend we explore these two options."

Fitness Xtreme

Naperville, Illinois, US

601
FULL
★★★

Post Case Review

Case Insights & Takeaways

- Since trainers may not be a stand-alone profit center, you had to think about whether they are valuable in other ways. Are they offering free help, cleaning equipment or being used as part of any promotions to members?

- Cutting the trainers completely did not save enough to be significant. On every case, look at revenue increases or cost savings in comparison to the overall size of the company.

Math & Logic Tips

- When faced with a difficult to measure question, like "Are trainers valuable?", look to measure usage. See Additional Info Quick Insight for a calculation you could have done.

- This "data dump" case literally had the interviewer dumping data on your head. Staying organized with small charts will help you keep it all straight. Don't worry if you can't make your charts to the right proportion. Even a "rough" version will help you ask better follow-up questions.

What to Expect with Cases Like These

- This case started with a very specific question and stayed on that topic. If you want to structure your initial plan with broader areas, like revenue growth or member expansion, do that after you address the interviewer's specific questions (trainer costs in this case).

- Estimate your math whenever possible.

- As you do the math, note takeaways that you want to use in your conclusion. Put a circle around the key facts for quick retrieval at the end.

My Takeaways

To build skills and improve, you must apply what you learned to future cases. Take a few moments and review the interviewer feedback and jot down some key insights about your performance in the space below.

Thinking Skills

My top 2 strengths are:

My top 2 soft spots are:

To address these problems I'll begin to:

VIDEO 3
*Recap & Tips
(David Ohrvall)*

My Performance During the Case

Add up your points. ➡ Total Score: _____ /15

F Form A Plan	**R** Read My Audience	**A** Anchor a Hypothesis	**M** Mine for Answers	**E** End the Case
points	points	points	points	points
③ Structured, clean	③ Good back & forth, caught clues	③ Solid hunch, pursued clue	③ Specific questions, solid analysis	③ Used facts and data, connected the dots
② Somewhat organized and logical	② Awkward, trouble with interviewer style	② Partial direction	② Missed some questions, some math mistakes	② Some data, mostly understood connections
① Messy, overlapping ideas	① Interviewer not interested, couldn't follow	① No hypothesis at all	① Vague questions, weak math, no linkages	① No data, no passion, no connections

Fitness Xtreme

Naperville, Illinois, US

Interviewer's Data Guide

There is a lot of information to give, so it is likely that you'll need to give it in pieces. All of the data is necessary, so if the candidate does not ask for it you may have to eventually give it. In each section, try to have the Candidate think through what data he needs before you give it. You should ask questions like, "What data would be relevant here?"

Table 1	Cost Data (monthly)	
Employee salaries	$150,000	(includes trainers and others, more detail below)
Internal maintenance & parts	$50,000	(repair of exercise machines, infrastructure, etc.)
Outsourced maintenance	$25 000	(landscaping, HVAC, paving, etc .)
Xtreme Café food	$12,000	(light fare ingredients and packaged foods)
Lease payments	$275,000	(long-term, non-negotiable)
Other	$50,000	(miscellaneous costs like new towels)
Total	**$562,000**	

Table 2	Revenue Data (monthly)	
Memberships	$616,000	(initial fee and monthly)
Xtreme Café	$30,000	
Spa/ Beauty Treatments	$60,000	
Family/ Individual Classes	$35,000	
Personal Training	$54,000	(see detail below)
Total	**$795,000**	

Table 3	Salary Cost Breakdown (monthly)	
Trainers	$52,500	(18 full-time x 35k)
Maintenance	$23,333	(8 full-time x 35k)
Spa/ Beauty	$30,000	(8 full time x 45k*) *includes tips
Part-time Admin	$31,250	(15 part-time x 25k)
Full-time Admin	$28,000	(7 full-time x 48k)
Sales Staff	$37,500	(15 part-time x 30k)
Total	**$202,583**	

Key Variables

Monthly Membership

14,000 members x $110 (average of monthly and start-up fees / 2.5 (ratio to account for families with kids)
= $616,000

Personal Trainers

18 trainers x $60 per session x 2.5 sessions per day x 20 average working days per month
= $54,000

Average Daily Trainer Activities:

One-on-one sessions	2.5 hours	31% (sessions booked by member, $60 per hour)
Introductory sessions	3 hours	38% (free to new member, may build trainer's book)
"Walking the aisles"	2.5 hours	31% (no set duties; lending ad hoc assistance to members)

WORKSHEET

CRACK THE CASE SYSTEM

Fitness Xtreme
Naperville, Illinois, US

FITNESS XTREME

My Initial Plan and Output

Today's date:

2. Be original with your data

1. Zone out your paper

3. Take clean and simple notes

4. Leave ample room for a structure and additional notes as the case progresses

WORKSHEET

CRACK THE CASE SYSTEM

Fitness Xtreme
Naperville, Illinois, US

601 FULL ★★★

Potential Plan and Output

FITNESS XTREME

Rev - ?

Costs - ?

Profit Margin -

Goal: cut costs

Profit issue!

- Fitness Extreme / Midwest / big
- 45k sg. ft.
- state of art / gym / dance
- rag ball / climb / swim
- day care, food
- spa
- econ slowdown - profit down
- 50/50 - cut or keep trainers

Should trainers be cut?

Costs

What are total costs?

How do trainer costs compare as a percent?

Are they varying due to usage or are they fixed?

Organization, People

How are the trainers structured?

What do they do to gain business? Are they fully utilized?

Can we structure their schedules to optimize usages and benefit to the gym?

HUNCH: day to day activities need to be changed. Likely underutilized.

Revenue

What is the total revenue for the gym?

If trainers are removed, how much will revenue drop?

Would members not join if trainers were not there?

Competitors

Do they have trainers?

Do we need them to match status and overall offerings?

Are there industry approaches we are not using?

Voiceover

"I'd like to approach this problem from several angles. First, let's review the costs and find out what kind of savings would be achieved by eliminating the trainers. They may be a small category and we'll need to look at other cost cutting. Next, I would like to understand the structure of the team and see if there are any win/win solutions to keeping people while still reducing costs. We might be able to realign their activities around attracting new members for example. Third, management is concerned about declining membership and total revenue. We should try to gauge the revenue impact of our decision and see if removing trainers would hurt revenue. Finally, it would be good to check on the competitors and industry standards for trainers. To get started do you have any data in the cost area?"

Additional Study: For more questions to consider, review Section 13: Roadmaps.

VIDEO 2 Plan & Structure (Candidate)

CRACK THE CASE SYSTEM

Muncie Mission Ministries

Muncie, Indiana, US

How far can the Muncie Mission spread its goodwill toward men?

602 START
★★★

MUNCIE CITY FACTS

▸ Home of Ball State University and Ball Corporation, and the birthplace of David Ohrvall

▸ Known as Middletown USA and often a favorite town among filmmakers, it is used to represent the archetypical Midwestern, small town

▸ Settled in 1770s by Delaware Indians

TRAIN Profile

Type	**R**egion	**A**nalysis	**I**ndustry	**N**umber
1 CASE START	MUNCIE, INDIANA, US Population: 65K Currency: Dollar, USD, $	ROADMAP **2** Growth Strategy	Non-profit	LEVEL **1**

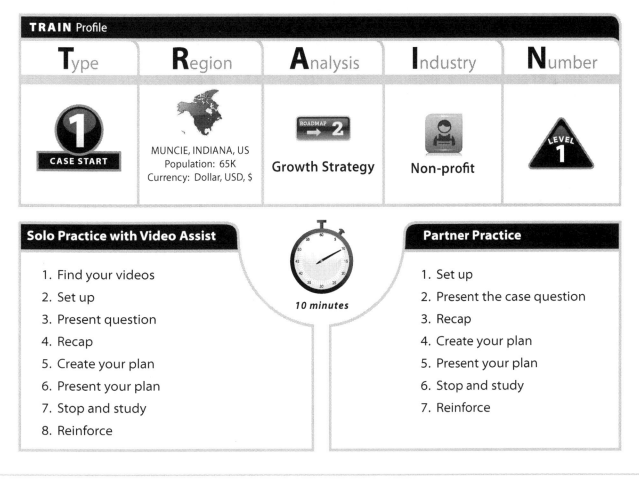

Solo Practice with Video Assist

1. Find your videos
2. Set up
3. Present question
4. Recap
5. Create your plan
6. Present your plan
7. Stop and study
8. Reinforce

10 minutes

Partner Practice

1. Set up
2. Present the case question
3. Recap
4. Create your plan
5. Present your plan
6. Stop and study
7. Reinforce

CRACK THE CASE
SYSTEM

Muncie Mission Ministries
Muncie, Indiana, US

602 START ★★★

Interview Guide

Case Situation & Question

Muncie Mission Ministries is a faith-based, not-for-profit agency that has brought hope to the poor, needy and homeless in East Central Indiana for over 80 years. They have programs for families and children and are now looking to expand to an additional location. They specialize in helping men with alcohol and drug addictions get back on track through their addiction recovery programs, job training and job placement. They think there is a growing need in nearby regions.

How would you help them pull together a strategy?

Case Twist

A tragic July 4th fire just burned a majority of the mission's main building in Muncie. It was insured but most of the building will need to be replaced.

How does this information affect your plan?

VIDEO 1
Case Question
(Interviewer)

Feedback

Physical Skills

	Weak		Strong
Body Language	①	②	③
Verbal	①	②	③
Listening	①	②	③

Thinking Skills

Hypothesis Generation	①	②	③
Initial Plan & Output	①	②	③
Data Gathering	①	②	③
Basic Business Intuition	①	②	③

Total Score _____ / 21

Case Start Self Study Reminders

Present Question	Recap & Ask for a Minute	Create Your Plan	Present Plan	Stop & Study	Reinforce
Read the question out loud like an interviewer or watch the MBACASE video interviewer.	Briefly recap the situation, the complication, and your task. Speak out loud just like you would in an interview.	Using the paper below, fill in the sections.	Turn your plan toward the interviewer (or mirror or webcam) and present it piece by piece .	Review the roadmaps and the Post Case Review page to see what you missed. Mark up your plan to make it better.	Do the start again with the video interviewer, or find a live partner and get some feedback. Incorporate what you learned the first time.

CRACK THE CASE SYSTEM

602 START ★ ★ ★

Muncie Mission Ministries

Muncie, Indiana, US

My Initial Plan and Output

Today's date:

Questions I'm thinking about:

Topics I know to cover:

Profit Tree Approach:

Topic Bucket Approach:

CRACK THE CASE SYSTEM

Muncie Mission Ministries

Muncie, Indiana, US

602 START ★★★

Post Case Review

Sample Case Starts

Profit Tree Approach:

$$\pi \rightarrow \begin{array}{c} \text{Revenues} \\ \\ \text{Costs} \end{array}$$

Revenues

$$P$$
$$\times$$
$$V$$

Costs

$$FC$$
$$+$$
$$VC$$
(unit VC × volume)

How to break even?

- Since, non-profit, pricing by "unit" may not be critical.
- Does funding source pay per individual?
- How does payment per person compare to other locations?

- What number of individuals need to be served to hit threshold for individual or flat fee funding?
- Where do additional volumes of people push up the costs?

- Do we need new facility? Buy, build or lease?
- Equipment? Bus, cars, tables, beds, kitchen, workrooms?
- Office equipment, computers

- Will new production require more man hours or input costs?
- What are the estimates in the short and mid-term?

Topic Bucket Approach: Should Muncie Mission grow by expanding to a new location?

Industry/Comp
- What is the trend with other non-profits?
- Is multi-location best?

Growth Options
- Serving more patients locally?
- Serving more in new location?
- Serve different demographics?

Funding
- Sources for MM?
- National, State, Local Gov't
- Companies, Charities
- Individual Donations

Costs
- Fixed – building, buy, build or lease
- Equipment – buses, beds, kitchen, tables, other
- People & materials – food, clothes, bedding, personal

Questions to Consider

- [ ] For a non-profit, what are sources of funding?
- [ ] How does the Muncie Mission define success? Number of men helped? Individual recovery?
- [ ] What risks are there when entering a market farther away from headquarters?

My Takeaways

I'm doing well with:

I need to work on:

Additional Study: For more questions to consider, review Section 13: Roadmaps.

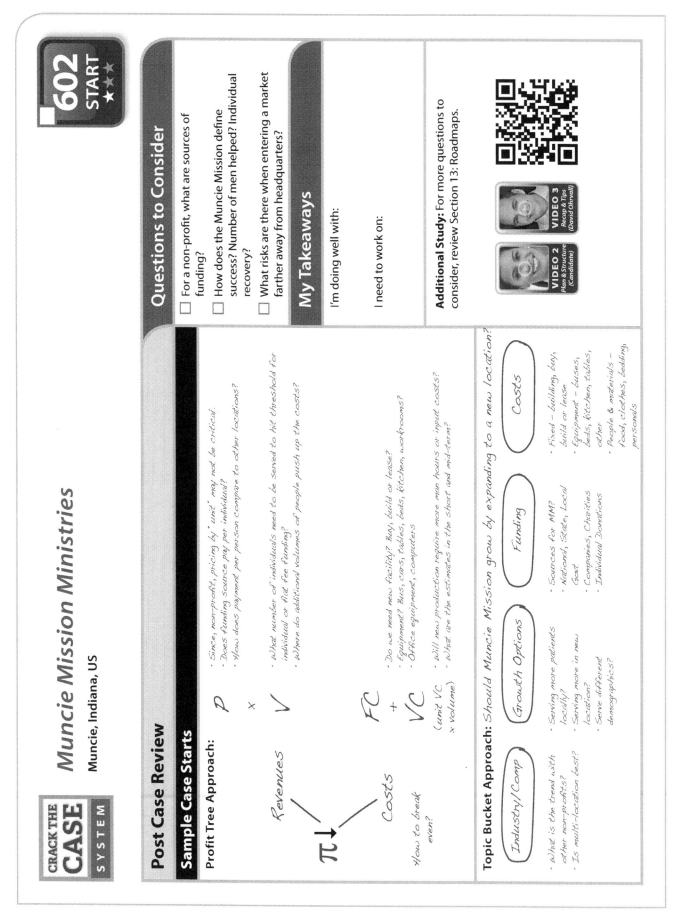

VIDEO 2
Plan & Structure
(Candidate)

VIDEO 3
Recap & Tips
(David Ohrvall)

CRACK THE CASE SYSTEM

Always Fresh

San Francisco, California, US

Determined to conquer the world with the power of deodorant, the Always Fresh team has set their sights on going abroad. Help them navigate the international intricacies of personal hygiene. Will success smell as sweet outside of North America?

603 FULL ★★★

SAN FRANCISCO CITY FACTS

▸ Famous landmarks: Golden Gate bridge, cable cars (the only moving National Historic Landmark), Chinatown

▸ Nicknames: City by the Bay, Paris of the West, Frisco

▸ Known as the center of liberal activism; has not voted more than 20% for a Republican presidential or senatorial candidate since 1988.

TRAIN Profile

Type	**R**egion	**A**nalysis	**I**ndustry	**N**umber
4 FULL BUSINESS	SAN FRANCISCO, CALIFORNIA, U.S. Population: 809K Currency: Dollar, USD, $	ROADMAP → **4** Enter a New Geography or Market	Consumer Products	LEVEL **3**

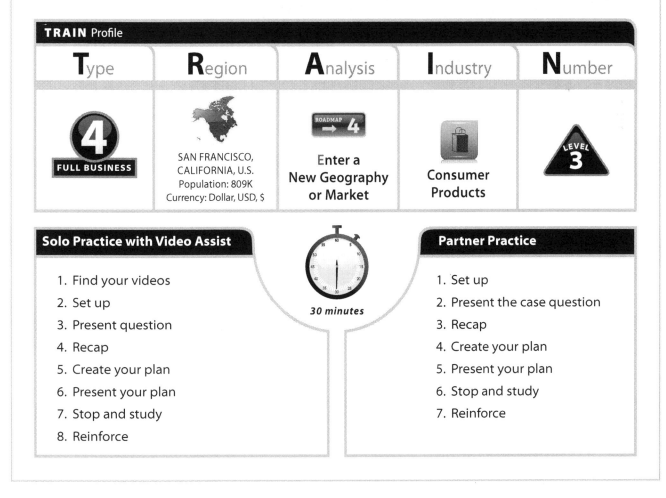

Solo Practice with Video Assist

1. Find your videos
2. Set up
3. Present question
4. Recap
5. Create your plan
6. Present your plan
7. Stop and study
8. Reinforce

30 minutes

Partner Practice

1. Set up
2. Present the case question
3. Recap
4. Create your plan
5. Present your plan
6. Stop and study
7. Reinforce

Always Fresh

San Francisco, California, US

603
FULL
★★★

Interview Guide

Case Situation and Question

Always Fresh is a subsidiary of a $30B consumer products conglomerate. The company's main product line is deodorant/anti-perspirant sprays, roll-ons and sticks. Sales over the last five years have been steadily growing in North America, and now the Always Fresh team is ready to take its products global.

As the team's leader, how would you assess whether or not international expansion is a good idea? If so, which countries offer the greatest three-year revenue opportunity?

Case Twist

You discover that another large consumer products company has decided to launch similar deodorant products in the countries you picked?

What would you do?

VIDEO 1
Case Question
(Interviewer)

Feedback

Physical Skills
	Weak		Strong
Body Language	①	②	③
Verbal	①	②	③
Listening	①	②	③

Thinking Skills

Hypothesis Generation	①	②	③
Comfort with Ambiguity	①	②	③
Initial Plan & Output	①	②	③
Data Analysis	①	②	③
Basic Business Intuition	①	②	③
Integration	①	②	③
2nd Level Insights	①	②	③
Creativity	①	②	③

Total Score _____ / 33

Intro Facts (Tell the Candidate if Asked)

Location preferences: None. Management wants the project team to tell them.

Product line: Any or all of the three deodorant types can be launched into new locations. Each product (stick, spray, roll-on) lasts 3 months long on average.

Team: Internal resources appear sufficient to handle this launch. Your interview candidate is the leader of the team.

Capital, production and distribution: Parent company will support any well-defined need. Worldwide production and distribution facilities will help. Relationships with retailers are good.

Financial targets: 25% annual revenue growth for 3 years and year one sales of at least $50M.

North American (NAM) sales: Last year's sales were $350M. NAM growth is about 10% per year.

Suppliers: Non-issue, North American suppliers.

Government/ Legislation: No barriers.

Financing this venture: Non-issue.

Key Insights (Do Not Tell the Candidate)

General tips: This is a basic market entry case with critical data scattered throughout four different handouts. "Star" candidates will be on a mission to find certain facts and pull them from the handouts.

Market potential: Three countries are much larger than the others in terms of overall size: Germany, Japan and Brazil.

Pricing: AF sells three different types of product that sell at different price points. Prices also vary by country. However, since the three product types are weighted about the same, you can average the prices to develop an average price for all units for a particular country.

Country-specific competitors: There are strong competitors in each market that AF wants to enter. Brazil and Japan are the most fragmented, which would enable AF to take market share from the small, local brands. Although AF is new, their large parent organization will make it possible for them to promote their products heavily and to use already established distribution relationships.

Global competitors: Mann and Rembrant each have solid market share in 3 different countries. They are well-established companies like AF and its parent company.

Mid-case Data (Tell Only at Appropriate Time)

Ask, "What is the primary metric by which you could judge each country?"

■ **Give the candidate Handout A.** Ask, "How would you describe what is happening?" Ask, "What kind of data would you need to best understand pricing?"

■ **Give the candidate Handout B.** Ask, "What do you notice about the price structure here?" Ask, "What kind of products would you want to offer in other countries?"

■ **Give the candidate Handout D,** product types by country. "Do certain countries tend to use one product type over another?" Ask, "How would you go about thinking about competitors? What information would you need to evaluate this threat?"

■ **Give the candidate Handout C,** competitor share by country. Ask, "Which countries provide the most opportunity and why?"

Always Fresh

San Francisco, California, US

603
FULL
★★★

Case Flow and Milestones

1 Present Main Question	**2** Answer Any Basics	**3** Ask for Clarification	**4** Guide Discussion	**5** Get Recommendation
Candidate takes notes, asks for a minute, forms a plan and presents it. Be sure to read through the handouts and the main question carefully to understand the flow.	These may come up after you read the question, or later. Read through the entire case noting areas where the candidate will likely have questions.	Prompt with questions: "Tell me more about this area (you choose). What are you thinking about here?" or "Tell me how the parts of your structure link to each other."	The "star" will get to business by assessing the full revenue and profit potential by country. Basic data that is necessary includes: size of the potential market, price per unit sold, usage rates and volume. Your goal is to provide handouts (A–D) so candidate can make a holistic decision. Review the calculations on Page 6.	During the Candidate's wrap-up, look for the following: • Good grasp of the facts from the slides and clear data-driven reasons for going abroad or not • Persuasion! Would you be ready to move ahead with the Candidate's suggestions? • Immediate next steps

---

Handout and Data Guide

Additional Info

Handout A:

Candidate: How big is the market by country? Or Do you have any market data?

Interviewer: Here's some market data. What do you see? What jumps out to you on this chart? Any countries you would consider over others?

Insight: Big markets to consider are Brazil, Japan and Germany.

Handout B:

Candidate: Do we have any pricing information?

Interviewer: Here's some pricing by country. What do you think? What pricing trends do you see by product?

Insight: Pricing for spray is often higher. In Japan roll-on prices are higher.

Handout C:
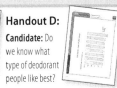
Candidate: Do you know who the competitors are by country and their market share?

Interviewer: These numbers are rough and represent what the team could pull together in a day. What jumps out at you? Who seems to be dominant by market place?

Insight: Brazil and Japan are fragmented, creating opportunity to take share.

Handout D:
Candidate: Do we know what type of deodorant people like best?

Interviewer: Here's some quick data we got from street interviews.

Insight: Spray is preferred by Brazil and Japan. France likes roll-on. No one deodorant type dominates across countries in terms of usage.

Redirect the discussion to these areas if necessary:

- In terms of market potential, Brazil, Germany and Japan are the largest.

- Each country is about equal in terms of deodorant usage rates.

- Prices do vary by country; but, in general, the price points by product type do not vary much.

- Spray tends to be the highest and stick is the cheapest.

- Certain markets are more crowded than others: France, Spain and Germany. The UK, Brazil and Japan have significant fragmentation with many small competitors.

- No one type of deodorant is dominant in terms of usage.

Re-routers | Questions to Keep Things on Track

- **What criteria would you use to rank one country over another?**

  ‣ Market size
  ‣ Competitor saturation and relative market share
  ‣ Customer needs

- **How would you go about determining the potential market size?**

  ‣ Start with all potential customers and slim down the field according to product preference and usage patterns.

- **Now that you have some target markets, what other issues should you consider?**

  ‣ Product distribution

‣ Product push (spray vs. stick vs. roll-on)
‣ Internal marketing support
‣ Sales rollout
‣ Retailer relationships and advertising

- **What internal organizational issues concern you most?**

  ‣ Leveraging our conglomerate's experience to support expansion
  ‣ IT systems to track the actual success of this venture
  ‣ Senior management support and patience
  ‣ Team dedication—this will be a lot of work

Always Fresh
San Francisco, California, US

603
FULL
★★★

Additional Study Using the FRAME Method

F – Form a Plan

MVM™

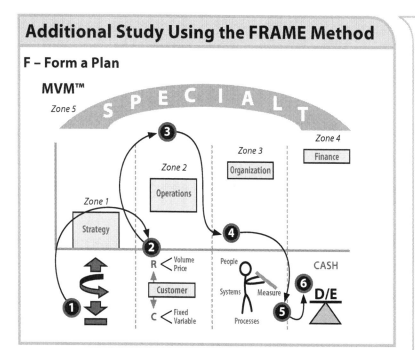

1. **Start in Zone 1, Strategy.** Always Fresh is changing direction and looking to start something new.

2. **Move to Zone 2, Operations.** How much demand is there, and what can we charge?

3. **Don't forget key external factors.** As you consider price and volume also consider:
   - Suppliers—are there any raw material problems in our future locations?
   - Competitors—how does our product compare to what they offer?
   - Industry—are there barriers to this industry in our new countries?

4. **Shift to AF's internal team.** Do we have enough people in place and good leaders?

5. **Discuss distribution processes.** How will they be leveraged in the new country?

6. **Move to financing.** What will happen with the company's debt/equity?

M—Mine for the Answer

Now you can mine for data. Use your plan as a guide, as well as your initial hypothesis. Try to ask 2-3 questions in each section you explore.

Demand	Product/ Competitors	Internal Support
■ **Do we have evidence that people want this product?** *Deodorant users are plentiful.*	■ **What is unique about our product?** *We have no information on what's unique.*	■ **Is the team in place? Do we have a strong leader?** *Yes. You are the leader.*
■ **Can we estimate demand? How about price?** *We do have rough demand and price.*	■ **How can we differentiate?** *Competitors are fragmented, so they may be slow to react.*	■ **How will we sell and distribute the product?** *Distribution relationships are in place. We can leverage the conglomerate's relationships.*
■ **Where do we see demand to be highest?** *Brazil, Japan and Germany provide the most opportunity.*	■ **How will competitors respond?** *There is a good opportunity to take market share.*	■ **Is our financing in place?** *Yes, there are no financing issues.*

Product Line	Financial Targets	Suppliers
■ **Does AF provide a product line that will work in several different countries?** *Yes. Every country they want to enter uses their main products: spray, roll-on and stick.*	■ **What are management's goals with this international expansion?** *Ultimately, management wants to see about half of AF's sales come from outside of North America. For the first 3 years, they expect 25% revenue growth.*	■ **Will our product be made abroad or in the local country?** *Initially, to take advantage of production efficiencies, all products will be made in the US. In the long term, making the products locally may be an option.*
■ **Do certain countries demand certain product attributes that the AF product line does not have?** *No. Initial research indicates that the AF product line will be well accepted in all the countries*	■ **Are there any other financial goals in place?** *None at this time.*	■ **Are there any suppliers who will react negatively to AF importing products?** *We have no information at this point. AF's parent does have good relationships with suppliers.*

A – Anchor a Hypothesis

Did you take advantage of some of your initial thoughts about this decision? By anchoring your thoughts around a hypothesis, you can give yourself a natural focus for your questions as you move through the different elements of your plan.

AF Should Expand

"Because of AF's parent conglomerate and its likely advantages with distributors and retailers in different countries, launching this product seems like a natural fit."

AF Should Wait

"Just because we have been successful in North America, this does not guarantee the same success abroad. I suspect that the costs will outweigh the advantages.

E – End the Case

"Always Fresh should definitely move ahead with international expansion. After assessing total potential market share, three countries—Brazil, Japan and Germany—rise to the top of the list. It appears that we can capture share quickly in the first two, with total projected conservative revenues for all three at about $160M the first year. Additional growth at 25% may be aggressive in Germany since the market there is less fragmented. Also, distribution, IT, and sales processes will need monitoring."

Always Fresh

San Francisco, California, US

603
FULL
★★★

Post Case Review

Case Insights & Takeaways

- In terms of market potential, Brazil, Germany and Japan are the largest.
- Prices do vary by country; but, in general, the price points by product type do not vary much.
- Spray tends to be the most expensive and stick is the cheapest. No one type of deodorant is dominant in terms of usage.
- Certain markets are more crowded than others: France, Spain and Germany. The UK, Brazil and Japan have significant fragmentation with many small competitors.

Tying it All Together

Looking for large markets makes good sense. Unless there are some unique barriers to a market that is larger, go there first.

When making calculations, you have to find ways to simplify the numbers. Try to "ballpark" your numbers (get them in the range) before going for detailed precision.

Volume: What is the common unit to count? Since each product (stick, spray or roll-on) is being used in the same manner, and likely lasts the same length of time, each sale can be counted as one unit. To get the number of units, you must know: Total Available Users x Market Share for AF x Units Used Per Year. You can get the user data from Handout A, the market share data from Handout C, and the number of units per year by asking the interviewer (4 units per year per person).

Price: As for price, a quick solution is to review the chart and come up with an average. If you have more time you could weight the price, but that is not necessary.

After determining the revenue potential, you need to apply some business judgment to the results. The Math Zone covers some of that logic.

When you present your final answer, it is natural to caveat some of your numbers and talk about what you would like to investigate if you had more time.

My Takeaways

To build skills and improve, you must apply what you learned to future cases. Take a few moments and review the interviewer feedback and jot down some key insights about your performance in the space below.

Thinking Skills

My top 2 strengths are:

My top 2 soft spots are:

To address these problems I'll begin to:

VIDEO 3
Recap & Tips
(David Ohrvall)

My Performance During the Case

Add up your points. ➡ Total Score: _____ / 15

F Form A Plan	**R** Read My Audience	**A** Anchor a Hypothesis	**M** Mine for Answers	**E** End the Case
points	points	points	points	points
③ Structured, clean	③ Good back & forth, caught clues	③ Solid hunch, pursued clue	③ Specific questions, solid analysis	③ Used facts and data, connected the dots
② Somewhat organized and logical	② Awkward, trouble with interviewer style	② Partial direction	② Missed some questions, some math mistakes	② Some data, mostly understood connections
① Messy, overlapping ideas	① Interviewer not interested, couldn't follow	① No hypothesis at all	① Vague questions, weak math, no linkages	① No data, no passion, no connections

Always Fresh
San Francisco, California, US

Interviewer's Data Guide

Math Zone

Potential Approach

Estimate the Market

	Brazil	Japan	Germany
Total market:	~84M customers	~90M customers	~60M customers
Average price:	$2 (weight toward spray)	$3 (weight toward spray)	$2 (even weighting)
Usage rate (no info):	4x (1 per quarter year)	4x (1 per quarter)	4x (1 per quarter year)
Est. market share:	10% (.25 of fragmented)	10% (.25 of fragmented)	5% (not fragmented)
Annual est. revenue:	~$70M	~$100M	~$24M

Total Annual Revenue: ~$194M (will vary according to your assumptions, e.g. how many units of deodorant do you use per year? Round this number to ~$200M)

Gut Check It

$200M for the first year seems high, given that after 5 years North America has $350M.

A sharp candidate will offer a plus or minus percent to safeguard their answer. In this case, 20% error in either direction would result in a range of ~$160M – $240M. Be conservative and go with $160M.

Calculate Required Growth

In the first year, sell about $160M. This number seems aggressive.

In the second year, grow at requested 25% ($40M), so sell ~$200M.

In the third year, grow at requested 25% ($50M), so sell ~$250M. After three years, Always Fresh would be about $250M (international), which seems reasonable since NAM is $350M after five years.

Interpret the Numbers

Establishing the business during the first year is important and will be difficult. Germany in particular is not fragmented, and gaining shelf space may prove difficult.

Growing at 25% may be possible, given that Brazil and Japan are so fragmented. It does seem aggressive, however, given NAM's 10% growth rate.

We may have the option of entering only two countries and still reaching our targets.

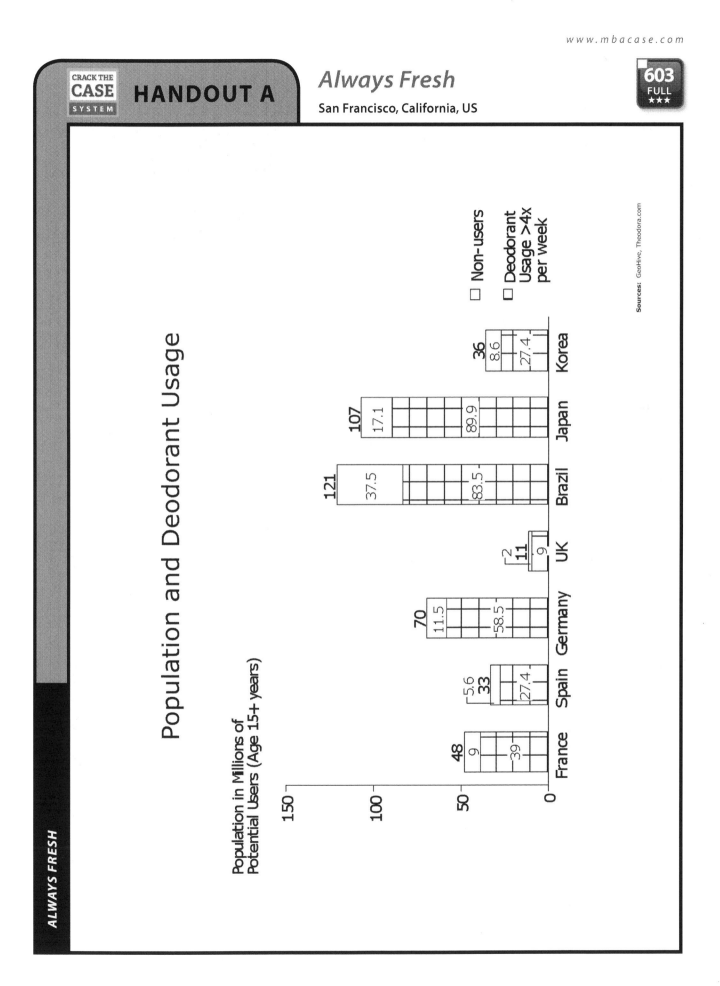

HANDOUT A

Always Fresh

San Francisco, California, US

Population and Deodorant Usage

Population in Millions of
Potential Users (Age 15+ years)

Non-users

Deodorant
Usage >4x
per week

Sources: GeoHive, Theodora.com

France: **48**, 9, 39
Spain: **33**, 5.6, 27.4
Germany: **70**, 11.5, 58.5
UK: **11**, 2, 9
Brazil: **121**, 37.5, 83.5
Japan: **107**, 17.1, 89.9
Korea: **36**, 8.6, 27.4

CRACK THE
CASE
SYSTEM
HANDOUT B

Always Fresh
San Francisco, California, US

603
FULL
★★★

ALWAYS FRESH

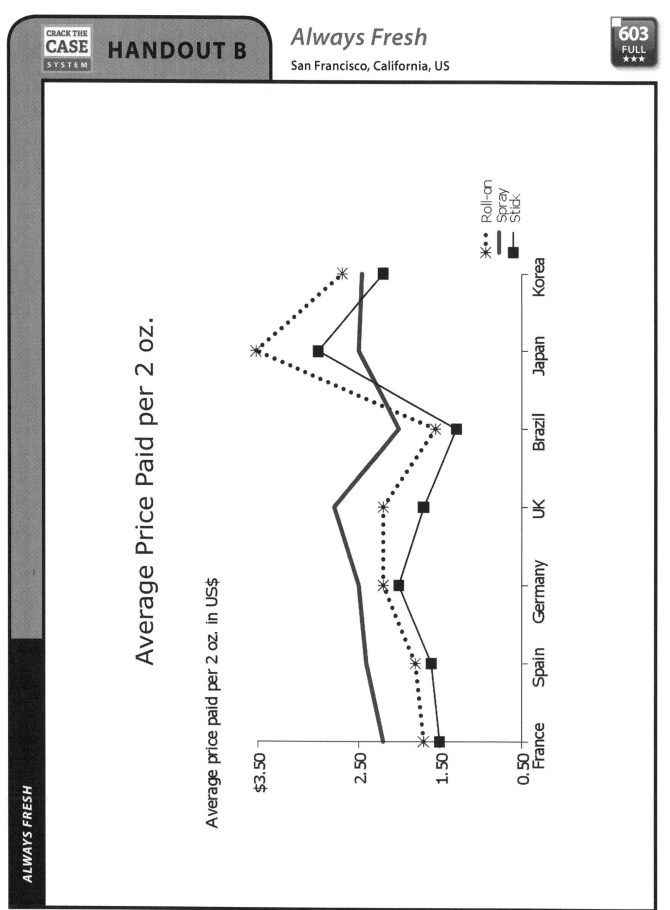

Average Price Paid per 2 oz.

Average price paid per 2 oz. in US$

Roll-on
Spray
Stick

$3.50

2.50

1.50

0.50

France   Spain   Germany   UK   Brazil   Japan   Korea

Always Fresh

San Francisco, California, US

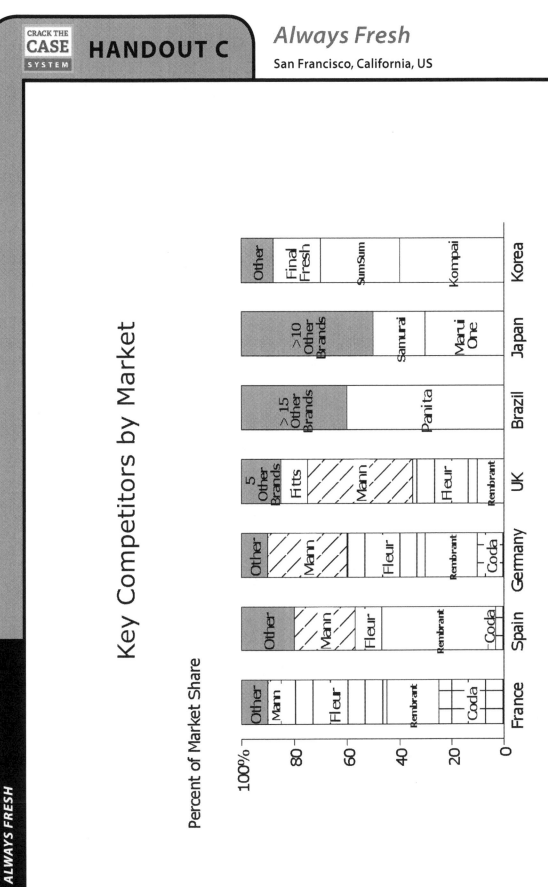

Key Competitors by Market

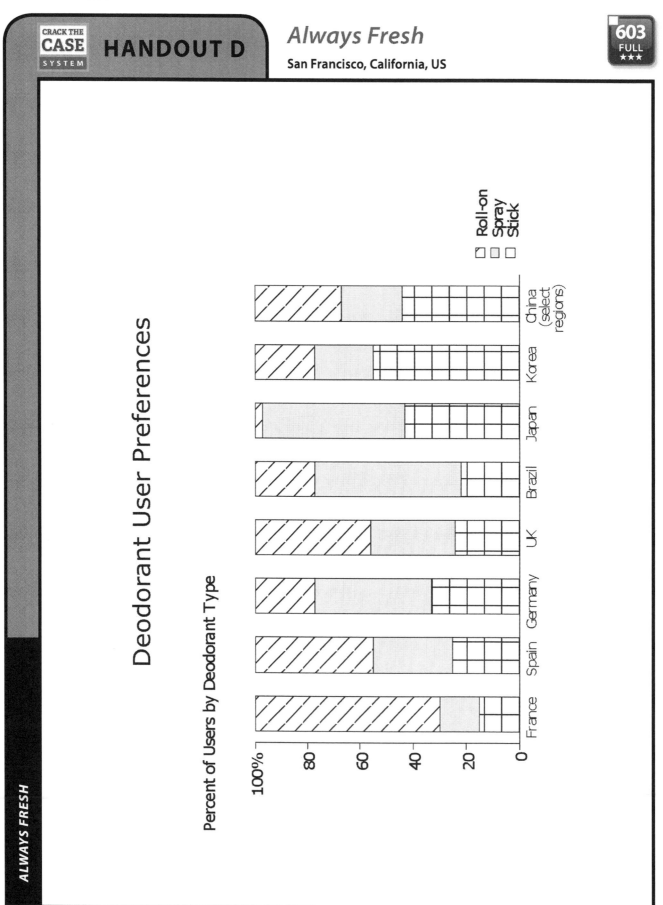

Deodorant User Preferences

Percent of Users by Deodorant Type

Legend: Roll-on, Spray, Stick

Countries: France, Spain, Germany, UK, Brazil, Japan, Korea, China (select regions)

WORKSHEET

Always Fresh
San Francisco, California, US

CRACK THE CASE SYSTEM

ALWAYS FRESH

My Initial Plan and Output

Today's date:

2. Be original with your data

4. Leave ample room for a structure and additional notes as the case progresses

1. Zone out your paper

3. Take clean and simple notes

Potential Plan and Output

WORKSHEET

Always Fresh

San Francisco, California, US

Is global expansion a good idea?

Which countries offer best 3 yr. rev. opp?

Rev / price

What are price points by country?

What is the pricing trend across products?

What pricing est. can we use?

HUNCH: AF will succeed — deodorant is global need. Stick to developed countries and take share.

Rev / volume

Deodorant market full potential by country?

What market share is possible?

What is predicted volume over 2 years?

Barriers & Competitors

What will we face by country? Have other CPG companies established themselves?

Country specific boundaries?

Support / Team / Suppliers / Financing

Do we have funding in place?

Does the conglom. team have experience?

Do we have "new entry" processes: marketing, sales and distribution

Rev — subsid. of $30B CPG

Costs — no data

Profit — no data

Goal: cut costs

Goal: Assess whether international expansion is good

Biggest 3 yr. opp?

Financial targets? Rev. or profit targets? Number of countries?

- Main prod. Deodorant
- anti-persp. / roll-ons / sticks
- Sales growing in N. A.
- Plan for global expansion

Voiceover

"Our goal is to enter a new country, so I want to determine which countries offer the best revenue and the simplest entry. Issues like suppliers, competitor response, and industry barriers will be important. I also would like to discuss internal support issues like our team, marketing, distribution, and financing. Before I go down this path, does management have any specific goals for our team? For instance, do you have the number of countries or revenue or profit targets?"

Additional Study: For more questions to consider, review Section 13: Roadmaps.

VIDEO 2 Plan & Structure (Candidate)

Granny's Organics

Cape Cod, Massachusetts, US

Everything was sunny side up for Granny, until the big shots came to town. Can you help Granny think through her sticky situation?

604 MINI ★★★

Cape Cod City Facts

▸ Known as "The Land of Lighthouses"; contains more lighthouses than any other county in the nation

▸ Famous for its cranberries, shellfish, beaches, lobstering, and whale sightings

▸ Provincetown, at the tip of Cape Cod, was site of Pilgrims' first landing

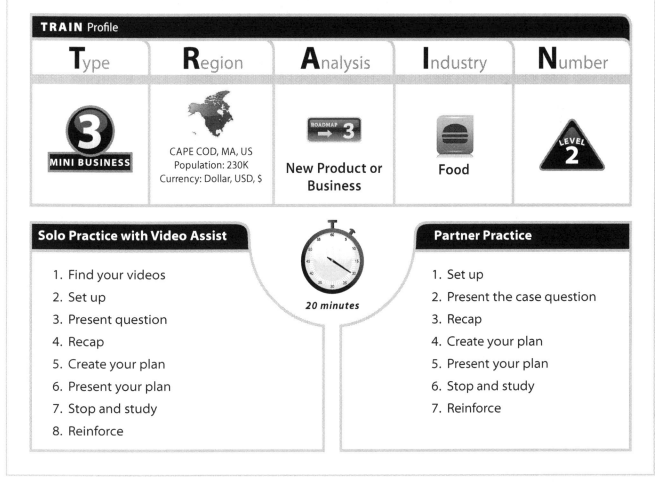

TRAIN Profile

Type	**R**egion	**A**nalysis	**I**ndustry	**N**umber
3 MINI BUSINESS	CAPE COD, MA, US Population: 230K Currency: Dollar, USD, $	ROADMAP → **3** New Product or Business	Food	LEVEL **2**

Solo Practice with Video Assist

1. Find your videos
2. Set up
3. Present question
4. Recap
5. Create your plan
6. Present your plan
7. Stop and study
8. Reinforce

20 minutes

Partner Practice

1. Set up
2. Present the case question
3. Recap
4. Create your plan
5. Present your plan
6. Stop and study
7. Reinforce

Granny's Organics

Cape Cod, Massachusetts, US

604 MINI ★★★

Interview Guide

Case Situation and Question

Granny O'Manny has become a local hero for her café and shop (Granny's Organics) offering wholesome, organic foods and gifts and crafts from around the world.

She's been in business for 10 years and has a strong network of local farmers who supply her with organic eggs, meats, fruits and vegetables. Her café offers a variety of specialties, including her famous organic buckwheat pancakes. She recently received a lot of press from a food critic hailing Granny's organic buckwheat pancakes as the "best in the universe."

A NYC venture capital team wants Granny to package the liquid batter and sell it nationwide in grocery stores. They think she should focus her energy on the pancake batter roll-out. They're offering financing, distribution and marketing expertise.

Case Twist

Check out the Crack the Case System videos on mbacase.com or scan the Video 3 QR code on the Post Case Review page to hear an additional challenge.

VIDEO 1
Case Question (Interviewer)

Feedback

Physical Skills

	Weak		Strong
Body Language	①	②	③
Verbal	①	②	③
Listening	①	②	③

Thinking Skills

Hypothesis Generation	①	②	③
Comfort with Ambiguity	①	②	③
Initial Plan & Output	①	②	③
Data Gathering	①	②	③
Data Analysis	①	②	③
Basic Business Intuition	①	②	③
Integration	①	②	③
2nd Level Insights	①	②	③
Creativity	①	②	③
Recommendation	①	②	③

Total Score _____ / 39

Intro Facts (Tell the Candidate if Asked)

Food Quality: Products are organic and customers are loyal.

Shop Products: Shop offerings vary yearly based on what Granny likes. She's opinionated and values high quality.

Café and Shop Revenue: Café and shop revenue is $7M. Net profit is 30%. Granny's thrives year-round.

Team: Staff are overwhelmed by the complexity of their business, with over 500 products and 30 entrees. Granny is 65.

Debt: Granny doesn't like debt; she would want the pancake batter roll-out to pay off all investments as quickly as possible.

Key Insights (Do Not Tell the Candidate)

Café and Shop Revenue: This information is necessary in order to compare the "batter roll-out" option vs. the "do nothing" option of continuing to manage the café and shop. You may have to prompt the candidate with this information.

Granny's Well Being: Granny is 65 and likely near the end of her business career. See if the candidate has considered broader issues such as her financial goals, her succession plans and her work style. Her new role with the VC option will be very different from her current role.

Mid-case Data (Tell Only at Appropriate Time)

After Start: After hearing the candidate's initial structure and plan, ask for more ideas. Use the Potential Plan and Output page to ask about missing pieces or areas that don't make sense. Thoroughly test her plan.

During the Plan Review: If necessary, hint about the topic of team. It's unlikely Granny will work for more than 5—10 years. She could be in a "make no changes" mode or a "hurry up and make money" mode. The candidate should talk about this. If necessary ask, "What objectives do you think Granny has for the future?"

Case Flow and Milestones

1 Present Main Question

Interviewer should read through the case and know the timing for questions, data, charts, and hints. Take on a personality (friendly, firm, or foe). Present the case question. Candidate will then likely recap and clarify, ask for time to think, form a plan on paper, and present his plan.

2 Assess Structure

Review the Potential Plan and Output page. The answer shown is only one way to approach the problem. The Topic Bucket Approach works well given the complexity of launching a new product, the VC involvement and unique succession issues. Look for gaps or overlaps.

3 Look for Specifics

Launching a new product involves sizing the revenue potential and counting investment costs. Look for a grasp of specific challenges: gaining shelf space, demand for pancake batter (vs. powdered mix), price sensitivity, investment in plant and equipment, and Granny's transition to a new role.

4 Guide Discussion

Test the candidate's ability to do simple math and compare and contrast two options. Follow the Data Guide and give the candidate data and ask questions in order. Ignore minor mistakes but give help where necessary to get to the options comparison.

GIVE DATA

5 Get Recommendation

After you ask for several options for Granny (Step 3, Interviewer's Data Guide), look for a firm recommendation with data. It should be well-supported with numbers and the pros and cons. After hearing the recommendation, ask for immediate next steps. Those should be clear, prioritized and action-oriented.

Granny's Organics

Cape Cod, Massachusetts, US

604
MINI
★★★

Interviewer's Data Guide

Step 1 – Give Revenue Data

- Test the candidate's ability to do some simple multiplication using growth rates.
- Say: "Let's look at some projections. Granny's venture capital team believes that they will sell 3 million units in year one. I also have some price and growth rates for you. I'd like you to calculate estimated revenue at the end of year three."
- Give the first 2 columns of data. The candidate will need to calculate the third column. Do not give any data in that column.

	Units, End of Year 1	End of Year 3	ANSWERS— Do Not Give
Granny's Organics	3,000,000	30% growth each year	5,070,000 units
Estimated price	6.99	12% growth each year	8.77
Total Revenue	$20,970,000	—	$44,455,058

Step 2 – Check Candidate's Calculations

Calculations
  Units: 3M x 1.3 x 1.3 = 5.07M
  Price: 6.99 x 1.12 x 1.12 = $8.77
  Total Revenue: 5.07 x $8.77 = $44,455,058

Give hints if the candidate is stuck. He needs this data for the next question.

Step 3 – Ask for an Options Analysis

Say: "Granny's pretty impressed with the kind of revenue the batter roll-out could make, but she's somewhat leery of dealing with outside investors. They want 30% of all revenue for five years and have talked about selling their shares at the end of that time. They also want her to take a $14M loan for plant and equipment. Net profit on the batter should be 40%. Please lay out several options that Granny can pursue."

Look for the candidate to struggle somewhat with creating options. The obvious ones are "do nothing" or "roll out batter". Review all the options listed below and give a few hints if necessary, like, "Does Granny have to go with this VC firm?"

OPTIONS	FINANCIAL IMPACT	PROS	CONS
Do Nothing	Annual Revenue x Net Profit x 5 yrs. (no time value) = $7M x .3 x 5 = **$10.5M**	Granny can keep her same lifestyle, enjoy her shop and customers and do what she loves.	Smallest financial reward. Granny may be tired of the business.
Work with VC	5 year gross revenue x net margin - VC gross revenue take - loan = Granny's 5 year estimated net profit take	Granny will make more money, build a brand that could be sold and get to do something new.	Granny's time will be stretched and she may have to limit her restaurant involvement. She may miss her shop and customers.
	Assume growth levels after year 3. (5 year revenue = $21M + $30.5M + $44.5M x 3 = $185M) x .4 - (185 x .3) - 14 = **$23M**		
Find New VC	Potentially more money for Granny	Granny has learned from this VC and can use her knowledge for a better deal.	Finding a new company may waste time and not be that much better.
Self Finance / Pilot	Most likely will not disturb the shop and café.	Will allow for slow and careful roll-out which Granny can control.	May be complicated to manage production, financing and marketing of the batter while running the current business.

Granny's Organics
Cape Cod, Massachusetts, US

604
MINI
★★★

Post Case Review

Case Insights & Takeaways

- Granny and her family were already "feeling overwhelmed" with the current business. This situation raised concerns about the best option on both the financial and non-financial dimensions.
- With the restaurant already succeeding one viable option was to do nothing.
- Investors were educating Granny at their own expense. She easily could move ahead with a new investment firm with no obligation to the first one.
- Start with the numbers, but don't forget to consider other things.

Math Tips

- For growth rates be sure to ask if it is an annual rate or not.
- Feel comfortable rounding the price of $6.99 to 7.00 and the revenue of $20.970M to $21M as long as you inform your interviewer.
- Incorporate time into your analysis whenever possible. You learned that the investment firm had a five year period before they wanted to exit. That number should have prompted you to do a five year comparison.
- Practice laying out the math comparison table several times.

What to Expect with Cases Like These

- With several layers to the problem (entrepreneur, thriving business, family involvement, investors and new product), use the bucket approach to manage the complexity in an organized manner.
- Mention how each part of your plan has a financial impact (e.g., Granny may not give up the restaurant and only be partially focused on the batter roll-out).
- Investor cases imply payback and exit so be ready to calculate everyone's gain or loss over a period of time.
- Lead with the numbers before talking about softer issues.

My Takeaways

To build skills and improve, you must apply what you learned to future cases. Take a few moments and review the interviewer feedback and jot down some key insights about your performance in the space below.

Thinking Skills

My top 2 strengths are:

My top 2 soft spots are:

To address these problems I'll begin to:

VIDEO 3
Recap & Tips
(David Ohrvall)

My Performance During the Case

Add up your points. → Total Score: _____ /15

F — Form A Plan	R — Read My Audience	A — Anchor a Hypothesis	M — Mine for Answers	E — End the Case
points	points	points	points	points
(3) Structured, clean	(3) Good back & forth, caught clues	(3) Solid hunch, pursued clue	(3) Specific questions, solid analysis	(3) Used facts and data, connected the dots
(2) Somewhat organized and logical	(2) Awkward, trouble with interviewer style	(2) Partial direction	(2) Missed some questions, some math mistakes	(2) Some data, mostly understood connections
(1) Messy, overlapping ideas	(1) Interviewer not interested, couldn't follow	(1) No hypothesis at all	(1) Vague questions, weak math, no linkages	(1) No data, no passion, no connections

WORKSHEET

Granny's Organics
Cape Cod, Massachusetts, US

GRANNY'S ORGANICS

My Initial Plan and Output

Today's date:

2. Be original with your data

1. Zone out your paper

3. Take clean and simple notes

4. Leave ample room for a structure and additional notes as the case progresses

CRACK THE CASE SYSTEM — WORKSHEET

Granny's Organics
Cape Cod, Massachusetts, US

604 MINI ★★★

VIDEO 2
Plan & Structure
(Candidate)

GRANNY'S ORGANICS

Potential Plan and Output

Should Granny go w/ VC offer?

Key elements to consider?

Market growth and stability for batter roll-out	Compet. for the batter roll-out	Risks to current shop/café	Team – Granny + family
• Growth projection – How fast grow?	• Do we know who we will compete against?	• Shop necess. for Granny's fame?	• Is Granny happy?
• Stability – Concerns? Is it a fad?	• Strong brands? Good dist?	• Granny's focus on batter hinder the café and shop's success?	• Why change?
• Distribution – What? How?	• Growth project?	• Consumers loyal long term?	• How important is money?
• International – pancakes US taste only?	• Will competitors launch copycat products? How fast?		• Others involved?
			Family biz

Financials café/ shop vs. batter
• Profit-margins for shop products, food and the batter?
• Revenues (V × P) minus Costs

• DATA shop/ café 2 yrs. by prod.
• Pricing – increase at shop? How set for batter? Competitor pricing?

• DATA hist. growth rates compet. shares

• Volume – How sensitive is volume to price for the batter?

• Costs – Which costs up most? Reduce?

Granny O'Manny (age?)

Café / shop organic gifts/ global? Where does she get them?

In biz 10 yrs.

Network organic farmers (meat, egg . . .)

Buckwheat pancakes (what is this?)

NYC VC – US dist.

Focus on batter roll-out

Offer fin., distr. and mkt.

Rev? Café & Shop
       Batter roll-out / total upside?

Costs? Will VC finance everything?

What does VC want?

Additional Study: For more questions to consider, review Section 13: Roadmaps.

Tattoo Redo

Panama City, Florida

Tattoo On You! wants to undo your old tattoos and replace them with new. But will the program end in red ink?

605 MINI ★★★

PANAMA CITY FACTS

▸ Has 27 miles of beaches, and an average of 320 days of sunshine per year

▸ Known as "The Seafood Capital of the South"

▸ Often impacted by hurricanes

▸ Popular tourist destination, with about 6 million tourists per year

TRAIN Profile

Type	**R**egion	**A**nalysis	**I**ndustry	**N**umber
3 MINI BUSINESS	PANAMA CITY, FLORIDA Population: 36,644 Currency: Dollar, USD, $	ROADMAP ➡ **7** Change Price	🛒 Retail	LEVEL **2**

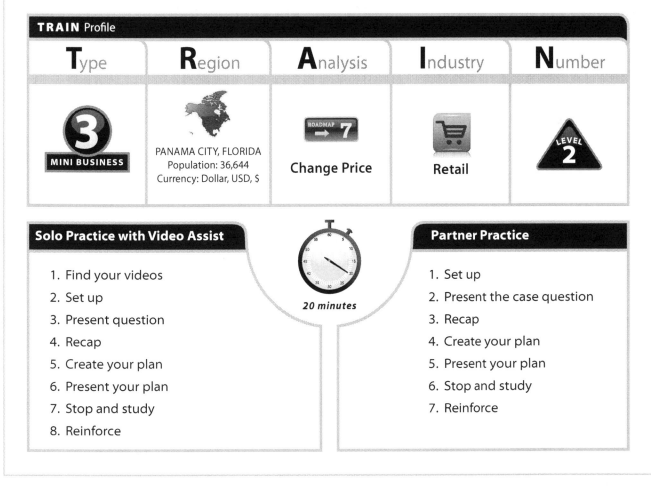

Solo Practice with Video Assist	**Partner Practice**
1. Find your videos	1. Set up
2. Set up	2. Present the case question
3. Present question	3. Recap
4. Recap	4. Create your plan
5. Create your plan	5. Present your plan
6. Present your plan	6. Stop and study
7. Stop and study	7. Reinforce
8. Reinforce	

20 minutes

Tattoo Redo
Panama City, Florida

Interview Guide

Case Situation and Question

Tattoo On You!, a chain of 45 tattoo shops, is trying to expand in a unique way. It wants to introduce the Tattoo Redo program. Customers can have old tattoos removed, clearing space for new tattoos. Their goal is to draw new customers and maintain loyalty among old customers.

Research shows that heavy tattoo users are most likely to want old tattoos removed to make room for new ones. To increase the likelihood of success, encourage users to focus on removing tattoos from smaller areas. Smaller areas can be cleared more cleanly, more quickly and for less money. Bundle the removal and application appointments. It is more profitable to offer the Tattoo Redo program to customers who want a new tattoo after the removal of an old tattoo.

Pilot the program. Purchase tattoo removal lasers for four pilot locations and market the program. If it goes well, expand the program.

You are asked to evaluate the pilot program and raise concerns. What do you think?

Case Twist

Check out the Crack the Case System videos on mbacase.com or scan the Video 3 QR code at the end of this case to hear an additional challenge.

VIDEO 1
Case Question
(Interviewer)

Feedback

Physical Skills   Weak   Strong

Body Language	①	②	③
Verbal	①	②	③
Listening	①	②	③

Thinking Skills

Hypothesis Generation	①	②	③
Comfort with Ambiguity	①	②	③
Initial Plan & Output	①	②	③
Data Gathering	①	②	③
Data Analysis	①	②	③
Basic Business Intuition	①	②	③
Integration	①	②	③
2nd Level Insights	①	②	③
Creativity	①	②	③
Recommendation	①	②	③

Total Score _____ / 39

Intro Facts (Tell the Candidate if Asked)	**Key Insights** (Do Not Tell the Candidate)	**Mid-case Data** (Tell Only at Appropriate Time)
Competitors: No competitor is promoting the combination tattoo removal and application process. **Laser removal machine cost:** Each machine costs $400k with annual maintenance fees of $30k and life expectancy of 4 years. **Pricing:** The average laser removal package will cost $750 in total and require 3 treatments.	**Profit tree structure:** A simple profit tree structure will help the candidate identify areas of further exploration. **Break-even Analysis:** The candidate should develop a break-even analysis to evaluate the program's feasibility (i.e. $750 price and $400k cost of laser machines). For simplification, ignore interest rates and the time value of money.	**After Start:** After hearing the candidate's initial structure and plan, ask the candidate to give you more ideas. Use the Potential Plan and Output page to ask about missing pieces or areas that don't make sense to you. Give feedback on the break-even analysis. **After initial break-even analysis:** Ask the candidate to provide a more detailed break-even calculation for each of 4 pilot locations, based on their specific pricing, labor and materials costs. (See Interviewer's Data Guide.)

Case Flow and Milestones

1 Present Main Question	**2** Assess Structure	**3** Look for Specifics	**4** Guide the Analysis	**5** Get Recommendation
Interviewer reads through the case and knows the timing for questions, data, charts, and hints. Take on a personality (friendly, firm, or foe). Present case question. Candidate should recap and clarify, ask for time to form a plan, and present his plan.	Review the Potential Plan and Output page. The answer shown is only one way to approach the problem. For an initial structure, expect to see a simple profit equation and the candidate drilling into each of the variables.	Candidate should develop follow-up questions for several pieces of the profit equation. For example, he may ask about price sensitivity (P), volume estimates (V) and labor costs (VC).	Test the candidate's ability to determine the break-even number of treatments at the $750 price. Follow the Data Guide and give him the revenue/ costs for pilot locations. Ignore minor mistakes. Help where necessary to arrive at a good location comparison.	Should the pilot program be expanded to all locations? After hearing the recommendation, ask for immediate next steps. Those should be clear, prioritized and action-oriented.

GIVE
DATA

CRACK THE CASE SYSTEM

605 MINI ★★★

Tattoo Redo
Panama City, Florida

Pilot Locations

Step 1 Table

	A	B	C	D
Fee for 3 treatment package	$750	$650	$750	$750
Labor (3 treatments)	$150	$150	$225	$150
Material (ointment, bandages)	$45	$45	$45	$70
Profit per treatment package	$555	$455	$480	$530
Margin per treatment package	74%	70%	64%	71%

Pilot Locations

Step 2 Table

	A	B	C	D
Initial Cost of Laser Machine	$400,000	$400,000	$400,000	$400,000
Maintenance over 4 years	$120,000	$120,000	$120,000	$120,000
Total Fixed Cost	$520,000	$520,000	$520,000	$520,000
Payback required per year (4 yrs total)	$130,000	$130,000	$130,000	$130,000
Profit per treatment package	$555	$455	$480	$530
# of treatments to break-even	234	286	271	245

Explanations

A is following corporate guidelines
B is running a special due to competition
C by law requires 2 people present for the treatment
D gives additional gauze and ointment

Interviewer's Data Guide

Step 1: Calculate profit per location

- Tell the candidate that you need to give her some data and want to know profit per treatment at each of 4 pilot program locations in dollars and percentages.

- Ask her to ask for the data she needs, like price ($750), labor and materials. Ignore overhead costs like rent and utilities. Give the "explanations" of differences among locations after giving the numbers.

- She should do the calculations (e.g. A = $555, 74%). Reasonable estimates are OK. If it is taking too long, give the unsolved numbers.

Step 2: Calculate volume needed to Break-even

- Tell the candidate that the project manager is concerned that some locations will not be able to pay off their laser machines. He believes that no store can do more than 250 treatments per year.

- What is the current number of break even treatments that each location needs given their current data? She should solve for the number of treatments (e.g. A = 234).

- Locations B and C aren't earning enough to break-even unless they expect demand to be higher than 250.

Step 3: Ask the candidate for ideas on how to solve the break-even problem.

- Raise price across all locations. Test price against current competition.

- Review Location D's concerns about extra bandages and ointments. Point out the profit impact with this approach.

- Consider training lower cost people at Location C to meet state guidelines more affordably.

CRACK THE CASE SYSTEM

WORSHEET

Tattoo Redo

Panama City, Florida

605 MINI ★★★

TATTOO REDO

My Initial Plan and Output

Today's date:

2. Be original with your data

4. Leave ample room for a structure and additional notes as the case progresses

1. Zone out your paper

3. Take clean and simple notes

CRACK THE CASE SYSTEM

WORKSHEET

Tattoo Redo
Panama City, Florida

605 MINI ★★★

Potential Plan and Output

TATTOO REDO

Tattoo Redo a Good Idea?

Revenues — minus — Costs

Revenues = $P \times V$

Costs = $FC \times VC$

PRICE	VOLUME	FIXED COSTS	VARIABLE COSTS
Will we charge enough to cover any new costs (beyond the machine, e.g. technician salaries)?	What kind of sales can we expect over the first year? Do we expect the sales to flatten out over time or grow as awareness grows? Do we see an increase in the average number of tattoos applied?	New investment in lasers	Technician training and salaries
How sensitive will the consumers be to price? Can the company lower the price to test sensitivity?		Special equipment in addition to lasers	New medical supplies required for each treatment
		Any special space needs for storage or use?	
		Is there a cheaper option to lease the lasers?	

---

45 shops

Tattoos – remove and do new one

3 sessions for $750

Laser – 4-yr life, $400k + $30k/yr

Pilot in 4 locations

Profitable?

B/E calc

$400k + $30k/yr × 4yr = $520k

= $130k/year

$130k/$750 per treatment

= Approx 175 treatments to b/e

VIDEO 3 Recap & Tips (David Ohrvall)

VIDEO 2 Plan & Structure (Candidate)

Additional Study: For more questions to consider, review Section 13: Roadmaps.

Slash & Burn Investors

New York City, New York, US

Tempers are flaring in NYC as the partners of Slash & Burn decide the fate of Tuttle Knox. To pay down debt, S&B must divest some of Tuttle Knox's assets. Help these sharks decide who sinks and who swims.

606
FULL
★★★

TRAIN Profile

Type	**R**egion	**A**nalysis	**I**ndustry	**N**umber
4 FULL BUSINESS	NEW YORK, NY, US Population: 8.5M Currency: Dollar, USD, $	ROADMAP → **5** Exit a Business or Market	Banking	LEVEL **3**

Solo Practice with Video Assist

1. Find your videos
2. Set up
3. Present question
4. Recap
5. Create your plan
6. Present your plan
7. Stop and study
8. Reinforce

30 minutes

Partner Practice

1. Set up
2. Present the case question
3. Recap
4. Create your plan
5. Present your plan
6. Stop and study
7. Reinforce

Slash & Burn Investors

New York City, New York, US

606 FULL ★★★

Interview Guide

Case Situation and Question

Slash & Burn is a New York City investment firm. Not known for being a "friendly fund" like some of their contemporaries, S&B is infamous for selling off acquired companies, or parts of companies, within 3 years of acquisition. Tuttle Knox Corp., a 2.5 year-old investment, is a hardware conglomerate designed to capture a high share of the home improvement market. TK is not doing well overall. Slash & Burn would like to reduce its debt burden by $500M, and has decided that Tuttle Knox must sell off assets to raise the funds. They would like you to determine which companies they should sell to raise the $500M. Select the companies you would divest, and give your logic for the choices.

Case Twist

If the investors came back and said they needed $750M rather than $500M, would you change your answer?

What would you do differently?

How can we improve the marketability of the assets we have left?

VIDEO 1
Case Question (Interviewer)

Feedback

Physical Skills

	Weak		Strong
Body Language	①	②	③
Verbal	①	②	③
Listening	①	②	③

Thinking Skills

Hypothesis Generation	①	②	③
Comfort with Ambiguity	①	②	③
Initial Plan & Output	①	②	③
Data Analysis	①	②	③
Basic Business Intuition	①	②	③
Integration	①	②	③
2nd Level Insights	①	②	③
Creativity	①	②	③

Total Score _____ / 33

Intro Facts (Tell the Candidate if Asked)

Slash and Burn Motto: "Grow or Be Sold"

TK Customers: TK was designed to penetrate Home Depot, Lowe's, and Menard's as well as Ace Hardware and other national hardware chains. The strategy was to gain leverage with retailers by supplying critical product lines in several store categories.

Sales Multiples and Timing: Assume that price per asset will be one times annual revenue, and that there are buyers for all assets.

Intention: S&B hopes to streamline TK, create a more focused business and then keep the smaller entity for 2–3 more years."

Key Insights (Do Not Tell the Candidate)

Tuttle Knox Management: They are deferring to the candidate's recommendations.

Low Growth Businesses: Heavy Lawn Equipment (HLE) and Tools are the lowest growth businesses, with HLE being the lowest. These two areas are clearly the place to focus, but the real question is which companies to choose.

Divestiture Combinations: There are several combinations within Heavy Lawn Equipment and Tools that will give S&B their stated goal of $500M. The key is to put a stake in the ground on the logic that seems best (see Interviewer's Data Guide).

Mid-case Data (Tell Only at Appropriate Time)

Understand the bottom-line impact. Some questions to ask after you hear the Candidate's approach:

- If there is a combination of tools and lawn equipment, how will they work together?

- Setting aside the heavy lawn equipment and tools,, what is the synergy between the remaining businesses?

- Will there be any new challenges in dealing with the home improvement centers after some assets are divested? If TK has any leverage with certain companies, will it be gone?

Slash & Burn Investors

New York City, New York, US

606
FULL
★★★

Case Flow and Milestones

1 Present Main Question	**2** Present Any Basics	**3** Ask for Clarification	**4** Guide Discussion	**5** Get Recommendation
Candidate takes notes, asks for a minute, forms a plan and presents it.	For this case the Candidate needs to interpret data from one chart and take notes on some additional facts. There may be a few questions before you get to the slide.	Be sure to make him explain anything you do not fully understand.	There is only one handout. The chart is called a marimekko. It enables you to quickly see two dimensions (in this case, total division revenue and percent of division by business). The candidate should look for combinations of businesses that total $500M in some logical form.	Look to see that it is data-driven and based on the facts of the case.

ASK QUESTIONS

PRESENT CASE TWIST

Handout and Data Guide

Handout:

Give the candidate the marimekko chart showing company revenue

Data to Read

Provide the candidate with the "Additional Info" from sidebar to the right when asked. Refer to the Interviewer's Data Guide and Post Case Review pages for calculations and potential case answers.

Re-routers | Questions to Keep Things on Track

- **When you look at this chart, what jumps out at you?**
  - ‣ A large number of companies are the same size.
  - ‣ Two categories have low growth and low profit margins.

- **How will you prioritize some assets over others?**
  - ‣ Look at net profit and growth percentages.
  - ‣ Consider the strategic implications.

- **What are the implications of the divestitures in their respective categories? Will Tuttle Knox be able to compete going forward?**
  - ‣ If either of the large lawn mowing companies is left, Tuttle Knox will not have trouble competing.
  - ‣ If the smaller lawn care companies are left then, Tuttle Knox may have trouble establishing market share.

Additional Info

Likely question from Candidate: Do you have any information on the businesses that Tuttle Knox owns?

Interviewer: "Here's a marimekko of 2002 revenue. If this chart type is new to you, just think of it as a square pie chart. The upper right corner shows the total revenue for the entire chart. The width of each column is proportional by product category (e.g. heavy lawn equipment is the largest). Each block within a column represents a business. The y axis shows % of category. For example, True Cut is about 40% of heavy lawn equipment."

Businesses under consideration:

- True Cut—Oldest, most prestigious line of lawn mowers. Some older technology. Loyal customers.
- LawnKraft—Second only to True Cut in terms of name and brand. Some think their quality is the best.
- Shaker Smith—Premium image. Less focused on lawn mowers; more focused on broad set of tools.
- Trim Assist—New to the mower space. Better technology, savvy marketing to hip suburbanites.
- Shinjuku—Japanese high-quality tool maker. Making strong inroad into the market.
- Fulcrum Tools—"Good Ole Boys" tool maker; strong loyalty among carpenters; slipping in quality.
- Congren—Consistently the also-ran brand. Dying a slow death as Shinjuku takes its share.

Slash & Burn Investors

New York City, New York, US

Additional Study

F – Form a Plan

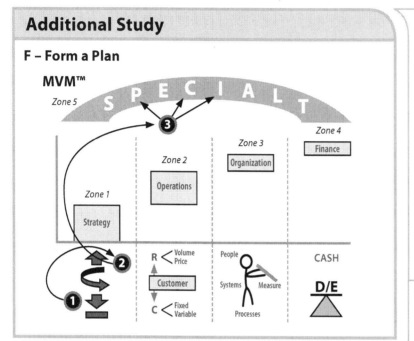

MVM™

M—Mine for the Answer

Where did you go looking for data? You needed to build a fact base around the companies. There were also some questions you could have asked about what is driving the company's performance today (e.g. size, innovation, etc.). Here are some examples:

Company Facts	Innovation	Performance
■ **What is the full list of companies owned by Tuttle Knox?** *See the marimekko chart. Each block represents one company and shows its sales.* ■ **Which companies are growing and which ones are not?** *See the marimekko chart and data distribution.* ■ **Are there distinct markets that we want to exit?** *The chart shows that Heavy Lawn Equipment and Tools are both low-growth and low-margin businesses.* ■ **Is it clear where to focus?** *Heavy Lawn Equipment and Tools are the poorest-performing areas.*	■ **Have the businesses had trouble innovating?** *Many managers have complained that the organization is too big. Heavy Lawn Equipment and Tools take a proportionally larger share of resources to manage.* ■ **Where have we seen evidence of innovation within the businesses?** *The paint businesses have been extremely innovative, capitalizing on the growing popularity of home decoration shows and interest in decorative painting projects.* ■ **What kind of support do the businesses need to be more innovative?** *Most advantages have come from relationships among senior executives at various business lines, from consolidated shipments, and from sharing insights about how to deal with troublesome customers.*	■ **Has our conglomerate model worked with home improvement stores?** *Each department typically has a different buyer, so the paint sales buyer doesn't care if we're an important lawn mower supplier. We gain little or nothing in terms of preferred pricing from our volume in several categories.* ■ **What advantages do we currently have, and will they continue after selling assets?** *The businesses want freedom to make independent decisions more quickly without having to obtain senior management's approval.*

1. **Start in Zone 1, Strategy/Divest:** Slash & Burn Investors want Tuttle Knox to divest $500M of assets. How much will buyers pay for the assets? How well will the remaining companies work together? Will competitors buy the assets and use them against us?

2. **Move to Zone 2, Operations:** To understand which businesses to divest, you'll need to know the basics about each business: annual revenue, net profit and historical and expected growth rates.

3. **Move to Zone 5, External Factors:** What about the industry for the remaining assets? Will growth projections continue for each business, or are there potential limits? Consider potential competitor response and public opinion.

A - Anchor a Hypothesis

Using a hypothesis does not have to be limited to the main question of the case (e.g. Which companies should you divest to reach the goal of $500M?). Use hypothesis thinking in sub-sections of a case where you may have to quickly form an opinion or develop a structure for finding more data.

For instance, once you found that mathematically there were several options you could choose to reach the $500M goal, you had a great opportunity to put a stake in the ground with a hunch about which deal would be best..

E - End the Case

How strong was your final conclusion? Make sure that you are answering the main question of the case and that you use data whenever possible.

In concluding this case, be direct and to the point. Also, be very clear about how you got to your answer. S&B partners will want to know the bottom line.

Slash & Burn Investors

New York City, New York, US

606 FULL ★★★

Post Case Review

Case Insights & Takeaways

- Heavy Lawn Equipment and Tools have weak profit and growth margins.
- Divesting the low margin businesses is a key priority.
- To divest anything in the Tools category before Heavy Lawn Equipment would mean a 3¢ loss of profit for every dollar of revenue.
  — Option 1: True Cut and LawnKraft, $529M, (sticking with specialty lawn equipment only).
  — Option 2: LawnKraft, Shaker, Trim, $469M, (placing bet on True Cut, tradition and loyalty).
  — Option 3: True Cut, Shaker, Trim, $508M, (placing bet on quality and making #2 into #1).

Math Tips

- Round your numbers to come up with estimates quickly.
- Scan the companies to see if a few options can quickly add up to about $500M.
- Think about the numbers of this case at a high level. $500M can be broken into 4 companies at $125M each, 3 companies at $133M each and 2 companies at $250M each. Each approach would imply different activities.

Tips for Reading Charts and Graphs

- Talk while reading through the chart to show that you are relaxed and could talk to a client.
- Start at the top, go around the edges, and finish up in the middle.
- Look at the big pieces first and see what would have the most impact.
- Think of simplicity first. Is there an obvious solution that you can tailor or refine?
- Use your paper along with the chart. Make sure you are calculating very early in the case to show your ease with calculations and numbers.

My Takeaways

To build skills and improve, you must apply what you learned to future cases. Take a few moments and review the interviewer feedback and jot down some key insights about your performance in the space below.

Thinking Skills

My top 2 strengths are:

My top 2 soft spots are:

To address these problems I'll begin to:

VIDEO 3
Recap & Tips (David Ohrvall)

My Performance During the Case

Add up your points. ➡ Total Score: _____ /15

F Form A Plan	**R** Read My Audience	**A** Anchor a Hypothesis	**M** Mine for Answers	**E** End the Case
points	points	points	points	points
③ Structured, clean	③ Good back & forth, caught clues	③ Solid hunch, pursued clue	③ Specific questions, solid analysis	③ Used facts and data, connected the dots
② Somewhat organized and logical	② Awkward, trouble with interviewer style	② Partial direction	② Missed some questions, some math mistakes	② Some data, mostly understood connections
① Messy, overlapping ideas	① Interviewer not interested, couldn't follow	① No hypothesis at all	① Vague questions, weak math, no linkages	① No data, no passion, no connections

Slash & Burn Investors

New York City, New York, US

Interviewer's Data Guide

Ask the following: Which companies would be on your short list to sell? Why?

- Main insights: Two categories have significantly lower growth than the others, Heavy Lawn Equipment and Tools. Both also have low margins.
- The other categories of product all have healthy profit margins and growth rates, so it is safe to focus on Heavy Lawn Equipment and Tools. The next question is which ones to eliminate.

Narrow down the choices

- Heavy Lawn Equipment and Tools have weak profit and growth margins. They are prime areas to examine, since the other areas appear to be growing and show healthier profit margins.
- When choosing between the two, choose Heavy Lawn Equipment. Divesting all tools ($356M of revenue) vs. divesting an equivalent amount in heavy equipment will result in a profit loss of 3% x $356M = $10.7M, due to the difference in profit margins (12% vs. 15%).
- Divesting the low margin businesses is a key priority. To divest anything in the Tools category before Heavy Lawn Equipment would mean a loss of 3¢ for every dollar of revenue.

Look for combinations that amount to $500M in the lawn category

What will add up to $500M?		What's the Implication
Option 1: True Cut and LawnKraft	$529	Sticking with specialty lawn equipment only
Option 2: LawnKraft, Shaker, Trim	$468	Placing bet on True Cut, tradition and loyalty.
Option 3: True Cut, Shaker, Trim	$508	Placing bet on quality and making #2 into #1

Since option 2 does not quite reach $500M, you could divest Congren (Tools) as well, which would bring the total to $556. Slash & Burn wouldn't mind the extra cash for debt payments and it might be best to take care of all the divestitures at one time. This plan leaves TK with True Cut, the traditional lawn mower company. High share would likely be sustained for a period of time, but it is very slow growth and not very profitable.

Option 1 leaves TK with two smaller specialty companies that are likely acquisition targets down the road. They could be packaged together and sold in a year or two. At that point, TK would be out of the slow-growth lawn business.

Option 3 hits the target and leaves TK with one lawn company to focus on and grow. However, it is questionable whether TK will want to grow a business in the lawn care field.

Follow-up Questions

Consider what is left after the company divests the assets

- If there is a combination of tools and lawn equipment, how will they work together?
- Setting aside the heavy lawn and tool equipment, what is the synergy between the remaining businesses?
- Will there be any new challenges in dealing with the home improvement centers after some assets are divested? If TK has any leverage with certain companies, will it be gone?

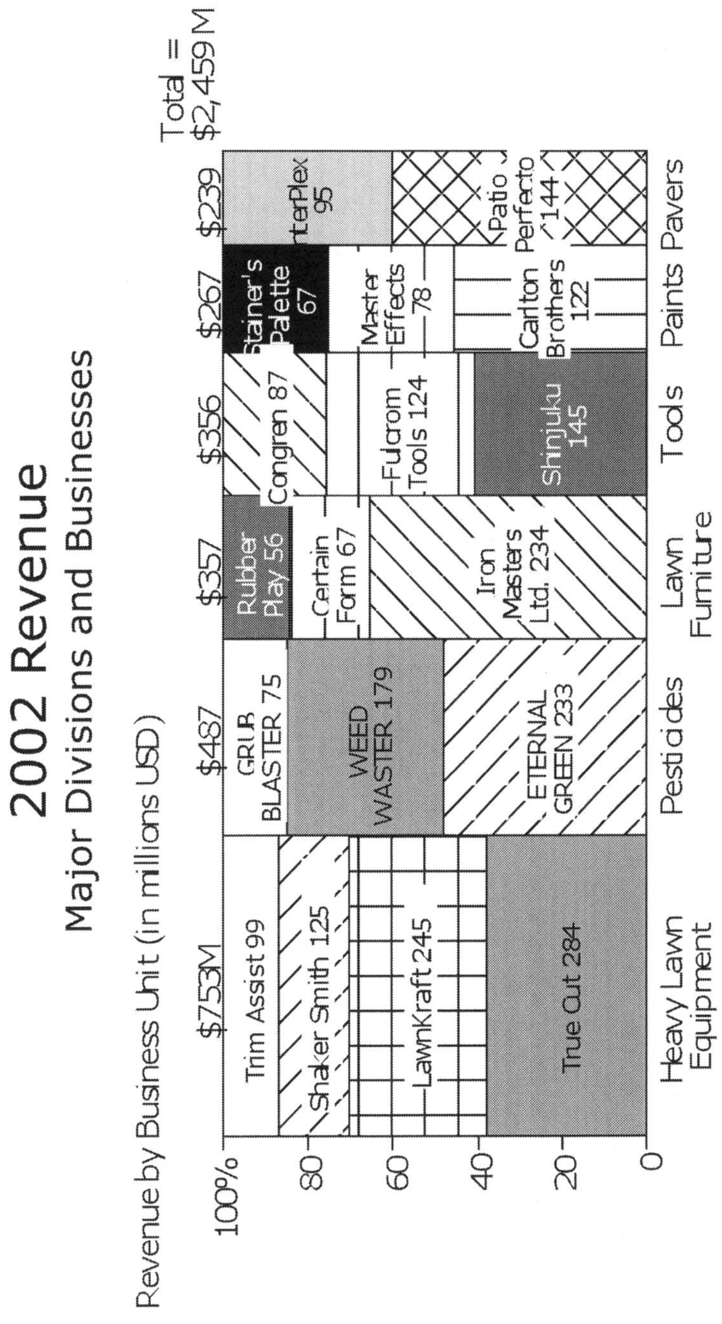

CRACK THE
CASE
SYSTEM

Slash & Burn Investors
New York City, New York, US

606
FULL
★★★

SLASH & BURN INVESTORS

2002 Revenue
Major Divisions and Businesses

Revenue by Business Unit (in millions USD)

Total =
$2,459 M

	Heavy Lawn Equipment	Pesticides	Lawn Furniture	Tools	Paints	Pavers
	$753M	$487	$357	$356	$267	$239
Net Profit Margin	12%	23%	27%	15%	42%	34%
Avg. Growth Rate	4%	9%	13%	5%	17%	31%

Trim Assist 99
Shaker Smith 125
LawnKraft 245
True Cut 284

GRU R BLASTER 75
WEED WASTER 179
ETERNAL GREEN 233

Rubber Play 56
Certain Form 67
Iron Masters Ltd. 234

Congren 87
Fulcrom Tools 124
Shinjuku 145

Stainer's Palette 67
Master Effects 78
Carlton Brothers 122

terPlex 95
Patio Perfecto 144

WORKSHEET

Slash & Burn Investors
New York City, New York, US

SLASH & BURN INVESTORS

My Initial Plan and Output

Today's date:

2. Be original with your data

4. Leave ample room for a structure and additional notes as the case progresses

1. Zone out your paper

3. Take clean and simple notes

WORKSHEET

CRACK THE CASE SYSTEM

Slash & Burn Investors

New York City, New York, US

606 FULL ★★★

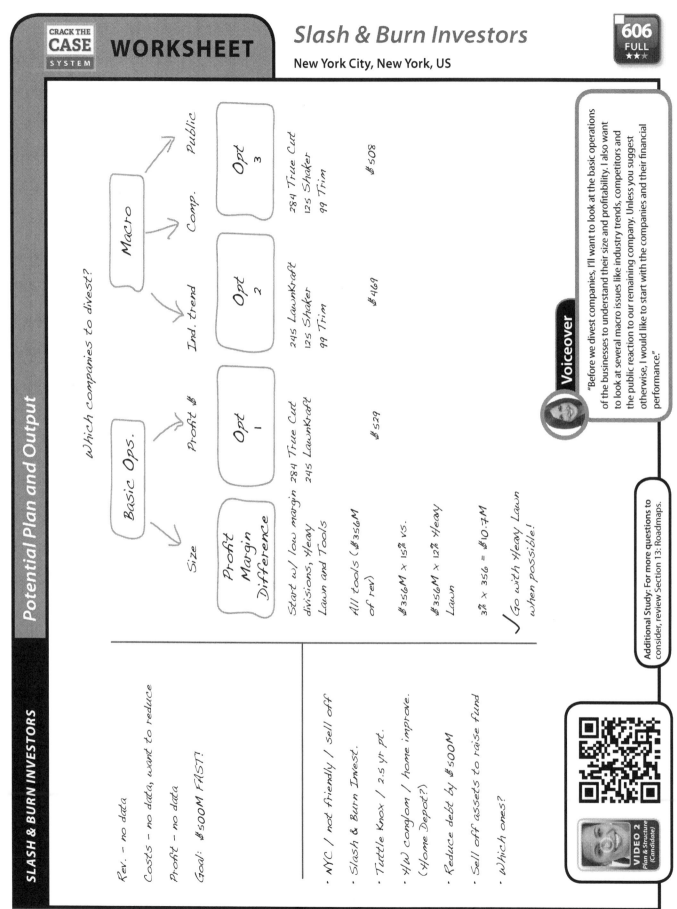

Potential Plan and Output

Which companies to divest?

Basic Ops.

Macro

Size — Profit $ — Ind. trend — Comp. — Public

Profit Margin Difference

Opt 1 — 284 True Cut / 245 LawnKraft

Opt 2 — 245 LawnKraft / 125 Shaker / 99 Trim

Opt 3 — 284 True Cut / 125 Shaker / 99 Trim

Start w/ low margin divisions, Heavy Lawn and Tools

All tools ($356M of rev)

$356M × 15% vs.

$356M × 12% Heavy Lawn

3% × 356 = $10.7M

✓ Go with Heavy Lawn when possible!

Opt 1: $529
Opt 2: $469
Opt 3: $508

SLASH & BURN INVESTORS

- Rev. — no data
- Costs — no data, want to reduce
- Profit — no data
- Goal: $500M FAST!

- NYC / not friendly / sell off
- Slash & Burn Invest.
- Tuttle Knox / 2.5 yr pt.
- H/w conglom / home improve. (Home Depot?)
- Reduce debt by $500M
- Sell off assets to raise fund
- Which ones?

Voiceover

"Before we divest companies, I'll want to look at the basic operations of the businesses to understand their size and profitability. I also want to look at several macro issues like industry trends, competitors and the public reaction to our remaining company. Unless you suggest otherwise, I would like to start with the companies and their financial performance."

Additional Study: For more questions to consider, review Section 13: Roadmaps.

VIDEO 2
Plan & Structure
(Candidate)

CRACK THE CASE SYSTEM

Office Everything

Dallas, Texas, US

Everything was running smoothly until the profit machine jammed.

607 MINI ★★★

DALLAS CITY FACTS

▶ Home to the Dallas Arts District, the largest urban arts district in the US

▶ Birthplace of the frozen margarita, invented here in 1971

▶ More shopping centers per capita than any other major U.S. city

▶ Four times more restaurants per capita than New York

TRAIN Profile

Type	**R**egion	**A**nalysis	**I**ndustry	**N**umber
3 MINI BUSINESS	DALLAS, TX, US Population: 1.3M Currency: Dollar, USD, $	ROADMAP → **6** Maximize Profit	Retail	LEVEL **2**

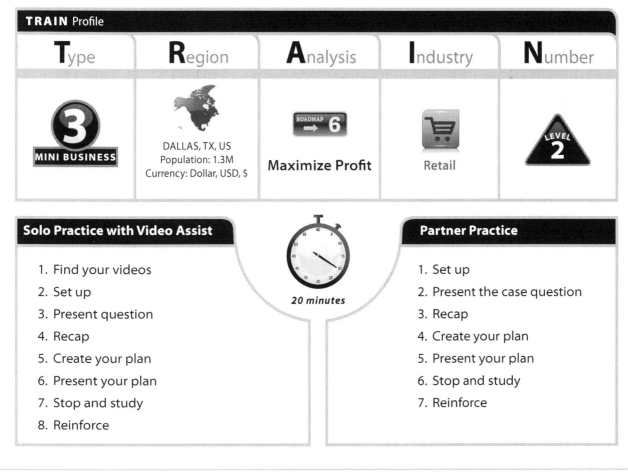

Solo Practice with Video Assist

1. Find your videos
2. Set up
3. Present question
4. Recap
5. Create your plan
6. Present your plan
7. Stop and study
8. Reinforce

20 minutes

Partner Practice

1. Set up
2. Present the case question
3. Recap
4. Create your plan
5. Present your plan
6. Stop and study
7. Reinforce

Office Everything

Dallas, Texas, US

Interview Guide

Case Situation and Question

Office Everything is a chain of 25 medium sized office stores throughout Texas and several southern states. They are a company owned chain and everything is standard. True to their name, they offer every kind of office product imaginable, from paper to shredders to filing cabinets. They are located in strip malls and are not "big box" stores like Staples.

Over the last year almost all of their stores have been consistently flat, growing revenue at about 1% per year. One of the stores, under a new district manager in charge of 10 stores, has had a steep decline in profit this last year.

Can you figure out what's going on?

Case Twist

Check out the Crack the Case System videos on mbacase.com or scan the Video 3 QR code on the Post Case Review page to hear an additional challenge.

Feedback

Physical Skills	Weak		Strong
Body Language	①	②	③
Verbal	①	②	③
Listening	①	②	③

Thinking Skills

Hypothesis Generation	①	②	③
Comfort with Ambiguity	①	②	③
Initial Plan & Output	①	②	③
Data Gathering	①	②	③
Data Analysis	①	②	③
Basic Business Intuition	①	②	③
Integration	①	②	③
2nd Level Insights	①	②	③
Creativity	①	②	③
Recommendation	①	②	③

Total Score _____ / 39

Intro Facts (Tell the Candidate if Asked)

Locations: All stores are the same in terms of size and products.

Competitors: There is no data on competitor sales..

Customers: There is no data indicating that customers have changed their opinions or tastes.

Industry shift: Ask, "Why were you thinking about the industry overall when we know that only one location has changed?" You have no data.

Prices: There are no changes; all pricing is standard.

Key Insights (Do Not Tell the Candidate)

Volume mix problem: People are still coming to the store and buying things, but they are buying lower-margin items. After the candidate does the calculation he should see that the volume of low-margin items is increasing.

Volume drivers: Expect the candidate to ask about why the volume has changed. Push him to think through various reasons before giving the mid-case data.

Mid-case Data (Tell Only at Appropriate Time)

Give handout: After discussing the initial plan, ask the candidate to review and interpret the Handout. Basically, customers are still coming, but buying different products.

Expect a precise answer: Have him calculate total store profit before and after the profit drop. Push him to get it right. If necessary, guide the math.

Give clue: After hearing his answer, ask why this is happening. This should lead to the increase in low-margin sales. Say that six months ago, the employees rearranged and put frequently-requested products toward the front.

Case Flow and Milestones

1 Present Main Question

Read all the notes in the Interview Guide. Understand when to ask certain questions and when to give charts, data and clues.

2 Present Any Basics

Take on a personality (friendly, firm, or foe). Ask one or two background questions. Present the question. Candidate will take notes, ask for a minute, form a plan and present it.

3 Ask for Clarification

This is a straightforward declining profit case. Answer initial questions by using the Intro Facts. If you don't see some major elements shown on page 3, ask why. As the candidate explains his plan, ask about connections between each part. Push for more info.

4 Guide Discussion

Give the handout and follow the Mid-case Data tips. After the candidate interprets the data, give the clue. This clue should trigger an understanding that customers are no longer upgrading and buying higher-margin products. They enter the store, buy what they see, and leave.

5 Get Recommendation

A good recommendation will have 3 parts: in the short term, put the store back; in the mid-term, train employees and promote high- margin products; in the long term, cut negative-margin products. Breaking even, through higher pricing or lower supply costs, would save $350k per year.

GIVE CHART **GIVE CLUE**

Office Everything

Dallas, Texas, US

607
MINI
★★★

Post Case Review

Case Insights & Takeaways

- Questions about the root causes should have focused on store-specific problems, since the other chain stores were doing well.
- Volume was dropping, but only for the low-margin products.
- Customers are still coming to the store, but they are buying different items.
- It wasn't clear whether the customer type stayed the same.

Math Tips

- Scan around the chart and then move to the middle to see that the shift was in revenue.
- A quick review shows that the percentages of revenue have shifted to low margin products.
- Calculate your "close to" estimates by thinking high quality products shrank by half, and low quality products almost doubled.
- Avoid lots of zeroes by picking a scale, like M for millions.
- Use 40% of 10M and 4M, as an anchor to quickly help you calculate the other revenue ($2.5M, $3.5M, etc.).

What to Expect with Cases Like These

- When volume is down, be sure to review mix. Many companies like to use mix problems.
- Remember that volume is also about supply. This case could have been about trucks not delivering to the unprofitable store.
- Present all of your areas and show that you have considered other options. Don't jump to the perceived answer too quickly.
- Show your work even for easy cases. Interviewers don't know that you know the profit elements.

My Takeaways

To build skills and improve, you must apply what you learned to future cases. Take a few moments and review the interviewer feedback and jot down some key insights about your performance in the space below.

Thinking Skills

My top 2 strengths are:

My top 2 soft spots are:

To address these problems I'll begin to:

VIDEO 3
*Recap & Tips
(David Ohrvall)*

My Performance During the Case

Add up your points. ➡ Total Score: _____ /15

F Form A Plan	**R** Read My Audience	**A** Anchor a Hypothesis	**M** Mine for Answers	**E** End the Case
points	points	points	points	points
③ Structured, clean	③ Good back & forth, caught clues	③ Solid hunch, pursued clue	③ Specific questions, solid analysis	③ Used facts and data, connected the dots
② Somewhat organized and logical	② Awkward, trouble with interviewer style	② Partial direction	② Missed some questions, some math mistakes	② Some data, mostly understood connections
① Messy, overlapping ideas	① Interviewer not interested, couldn't follow	① No hypothesis at all	① Vague questions, weak math, no linkages	① No data, no passion, no connections

HANDOUT

CRACK THE CASE SYSTEM

Office Everything

Dallas, Texas, US

607 MINI ★★☆

Office Everything Annual Sales

Total Store Revenue: $10M

BEFORE PROFIT DROP

	Margin	Revenue Breakdown	Profit
High quality	15%	40%	?
Medium quality	5%	25%	?
Low quality	-10%	35%	?
			Total?

Total Store Revenue: $10M

AFTER PROFIT DROP

	Margin	Revenue Breakdown	Profit
High quality	15%	20%	?
Medium quality	5%	30%	?
Low quality	-10%	50%	?
			Total?

WORKSHEET

Office Everything

Dallas, Texas, US

607
MINI
★★★

OFFICE EVERYTHING

My Initial Plan and Output

Today's date:

2. Be original with your data

4. Leave ample room for a structure and additional notes as the case progresses

1. Zone out your paper

3. Take clean and simple notes

WORKSHEET

Office Everything

Dallas, Texas, US

Potential Plan and Output

Single store profit is down. Why?

Profit ↑↑

$$Profit = Revenues - Costs$$

Revenues (P × VOL.)

$$P \times V$$

P (× VOL.) PRICE

- Price change for lots of prod?

- Change pricing philosophy? (e.g. cost plus vs. market based)

VOLUME

- Sold fewer units per cust? (e.g. no specials or bundles anymore)

- Has the type of product sold changed? Is the mix different?

- One off issues?
  – local economy
  – bad employees
  – supplier vol. down?

Costs

$$- FC + VC$$

Fixed Costs

- Has a fixed cost changed this last year?

- Rent
- Equipment
- Utilities
- Leases
- Supplier contracts

VARIABLE COSTS

- labor change?
- wages?
- product costs?

OFFICE EVERYTHING

Rev. – no data

Costs – no data

Profit down, no specifics

25 locations

east coast

lots of products

one store ——→ trouble

profit down

revenue flat / 1%

Additional Study: For more questions to consider, review Section 13: Roadmaps.

CRACK THE CASE SYSTEM

Green Thumb

Newark, New Jersey, US

Green Thumb is having trouble keeping up with the "greening" of America. Can you help management find a future in this changing landscape?

608 FULL ★★★

NEWARK CITY FACTS

▸ America's third oldest major city

▸ Nickname: "The Brick City"

▸ Regarded as the car theft capital of the world with more cars stolen in Newark than in any other US city.

▸ Port Newark, is the primary shipping facility for New York and the surrounding areas.

TRAIN Profile

Type	**R**egion	**A**nalysis	**I**ndustry	**N**umber
4 FULL BUSINESS	NEWARK, NEW JERSEY, US Population: 277K Currency: Dollar, USD, $	ROADMAP → **13** **Market Shift**	**Chemicals**	LEVEL **2**

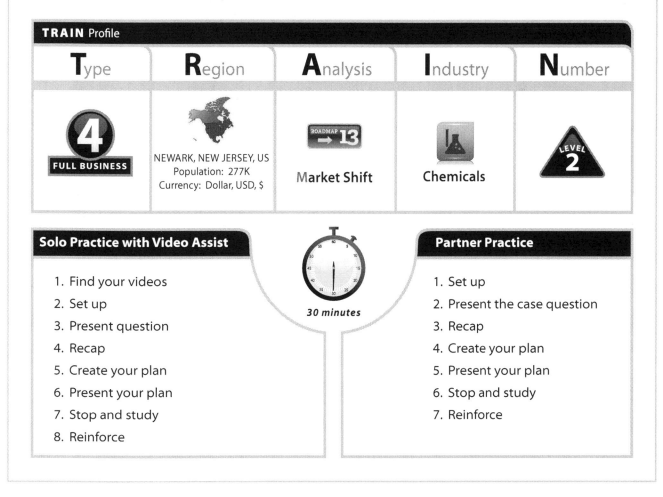

Solo Practice with Video Assist

1. Find your videos
2. Set up
3. Present question
4. Recap
5. Create your plan
6. Present your plan
7. Stop and study
8. Reinforce

30 minutes

Partner Practice

1. Set up
2. Present the case question
3. Recap
4. Create your plan
5. Present your plan
6. Stop and study
7. Reinforce

Green Thumb

Newark, New Jersey, US

608
FULL
★★★

Interview Guide

Case Situation and Question

Green Thumb, an $800M US-based lawn and garden supply manufacturer, has been the dominant player in the U.S. lawn fertilizer market for the last 25 years. The company has led this segment through the consistent marketing of a five-step approach to lawn care. GT's focus has been to demystify the art of having a plush, healthy green lawn, setting the "gold standard" for lawn care in the suburbs. Management is worried that environmental concerns will errode GT's customer base and profitabiity. In their view, this threat has three parts: water conservation, "back to nature" landscaping and the anti-chemical movement.

Help management determine how big these threats are, and what GT should do to counter them.

Case Twist

It turns out that the Total Gardening Survey may have been administered incorrectly and the data is questionable.

Does this change your answer?

VIDEO 1
Case Question
(Interviewer)

Feedback

Physical Skills	Weak		Strong
Body Language	①	②	③
Verbal	①	②	③
Listening	①	②	③

Thinking Skills

| | | |
---|---|---|---
Hypothesis Generation | ① | ② | ③
Comfort with Ambiguity | ① | ② | ③
Initial Plan & Output | ① | ② | ③
Data Analysis | ① | ② | ③
Basic Business Intuition | ① | ② | ③
Integration | ① | ② | ③
2nd Level Insights | ① | ② | ③
Creativity | ① | ② | ③

Total Score _____ / 33

Intro Facts (Tell the Candidate if Asked)

Customer buying patterns: There is some public attitude survey data on the Interviewer's Data Guide.

Causes for revenue decline in California (CA) and Oregon (OR): We don't know why revenue has dropped off.

Competitors: Everyone is facing the same issues, but Green Thumb is the market leader; thus, the competitors will follow whatever Green Thumb does.

Research & Development: Internal R&D at Green Thumb is focused mainly on solving problems through the use of traditional chemicals, not "green" solutions.

Marketing: Recent leadership change in this department has given the marketing team new enthusiasm for growing share.

Sales: Most products are sold in mass market outlets like home improvement centers and hardware stores.

Key Insights (Do Not Tell the Candidate)

General tips: Your Candidate may feel overloaded with the data. There are no data handouts, yet you have to give quite a bit.

Balance the discussion between framing vs. giving the data. The data is critical to solving the case, so don't hold it back if he gets lost or confused. Use the Re-router questions to keep him on track.

Size the Issues First: To do a good job developing a sense of each issue's size, the Candidate has to quickly sort through the data. Give these tips:

- For water conservation, use water restriction data.

- For back-to-nature landscaping, use percentage of customers changing over.

- For anti-chemical movement, estimate the number of homes cutting back.

Significance of Threats:

- 1/3 of our revenue comes from states with a "high awareness" of environmentalism.

- Soon 40% of all communities will have restrictions in place.

- 1/3 of polled customers want to limit chemical usage.

- Revenue is dropping in key states like California.

Mid-case Data (Tell Only at Appropriate Time)

You will be busy reading the data to the Candidate. All data is located on the Data Distribution page. To make it more interactive, consider asking these questions before giving the data sets:

In the beginning: "What kind of data would you need to best understand the threat of each issue?"

Before giving Data Set A, ask: "For chemical usage, what kind of information would be relevant?"

Give the sales trends (B), public awareness information (C), and the hotline info (F). After giving the data, ask: "How would you best interpret these data sets together."

Before giving Data Set D, ask: "With water reduction, where do you want to focus? Is this a consumer issue or a municipality one?"

Before giving Data Set E, ask: "Natural gardening as a trend seems tough to measure. How could you size this problem?"

Green Thumb

Newark, New Jersey, US

608
FULL
★★★

Case Flow and Milestones

1 Present Main Question	**2** Answer Any Basics	**3** Ask for Clarification	**4** Guide Discussion	**5** Get Recommendation
Candidate takes notes, asks for a minute, forms a plan and presents it.	This case has no handouts, but be prepared to give quite a bit of information. Review all the data on the Interview Guide to ensure you understand the flow. Also review potential questions on the Mine for the Answer section under the Additional Study Using the FRAME Method page.	Be sure to make him explain anything you do not fully understand. Look for clear connections between each part of the plan and an understanding of how each part contributes to the whole. Ask questions about his approach.	The Candidate may start in several different areas, but the "star" knows that he has to size the issues quickly. Without any dollar significance attached to each one, the case will just become an interesting discussion. Follow his lead to some degree and dole out the data appropriately.	Ask these questions if you have time: • What additional data would you need to refine your analysis? • If you had to recommend some adjacent business opportunities to Green Thumb, what would they be?

Handout and Data Guide

Data Set A: Revenue by Region and Product Type

Sales by Region
(Lawn Chemicals, $560M)

West Coast	33%
Central	15%
Mid-west	30%
East Coast	22%

Sales by West Coast State

California	45%
Oregon	33%
Washington	22%

Sales by Product
(Total Company Sales, $800M)

Lawn Chemicals	70%
Soils and Mulches	10%
Flower Chemicals	20%

Sales by East Coast State

New York	40%
Massachusetts	20%
Maine	10%
New Hampshire	5%

More Data

Data Set B: Sales Trends (Last 2 Years)
- California down 5%
- Colorado down 4%
- Maine down 1%

Data Set C: Public awareness of chemicals and water
Survey of residents in 50 states found that California (CA), Oregon (OR), Maine (ME), New Hampshire (NH) and Colorado (CO) all show high awareness (>30% of population) of environmental issues. "High Awareness" individuals tended to cut back on chemical and water consumption.

Data Set D: Legislation
30% of all communities have water conservation policies in place, which may grow to be 40% in two more years. These policies usually restrict the times lawns can be watered and, sometimes, the amount of water. Studies have shown that as people water their lawn less, they tend to ignore it more, using fewer chemical maintenance products.

Data Set E: Public "attitudes toward gardening" survey data
- 35% of respondents want to reduce lawn and garden chemicals
- 15% want to reduce lawn and garden water consumption
- 5% are considering diminishing the size of their lawn

Data Set F: Internal metrics
Green Thumb Hotline has shown a 50% increase in the number of calls related to chemical content and product safety. These calls are 40% of total calls

Re-routers | Questions to Keep Things on Track

- **This is a lot of data. How are you sorting through it all?**
  ‣ Looking for 80/20 insights
  ‣ Trying to see if our major regions are affected by the adverse trends
  ‣ Checking for multiple trends occurring in one location
- **Do you think that we should look at these environmental issues as one trend or as separate issues?**
  ‣ Making it one issue can over-simplify

the effects and hide areas that are worth exploring. For instance, water consumption should be analyzed separately from the anti-chemical movement, as they may be present in different degrees across geographic areas.
- **What additional data would you like to see?**
- **How can you make your answer more quantitative?**

Green Thumb

Newark, New Jersey, US

608
FULL
★★★

Additional Study Using the FRAME Method

F – Form a Plan

MVM™

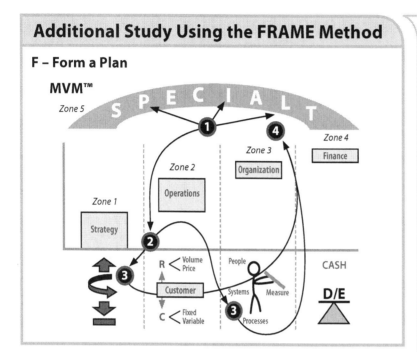

M—Mine for the Answer

As you worked your way through the data, were you looking for answers?
Try to ask 2–3 questions in each section you explore.

Reality of Threat	Revenue Impact	Ability to Respond
■ In what regions have these trends already affected revenue? *Western states are leading in terms of water restriction and public awareness.*	■ Where in the country are legislators most concerned about green issues? *Western states have the largest number of current/proposed laws.*	■ Who is more advanced than GT in developing green solutions? *A few small companies are using new technology and greener chemicals.*
■ What percentage of our customers want "green" chemicals? *California and Colorado sales have declined.*	■ What kind of legislation will affect our sales? *Water restriction would have the largest impact on revenue.*	■ What companies could GT acquire or form a joint venture? *Some of these small ones may be easily acquired.*
■ How about low water-use yards? *Recent polls indicate that 35% want to "reduce chemical usage" and 15% want to "reduce water consumption."*	■ Where has customer opinion begun to change? *Customer opinion toward "green" is growing in CA, OR, NH, ME and CO.*	■ How should GT market its products to align better with green philosophies? *Any slight reduction in hazardous chemicals should be heavily marketed.*
■ How about eliminating yards? *Only 5% are considering "greatly diminishing the size of their lawn."*	■ How much will those changes influence buying patterns? *These states together represent 40% of sales.*	■ Are there any other products GT should begin to develop? *GT explored "desert-scape" products like mulches and soils, but margins are much smaller than chemicals.*

1. **Start in Zone 5, External Issues.** Several factors are under consideration. Ask for data on each one to determine the extent of the problems:

   • Industry – There is a shift away from chemicals. How many companies have begun to make a change in what they sell?

   • Public – Opinion is changing quickly about what makes for an attractive landscape. To what degree have these new trends caught on? Are people really shunning chemicals?

   • Legislation – Water restrictions are more common now. How have these pressures forced the homeowners to change their approach?

2. **Move to Zone 2, Operations.** To what degree will these trends affect our future revenue?

3. **Move to Zone 1 Strategy or Zone 3 Processes.** Discuss alternate solutions to the problems. Green Thumb may need to acquire a company to help develop "greener" (chemical free) solutions, or it may need to change the way it develops new products internally.

4. **Move to Zone 5, Technology.** Explore new, environmentally friendly chemical technologies.

A – Anchor a Hypothesis

Did you have any hunches here? When a case topic is unfamiliar, stick to a "yes/no" format. In this case, either the threats are real or they are not. Positioning your mind ahead of time in one of those zones will help you anticipate the data.

These Threats are Real and Big

"Since GT has a good understanding of the industry, it is likely that their sources are accurate. I bet they'll have to refocus their business and explore new products and potentially new channels."

E – End the Case

"In sum, these issues are serious: 1/3 of our revenue comes from high-awareness states, legislation to limit watering is increasing, and about 1/3 of polled customers want to limit chemical usage. We are also seeing revenue drops in key states like California, which may be attributed to these environmental concerns.
I recommend we focus on two areas: 1. Identify acquisition targets and/or find a way to partner with them; 2. Market our push toward "green" solutions and show our concern for the environment. As for next steps, I would pursue further analysis of the drivers of revenue decline in our key states."

Green Thumb

Newark, New Jersey, US

608
FULL
★★★

Post Case Review	**My Takeaways**

Case Insights & Takeaways

Review the Additional Candidate Tips page for more a detailed explanation of insights.

- Several states fall in the High Awareness category.
- Together those states represent about 30% of chemical sales.
- Legislation for reducing water consumption for lawns and gardens is increasing.
- Consumers want to reduce the amount of water and chemicals used.
- A large percentage of hotline calls are related to chemical concerns.

Math Tips

- Create small graphs to keep all the data organized.
- Don't be shy about explaining how you are using the data to conclude your thinking. Interviewers want to see how you think.
- Look for insights quickly by using 80/20 estimates or checking to see if one "common sense" answer (e.g. west coast people will conserve more water) is the right one.

What to Expect with Cases Like These

- Expect to be frustrated! No one likes to do this much math under pressure. Practice this case again several times to rehearse how you could ask for more data, take notes, do math and create charts.
- Plan to fully extract the data once you realize your interviewer has data sets. Review the questions you could have asked to accelerate the analysis. Focus on making cases like these a conversation with your interviewer.

To build skills and improve, you must apply what you learned to future cases. Take a few moments and review the interviewer feedback and jot down some key insights about your performance in the space below.

Thinking Skills

My top 2 strengths are:

My top 2 soft spots are:

To address these problems I'll begin to:

VIDEO 3
Recap & Tips
(David Ohrvall)

My Performance During the Case   Add up your points. ➡ Total Score: _____ /15

F Form A Plan	**R** Read My Audience	**A** Anchor a Hypothesis	**M** Mine for Answers	**E** End the Case
points	points	points	points	points
③ Structured, clean	③ Good back & forth, caught clues	③ Solid hunch, pursued clue	③ Specific questions, solid analysis	③ Used facts and data, connected the dots
② Somewhat organized and logical	② Awkward, trouble with interviewer style	② Partial direction	② Missed some questions, some math mistakes	② Some data, mostly understood connections
① Messy, overlapping ideas	① Interviewer not interested, couldn't follow	① No hypothesis at all	① Vague questions, weak math, no linkages	① No data, no passion, no connections

Green Thumb
Newark, New Jersey, US

Additional Candidate Tips

Plot Your Data

Make simple charts to keep it all organized

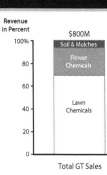

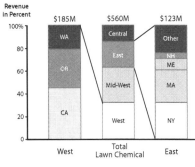

Look for Insights

States that have "High Awareness" to environmental issues include:

Oregon and CA: ~80% x $185M = $148M

Maine and NH: ~15% x $123M = $18M

Colorado: no data

Together these represent about 30% (($148 + $18)/$560M) of our chemical sales, which seems like a high percentage to have at risk.

Plot Your Data

Water reduction trend?

Serious. 40% of all communities will soon have water restrictions.

Implications?

Serious. Over 30% of states have high awareness of this issue.

Lawn reduction?

Not Serious. The data we have indicates a mere 5% considering it.

Urgency?

High. These percentages are likely to grow rather than shrink.

Sure these will happen?

No. However, this is a large enough issue to explore remedies.

Other indicators?

Hotline, gardening survey, and legislation all point the same way.

Develop Revenue Growth Scenarios

Overall, Green Thumb must protect its revenue streams.

Acquisitions: Green Thumb has researched companies that are making advances in the use of safer chemicals for lawns. Many of them want to stay independent.

New Marketing: Green Thumb would like to market the safety of their products, but they can't do so until they reformulate them.

Develop less harsh chemicals for lawn management: Green Thumb has looked into this. If these "greener" chemicals can be commercialized they will increase the overall expense of production.

Explore selling more non-chemical products: Green Thumb has already entered the mulch and soil business. Margins from these products are not as high as for chemicals (no details on margins available). The company would consider creating other products, but is concerned about moving away from its core business—chemicals. What products, if any, do you think they should pursue?

CRACK THE CASE SYSTEM

WORKSHEET

Green Thumb

Newark, New Jersey, US

608 FULL ★★★

GREEN THUMB

My Initial Plan and Output

Today's date:

2. Be original with your data

1. Zone out your paper

3. Take clean and simple notes

4. Leave ample room for a structure and additional notes as the case progresses

CRACK THE CASE SYSTEM — WORKSHEET

Green Thumb
Newark, New Jersey, US

608 FULL ★★★

Potential Plan and Output

GREEN THUMB

Today's date:

How big are these threats?
How should they counter them?

External	Operations	Strategy	Process & Technology
Industry shift? Producers moving away from chemicals? Change products?	Size of impact on revenue?	Acquisitions? Are there growing companies that offer alternatives?	Can GT develop new chemicals?
Public pressure? Are people avoiding chemicals?	Price changes. Will we have to lower prices?	New production techniques.	How strong is R&D?
Legislation for water. How big? How strict? Trend?	Volume drops. Which products will be hit hardest?	New products.	What changes are necessary to company processes?

HUNCH: volume of current products will drop. GT needs to make alternative products.

- Rev. ~ $800M
- Costs - ?
- Profit Margin -
- Goal: size and determine threats
- Competitor threat! Is it real?

- Green Thumb
- US – lawn / garden supplier
- Dominant for 25 yrs.
- 5 step program / mkt. well
- Threat – environmentalism
- water / back to nature / anti-chemical

Voiceover

"I would first like to assess the potential size of each of these problems using the data we have available. Once we have an estimate of the impact and timing of each problem, I would like to understand how each one may affect revenue and costs. If we have time, it would be interesting to explore potential solutions for each of these. Before we begin, is there any one area where you would like me to focus first?"

Additional Study: For more questions to consider, review Section 13: Roadmaps.

VIDEO 2 Plan & Structure (Candidate)

Plainfield Industries

Bismarck, North Dakota, US

Plainfield wants to plant their new seed. Will it grow?

609 START
★★★

BISMARCK CITY FACTS

▸ In 1773, changed the name to Bismarck after German chancellor Otto van Bismarck to gain German investment in Northern Pacific Railway

▸ In February 2007, Bismarck set a national record for the most snow angels made in one place: 8, 962

▸ The top three ancestries in Bismarck are German (57.9%) Norwegian (18.2%) and Russian (7.7 %)

TRAIN Profile

Type	**R**egion	**A**nalysis	**I**ndustry	**N**umber
1 CASE START	BISMARCK, NORTH DAKOTA Population: 104,944 Currency: Dollar, USD, $	ROADMAP ➡ 3 New Business or Product	Agriculture	LEVEL 1

Solo Practice with Video Assist

1. Find your videos
2. Set up
3. Present question
4. Recap
5. Create your plan
6. Present your plan
7. Stop and study
8. Reinforce

10 minutes

Partner Practice

1. Set up
2. Present the case question
3. Recap
4. Create your plan
5. Present your plan
6. Stop and study
7. Reinforce

609
START ★★☆

Plainfield Industries

Bismarck, North Dakota, US

Interview Guide

Case Situation & Question

Plainfield Industries has had a new breakthrough. They have just developed a genetically engineered corn kernel that produces crops of drought-resistant corn. Overwhelmed with the possibilities of revenue growth, they want to get this product to market ASAP. They realize they have a lot of options and need your help to prioritize.

What's the best and fastest way to launch this new product?

Case Twist

Two other competitors, one in Europe and another in Asia, have discovered similar products.

How do these announcements impact your strategy?

VIDEO 1
Case Question
(Interviewer)

Feedback

Physical Skills

	Weak		Strong
Body Language	①	②	③
Verbal	①	②	③
Listening	①	②	③

Thinking Skills

	Weak		Strong
Hypothesis Generation	①	②	③
Initial Plan & Output	①	②	③
Data Gathering	①	②	③
Basic Business Intuition	①	②	③

Total Score _____ / 21

Case Start Self Study Reminders

Present Question	Recap & Ask for a Minute	Create Your Plan	Present Plan	Stop & Study	Reinforce
Read the question out loud like an interviewer or watch the MBACASE video interviewer.	Briefly recap the situation, the complication, and your task. Speak out loud just like you would in an interview.	Using the paper below, fill in the sections.	Turn your plan toward the interviewer (or mirror or webcam) and present it piece by piece .	Review the roadmaps and the Post Case Review page to see what you missed. Mark up your plan to make it better.	Do the start again with the video interviewer, or find a live partner and get some feedback. Incorporate what you learned the first time.

609 START ★★ ★

CRACK THE CASE SYSTEM

Plainfield Industries
Bismarck, North Dakota, US

Today's date:

My Initial Plan and Output

Questions I'm thinking about:

Topics I know to cover:

Profit Tree Approach:

Topic Bucket Approach:

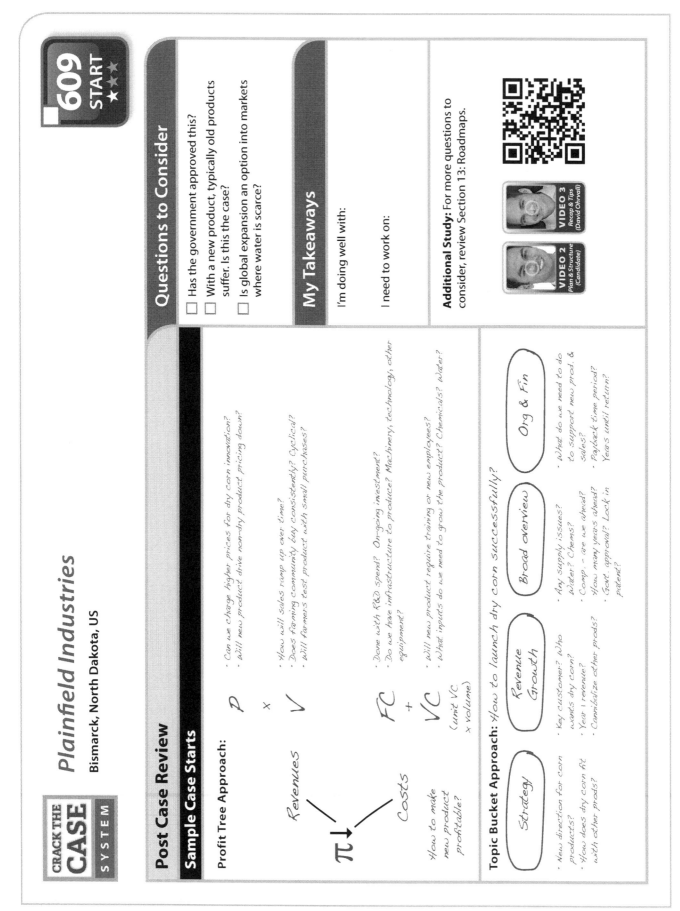

CRACK THE CASE SYSTEM

609 START ★★ ★

Plainfield Industries
Bismarck, North Dakota, US

Post Case Review

Sample Case Starts

Profit Tree Approach:

$$\pi \to \text{Revenues} \begin{cases} P \\ \times \\ V \end{cases}$$

$$\text{Costs} \begin{cases} FC \\ + \\ VC \\ \text{(unit VC} \\ \times \text{volume)} \end{cases}$$

How to make new product profitable?

- Can we charge higher prices for dry corn innovation?
- Will new product drive non-dry product pricing down?

- How will sales ramp up over time?
- Does farming community buy consistently? Cyclical?
- Will farmers test product with small purchases?

- Done with R&D spend? On-going investment?
- Do we have infrastructure to produce? Machinery, technology, other equipment?

- Will new product require training or new employees?
- What inputs do we need to grow the product? Chemicals? Water?

Topic Bucket Approach: *How to launch dry corn successfully?*

Strategy
- New direction for corn products?
- How does dry corn fit with other prods?

Revenue Growth
- Key customer? Who wants dry corn?
- Year 1 revenue?
- Cannibalize other prods?

Broad overview
- Any supply issues? Water? Chems?
- Comp. – are we ahead?
- How many years ahead?
- Govt. approval? Lock in patent?

Org & Fin
- What do we need to do to support new prod. & sales?
- Payback time period? Years until return?

Questions to Consider

- ☐ Has the government approved this?
- ☐ With a new product, typically old products suffer. Is this the case?
- ☐ Is global expansion an option into markets where water is scarce?

My Takeaways

I'm doing well with:

I need to work on:

Additional Study: For more questions to consider, review Section 13: Roadmaps.

VIDEO 2
Plan & Structure
(Candidate)

VIDEO 3
Recap & Tips
(David Ohrvall)

CRACK THE
CASE
SYSTEM

Room with a View

Princeville, Kauai, US

How many timeshare units are in Hawaii?

610
SIZING
★★★

TRAIN Profile

Type	**R**egion	**A**nalysis	**I**ndustry	**N**umber
2 MARKET SIZING	PRINCEVILLE, KAUAI, US Population: 1.7K Currency: Dollar, USD, $	Observe, Range	Real Estate	LEVEL **2**

Solo Practice with Video Assist

1. Find your videos
2. Set up
3. Present question
4. Recap
5. Create your plan
6. Present your plan
7. Stop and study
8. Reinforce

15 minutes

Partner Practice

1. Set up
2. Present the case question
3. Recap
4. Create your plan
5. Present your plan
6. Stop and study
7. Reinforce

Room with a View

Princeville, Kauai, US

610
SIZING
★★★

Interview Guide

Initial Question

Your client is a large real estate services provider trying to grow its timeshare service offering. It would like to determine the size of the timeshare market in Hawaii as it may invest more in the Pacific Rim. It plans to open an office in Princeville, Kauai. How many timeshare units are in Hawaii? Assume that there are 7.5M visitors per year and that timeshare units represent 10% of all potential lodging inventory.

VIDEO 1
Case Question
(Interviewer)

Feedback

Physical Skills	Weak		Strong
Body Language	①	②	③
Verbal	①	②	③
Listening	①	②	③

Thinking Skills

Initial Plan & Output	①	②	③
Data Gathering	①	②	③
Data Analysis	①	②	③

Total Score _____ / 18

Intro Facts (Tell the Candidate if Asked)	**Key Insights** (Do Not Tell the Candidate)	**Mid-case Data** (Tell Only at Appropriate Time)
The average length of stay is a week with two people per room.	**Funneling:** Candidate must understand how the length of the visit and number of people per room will affect the overall equation.	Assume that the lodging industry runs at 75% capacity.

Case Flow and Milestones

1 Prep and Review	**2** Present Main Question	**3** Answer & Ask	**4** Guide Discussion	**5** Get Recommendation
Read all the notes in the Interviewer Guide. Understand when to ask certain questions and when to give charts, data and clues.	Take on a personality (friendly, firm or foe). Ask one or two background questions. Present the question. Candidate will take notes and ask for time to think or begin talking. Discourage silence as market sizing cases are meant to be interactive.	This is an ambiguous problem. Try to help the candidate by offering ideas if he is stuck. Continue to ask why he is thinking a certain way.	Give any missing data if necessary and the Mid-case Data tips. Review the answer on page 4 of the case pack and offer suggestions if the candidate needs help.	Be firm and expect a final number. To see if the candidate is thinking about broader business issues ask what he would do with this information.

GIVE CLUE

CRACK THE CASE SYSTEM

Room with a View
Princeville, Kauai, US

610
SIZING
★★★
★

My Initial Plan and Output
Use the space below to write your thoughts.

My Numbers

What are some simple estimates for getting started?

How might you refine these numbers?

State your assumptions

Pick your main metrics and approach

Estimate quickly and with round numbers

Assess your approach and answer

Keep exceptions and next steps in mind.

Room with a View

Princeville, Kauai, US

Post Case Review	My Score	
Potential Solution & Output	Weak	Strong

State your assumptions ①②③

- Everyone who visits Hawaii will stay in a lodging room of some sort.

- Occupancy rates are the same across the board.

Pick your main metrics and approach ①②③

- Top-down based on the number of visitors to the state.

Estimate quickly and with round numbers ①②③

- 7.5M visitors per year / 2 visitors per room = 3.75M rooms per year

- 3.75M rooms per year / 50 weeks = 75K rooms required

- 75% occupancy = 100K rooms required

- 10% of 100K rooms = 10K timeshare units

Assess your approach and answer ①②③

- 10,000 timeshare units is a challenge to assess without any other context. However, considering that the ratio is one timeshare for every 750 visitors, this seems reasonable.

Keep exceptions and next steps in mind ①②③

- The 75% occupancy rate would change for different types of lodging inventory. If residents in Hawaii also vacation on other islands, there would be a higher demand for rooms and timeshares.

Total:

Case Twist

- Due to recent volcanic and tectonic activity, the government has required a regulation of no buildings higher than 20 stories on the island. All floors above 20 must be vacated immediately, with no foreseeable end in sight. Right now, the tallest hotel in Hawaii is 50 floors high. Assume a normal distribution of hotel size.

Tips and Takeaways

- If not using a population-based approach, use population as a sanity check.

VIDEO 2
Plan & Structure (Candidate)

VIDEO 3
Recap & Tips (David Ohrvall)

Yellow Brick Road Distribution

CRACK THE CASE SYSTEM

Los Angeles, California, US

Yellow Brick's road is no longer paved in gold. Can you help them navigate?

611 START ★★☆

LOS ANGELES CITY FACTS

▸ Second largest city in the US and the largest city in California

▸ Home to Hollywood and known as "The Entertainment Capital of the World"

▸ There are 851 museums in L.A., more museums per capita than any other city in the world

TRAIN Profile

Type	**R**egion	**A**nalysis	**I**ndustry	**N**umber
1 CASE START	LOS ANGELES, CALIFORNIA Population: 3.8M Currency: Dollar, USD, $	ROADMAP **1** Change Price	Entertainment	LEVEL **1**

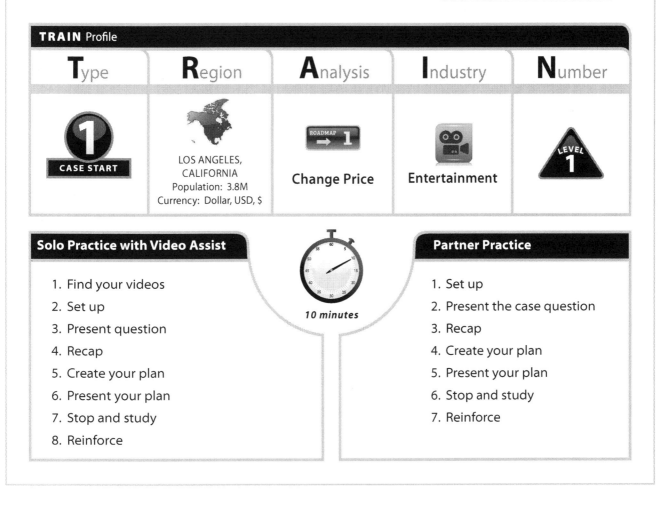

Solo Practice with Video Assist

1. Find your videos
2. Set up
3. Present question
4. Recap
5. Create your plan
6. Present your plan
7. Stop and study
8. Reinforce

10 minutes

Partner Practice

1. Set up
2. Present the case question
3. Recap
4. Create your plan
5. Present your plan
6. Stop and study
7. Reinforce

611
START
★★★

Interview Guide

Yellow Brick Road Distribution

Los Angeles, California, US

CRACK THE
CASE
S Y S T E M

Case Situation & Question

Yellow Brick Road Distribution (known as Yellow Brick) is the distribution arm for several major Hollywood studios. They are responsible for launching the domestic and international roll-out of DVDs, typically within 3–5 months of a film's release. They are constantly challenged by an ever-shifting entertainment, technology and consumer landscape. Their latest challenge is pricing. Due to the instant access of downloadable movies, DVD sales are declining rapidly. They think that in the next 12 months they will discontinue DVD sales of 1/3 of their titles. Also, retailers are expecting a price reduction for all titles to make the products more competitive.

How would you help them think through their pricing strategy?

Case Twist

Yellow Brick has now decided to phase out 50% of their titles.

How would that information change your perspective?

VIDEO 1
*Case Question
(Interviewer)*

Feedback

Physical Skills

	Weak		Strong
Body Language	①	②	③
Verbal	①	②	③
Listening	①	②	③

Thinking Skills

	Weak		Strong
Hypothesis Generation	①	②	③
Initial Plan & Output	①	②	③
Data Gathering	①	②	③
Basic Business Intuition	①	②	③

Total Score _____ / 21

Case Start Self Study Reminders

Present Question	Recap & Ask for a Minute	Create Your Plan	Present Plan	Stop & Study	Reinforce
Read the question out loud like an interviewer or watch the MBACASE video interviewer.	Briefly recap the situation, the complication, and your task. Speak out loud just like you would in an interview.	Using the paper below, fill in the sections.	Turn your plan toward the interviewer (or mirror or webcam) and present it piece by piece.	Review the roadmaps and the Post Case Review page to see what you missed. Mark up your plan to make it better.	Do the start again with the video interviewer, or find a live partner and get some feedback. Incorporate what you learned the first time.

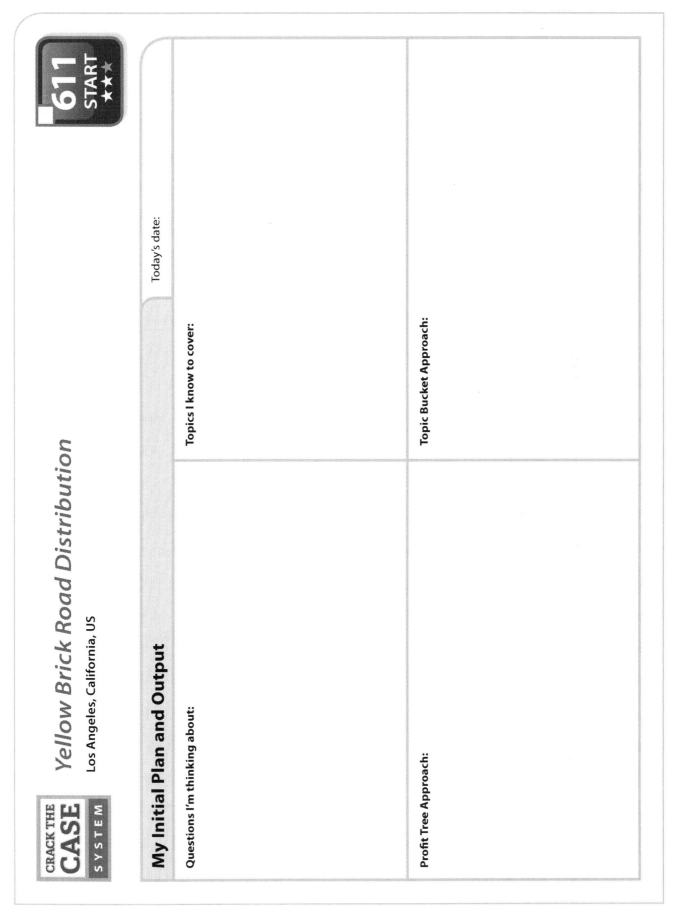

CRACK THE CASE SYSTEM

611
START
★★★

Yellow Brick Road Distribution

Los Angeles, California, US

Today's date:

My Initial Plan and Output

Questions I'm thinking about:

Topics I know to cover:

Profit Tree Approach:

Topic Bucket Approach:

www.mbacase.com

Yellow Brick Road Distribution

Los Angeles, California, US

611
START
★ ★ ★

Questions to Consider

☐ With a pricing case, can you determine what basic type of pricing is the focus? Customer driven, competitive or cost plus?

☐ Can we charge a premium?

☐ Should we take a loss and be lower than competitors?

My Takeaways

I'm doing well with:

I need to work on:

Additional Study: For more questions to consider, review Section 13: Roadmaps.

VIDEO 2
Plan & Structure
(Candidate)

VIDEO 3
Recap & Tips
(David Ohrvall)

Post Case Review

Sample Case Starts

Profit Tree Approach:

$\pi \rightarrow$

$P \times V$ — Revenues

$FC + VC$ (unit VC × volume) — Costs

- What are YBR's current prices by product?
- What are the potential new price levels?
- Can we offset price decrease with new premiums for other products?

- How to keep customers loyal? Product differentiation?
- Look for ways to give customers more benefits with products (and services)?

- As the product portfolio decreases, which FC will be underutilized?

- After selling off product lines, will input costs go up (e.g. discs)?
- Can we renegotiate with employees and suppliers?

How to change pricing to meet new demands?

Topic Bucket Approach: How Should Yellow Brick Price?

(Customers)   (Competitors)   (Price)   (Measure)

- Historical response to price changes for DVDs?
- Are they demanding a certain price level?

- How are they pricing products today?

- What is the price volume relationship?
- Do we have to match prices of competitor's DVDs?

- How will we know our strategy worked?
- How will we measure?

CRACK THE CASE SYSTEM

Mexican Impasse

Mexico City, Mexico

Mexican insurance companies are feeling effects of foreign competition. They know they have to move quickly. Can you underwrite their success?

612 START
★ ★ ★

MEXICO CITY FACTS

▸ Largest metropolitan area in the Americas

▸ Nickname: The City of Palaces

▸ In 2005 Mexico City ranked as the 8th richest city in the world, with a GDP of $315 billion

TRAIN Profile

Type	**R**egion	**A**nalysis	**I**ndustry	**N**umber
1 CASE START	MEXICO CITY, MEXICO Population: 8.8M Currency: Mexican New Peso (MXN)	ROADMAP → **8** Streamline a Process	**J** Insurance	LEVEL **1**

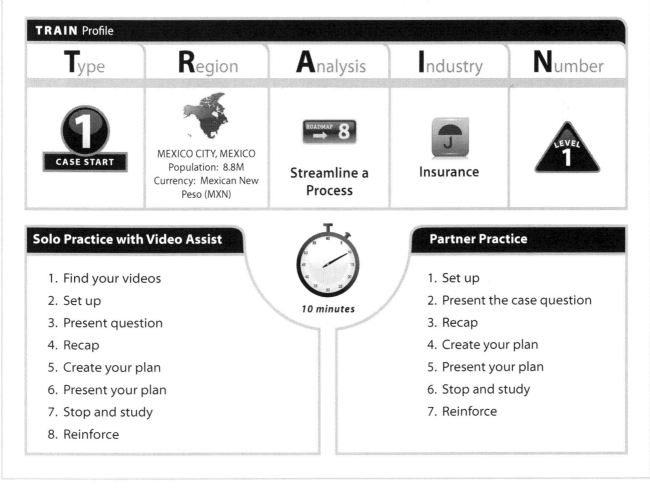

Solo Practice with Video Assist	**10 minutes**	**Partner Practice**
1. Find your videos		1. Set up
2. Set up		2. Present the case question
3. Present question		3. Recap
4. Recap		4. Create your plan
5. Create your plan		5. Present your plan
6. Present your plan		6. Stop and study
7. Stop and study		7. Reinforce
8. Reinforce		

CRACK THE CASE
SYSTEM

Mexican Impasse

Mexico City, Mexico

Interview Guide

Case Situation & Question

Mexican insurance companies are seeing healthy growth in both the life and non-life products. But the recent liberalization of their industry has led to many competitors moving in and taking share.

Several insurance companies think the winning strategy is to speed up their insurance sign-up process. They feel that individual clients are attracted to a quick approval process when initially signing up.

How would you help speed up the sign-up process?

Case Twist

Several insurance companies are finding that rolling out process improvements is more difficult than expected. Employees are resistant to change and measurement. They are questioning the value of the improvements.

What would you do to ensure your plan is successful?

VIDEO 1
Case Question
(Interviewer)

612
START
★ ★
★ ★ ★

Feedback

Physical Skills	Weak		Strong
Body Language	①	②	③
Verbal	①	②	③
Listening	①	②	③

Thinking Skills			
Hypothesis Generation	①	②	③
Initial Plan & Output	①	②	③
Data Gathering	①	②	③
Basic Business Intuition	①	②	③

Total Score _____ / 21

Case Start Self Study Reminders

Present Question	Recap & Ask for a Minute	Create Your Plan	Present Plan	Stop & Study	Reinforce
Read the question out loud like an interviewer or watch the MBACASE video interviewer.	Briefly recap the situation, the complication, and your task. Speak out loud just like you would in an interview.	Using the paper below, fill in the sections.	Turn your plan toward the interviewer (or mirror or webcam) and present it piece by piece.	Review the roadmaps and the Post Case Review page to see what you missed. Mark up your plan to make it better.	Do the start again with the video interviewer, or find a live partner and get some feedback. Incorporate what you learned the first time.

612 START ★★★

Mexican Impasse

Mexico City, Mexico

My Initial Plan and Output

Today's date:

Questions I'm thinking about:

Topics I know to cover:

Profit Tree Approach:

Topic Bucket Approach:

CRACK THE CASE SYSTEM

612 START ★★★

Mexican Impasse
Mexico City, Mexico

Post Case Review

Sample Case Starts

Profit Tree Approach:

$$\pi \quad \begin{cases} \text{Revenues} \quad \begin{cases} P \\ \times \\ V \end{cases} \\ \text{Costs} \quad \begin{cases} FC \\ + \\ VC \end{cases} \end{cases}$$

How to increase profit with a new process?

- Can insurance companies charge a premium for faster processing?
- How competitive is the pricing (typically, very!)?

- With faster approvals, what new volume do we expect?
- As volume increases, will costs go up? Staff in place to handle?

- Are all the support systems in place? Space/rent, equipment, computer systems
- Is the process hindered due to a lack of fixed assets?

(unit VC × volume)
- What are the plans to handle increased volume?
- Do we need to add people? Supplies?

Topic Bucket Approach: Mexican Insurance Co. – How change process?

(People/Flow) (Competitors) (Revenue/Cost) (Measure)

- Who supports this process?
- What is the flow overall?

- Do lead competitors have a faster process?
- How about banks?
- Other benchmarks?

- How can we measure costs?
- Time per application?
- New costs to increase revenue?

- How will we track the speed improvements?
- What is a good goal re: processing time?

Questions to Consider

☐ What are the major steps in the insurance approval process?

☐ Which steps are likely to be bottlenecks?

☐ What baseline measurements need to be in place to track improvements?

My Takeaways

I'm doing well with:

I need to work on:

Additional Study: For more questions to consider, review Section 13: Roadmaps.

VIDEO 2
Plan & Structure
(Candidate)

VIDEO 3
Recap & Tips
(David Ohrvall)

Windy Island

Kingston, Ontario, Canada

Islanders seem to be blowing a lot of hot air while investors are crunching the numbers. Can you bring the two sides together?

613
MINI
★★★

KINGSTON CITY FACTS

▶ Famous for its yearly cultural festivals, including film, jazz, and art.

▶ Claims (controversially) to be the birthplace of ice hockey, and is home to the International Hockey Hall of Fame

▶ The original capital of Canada

▶ Motto: "Where history and innovation thrive"

TRAIN Profile

Type	**R**egion	**A**nalysis	**I**ndustry	**N**umber
3 MINI BUSINESS	KINGSTON, ONTARIO Population: 117.2K Currency: Canadian Dollar, CAD	ROADMAP **2** **Growth Strategy**	**Energy**	LEVEL **4 & 5**

Solo Practice with Video Assist

1. Find your videos
2. Set up
3. Present question
4. Recap
5. Create your plan
6. Present your plan
7. Stop and study
8. Reinforce

20 minutes

Partner Practice

1. Set up
2. Present the case question
3. Recap
4. Create your plan
5. Present your plan
6. Stop and study
7. Reinforce

Windy Island
Kingston, Ontario, Canada

613 MINI ★★☆

Interview Guide

Initial Question

Windy Islands, Inc. operates windmill farms across different cities in Canada. They are exploring setting up another wind farm to produce electricity on Wolfe Island (Kingston). The government already operates a good power distribution grid in the form of submarine cable for transmitting power from the island to the mainland. This cable can be used for distributing electricity produced from the windmills.

Should they set up a wind farm on Wolfe Island? What will a 15-year NPV look like? Should they move ahead?

Case Twist

Check out the Crack the Case System videos on mbacase.com or scan the Video 3 QR code on the Post Case Review page to hear an additional challenge.

VIDEO 1
Case Question
(Interviewer)

Feedback

Physical Skills	Weak		Strong
Body Language	①	②	③
Verbal	①	②	③
Listening	①	②	③

Thinking Skills

Hypothesis Generation	①	②	③
Comfort with Ambiguity	①	②	③
Initial Plan & Output	①	②	③
Data Gathering	①	②	③
Data Analysis	①	②	③
Basic Business Intuition	①	②	③
Integration	①	②	③
2nd Level Insights	①	②	③
Creativity	①	②	③
Recommendation	①	②	③

Total Score _____ / 39

Intro Facts (Tell the Candidate if Asked)

Costs: A windmill costs almost $5.5 Million (including turbine cost) to set up and a wind farm would require about 86-90 windmills. On-going maintenance and taxes would cost 15%.

Rent: Land rent to local farmers will be to the tune of $7500 per annum / per turbine.

Output: A typical turbine can generate 2300 Kilowatts of energy, or 3,050 hours of electricity per year. 1 megawatt hour (MWh) = 1,000 Kilowatts (kWh). It can be sold to the government grid for 9 cents per kilowatt hour.

Discount Factor: Prevalent interest rates can be assumed at 4%.

Key Insights (Do Not Tell the Candidate)

Revenue: A windmill farm costs about $473M to set up after deducting land rent expenses. The farm will be able to generate 603,900 MWh hours of energy per annum, or $54M revenue.

Cash Flow: Post admin, maintenance and tax expenses, cash flow will be about $46M.

Pay Back Period: With a discount rate of 4%, it will take about 15 years for the windmill farm to recover the $475M set-up cost (assuming constant 4%, revenues and costs).

Quick NPV calculation: The candidate need not find the exact number of payback years. Review the extrapolation approach in Step 6 of the Interviewer's Data Guide.

Mid-case Data (Tell Only at Appropriate Time)

Prompt with Tips: Review the Interviewer's Data Guide to fully understand the math flow. It will be important for you to be ready to prompt with tips when the candidate is stuck.

Give handout: After hearing the candidate's financial evaluation and asking questions, show the candidate the Handout. Ask whether these issues affect his decision about moving ahead with the wind farm.

Discuss: All the potential issues raised by the locals and resistance groups have a valid solution. To succeed, Windy Islands will need to communicate the benefits that the wind farms will generate ($3M annually) and seek affordable solutions to any problems created.

Case Flow and Milestones

1 Prep and Review

Read all the notes in the Interviewer Guide. Understand when to ask certain questions and when to give charts, data and clues.

2 Present Main Question

Take on a personality (friendly, firm or foe). Present the case question. Candidate will take notes, ask for a minute, form a plan and present it.

3 Guide the Analysis

The candidate must calculate the NPV. Make sure he has all the key elements (like discount rate, energy per turbine, and price per output) to do the math.

4 Guide Discussion

Give information and handout and follow the Mid-case Data tips. After the candidate reviews the data, give clues to guide the calculations. It takes about 15 years for Windy Islands, Inc. to recover the set-up cost. Discuss ways to address the community's concerns.

5 Get Recommendation

A good recommendation here will have 2 parts:

The project is financially viable for all stakeholders involved with 15 years to recover the set up cost. Financial benefits to locals in terms of monthly income are also substantial.

Windy Island

Kingston, Ontario, Canada

Interviewer's Data Guide

Step 1 – Calculate the cost of setting up the wind farm

- Total turbines / windmills: 86 (use low number of range)
- Cost of each windmill = $5.5M
- Multiply 86 windmills x $5.5M
- Total windmill farm cost: $473M

Step 2 – Consider other costs

- Land rent per turbine $7,500
- Multiply 86 windmills x $7,500 = $645,000

Step 3 – Calculate the wind farm energy output and be ready to help explain the metrics

- Energy per turbine: 2300 Kilowatts
- Energy per turbine / per year: 2.3 Megawatts
- Typical electricity per turbine / per year 3050 hours of electricity
- Multiply 86 windmills x 2.3 MWh = 198 Megawatts
- Multiply total wind farm MW x electricity per turbine = 603,900 MWH per year

Step 4 – Calculate the full revenue potential

- Revenue per kilowatt hour = 9 cents per kWh
- Translate revenue into $ per MWh = $90 per MWh
- Multiply total wind output x revenue per MWh = $54,351,000 per year
- Translate gross revenue into millions for easier NPV calculations = $54.35M

Step 5 – Calculate net revenue

- Gross revenue = $54.4M
- Reduce by 15% due to taxes and maintenance to find net revenue = $46.2M
- Reduce by $645,000 for land rent to calculate cash flow = $45.6M

Step 6 – Calculate NPV using a quick estimate method

- Calculate the rough number of years with no discounting by taking $473M (total farm cost) / $45.5M (cash flow) = almost 10 years
- Rough out sample present values using the discount rate of 4%:
  - $45M in Year 2 has NPV of $43M (45/1.04)
  - $45M in Year 3 has NPV of $41M (45/1.04/1.04)
- Extrapolating this method, 15 years is a good estimate to recover the full $473M.

CRACK THE CASE SYSTEM **HANDOUT**

Windy Island
Kingston, Ontario, Canada

613 MINI ★★☆

WINDY ISLAND

Issues & Concerns

- Several concerns have been cited regarding the use of wind energy: aesthetics, land space, bird kills, and noise.

- Some people consider wind turbines unattractive, although others find the rotating blades visually appealing.

- Concern related to agricultural land space seems to have been resolved because once constructed, the wind turbines occupy less than one percent of the space.

- Bird kills by wind turbine blades are usually small; however, Wolfe Island is in the path of migrating bird species.

- Therefore bird mortality is one of the key issues of the environmental impact assessment, and must be satisfactorily addressed before regulators will grant approval to construct and operate a wind farm.

- The new turbines operate quietly enough that noise does not seem to be a problem.

- The estimated economic benefit, including royalties, taxes, amenities agreement, and operating and maintenance expenses, equates to over $3 million annually for decades to come.

Windy Island

Kingston, Ontario, Canada

613
MINI
★ ★ ★

Post Case Review

Case Insights & Takeaways

- The project is financially viable for all stakeholders involved. Windy Islands, Inc. will be able to recover the high set-up costs in approximately 15 years.
- The issues and opposition is based largely on traditional view of the windmills, but the latest technology and solutions have addressed most of them. Windy Islands should educate the locals about these facts to improve public perception of the benefits of the project.

Math Tips

- Review the Interviewer's Data Guide.
- The set-up costs divided by the annual cash flow comes to about 10 years.
- Instead of calculating the NPV for 15 years, a sample NPV for 2–3 years can help you project the total range of years necessary to pay back the initial investment.
- Avoid lots of zeroes by picking a scale like M for millions

What to Expect with Cases Like These

- This is a numbers-intensive case which combines local social issues as well. Be ready to take a purely financial answer and make it more realistic by discussing challenges with the roll-out.
- To move through the math quickly, learn to make estimates and extrapolations to reach an initial recommendation. You can fine-tune the numbers after you have a rough calculation.
- Always show your work to help the interviewer interact with you. It's important to keep the discussion going and not be silent for too long. In addition, the interviewer can help you if he understands what you are doing.

My Takeaways

To build skills and improve, you must apply what you learned to future cases. Take a few moments and review the interviewer feedback and jot down some key insights about your performance in the space below.

Thinking Skills

My top 2 strengths are:

My top 2 soft spots are:

To address these problems I'll begin to:

VIDEO 3
*Recap & Tips
(David Ohrvall)*

My Performance During the Case

Add up your points. → Total Score: _____ /15

F Form A Plan	**R** Read My Audience	**A** Anchor a Hypothesis	**M** Mine for Answers	**E** End the Case
points	points	points	points	points
③ Structured, clean	③ Good back & forth, caught clues	③ Solid hunch, pursued clue	③ Specific questions, solid analysis	③ Used facts and data, connected the dots
② Somewhat organized and logical	② Awkward, trouble with interviewer style	② Partial direction	② Missed some questions, some math mistakes	② Some data, mostly understood connections
① Messy, overlapping ideas	① Interviewer not interested, couldn't follow	① No hypothesis at all	① Vague questions, weak math, no linkages	① No data, no passion, no connections

CRACK THE CASE SYSTEM

WORKSHEET

Windy Island

Kingston, Ontario, Canada

613 MINI ★★★

My Initial Plan and Output

WINDY ISLAND

Today's date:

1. Zone out your paper
2. Be original with your data
3. Take clean and simple notes
4. Leave ample room for a structure and additional notes as the case progresses

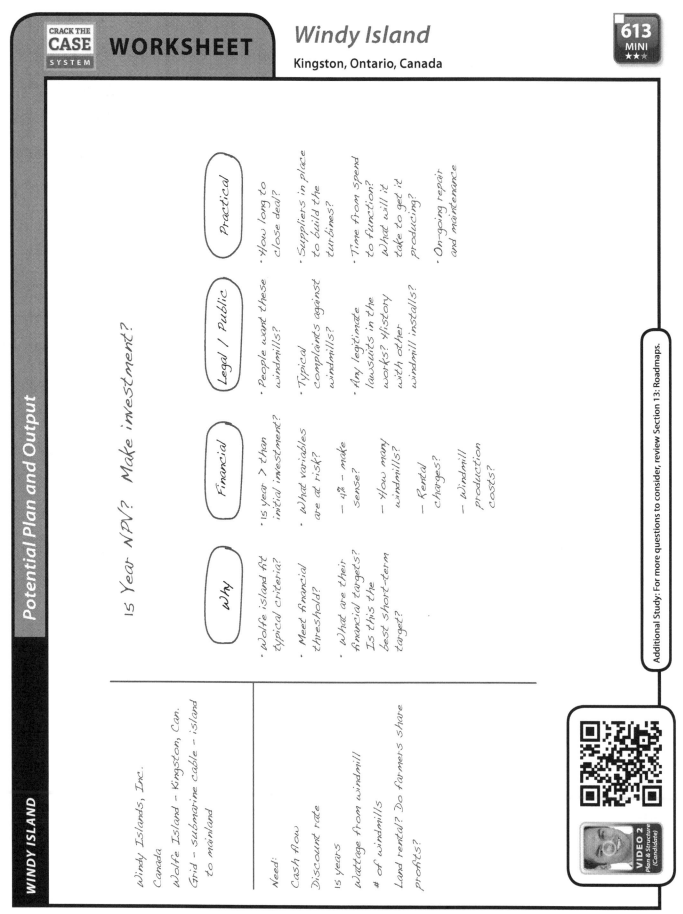

WORKSHEET

CRACK THE CASE SYSTEM

Windy Island
Kingston, Ontario, Canada

613 MINI ★★★

Potential Plan and Output

WINDY ISLAND

15 Year NPV? Make investment?

Why
- Wolfe island fit typical criteria?
- Meet financial threshold?
- What are their financial targets? Is this the best short-term target?

Financial
- Is year > than initial investment?
- What variables are at risk?
  - 4% - make sense?
  - How many windmills?
  - Rental charges?
  - Windmill production costs?

Legal / Public
- People want these windmills?
- Typical complaints against windmills?
- Any legitimate lawsuits in the works? History with other windmill installs?

Practical
- How long to close deal?
- Suppliers in place to build the turbines?
- Time from spend to function? What will it take to get it producing?
- On-going repair and maintenance

Windy Islands, Inc.
Canada
Wolfe Island - Kingston, Can.
Grid - submarine cable - island to mainland

Need:
Cash flow
Discount rate
15 years
Wattage from windmill
# of windmills
Land rental? Do farmers share profits?

Additional Study: For more questions to consider, review Section 13: Roadmaps.

VIDEO 2 Plan & Structure (Candidate)

516

Border out of Control

Toronto, Canada

How many freight trucks cross the border of Canada every day?

TORONTO CITY FACTS

- Fifth most populous city in North America
- Canada's economic capital, it is home to the Toronto Stock Exchange
- Half the population is foreign born, making it one of the most diverse cities in the world
- With an extremely low crime-rate, it is also one of the safest cities in the world

TRAIN Profile

Type	**R**egion	**A**nalysis	**I**ndustry	**N**umber
2 MARKET SIZING	TORONTO, ONTARIO Population: 2.5M Currency: Canadian Dollar, CAD	Funnel	Government	LEVEL 1

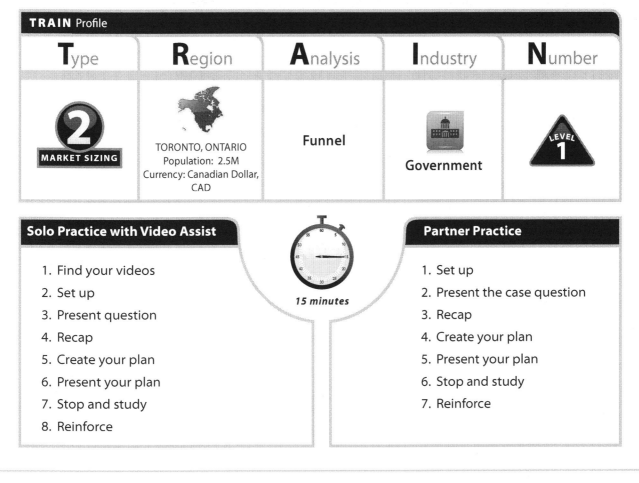

Solo Practice with Video Assist

1. Find your videos
2. Set up
3. Present question
4. Recap
5. Create your plan
6. Present your plan
7. Stop and study
8. Reinforce

15 minutes

Partner Practice

1. Set up
2. Present the case question
3. Recap
4. Create your plan
5. Present your plan
6. Stop and study
7. Reinforce

Border out of Control
Toronto, Canada

614
SIZING
★★★

Interview Guide

Initial Question

The Government of Canada would like to install retina scanners at the border so that frequent freight truckers from the US can choose to stop, turn, and quickly scan their eye and move forward. How many freight trucks cross the border into Canada every day? Assume there are 3.5M truckers in the US.

VIDEO 1
Case Question (Interviewer)

Feedback

Physical Skills	Weak		Strong
Body Language	①	②	③
Verbal	①	②	③
Listening	①	②	③

Thinking Skills			
Initial Plan & Output	①	②	③
Data Gathering	①	②	③
Data Analysis	①	②	③

Total Score _____ / 18

Intro Facts (Tell the Candidate if Asked)	**Key Insights** (Do Not Tell the Candidate)	**Mid-case Data** (Tell Only at Appropriate Time)
10% of truckers on the road are Canada-bound. Border-bound truckers typically visit Canada once per month.	**Problem setup:** Candidate will have to set up the appropriate equation to determine the total freight traffic (Truckers who cross x frequency of crossing).	If the candidate is stuck, then suggest that they set up an equation that will determine the freight trucks per year and look for the data that will solve it.

Case Flow and Milestones

1 Prep and Review	**2** Present Main Question	**3** Answer & Ask	**4** Guide Discussion	**5** Get Recommendation
Read all the notes in the Interviewer Guide. Understand when to ask certain questions and when to give data and clues.	Take on a personality (friendly, firm or foe). Ask one or two background questions. Present the question. Candidate will take notes and ask for time to think or begin talking. Discourage silence as market sizing cases are meant to be interactive.	This is an ambiguous problem. Try to help the candidate by offering ideas if he is stuck. Continue to ask why he is thinking a certain way.	Give any missing data if necessary and the Mid-case Data tips. Review the answer on page 4 of the case pack and offer suggestions if the candidate needs help.	Be firm and expect a final number. To see if the candidate is thinking about broader business issues ask what he would do with this information.

GIVE CLUE

CRACK THE CASE SYSTEM

614 SIZING ★★★

Border out of Control
Toronto, Canada

My Initial Plan and Output   Use the space below to write your thoughts.

My Numbers
What are some simple estimates for getting started?
How might you refine these numbers?

State your assumptions

Pick your main metrics and approach

Estimate quickly and with round numbers

Assess your approach and answer

Keep exceptions and next steps in mind.

Border out of Control

Toronto, Canada

Post Case Review	My Score	
Potential Solution & Output	**Weak**	**Strong**
State your assumptions • Northbound freight traffic from Mexico or other countries is not a significant consideration.	① ② ③	
Pick your main metrics and approach • Top-down approach based on Canada-bound truckers from the US.	① ② ③	
Estimate quickly and with round numbers • 3.5M US truckers * 10% "border-bound" = 350K border bound truckers. • 350K border bound truckers * 1 visit/month * 12 months = 4.2M visits/year. • Total freight crossings = 4.2M/year.	① ② ③	
Assess your approach and answer • 4.2M freight crossings means about 12,000 crossings per day. • Assuming 20 border cities, this is about 600 crossings per day per gateway. This seems reasonable.	① ② ③	
Keep exceptions and next steps in mind • Freight crossing traffic will likely be affected by gas prices as well as by the economy. • Security concerns around boat/rail traffic may drive further traffic to trucks.	① ② ③	
Total:		

Different Approaches to Consider

- Compare total freight crossings with those of other similar land masses (such as Mexico).

Tips and Takeaways

- Do sanity check to get a total number to a digestible "real world" piece – such as crossings per gate.

VIDEO 2 *Plan & Structure (Candidate)*

VIDEO 3 *Recap & Tips (David Ohrvall)*

CRACK THE CASE SYSTEM

Enrique De Chocolate

Bogota, Colombia

Enrique has tasted sweet success but now wants more. Do they have the right team to pull it off?

701 START
★★★

BOGOTA CITY FACTS

▶ The Athens of South America (title given in the 1800s because of its many libraries and universities)

▶ Bogota has one of the most extensive bike routes of any city in the world

▶ Bogota's airport is the largest and most expensive in South America

TRAIN Profile

Type	**R**egion	**A**nalysis	**I**ndustry	**N**umber
1 CASE START	BOGOTA, COLOMBIA Population: 7.3M Currency: Colombian Peso (COP)	ROADMAP → 9 **Restructure the Team**	**Food**	LEVEL **1**

Solo Practice with Video Assist

1. Find your videos
2. Set up
3. Present question
4. Recap
5. Create your plan
6. Present your plan
7. Stop and study
8. Reinforce

10 minutes

Partner Practice

1. Set up
2. Present the case question
3. Recap
4. Create your plan
5. Present your plan
6. Stop and study
7. Reinforce

CRACK THE CASE SYSTEM

701
START
★ ★
★

Enrique De Chocolate
Bogota, Colombia

Interview Guide

Case Situation & Question

Enrique de Chocolate is a maker of fine chocolates with boutique chocolate stores throughout South and North America. They have grown rapidly due to their ability to create unique chocolate that is well branded and sold in their exclusive stores. To further their expansion, they are debating whether to backward integrate, and begin buying their own cocoa beans and extract their own cocoa liquor, powder and butter. Or should they reorganize to respond to a request from Walmart North America, to make a private label, chocolate line for all of their stores.

How would you restructure the team to best support either option?

Case Twist

Despite your amazing analysis, the team is revolting and wanting to pursue the other option (you must pick Walmart or backward integration).

What data would you collect to prove out that your thinking is correct?

VIDEO 1
Case Question
(Interviewer)

Feedback

Physical Skills	Weak		Strong
Body Language	①	②	③
Verbal	①	②	③
Listening	①	②	③

Thinking Skills			
Hypothesis Generation	①	②	③
Initial Plan & Output	①	②	③
Data Gathering	①	②	③
Basic Business Intuition	①	②	③

Total Score _____ / 21

Case Start Self Study Reminders

Present Question	Recap & Ask for a Minute	Create Your Plan	Present Plan	Stop & Study	Reinforce
Read the question out loud like an interviewer or watch the MBACASE video interviewer.	Briefly recap the situation, the complication, and your task. Speak out loud just like you would in an interview.	Using the paper below, fill in the sections.	Turn your plan toward the interviewer (or mirror or webcam) and present it piece by piece .	Review the roadmaps and the Post Case Review page to see what you missed. Mark up your plan to make it better.	Do the start again with the video interviewer, or find a live partner and get some feedback. Incorporate what you learned the first time.

701
START
★★★

Enrique De Chocolate

Bogota, Colombia

My Initial Plan and Output

Today's date:

Questions I'm thinking about:

Topics I know to cover:

Profit Tree Approach:

Topic Bucket Approach:

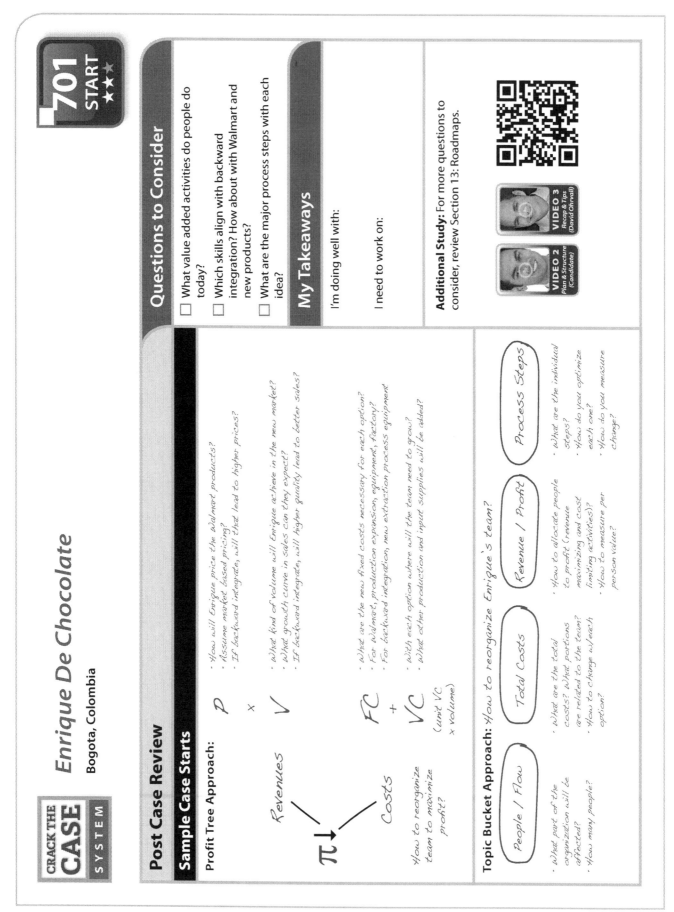

Enrique De Chocolate
Bogota, Colombia

CRACK THE CASE S Y S T E M

701 START ★★ ★★★

Post Case Review

Sample Case Starts

Profit Tree Approach:

$$\pi \rightarrow \begin{matrix} Revenues \\ Costs \end{matrix}$$

How to reorganize team to maximize profit?

Revenues:
$$P \times V$$

- How will Enrique price the Walmart products?
- Assume market based pricing?
- If backward integrate, will that lead to higher prices?

- What kind of volume will Enrique achieve in the new market?
- What growth curve in sales can they expect?
- If backward integrate, will higher quality lead to better sales?

Costs:
$$FC + VC$$
(unit VC x volume)

- What are the new fixed costs necessary for each option?
- For Walmart, production expansion equipment, factory?
- For backward integration, new extraction process equipment

- With each option where will the team need to grow?
- What other production and input supplies will be added?

Topic Bucket Approach: How to reorganize Enrique's team?

(People / Flow)
- What part of the organization will be affected?
- How many people?

(Total Costs)
- What are the total costs? What portions are related to the team?
- How to change w/each option?

(Revenue / Profit)
- How to allocate people to profit (revenue maximizing and cost limiting activities)?
- How to measure per person value?

(Process Steps)
- What are the individual steps?
- How do you optimize each one?
- How do you measure change?

Questions to Consider

- [ ] What value added activities do people do today?
- [ ] Which skills align with backward integration? How about with Walmart and new products?
- [ ] What are the major process steps with each idea?

My Takeaways

I'm doing well with:

I need to work on:

Additional Study: For more questions to consider, review Section 13: Roadmaps.

VIDEO 2
Plan & Structure
(Candidate)

VIDEO 3
Recap & Tips
(David Ohrvall)

Houdini Pretzel

702 FULL ★★★

Santiago, Chile

Houdini Pretzel is all tied up in knots about what to do. Branded profits are falling and private label competitors may be the culprit. See if you can unravel this twisted tale.

SANTIAGO CITY FACTS

▸ Located at the foot of the Andean Mountain Range

▸ One of the few cities in the world with access to both beaches and ski slopes

▸ Generates 45% of the country's GDP

TRAIN Profile

Type	**R**egion	**A**nalysis	**I**ndustry	**N**umber
4 FULL BUSINESS	SANTIAGO, CHILE Population: 5M Currency: Chilean peso	ROADMAP → 12 Competitor Attack	Outsourcing	LEVEL 3

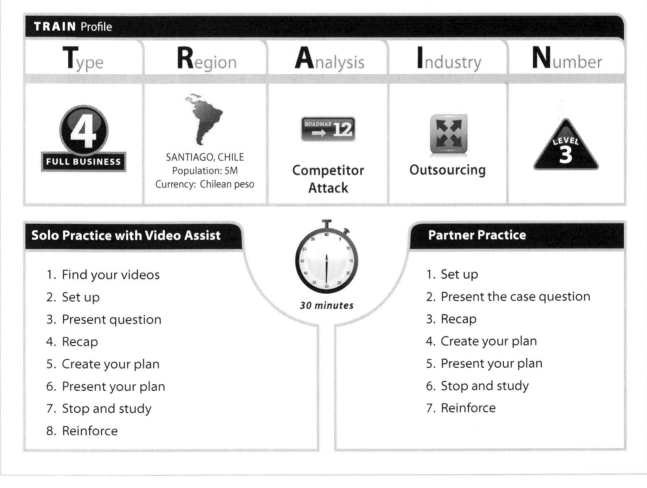

Solo Practice with Video Assist

1. Find your videos
2. Set up
3. Present question
4. Recap
5. Create your plan
6. Present your plan
7. Stop and study
8. Reinforce

30 minutes

Partner Practice

1. Set up
2. Present the case question
3. Recap
4. Create your plan
5. Present your plan
6. Stop and study
7. Reinforce

Houdini Pretzel

Santiago, Chile

702
FULL
★★★

Interview Guide

Case Situation and Question

Houdini Pretzel, maker of Pretzel Twists and Ties, is a $175M division of a large snack food conglomerate. Houdini is the largest manufacturer of pretzels in Chile. Sabroso, S.A. is second, with approximately $145M in sales. Like most manufacturers, Houdini improves factory utilization by making private label products for grocery chains. These chains sell private label pretzels that compete directly with Houdini and Sabroso. In recent months, Houdini management has seen sales slip, largely due to a drop in private label prices. Also, Houdini has had to fight to maintain shelf space, as grocery chains are featuring their own products more prominently.

What should Houdini do to reverse this trend and increase their sales?

Case Twist

This situation turns nasty. Several grocery chains threaten to drastically reduce shelf space unless Houdini continues the reduced production pricing.

What would you do?

VIDEO 1
Case Question
(Interviewer)

Feedback

Physical Skills   Weak   Strong

Body Language	①	②	③
Verbal	①	②	③
Listening	①	②	③

Thinking Skills

Hypothesis Generation	①	②	③
Comfort with Ambiguity	①	②	③
Initial Plan & Output	①	②	③
Data Analysis	①	②	③
Basic Business Intuition	①	②	③
Integration	①	②	③
2nd Level Insights	①	②	③
Creativity	①	②	③

Total Score _____ / 33

Intro Facts (Tell the Candidate if Asked)

Products: Pretzel twists, ties and rods packaged in party-sized bags

Competitors: Houdini Pretzel and Sabroso make up over 70% of industry revenue. Private label products contribute an additional 15%.

How Private Label (PL) Works:
Private label products are the generic products you find in your grocery stores. They typically are sold under a brand name that matches the store name (e.g. "Acme Foods"). Grocery stores have their generic products produced by the same manufacturers that make branded product. Usually the generic recipes are slightly different and often of lesser quality.

Branded Company Perspective on PL: Companies that have branded products try to fill the excess capacity in their plants with private label products. They don't like to compete with these private label products, but often regard them as a necessary evil.

Key Insights (Do Not Tell the Candidate)

Historical Pricing: In slide Handout A, prices for private label have begun to fall since October Year 1. Houdini and Sabroso have stayed relatively constant.

Pricing Gap: Since October Year 1, the pricing gap between Houdini's pretzels and private labels has exceeded 15 cents. When the savings per unit is this large, consumers switch from Houdini's to private label products.

Volume Change: The shift in pricing gap has caused a reduction in the volume of pretzels Houdini sells.

Plant Manger Incentives: Plant managers have an incentive structure that affects their personal bonus. If they keep plant capacity above 90% then there are no "losses" to the company. If the plant utilization falls below 90% then the company loses money. These "losses" are accounting measures though, and are not necessarily actual bottom-line dollars.

Mid-case Data (Tell Only at Appropriate Time)

After giving Handouts A, B and C, check for these insights:

- Houdini has lost $7.2M since this problem began.
- Volume has been declining steadily since October Year 1. Something happened in October.
- When the price gap between Houdini and private label exceeds 15 cents, customers switch to private label. At that price point the private label product is too cheap to pass up.

After checking for the insights, say this and give Handout D:

- "Let me tell you about some other changes at Houdini. About 10 months ago they finished implementing some new plant equipment, designed to increase efficiency. You should know that for every point below 90%, Houdini's accounting system assumes a loss of $50,000 per month. Given that metric, how much have they lost since October of Year 1?"

After giving Handout D, check for these insights:

- Plants that installed the new equipment to be more efficient saw their plant utilization drop as more product was going through the plant faster.
- Because of this drop in utilization, Houdini has lost $6M according to internal accounting metrics.
- Managers gave these discounts, without the knowledge of senior management, to protect their bonuses.

Houdini Pretzel

Santiago, Chile

702 FULL
★★★

Case Flow and Milestones

1 Present Main Question

Candidate takes notes, asks for a minute, forms a plan and presents it.

2 Answer Any Basics

Questions may come up after you read the main question. Look for those answers under Intro Facts.

3 Ask for Clarification

Prompt for clarification with questions like, "Tell me more about this area (you choose). What are you thinking about here?" or "Tell me how the parts of your structure link to each other." Look for clear connections between each part of the plan.

4 Guide Discussion

Direct the Candidate by giving handouts A, B and C. Check the Handout and Data Guide for more details. Also, it is important before giving Handout D to update the Candidate on some changes that the company has made to their plants.

5 Get Recommendation

Once the insights from all the slides have sunk in, the Candidate should be able to integrate and come to a conclusion. Test to see that he has a prioritized list. Refer to the Case Insights & Takeaways to understand a logical path forward.

Handout and Data Guide

Additional Info

Handout A:

Candidate: Do you have any pricing data?

Interviewer: Here's some unit volume and price data for the past 2 years. What trend do you see?

Insight: As private label prices declined, total Houdini sales volume also declined.

Volume is down considerably. Prices for both Houdini and Sabroso have remained stable.

Handout B:

Candidate: Do you have Houdini prices vs private vs. label prices?

Interviewer: Here's another way to look at the price gap (Handout A) between Houdini and the private label brands. What jumps out at you?

Insight: The gap increased for several months and then leveled off. The price gap correlates to the volume drop (Handout A).

Handout C:

Candidate: Do you have any more detail on the unit sales?

Interviewer: Here's a detailed view of the volume on slide A. What's the insight here?

Insight: Unit sales have been off consistently since the end of Year 1 and into Year 2. The volume drop corresponds to the increase in price gap between Houdini and the PL brands.

Handout D:

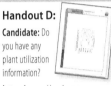

Candidate: Do you have any plant utilization information?

Interviewer: Here is some utilization information by plant that you may want to review.

How much is the loss? Why do you think the utilization rates went down?

Insight: 15 points x $50K = $750K x 8 months = $6M. Utilization rates fell because the new equipment was considerably more efficient.

When you press the candidate for a final answer, he may be tempted to fix the internal incentive problem. It seems that the plant managers made a poor decision so it makes sense to realign incentives. But, the real priority is to get sales back in line to their levels of 10 months ago. The internal metrics change is important, but it will not boost sales.

You may want to prompt the candidate with a question or comment like this:

- " What is the most important problem you should solve first?"
  or
- "Which problem is costing the company more?"
  or
- "Which problem is hurting the company's future growth the most?"

Re-routers | Questions to Keep Things on Track

- **Do you think there is a direct cause for the private label reduction in retail prices?**
  - We know that the price drop is consistent for all private label.
  - We know that Houdini supplies almost 80% of all private label.
  - Cause and effect is likely.
- **Do you think that customers will behave in a consistent pattern?**
  - Customers tend to change behavior when prices reach a certain level.

- Food products are especially sensitive to these changes.

- **What additional data would you like to see?**
- **How can you make your answer more quantitative?**
- **What specific insight does this data give you?**

Houdini Pretzel

Santiago, Chile

Additional Study Using the FRAME Method

F – Form a Plan

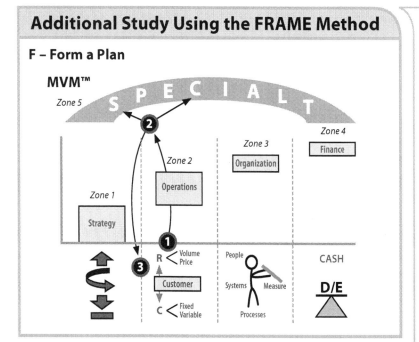

M—Mine for the Answer

How good were your questions? Typically it is good to try to ask 2–3 questions in any section you explore. Here are some good areas and examples.

Houdini Volume	PL Company Costs	Supplier Power
■ **Have private label prices dropped?** *Yes. Sharp downturn in Oct Year 1 (Handout A).*	■ **What have PL companies historically been charged for production?** *There's no data on typical charges.*	■ **Do private label companies have many options for production?** *No. Houdini produces 80% of the product. Sabroso can't take on more PL.*
■ **Do the PL price drop and the Houdini volume drop correlate?** *Yes. When the price gap between branded and PL exceeds 15¢, customers switch to PL.*	■ **Does Houdini sell much product to PL companies?** *Yes, several plants produce a large portion of PL.*	■ **Can Houdini control how much they charge PL manufacturers?** *Yes. Contracts are not long-term; many Houdini plants recently reduced the price they charge PL companies.*
■ **Does volume fluctuate seasonally?** *Yes. There's a slight increase in summer.*	■ **Is the manufacturing cost the majority of the costs to produce?** *Yes. PL companies leverage the labor force and distribution channels in place.*	

Competitors	Industry Trends	Shelf Space
■ **Has Sabroso's volume dropped over the last 10 months?** *No. Sabroso produces little PL product. Their branded product is stable.*	■ **Have overall pretzel sales dropped or been displaced?** *No data to indicate anything has changed in overall industry pretzel sales.*	■ **Has Houdini shelf space dropped at grocery chains?** *No. They have had pressure in that direction but it has not been consistent across stores.*
■ **Are grocery stores pushing out Houdini's product?** *No. They are pushing their own but understand Houdini's draw. Pretzel sales push high-margin soft drink sales.*	■ **Are consumers eating cheaper brands of pretzels?** *No macro trend exists. Some consumers will keep switching between branded pretzels and private label depending on the price.*	■ **Would a reduction in display space affect the volume of product sold?** *It would have minimal impact since Houdini's distribution process keeps fresh product in stock.*

1. Start in Zone 2, Operations/Revenue:
Review volume and price to assess the size of the problem.

- Volume – When did units start dropping off? Was it sharp or gradual?
- Price – What is the price gap between Houdini and the PL companies? When did it change? Does it correlate to the volume change?

2. Move to Zone 5, External Forces:
Explore two areas:

- Supplier – Houdini supplies some PL brands. Has Houdini changed its pricing for PL customers?
- Competitors – Houdini competes with the grocery stores' PL products but also needs the stores' shelf space. If Houdini charges more to produce PL products, how will Sabroso respond?

3. Return to Zone 2, Price:
Can Houdini increase manufacturing prices? If time permits, look for additional costs to cut. Cost reductions will shield Houdini from additional price decreases.

A – Anchor a Hypothesis

You do not need to explain your hypothesis to the interviewer, but use this mental anchor to help you structure your questions as you move through your plan. Here are some potential hunches:

Pricing: "Houdini is getting beaten at price. Maybe they should consider lowering price to get their market share back."

Supplier Power: "Since Houdini produces product for private label companies, I wonder what kind of control they have over the price they offer the PL companies."

Competitors: "PL companies may be getting better prices from competitors, who are trying to erode Houdini's market share."

E – End the Case

Be firm and use data. Here's an option: "Houdini is looking at an erosion of about $7M of revenue over eight months, or a little less than 5% of sales. The cause of the decline was a bad decision on the part of the plant managers to give the grocery chains a 5¢ per unit reduction. This seemingly small discount gave private label the ability to siphon some of our customers and reduce our sales volume. Our first priority is to get volume back. Since Sabroso is at full capacity, we control most of the private label production. My conclusion is that we should raise prices. To address the utilization problem in the plant we should consider plant consolidation and new business leads."

Houdini Pretzel

Santiago, Chile

Post Case Review

Case Insights & Takeaways

Ideas to consider in order of importance:

1. **Stop bleeding revenue.** Houdini's revenue decline is the result of special pricing for private label companies. If the price gap becomes less than 15 cents, customers will likely return. Houdini has capacity their competitors lack, so Houdini can name its price with grocery chains needing private label production.

2. **Fix internal metrics and accountability.** Plant managers chose poorly because their performance measurements did not account for new equipment. They need new measurement systems and more checks and balances on decisions.

3. **Protect shelf space.** As market leader, Houdini commands prime retail shelf space. To maintain shelf space as pretzel sales climb, Houdini should give stores more marketing incentives, or develop other negotiating tactics.

How Does It Tie Together?

Houdini is in the driver's seat in this situation:

- They gave the price break to the private label companies (and can take it back).
- They are the largest manufacturer for PL and can control price.
- Losing shelf space is not a huge threat since the Houdini product is in demand.

Houdini's priority is to reduce the volume drop and persuade consumers to switch back:

- Pushing PL price back to its historical levels will most likely work.
- Consumers may not readily switch back to Houdini. They may find the private label quality to be acceptable.

My Takeaways

To build skills and improve, you must apply what you learned to future cases. Take a few moments and review the interviewer feedback and jot down some key insights about your performance in the space below.

Thinking Skills

My top 2 strengths are:

My top 2 soft spots are:

To address these problems I'll begin to:

VIDEO 3
Recap & Tips
(David Ohrvall)

My Performance During the Case

Add up your points. ➡ Total Score: _____ /15

F Form A Plan	**R** Read My Audience	**A** Anchor a Hypothesis	**M** Mine for Answers	**E** End the Case
points	points	points	points	points
③ Structured, clean	③ Good back & forth, caught clues	③ Solid hunch, pursued clue	③ Specific questions, solid analysis	③ Used facts and data, connected the dots
② Somewhat organized and logical	② Awkward, trouble with interviewer style	② Partial direction	② Missed some questions, some math mistakes	② Some data, mostly understood connections
① Messy, overlapping ideas	① Interviewer not interested, couldn't follow	① No hypothesis at all	① Vague questions, weak math, no linkages	① No data, no passion, no connections

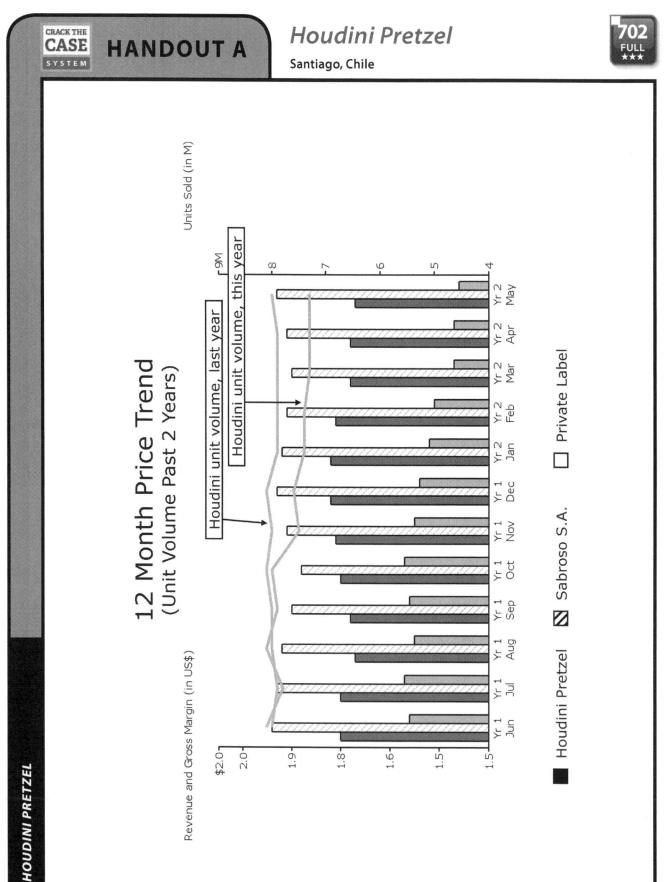

HANDOUT A

Houdini Pretzel

Santiago, Chile

702 FULL ★★★

12 Month Price Trend
(Unit Volume Past 2 Years)

Units Sold (in M)

Revenue and Gross Margin (in US$)

Houdini unit volume, last year

Houdini unit volume, this year

Houdini Pretzel   Sabroso S.A.   Private Label

Houdini Pretzel
Santiago, Chile

702
FULL
★★★

HOUDINI PRETZEL

Houdini Minus Private Label
12 Month Price Gap

Gap in Cents

	Yr 1 Jun	Yr 1 Jul	Yr 1 Aug	Yr 1 Sep	Yr 1 Oct	Yr 1 Nov	Yr 1 Dec	Yr 2 Jan	Yr 2 Feb	Yr 2 Mar	Yr 2 Apr	Yr 2 May
Price Gap (in cents per unit)	0.1	0.1	0.1	0.1	0.1	0.2	0.2	0.2	0.2	0.2	0.2	0.2

0.30Cents

0.20

0.10

0.00

Houdini Pretzel
Santiago, Chile

HOUDINI PRETZEL

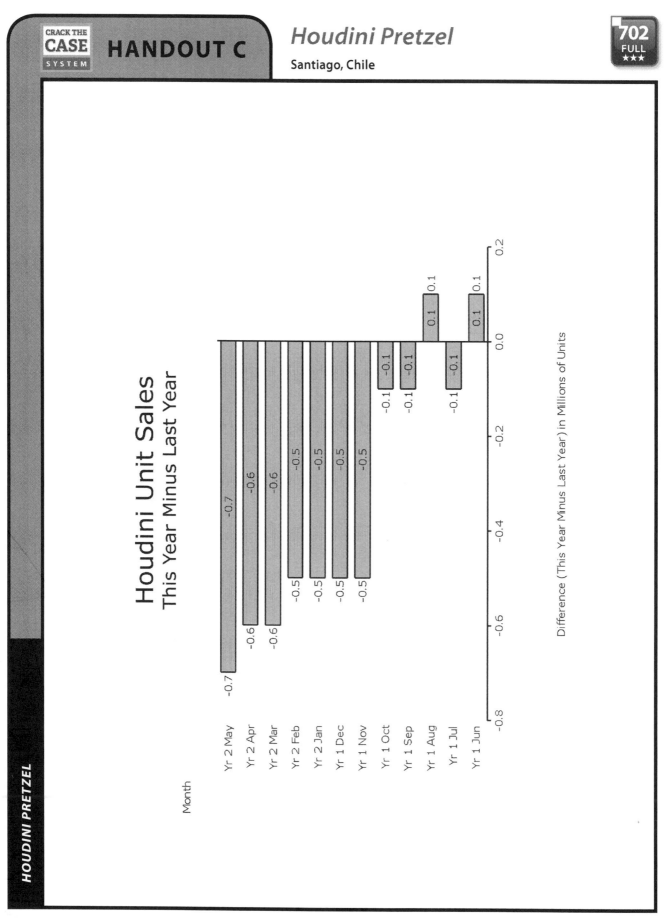

Houdini Unit Sales
This Year Minus Last Year

Month

	Difference
Yr 2 May	-0.7
Yr 2 Apr	-0.6
Yr 2 Mar	-0.6
Yr 2 Feb	-0.5
Yr 2 Jan	-0.5
Yr 1 Dec	-0.5
Yr 1 Nov	-0.5
Yr 1 Oct	-0.1
Yr 1 Sep	-0.1
Yr 1 Aug	0.1
Yr 1 Jul	-0.1
Yr 1 Jun	0.1

Difference (This Year Minus Last Year) in Millions of Units

Houdini Pretzel

Santiago, Chile

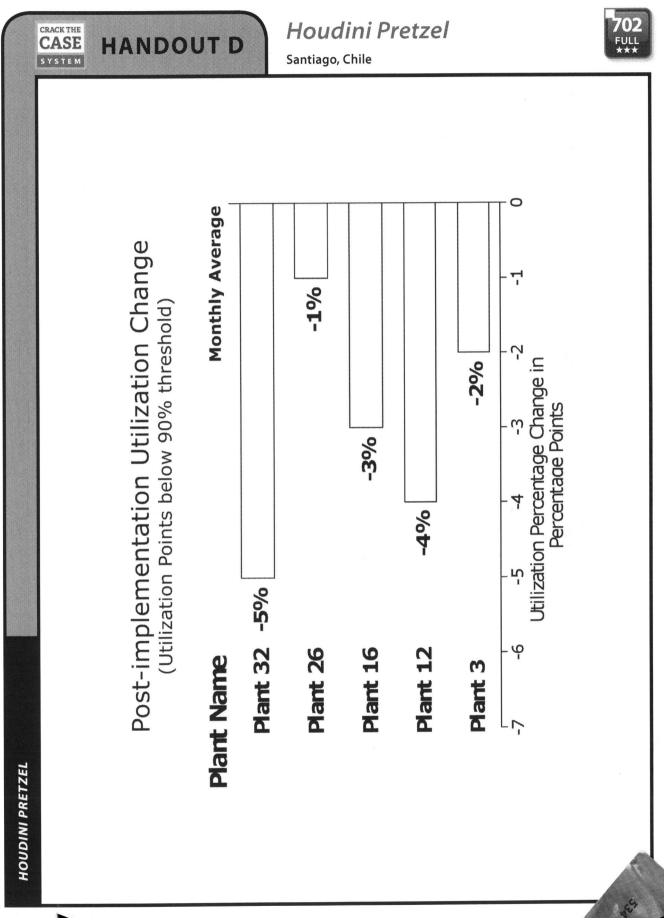

Post-implementation Utilization Change
(Utilization Points below 90% threshold)

Plant Name

Monthly Average

Plant 32 -5%

Plant 26 -1%

Plant 16 -3%

Plant 12 -4%

Plant 3 -2%

Utilization Percentage Change in Percentage Points

-7 -6 -5 -4 -3 -2 -1 0

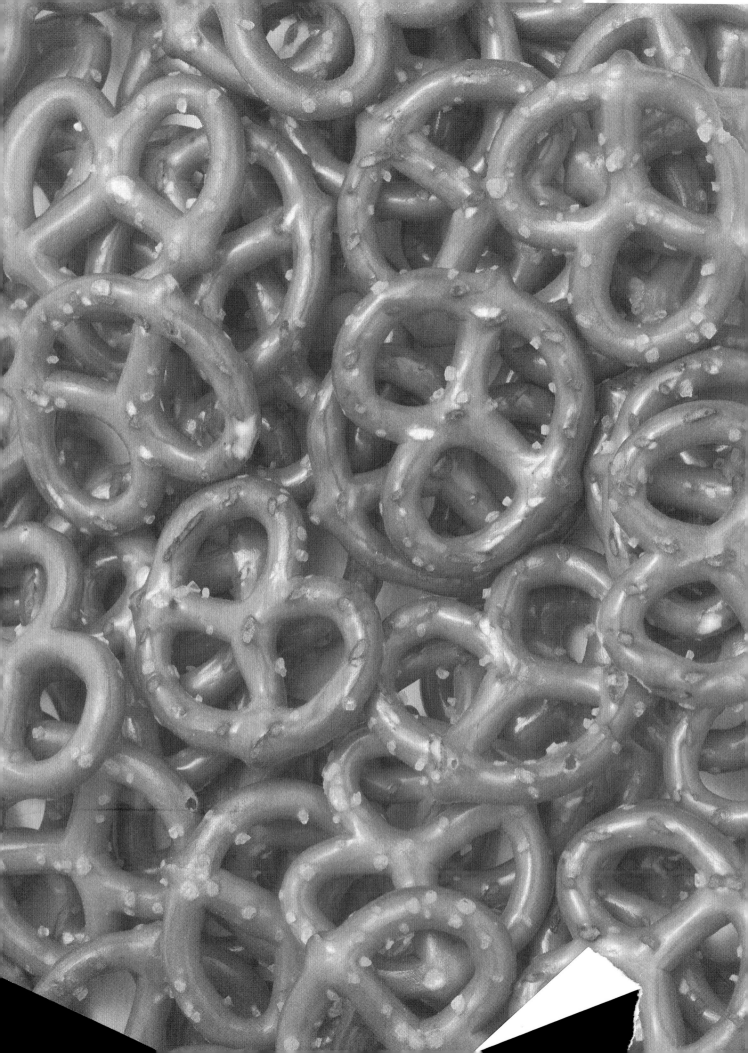

WORKSHEET

CRACK THE CASE SYSTEM

Houdini Pretzel
Santiago, Chile

HOUDINI PRETZEL

My Initial Plan and Output

Today's date:

2. Be original with your data

4. Leave ample room for a structure and additional notes as the case progresses

1. Zone out your paper

3. Take clean and simple notes

CRACK THE CASE SYSTEM — WORKSHEET

Houdini Pretzel
Santiago, Chile

Potential Plan and Output

HOUDINI PRETZEL

How can Houdini reverse the drop in sales?

Revenue drop / Price

Price – how much change? Has Houdini matched price drop?

Are they matching PL's pricing?

Revenue drop / Volume

How much volume dropped over last year?

Are consumers choosing PL due to lower price?

What's the price/volume relationship?

HUNCH: PL prices are down and customers are price sensitive. Houdini may have to lower price.

Suppliers

Have ingredients changed? Other raw material prices?

Shipping or storage costs from suppliers up?

Competitors

Is PL the only issue?

Has Sabroso made changes?

Why are grocery stores limiting shelf space?

Rev – $175M division

Large snack food conglom.

Sabroso, SA, $145M

Profit?

Goal: reverse drop in sales

· Pretzel twists and ties

· Houdini makes private label

· PL competes with Houdini & Sabroso

· Sales down due to PL price drop

· Shelf space becoming an issue

Voiceover

"There are several issues I would like to explore: the reasons for the revenue decrease, how price and volume have changed over time; and I'd like to know more about external factors like suppliers and competitors. Together I think these issues will get to the bottom of the problem. If we have time we can also talk about any actions that competitors are taking. I would like to start with revenue, unless you would prefer me to begin elsewhere."

Additional Study: For more questions to consider, review Section 13: Roadmaps.

VIDEO 2
Plan & Structure
(Candidate)